NEW DIRECTIONS IN GERMAN STUDIES

Vol. 14

Series Editor:

Imke Meyer

D1453789

Volumes in the series:

Thomas Mann and Shakespeare

Something Rich and Strange

Edited by
Tobias Döring and Ewan Fernie

Bloomsbury Academic
An imprint of Bloomsbury Publishing Inc

B L O O M S B U R Y
NEW YORK · LONDON · OXFORD · NEW DELHI · SYDNEY

Bloomsbury Academic
An imprint of Bloomsbury Publishing Inc

1385 Broadway	50 Bedford Square
New York	London
NY 10018	WC1B 3DP
USA	UK

www.bloomsbury.com

BLOOMSBURY and the Diana logo are trademarks of Bloomsbury Publishing Plc

First published 2015
Paperback edition first published 2017

Library of Congress Cataloging-in-Publication Data
Thomas Mann and Shakespeare : something rich and strange / edited by Tobias Döring, Ewan Fernie.
pages cm. -- (New directions in German studies)
Summary: "The first ever comparative reading of Shakespeare and Thomas Mann in view of key questions in modern culture"-- Provided by publisher.
Includes bibliographical references and index.
ISBN 978-1-62892-209-7 (hardback) -- ISBN 978-1-62892-210-3 (epub) -- ISBN 978-1-62892-211-0 (epdf) 1. Mann, Thomas, 1875-1955--Criticism and interpretation. 2. Shakespeare, William, 1564-1616--Criticism and interpretation. 3. Mann, Thomas, 1875-1955--Themes, motives. 4. Shakespeare, William, 1564-1616--Themes, motives. 5. Comparative literature--German and English. 6. Comparative literature--English and German. I. Döring, Tobias, editor, author. II. Fernie, Ewan, 1971- editor, author.
PT2625.A44Z891666 2015
833'.912--dc23
2015011135

ISBN: HB: 978-1-6289-2209-7
PB: 978-1-5013-3608-9
epub: 978-1-6289-2210-3
ePDF: 978-1-6289-2211-0

Series: New Directions in German Studies

Typeset by Fakenham Prepress Solutions, Fakenham, Norfolk NR21 8NN

Contents

Acknowledgements

This volume started life as a remarkable conference, generously supported by the Center for Advanced Studies, Ludwig-Maximilians-Universität München. We are profoundly grateful to Sonja Asal and to our speakers for doing so much to make it as stimulating, fulfilling and enjoyable as it was. We should also like to acknowledge the gracious contribution of Regina Schwojer in running the conference, and the crucial efforts of Elisa Leroy and Johannes Ungelenk in preparing it, which extended to providing elegant as well as accurate translations for the book. Yola Schmitz's labours as editorial assistant on a sometimes fiendishly difficult bilingual undertaking are greater than that modest title can express. And Martina Kübler made a decisive intervention as we finished preparing the manuscript. Karin Brown offered expert help at the Shakespeare Institute Library. We are grateful to Haaris Naqvi at Bloomsbury for being so genially encouraging and efficient an editor. And finally for enabling this particular pioneering conversation between English Studies and *Germanistik*, between criticism and creativity, and between Germany, Switzerland, the UK and the United States, we should like to express our sincere and continuing gratitude to Thomas Mann and Shakespeare.

Tobias Döring and Ewan Fernie

Notes on Contributors

Elisabeth Bronfen is Chair of English and American Studies at Universität Zürich, Switzerland, as well as Global Distinguished Professor at New York University, USA. Her many books include the influential *Over Her Dead Body: Death, Femininity and the Aesthetic* and the recent collection of essays (edited with Beate Neumeier) *Gothic Renaissance: A Reassessment.*

Jonathan Dollimore is among the foremost critics and theorists of his generation. Works such as *Sexual Dissidence, Death, Desire and Loss in Western Culture* and *Sex, Literature and Censorship* make connections between Shakespeare and Mann.

Tobias Döring is Chair of English Literature, LMU München, Germany, and past President of the German Shakespeare Society. His latest books are (ed. with Virginia Mason Vaughan) *Critical and Cultural Transformations: Shakespeare's* The Tempest *– 1611 to the Present* and (ed. with Mark Stein) *Edward Said's Translocations: Essays in Secular Criticism.*

Ulrike Draesner is a major contemporary German novelist, poet, translator and essayist. Her latest novel is the celebrated *Sieben Sprünge vom Rand der Welt.* She has written about Mann (in *Heimliche Helden*) and after Shakespeare (in *Twin Spin*).

Ewan Fernie is Chair, Professor and Fellow at the Shakespeare Institute, University of Birmingham, UK. His latest book, *The Demonic: Literature and Experience*, gives considerable attention to Shakespeare and Mann.

David Fuller is Emeritus Professor of English at the University of Durham, UK. His books include *The Life in the Sonnets*, which explores a significant resonance between Shakespeare and Mann.

John Hamilton is Chair of the Department of Germanic Languages and Literatures and Professor of German and Comparative Literature at Harvard University, USA. His books include *Music, Madness, and the Unworking of Language* and *Security: Politics, Humanity, and the Philology of Care.*

Alexander Honold is Chair of German Literature, Universität Basel, Switzerland. His latest book is *Die Zeit schreiben. Jahreszeiten, Uhren und Kalender als Taktgeber der Literatur;* together with Niels Weber he is co-editor of *Deconstructing Thomas Mann.*

Heather Love is R. Jean Brownlee Term Associate Professor, School of Arts and Sciences, University of Pennsylvania, USA. Her books include *Feeling Backward: Loss and the Politics of Queer History.*

Friedhelm Marx is Chair of German Literature, Universität Bamberg, Germany, and Vice-President of the Thomas-Mann-Gesellschaft. His books include *"Ich aber sage Ihnen...". Christusfigurationen im Werk Thomas Manns* and, most recently, *Thomas Mann Handbuch* (ed. with Andreas Blödorn).

Dave Paxton is a doctoral candidate at the Shakespeare Institute, University of Birmingham, UK. His thesis addresses the relationship between Shakespeare and Wagner and it also considers Mann.

Richard Wilson is the Sir Peter Hall Professor of Shakespeare Studies at Kingston University, UK. *Free Will: Art and Power on Shakespeare's Stage* is his latest work in a career which has brought a vigorous historicism together with an equally vigorous commitment to contemporary European thought.

Introduction: Something Rich and Strange
Ewan Fernie

One point of departure for this volume is found in Norman Rabkin's intellectually interesting but rather forgotten book *Shakespeare and the Problem of Meaning*, which concludes by means of a startling and revelatory comparison of Shakespeare with Thomas Mann. Rabkin recognizes that it may seem strange to yoke together the great English Renaissance dramatist with the most celebrated twentieth-century German novelist, but he insists that the great difference between them actually only 'makes the essential similarities of the two bodies of work all the more extraordinary' (Rabkin 1981: 122). These, Rabkin contends, add up to nothing less than a common vision of experience, a vision, he goes on to explain, whereby life is understood as: one, immanently and entirely absorbing, in all its sensuous and moral immediacy; and yet, at the same time, two, always strangely analogous to the work-of-art. In Mann, aesthetic self-consciousness penetrates into life itself. Indeed, it enters into its most intimate and intense experiences, which Rabkin illustrates by turning to Mann's *Der Erwählte* (*The Holy Sinner*), with its portrayal of the sexual relationship between Gregorius – already the child of an incestuous union between brother and sister – and Sibylla, his mother/aunt. Rabkin focuses especially on the moment when both characters confess that, as they broke the incest taboo for the second time, each of them darkly knew what they were doing. In pretending to be lovers, they in fact 'play acted'; or, as Gregorius suggests grimly, 'thought to offer God an entertainment' (ibid.: 127).[1]

For Rabkin, Mann's vision of life as simultaneously standing inside and, strangely, outside itself at last unlocks 'the problem' of Shakespearean meaning:

It explains the *otherwise* inexplicable insistence in the plays that the life presented as a version of our lives is itself like art, the recurrent suggestion that as people who act we are like actors in a play, the haunting analogies between Prospero's mastery and Shakespeare's.

(ibid.)

It even reveals how, in his late plays, Shakespeare is able to present the most terrible moral conundrums and outrage as 'part of an enchanting landscape, a spectacle to amuse us as well as an image of our lives' reality' (ibid.). And all of this is of more than intellectual benefit. For ultimately, reading Thomas Mann and Shakespeare together teaches a crucial existential lesson, helping us recognize that our lives are at the same time overwhelmingly important and utterly trivial: 'an inconsequential ripple on the flux of time' (ibid.: 139).

Rabkin's book was published in 1981. The year before saw the publication of Stephen Greenblatt's *Renaissance Self-Fashioning*, which famously inaugurated the new-historicist approach that was shortly to sweep through not just Renaissance but literary studies in general. *Renaissance Self-Fashioning* is ironically advertised as of 'related interest' on the fly-leaf of Rabkin's book. Looking back, it seems truer to think of it as of *un*related or alternative interest. For the new-historicist preference for local historical contexts, albeit interlarded with a certain amount of contemporary theory, more or less outlawed the sort of bold transhistorical connection Rabkin makes between Shakespeare and Mann. And yet, it is also clear from rereading Rabkin's thoughtful and engaging work now, that Mann strikes extraordinary lights with Shakespeare, and in ways that freshly and deeply illuminate them both. The present volume therefore seeks to reopen the account between these two major authors.

*

Another starting point for our book lies in Shakespeare's exceptional importance within German culture. In *Buddenbrooks*, Hugo Weinschenk is exposed as an uncultivated person when venturing 'the opinion that *Romeo and Juliet* was a play by Schiller' (Mann 1994: 434).[2] Roger Paulin's magisterial study (2003) on the critical reception of Shakespeare in Germany shows how Shakespeare had come to be adopted as a German classic: one-third of a great trinity also including Schiller and Goethe. 'Er ist unser' (i.e. 'He is ours'), said the Romantic critic and translator A. W. Schlegel in 1796, and in 1844 Ferdinand von Freiligrath opened a famous revolutionary poem with the bold claim 'Deutschland ist Hamlet' ('Germany is Hamlet') – even though this was, in fact, a critical identification which the poem as a whole desperately tried to revoke. By 1911 Friedrich Gundolf had made Shakespeare consubstantial with 'der deutsche Geist' (the German spirit) – an important intellectual legacy also for Thomas Mann (see Note on Mann's Shakespeare, below).[3] But Paulin doesn't engage with Mann, whose career extends beyond his remit. In his still classic study, *The Ironic German*, Erich Heller points out that Tonio Kröger, the titular hero of Mann's early novella, is 'sick of knowledge', as is also 'the case of Hamlet' (Heller 1979: 13); and this invokes not just Nietzsche's comparable reading of the Shakespeare play, but also Freiligrath's equation of an excessively cerebral Teutonic culture with Shakespeare's tormented Dane.[4] Here a condition of self-conscious knowledge and alienation is not resolved in what Rabkin understands as a morally mature double-take on life, which allows us simultaneously to own it and to let it go, but is instead experienced as 'infamous, indecent, outrageous' (ibid.: 14).[5] Hamlet/ Tonio constitutes a traditional and powerful symbiosis of Shakespeare and German culture and, at the same time, a vivid expression of the problematic we live now. And yet, major studies of Shakespeare and modernity such as Hugh Grady's *The Modernist Shakespeare* (1994) and Richard Halpern's *Shakespeare among the Moderns* (1997) do not engage with Mann at all. This volume attempts to fill the gap.

*

Mann's most extended and explicit engagement with Shakespeare is also his most sensational, for Shakespeare is strangely pivotal to the damnation of Adrian Leverkühn, Mann's representative modern artist in his diasporic wartime novel, *Doktor Faustus*. Even more sensationally, Mann associates Adrian's fall with Nazism, to the effect that in the end it is hard to separate Shakespeare from even that dreadful guilt. And yet, these shocking imputations have not been very fully considered in literary criticism. There are only a few, pioneering but rather neglected articles (cf. especially Cerf and Gremler), and I have myself published a more extended treatment in my more generally oriented *The Demonic: Literature and Experience* (2012: 115–41). But the further shock of the coming together of Mann and Shakespeare in Mann's *Faustus* is that Leverkühn derives demonic inspiration not from one of Shakespeare's most obviously demonic plays, such as *Macbeth* or *King Lear*, but rather from his early, baroque comedy *Love's Labour's Lost*.

Two compelling reasons for a book-length study therefore emerge from the most central and demonstrable connection between Shakespeare and Mann. One is its extraordinary and shocking seriousness, with Mann giving us nothing less than a demonic Shakespeare, in part responsible for the most terrible crisis in Western history and culture. There is surely more to be said about such a disturbing appropriation, and the ethically toxic connection it makes between Shakespeare and the demonic requires to be contextualized within Mann's other neglected engagements with the English dramatist. But the other reason for a sustained consideration of the Mann–Shakespeare connection is its sheer curiosity, deriving from the strangeness – the almost *comical* inappropriateness – of Mann's taking *Love's Labour's Lost* as a demonic source. The relation between Mann and Shakespeare has the aspect of an urgent and neglected intellectual puzzle, and this above all constitutes the opening for and interest of this book.

*

Some will still ask whether the conjunction of Mann and Shakespeare isn't in the end *just* a literary curiosity? Whether it isn't perhaps just a morbid modernist joke to associate Shakespeare's early comedy with the demonic guilt of Nazism? We can't entirely rule that out, but nor does it let us off the hook. For in *Doktor Faustus* Mann diagnoses irony and laughter as themselves symptomatic of the demonic trajectory of modern life which culminates in the German catastrophe. The novel makes much of the following couplet from *Love's Labour's Lost*: 'The blood of youth burns not with such excess / As gravity's revolt to wantonness' (5.2.73–4). In the curious business of Shakespeare's comedy, Mann discerns a signally modern alienation of mind from life. On the one hand, this spells liberation from the restrictions of life's givenness: it is an opening for creative freedom. On the other, unmoored from life, mind will tend to delirious, unhealthy abstraction, seen at its fascinating worst in the disorientating ironies, hysterical laughter and shrill, filigree nonsense of *Love's Labour's Lost*. That is one kind of 'wantonness': gravity revolting from life and getting lost in its own freedom. Yet this revolt from life simultaneously produces a perversely intensified hunger for it. Mann, then, describes a twofold movement: gravity revolts from life; then, lustily, revolts from gravity. It sins against life *twice*: by rejecting it then wrecking it in its distempered desire to repossess it again. And this, according to Mann, constitutes a revolt against God as the Creator and epitome of Being, which is why, when Leverkühn is working on his *Love's Labour's Lost* opera, the Devil walks in.

God certainly doesn't walk into the novel. For all the theology in the book, He is not obviously present at all. In this the greatest of Mann's late works, it is as if the demonic is the last religious gesture, perhaps violating God into being. And that explains something of Leverkühn's sacred aura, and is perhaps what the novel's official theologian Schleppfuß has in mind when he declares 'the vicious to be a necessary and inseparable concomitant of the holy, and the holy a constant satanic temptation, an almost irresistible challenge to violation' (Mann 1968: 98).[6] But the stakes are high, for Leverkühn's religiously creative violation which begins in an intellectual interest in the weird comedy of *Love's Labour's Lost*, Mann insists, obscurely but certainly culminates in the inhumane abstraction and perverse lusts of German fascism.

In the end then, Mann's choice of *Love's Labour's Lost* as the demonic inspiration for his *Doktor Faustus* is as brilliant as it is strange. Such is the novel's original reading of the Shakespeare play that Mann's ironic distance from Shakespeare's ironic distance compounds the atmosphere of existential dislocation and ethical crisis. And the seriousness and intensity with which Mann reads even an apparently minor Shakespearean comedy suggests the seriousness and intensity with which we should read Mann, perhaps especially when he is being most ironic.

We have already seen that, according to Rabkin, the Mann–Shakespeare connection offers deep insight into human experience. It is worth stressing the extraordinary truth that in Mann's work Shakespeare, our central and most representative artist, becomes demonic, and of course in *Doktor Faustus* Mann is revealing his own demonic nakedness as well.[7] Rejoining Shakespeare and Mann leads us through the perhaps by now overfamiliar territory of modern and postmodern irony into what one of our contributors, Jonathan Dollimore, calls 'the Big Stuff', enabling a major potential recovery of philosophical seriousness. If at a 'postmodern' distance from experience life can be understood as 'just gaming' (Lyotard 1985), the conjunction of Shakespeare and Mann reminds us the game is in deadly earnest. As this volume will show, art, religion and desire are all at stake. And our perspective is not unhistorical: one of our major concerns is with how the Mann–Shakespeare connection helps to define modernity in Germany, Europe, and America. Mann himself pinpoints the beginning of modernity and cultural crisis in Shakespeare, and we contend that this conjunction of Shakespeare and Mann offers something unusual and important to contemporary theoretical debates about modern life.

Mann connected Shakespeare with dark and demonic themes in works other than *Doktor Faustus*. Friedhelm Marx shows how the German author, who attended and wrote about important German productions of Shakespeare's *Othello*, related to the Moor as a 'dark exception among the rule-abiding' ('eine dunkle Ausnahme unter den Regelrechten').[8] Another of the essays in our volume demonstrates that Wagner provides a bridge between *Der Tod in Venedig* (*Death in Venice*) and Shakespeare's *Measure for Measure*, and between troubling, demonically tinged motifs of yearning, regression and ethics in all three artists.

John Hamilton reveals how the impasto of that same work of Mann's is thickened with echoes of Shakespeare's *The Merchant of Venice*, which in turn casts an unfamiliarly dark light back onto Shakespeare's play. Jonathan Dollimore offers a tour-de-force connecting the violence of desire in Shakespeare, Mann and Nietzsche, formulating in the process a new concept of 'radical theodicy', where the suffering subject gets actively to grips with evil and pain in a universe that God has vacated. In such essays, the disturbing connection which Mann forges in *Doktor Faustus* is shown to be relevant across the oeuvres of both authors.

*

This book is premised on a conviction that the challenge Mann finds in Shakespeare has, in fact, become freshly relevant in our time. At the centre of *Der Zauberberg* (*The Magic Mountain*) are two figures who emerge directly out of what Patrick Cruttwell (1954) calls 'the Shakespearean moment', and which we may define in historical terms of Renaissance humanism and religious crisis. These contend for the soul of Hans Castorp in a disturbingly prescient dramatization of the weak position of liberal thought when confronted with a passionate irrationalism that extends so far as demonic terror. But if Mann was right about the weakness of liberalism in 1924, and the Nazis rose to power in Germany, he is also right in the early twenty-first century, when his fiction strikes obvious lights with the revival of religious terrorism.

In *Der Zauberberg*, humanism and religious renovation are defined as the two poles of modern civilization, from 'the Shakespearean moment' to that in which the novel was written. The first contestant for Castorp's soul is Herr Settembrini, a shabbily chic humanist. The second is Herr Naphta, a peculiar kind of Jesuit, at once ascetic and voluptuous, unworldly and violent; a man of the cloth but clearly on the church's outermost fringe; an advocate of total immersion in a transcendent reality that encompasses both good and evil. This figure represents the continued, unpredicted ructions of Reformation and religious revival in modernity.

Settembrini is the liberal man of progress. Everything he believes in – liberty, education, pleasure – suggests he is one of us, the exemplarily modern man; whereas everything about Naphta confirms he is a throwback, perhaps a pervert, fascinating in his limited pathological way but only as a fossil or curiosity. The Renaissance remains a guiding light, it would seem, while the Reformation fades into its own backward gloominess. And yet, *Der Zauberberg* tells us how much more power-fully the darkly insinuating Naptha speaks to humanity's ordinary soul as it is embodied in Hans Castorp, foretelling the unpredictable, sometimes violent return of the spiritual, which Mann related to the Nazi crisis in *Doktor Faustus*, but which is also an unexpected and alarming feature of our contemporary life.

Settembrini would have no difficulty in signing up to today's ethics of difference – that late species of democratic humanism which was intellectually revived by post-structuralist thought and which plays out beyond the academy in, for example, the diversity agenda. But the ethics of difference tends to gloss over the violent negativity to which it tends. Pushed to its logical extreme, it involves the repudiation of what is in favour for what is not, which amounts to nothing less than, as Philip Blond perceives, 'an erasure of existents from existence' (1998: 218–9) and accords with great classical and literary accounts of the demonic. Naphta is on to this: 'For the progress was pure nihilism, the liberal citizen was quite precisely the advocate of nothingness and the Devil' (*The Magic Mountain*, hereafter referred to as *MM*, 525).[9] Thus does liberal humanism shade into utter negativity.

But Settembrini is in denial about this, and Mann insinuates that we are too. Instead of embracing negativity, Settembrini presents himself as the champion of life, but Naphta pitilessly demonstrates that the life which Settembrini champions is so vitiated and abstracted as to be no real life at all: 'he was anything other than pious, he was a traitor to life' (*MM* 525).[10] Settembrini is a traitor to life partly because of the displacement from life involved in abstract enthusiasm for democracy and the nascent ethics of difference, but also because he has no higher ideal than life. For, as Naphta says:

> this morality of Herr Settembrini's, what was it, what did it want? It was life-bound, and thus entirely utilitarian; it was pathetically unheroic. Its end and aim was to make men grow old and happy, rich and comfortable – and that was all there was to it. And this Philistine philosophy, this gospel of work and reason, served Herr Settembrini as an ethical system. As far as he, Naphta, was concerned, he would continue to deny it was anything but the sheerest and shabbiest bourgeoisiedom.
>
> (*MM* 464)[11]

But what's the alternative? The desublimated demonic, where nothingness becomes a positive passion? In a sense, yes. But what Naphta recognizes and embodies is that such a demonic intensification of life equally involves a re-ignition of the possibility of God. As he says, 'God and the Devil were at one in being opposed to life, to bourgeoisiedom, reason and virtue, since they together represented the religious principle' (*MM* 464).[12] Settembrini responds with hygienic disgust:

'What a disgusting hodge-podge – *che guazzabuglio proprio stomachevole!*' Good and evil, sanctification and criminal conduct, all mixed up together! Without judgement! Without direction! Without the possibility of repudiating what was vile! Did Herr Naphta realize what it was he denied and disavowed in the presence of youth, when he flung God and the Devil together and in the name of this mad two-in-oneness refused to admit even the existence of an ethical principle? He denied every standard of values, he denied goodness! Horrible! – Very well, then there existed neither good nor evil, nothing but a morally chaotic All! There was not even the individual in possession of a critical faculty – there was only the all-consuming, the all-levelling universal communality, and mystic immersion in her!

(*MM* 464)[13]

But what Naphta has on his side is the significant intuition that life – or at least any life that is worth having – is beyond the small concerns of ordinary individuated existence, and beyond the tidy demarcations of decorum and virtue. This is the positive force in the Freudian death-drive as Lacan and Žižek have unfolded it and, as Naphta sees, it is a significant impulse of religion as such insofar as religion involves metaphysical aspiration.[14]

This spiritual intensification of life Naphta foresees foretells both the horrors of the twentieth century and the nightmares of today. 'Liberation and development of the individual are not the key to our age,' he says, 'they are not what our age demands. What it needs, what it wrestles after, what it will create – is Terror' (*MM* 400).[15] That of course foretells Leverkühn's Shakespeare-fuelled adventures into the dark; and, in the epoch of Al-Qaeda and counterterrorism, it is once again a particularly chilling thought. Naphta elaborates as follows:

That power is evil we know. But if the kingdom is to come, then it is necessary that the dualism between good and evil, between power and the spirit, here and hereafter, must be for the time abrogated to make way for a single principle.

(*MM* 402)[16]

That principle will be one 'asserting the ideals of the *Civitas Dei* in opposition to the discredited and decadent standards of the capitalistic bourgeoisie' (*MM* 404).[17] It is not, one imagines, entirely different from the rationale of today's terrorists. The task, Naptha urges, 'is to strike terror into the world for the healing of the world, that man may finally achieve salvation and deliverance, and win back at length from law and from distinction of classes, to his original status as child of God' (*MM* 404).[18]

Der Zauberberg does not permit us just to hold this at horrified arm's length. Mann is exemplarily brave in admitting the power of demonic temptation in *Doktor Faustus*, and it is no different here. That is why Mann's ingenuous Castorp confesses, 'the temptation grew well-nigh irresistible to plunge head foremost into Naphta's "morally chaotic All"'(*MM* 468).[19] He contemplates first Settembrini and then Naphta as follows:

> You are a wind-bag and a hand-organ man, to be sure. But you mean well, you mean much better, and more to my mind, than that knife-edged little Jesuit and Terrorist, apologist of the Inquisition and the knout, with his round eye-glasses – though he is nearly always right when you and he come to grips over my paltry soul, like God and the Devil in the mediaeval legends.
>
> (*MM* 478)[20]

Naphta is so soul-shakingly right in spiritual matters, even where the soul concerned is as ordinary as Hans Castorp's, because his thought offers a real if terrible solution to the burden of modern negativity and alienation. Settembrini's more hygienic humanism is revealed as essentially an evasion of that problem.

You might think that Shakespeare can be kept out of it, but of course Renaissance and Reformation are the great traditions he works with and inherits, and the spirituality of horror for which Naphta speaks is ultimately given an explicitly Shakespearean form. At the visionary centre of the novel, when he is lost in a snowstorm on the magic mountain, Hans is ravished by beautiful visions of humanity. Yet when he reaches 'the sanctuary' that promises to disclose the mystical truth of his dream, 'the poor soul's knees all but gave way beneath him at the sight within. Two grey old women, witchlike, with hanging breasts and dugs of finger-length, were busy there, between flaming braziers, most horribly. They were dismembering a child' (*MM* 494).[21] You can almost see the cauldron steaming behind them:

> Double, double, toil and trouble,
> Fire burn, and cauldron bubble.

You can almost hear the old crone's toothless but fervent whisper as she drops the first severed digit from a height:

> Finger of birth-strangled babe
> Ditch-delivered by a drab.[22]

Hans Castorp has stumbled into a scene from *Macbeth*. Naphta and negativity seem horribly hard to overcome, primordial evil seems irreducibly involved in the demonic intensification of life, in *Der Zauberberg*. And it seems that, as with *Doktor Faustus*, Shakespeare is inextricably stirred into the mix.

But surely there is a further alternative to the unappealing choice between Settembrini's weak and fraudulent humanism and Naphta's terrible negativity? Mann certainly attempts to find one, and in such a way as, again, powerfully remembers Shakespeare. In his principled drunkenness, advanced age, defiant sexiness and great physical bulk, Mynheer Peeperkorn, who is generally understood as an unflattering portrait of Mann's great rival Gerhardt Hauptmann, in fact equally resembles Shakespeare's Falstaff. And both Peeperkorn and Falstaff stand for what Castorp calls 'the mystery of personality' (*MM* 583).[23] Falstaff crows: 'give me life' (*1 Henry IV*, 5.3.58). And Peeperkorn, according to his own impressive credo, stands for the power and positivity of life as experienced:

> 'Man is godlike, in that he feels. He is the feeling of God. God created him in order to feel through him. Man is nothing but the organ through which God consummates his marriage with roused and intoxicated life. If man fails in feeling, it is blasphemy; it is the surrender of His masculinity, a cosmic catastrophe, an irreconcileable horror –' He drank.
>
> (*MM* 603)[24]

This boozy philosopher is Falstaff rendered freshly, and Castorp insists that even if what he says is tomfoolery, it is 'majestic tomfoolery' whereby 'things that sound crass and irreverent ... are after all more solemn than the conventional religious formulas' (*MM* 624).[25]

Der Zauberberg begs the question: can Falstaff stand against Macbeth? It is, in fact, a brilliant, existentially provoking thought, of a sort arguably not asked enough in contemporary Shakespeare studies: a vouch of the important perspectives on Shakespeare that can arise from reading Mann. And yet, the truth is that Peeperkorn is a powerful sketch of a positive, Shakespearean alternative to the negativity of modern life, but a sketch merely, and something of an *opera buffa* sketch at that. Naphta's suicide in a climactic duel with Settimbrini leaves at least as lingering an impression, and Mann will have to do better than Peeperkorn, majestic tomfool though he is, to stave off his own most terrible and tempting nightmares of modern religious negativity. For now the road to *Doktor Faustus* – and to Hell – rolls out like a red carpet.

*

I hope the above will at least stand for something of the powerfully interesting Mann–Shakespeare conjunction, and its capacity to refresh discussion of both authors. Such a subject of course permits various approaches and this book therefore combines the strong through-line of an adventurous – as well as aesthetically, ethically and politically serious – consideration of the Mann–Shakespeare connection with scope for considerable differences of opinion. The essays worry at the urgent intellectual puzzle provided by the conjunction of these two authors in their own ways. Richard Wilson, for instance, finds the gnomic qualities of Mann's appropriation of *Love's Labour's Lost* bespeak a premonition of the modernist crisis of language, and a response in particular to Theodor Adorno's view that Auschwitz had murdered poetry.[26] And the failure of words which he takes up also relates to Tobias Döring's analysis of Mann as 'der Zauberer' in relation to the Shakespearean magus, Prospero, a consideration which leads Döring to wonder whether the Mann–Shakespeare connection doesn't ultimately reveal that the 'magic fountain' of efficacious authorship has actually dried up in modernity. My own essay suggests that, though Mann's Falstaffian answer to the challenge of the demonic ultimately fails in *Der Zauberberg*, he attempts to improve on it in his monumental but rather neglected four-part epic, *Joseph und seine Brüder* (*Joseph and his Brothers*). This is not a Shakespeare-inspired work but I argue that it can nonetheless 'bounce' us into a new view of one of Shakespeare's major comedies – *As You Like It* – as an analogous effort to make a life which positively draws the negative into its own texture, and as a result can comprehensively be affirmed. The comparative method of this contribution shows how our volume as a whole follows Rabkin in not restricting itself to 'Shakespeare-spotting' in Mann's oeuvre but rather extending into wider considerations of shared concerns and affinities in an effort to cast real light on both authors.

But if the main purpose of this book is its reciprocal illumination of Mann and Shakespeare, its bringing together two important artists from normally separated periods and traditions is also intended as an intervention in favour of expanding the horizons of mainstream criticism as it is practised in the academy today. We would, first, like the volume to highlight the possibilities for making productive European connections in a context where the recent dominance of the Anglo-American academy has combined with a timely interest in wider globalization to obscure them. *Thomas Mann and Shakespeare: Something Rich and Strange* brings together scholars from different fields – English, German and Comparative Literature – and from different countries – the UK, the USA, Germany and Switzerland – in an attempt to open up a particular nexus of European exchange which also, of course, involves negotiating two different languages. Moreover, to read Shakespeare and Mann together is to defy the increasingly walled-in specialism of literary topics and periodization, suggesting the scope for more adventurous conjunctions. Of course there are honourable precedents for this, and not least in the work of some of our own contributors. There is the transhistorical work of Jonathan Dollimore, and 'Comp Lit', as evidenced in Hamilton's work, is also exemplary. Apart from anything else, adventurous conjunctions are truer to the complex, even mysterious, processes of intellectual life. Writers often take inspiration from beyond scholarship's tidy curricula, and readers and critics need the flex, breadth and imagination to follow them. This volume takes the demonstrable connection between Mann and Shakespeare as an occasion to track at least one aesthetic impulse hitherto unaccommodated by critical analysis, and it equally attempts to show how Shakespeare's influence on Mann can help us to understand Shakespeare. This also involves bringing various intermediary figures, such as Wagner, into new constellations with our two major authors. The intellectual connections between Mann and Shakespeare broaden the focus out to philosophers from Friedrich Nietzsche to Gillian Rose, and some of these interlocutors and contexts are unfamiliar in either Shakespeare or Mann studies. Furthermore, the Shakespeare–Mann conjunction has its literary inheritors, as Heather Love shows in her treatment of how Willa Cather and Susan Sontag negotiated these great patriarchal queer influences, in the process importantly opening up what otherwise may seem an all-too-exclusively male milieu. Ulrike Draesner extends this broadening out in gender terms by showing how the works of both Shakespeare and Mann actually themselves solicit and thus can be transformed by female libido.

Mann and Shakespeare are of course practitioners of different literary arts, but our book ventures to suggest that, precisely as a result, their juxtaposition can cast unfamiliar light on poetry, drama and the novel. Alexander Honold's essay focuses on what happens to Shakespearean comic drama when it is drawn into Mann's great musical novel of cultural – and gender – crisis. And as a major practising poet, essayist and novelist, Draesner demonstrates some of the delicate and telling processes whereby the genre-crossing Shakespeare–Mann connection may play into new forms of creative thinking and writing. Throughout, then, this volume hopes to show how fertile a conjunction from outside the given intellectual doxa can be, and to encourage work in the same spirit on other couplings just as odd as that between Mann and Shakespeare. It contends that such neglected conjunctions across academic barriers can open up whole new worlds of intellectual possibility.

Finally, it also contends that what goes for writers, goes for readers too: that their imaginations and thought processes are richer and more apparently accidental than can be mapped onto given critical contexts, and that those contexts might have to stretch, shift and combine to do justice to the complexity of reading. In *Die Entstehung des Doktor Faustus* (*The Genesis of a Novel*), his record of composing his late great book, Mann tells how, even as he brooded on the endgame of World War II, he read *Love's Labour's Lost* in the evening – and he insists, quite unironically here, that the Shakespeare play falls within 'the charmed circle' (Mann 1961: 26–7).[27] This is Mann speaking as a reader for the unpredictable responsiveness of critical thinking. In our book, David Fuller analyses Hans Castorp's rapturous discovery of the gramophone as symbolic of the ways that such wild susceptibility combines with strict attentiveness in aesthetic response, relating this to his own responses to both Mann and Shakespeare. Certainly, if you add the unpredictability of aesthetic influence and composition to the unpredictability of reading, what you will get is very particular and surprising indeed, and as such closer to the pleasure and appeal books actually have for their readers. Of course, it is the responsibility of criticism to be available and shareable. But it is equally the responsibility of criticism to tell the truth about art, which is at least in part irreducibly subjective.

Thus even as it tries to do justice to the shareable 'Big Stuff' concerns into which Mann and Shakespeare lead us, this book attempts to suggest some of the open-ended contingency involved in reading these authors together. Both are so monumentally established and celebrated – Shakespeare of course even more so than Mann – that one perhaps *needs* to approach them from an odd angle in order to rediscover the inimitable power on which their elevated reputations depend, and which alone can justify them. In Mann, this book suggests, Shakespeare again becomes rich and strange, even as Shakespeare contributes to and renews Mann's own rich strangeness.

A Note on Mann's Shakespeare, by Tobias Döring

Authors choose and make their ancestors, rather than simply follow them. Thomas Mann was passionately concerned to present, invent and position himself as a modern artist in relation to key ancestral figures, both from German traditions and beyond, as evinced in the intertextual networks of so much of his work. The relevance of forebears such as Goethe, Schopenhauer, Wagner or Nietzsche has long been noted, and indeed is amply attested to in Mann's own fiction, essays, diaries or letters. The critical significance of Shakespeare's work for Mann, by contrast, has not yet been extensively explored.[28] Yet, arguably, Mann's writing also involves strong engagements with – and reinventions of – Shakespearean legacies whose uses for a modern age of crisis are tapped and crucially reworked. As indicated in the thematic introduction above, the contributions to this volume set out to explore these critical interrelations in a double perspective of mutual reconfiguration: their concern is not only with issues of how Mann reads Shakespeare but also how Shakespeare, as it were, reads Mann as well as us and our modern sense of crisis – or rather, how we today read Shakespeare differently after having also read Mann. In the words of Elizabeth Bronfen (in the 'Afterword' to our volume), this is 'an investigation into literary correspondences and connections, transcending ... issues of acknowledged influence and explicit citation' (p. 246), a project which she ingeniously terms *crossmapping*.

To begin with, however, before tracing this web of interconnections more fully, it may be useful to provide a rough map of the more obvious historical relation and briefly sketch what kind of Shakespeare Mann would actually have known – i.e. what Shakespearean studies he must have been familiar with and drew on in his work – and in what ways his own Shakespearean responses relate to dominant German Shakespeare notions at his time. Three names in particular are significant as writers formative for Mann's understanding, and creative use, of Shakespeare: Georg Brandes, Frank Harris and Friedrich Gundolf. More generally speaking, and as Fernie suggests above, Mann's Shakespeare engagements follow two centuries of intense German efforts in translating, adapting, adoring, appropriating, idealizing and naturalizing Shakespeare – a remarkable process of cultural domestication whose story has often been told.[29] At least since Christoph Martin Wieland published his first prose translations in the 1760s and since Lessing, around the same time, championed Shakespeare as a liberator from the dogma of neoclassical poetics, German literary culture celebrated and used Shakespeare's work as a weapon against what was seen as the narrow-minded norms and well-worn bonds of a received tradition, specifically identified with a French *ancien regime*. It is therefore no exaggeration to call Shakespeare *the* enabling, if not the actually originating, force of German cultural self-inventions, from the later eighteenth well into the twentieth century. With the romantic age and, especially, the later nineteenth century, this powerful literary development gained more and more political and nationalistic resonances, culminating in April 1864, at the Shakespeare Tercentenary, with the foundation of the German Shakespeare Society at Weimar – a key event indicating the then reigning *Dichterreligion* (religious poet worship) in Germany, combined with aggressively patriotic pronouncements to claim Shakespeare as 'fully ours', a strategy known as *nostrification*.[30] This, finally and lastingly, made Shakespeare – and especially Shakespearean tragic heroes like, above all others, Hamlet – the mirror which German culture held up to itself.

It also made Shakespeare a popular presence. One of the most far-reaching and far-sighted activities of the German Shakespeare

Society was to sponsor and circulate inexpensive popular editions in translation, available for a broad readership, which turned Shakespeare, alongside Schiller and Goethe, into a household name and obligatory item on the bookshelves of respectable middle-class families – hence Weinschenk's blunder, in *Buddenbrooks* (as cited above, see note 2), betraying his lowly origin and lack of *Bildung*. As a necessary element in the canon of bourgeois self-esteem, Shakespeare functioned henceforth as a proof of education, culture and refinement.

Against this background, Thomas Mann's own early engagements with Shakespeare can be placed. As a nineteen-year-old, in 1895, he wrote in his notebook:

> Hamlet's soul is not at all troubled by the question of how to take revenge on the King. In his innermost depth, he suffers from a breakdown by which he has lost the lighthearted view on life prevalent in his youth. He stands at a critical juncture of human life: at the transition from the enthusiasm and confidence of youth to the darker worldview of his more mature manhood. His faith and his confidence in men are blasted. This is the tragedy, this above all.
>
> (Georg Brandes)

(Notizbuch 1, pp. 38–9, Mann 1991: 27)[31]

This note lingers in the melancholy self-mirroring in Hamlet in such a way as will re-emerge in the novella *Tonio Kröger* a decade later. At the same time, it gives evidence of Mann's early contact both with Shakespeare and with one of his most powerful contemporary critics, the Danish writer Georg Brandes, restless campaigner for the modern breakthrough and author of a highly influential biographical study that defined the dominant image of Shakespeare in the early twentieth century. In 1927, when Brandes died, Mann paid public tribute to him as 'the last of the European generation to whom we fifty-year-olds owe our education' (quoted in Sandberg 1972: 157, trans. TD). The Shakespeare education Brandes offered was resolutely biographical and grounded in a general belief that exceptional creations must derive from exceptional personalities and their extraordinary lives. His *William Shakespeare: A Critical Study* (first published in 1895, German edition the same year, English edition in 1898) therefore combined a romantic reading of Shakespearean genius with severe historicist positivism, seeking and finding in the artist's biography the explanatory matrix of his work.[32]

Along the same romantic lines of biographical speculation, but without the rigour of historical considerations, let alone verification, Frank Harris's various Shakespeare engagements proceeded to suggest extremely intimate interrelations between life and work, with special emphasis on Shakespeare's love life. Unlike Brandes, Harris – an Irish-English journalist straddling a hectic business life as publisher and writer between London and New York – has no credit as a scholar, but his work gained remarkable prominence in popularizing neo-romantic Shakespeare myths, in particular reading the sonnets as an erotic diary, following Wordsworth's notorious notion that they must be the 'key' by which the bard unlocked his heart. In 1904, Harris published a stage play entitled *Shakespeare and His Love*. In 1909, he went on to transfer his main idea – Shakespeare's lifelong obsession with Mary Fitton, Queen Elizabeth's capricious maid of honour – from the realm of fiction into biography: his *The Man Shakespeare and His Tragic Life Story* casts Fitton in the role of the Dark Lady of the sonnets as well as Rosaline from *Love's Labour's Lost* and retells the sad story of Shakespeare's continued, yet frustrated, courtship of her, allegedly reflected in his plays and poems. With a true sense for dramatic possibilities, Harris also invents the figure of a go-between, the Fair Youth as messenger of love, whom Shakespeare supposedly employed for this purpose. This had the added advantage of making the male addressee of sonnets 1 to 123 a mediator, not the target, of Shakespeare's own true love, thus rescuing the bard from 'buggery' and supporting Harris's staunch homophobia.

Still, it was this triangular construction – wooing by proxy – that caught Mann's special interest and attention, as explicitly acknowledged in *Die Entstehung*, when he read the German version of Harris's book (which had come out in 1928 with Mann's own publisher, S. Fischer) while working on *Doktor Faustus*. In March 1943 he noted in his diary (Mann 1982: 544) apropos of *Der Mensch Shakespeare*: 'stimulating, a lot of truth, often doubtful' ('anregend, viel Wahres, oft zu bezweifeln', trans. TD). And yet it must have been precisely this kind of doubtfulness or dubiousness that made such speculative erotic-biographical fiction so productive for Mann's Faustus novel with its Nietzschean overtones and various love triangles – including reminiscences of Nietzsche's hapless courtship for Lou von Salomé using his friend Rée as go-between; a novel steeped in genre and in gender ambiguities, as argued in Alexander Honold's chapter. In fact, according to a recent book-length study of Harris as a source for Mann (Stürmer 2014), *Doktor Faustus* may even owe its generic biographical format to Harris's Shakespeare fantasy.[33]

By contrast, the third contemporary authority, whose impact on German Shakespeare notions from the 1910s to '30s cannot be overestimated, rejected all the narrow, lowly, mundane nitty-gritty of conventional biography; for him, genuine artists – Dante, Shakespeare, Goethe and so on – would rise above such frivolous contingencies and prove their mastery to the happy few by reconnecting them with the aura of eternal art. Friedrich Gundolf published *Shakespeare und der deutsche Geist* ('Shakespeare and the German Spirit') in 1911, when he was thirty and had just established himself as literature professor at the University of Heidelberg. It was the first of three literary monuments – the other two were on Goethe (1916) and on Stefan George (1920) – by which he formulated and propagated the aesthetic ethos of the George circle, as charismatic and exclusive as it was elusive and arcane, to which he had belonged since 1899. The book was also part of Gundolf's current efforts, together with George, to translate Shakespeare works anew, resolutely reworking the romantic Schlegel-Tieck versions, so as to bring them poetically into tune with the modern German genius (cf. Karlauf 2007: 373–5). Their Shakespeare is a vatic force of spiritual initiation who leads them into higher forms of life. As Gundolf writes in conclusion:

> What almost all of us lack is power for actuality [*Kraft zur Wirklichkeit*]. And when we look for a master who can give us actuality and, at the same time, the power to endure it, this again is Shakespeare. To conquer and shape his actuality for our own attitude to life [*Lebensgefühl*] is one of the missions of the new German spirit.
>
> (Gundolf 1920: 358)[34]

Mann, who owned a copy of George's 1909 translation of the sonnets, kept a lifelong distance from his circle, viewing George with guarded fascination and increasing political misgivings (cf. Marx 2006/7). But Gundolf's emphatic celebration of Shakespeare's supreme leadership, as both guardian and guide of the new German spirit, may not be quite irrelevant for Mann's later portrait, through the mask of modest Zeitblom, of Leverkühn, the German composer with his Shakespearean obsessions. To say the least, the Shakespeare legacy from Brandes, Harris and Gudolf formed a complex constellation of artistic creativity, exceptional biography and national destiny – certainly a suggestive field for subsequent generations to triangulate their Shakespeare notions. These resonated richly with Mann's lifelong interest in triangular constructions and in the social stigma of the modern artist figure, blurring boundaries between art and life and politics, in favour of their mutual mirroring – making Leverkühn a Prospero-like playmaster both of Germany's and of his own life drama, and turning the amorous Madame Houpflé in *Felix Krull* into a parodistic version of the sonneteering Shakespeare promising the beloved youth immortality through art.

However, all such crossmappings are now to be explored more fully in the dozen contributions to our book.

Notes

1   Rabkin is quoting from *The Holy Sinner* (Mann 1951: 332); *wir gedachten Gott eine Unterhaltung damit zu bieten* (Mann 1960: 257).

2   *oder wenn er der Meinung Ausdruck gab, 'Romeo und Julia' sei ein Stück von Schiller* (Mann 2002a: 485).

3   For these references, see Paulin (2003: 280, 443–5, 448–95).

4   For Paulin's discussion of Nietzsche on *Hamlet*, see (2003: 454–8).

5   Heller is quoting from Mann (1936: 106–7).

6   *erklärte das Verruchte für ein notwendiges und mitgeborenes Korrelat des Heiligen und dieses für eine beständige satanische Versuchung, eine fast unwiderstehliche Herausforderung zur Schändung* (Mann 2007: 148).

7   He himself called the book 'a radical confession' (Mann 1961: 124): *ein radikales Bekenntnis*, as noted also in his diary on 1 January 1946 (Mann 1986: 295).

8   The phrase is from Mann's programmatic 1907 essay 'Das Theater als Tempel' ('The Theatre as Temple'), an early version of the longer and better known 'Versuch über das Theater' ('Essay on the Theatre'); see the chapter by Friedhelm Marx for detailed references and discussion.

9   *Denn der Fortschritt sei reiner Nihilismus und der liberale Bürger ganz eigentlich der Mann des Nichts und des Teufels* (*Der Zauberberg*, hereafter referred to as GKFA 5: 791).

10   *Er sei aber nichts weniger als fromm, sondern ein Hochverbrecher am Leben* (ibid.).

11   *Was sie denn sei und wolle, die Sittlichkeit des Herrn Settembrini? Sie sei lebengebunden, also nichts als nützlich, also unheroisch in erbarmungswürdigem Grade. Sie sei dazu da, daß man alt und glücklich, reich und gesund damit werde und damit Punktum. Diese Vernunft- und Arbeisphilisterei gelte ihm als Ethik. Was dagegen Naphta betreffe, so erlaube er sich wiederholt, sie als schäbige Lebensbürgerlichkeit zu kennzeichnen* (ibid.: 698–9).

12   *In Wirklichkeit aber seien sie eins und einig dem Leben entgegengesetzt, der Lebensbürgerlichkeit, der Ethik, der Vernunft, der Tugend, – als das religiöse Prinzip, das sie gemeinsam darstellten* (ibid.: 698).

13   *'Was für ein ekelhafter Mischmasch – che guazzabuglio proprio stomachevole!' rief Settembrini. Gut und Böse, Heiligkeit und Missetat, alles vermengt! Ohne Urteil! Ohne Willen! Ohne die Fähigkeit, zu verwerfen, was verworfen sei. Ob Herr Naphta denn wisse, was er leugne, indem er vor den Ohren der Jugend Gott und Teufel zusammenwerfe und im Namen dieser wüsten Zweieinigkeit das ethische Prinzip verneine! Er leugne den Wert, – jede Wertsetzung, – abscheulich zu sagen. Schön, es gab also nicht Gut noch Böse, sondern nur das sittlich ungeordnete All! Es gab auch nicht den einzelnen in seiner kritischen Würde, sondern nur die alles verschlingende und ausgleichende Gemeinschaft, den mystischen Untergang in ihr!* (ibid.).

14   Jacques Lacan suggests that life is 'between two deaths', the first being involved in the necessary break beyond merely conventional identity, the second being our mortal end (see Lacan 1999: 282); Slavoj Žižek develops this idea in *The Ticklish Subject* (1999).

15 *Nicht Befreiung und Entfaltung des Ich sind das Geheimnis und das Gebot der Zeit. Was sie braucht, wonach sie verlangt, was sie sich schaffen wird, das ist – Terror* (GKFA 5: 604).

16 *Daß die Macht böse ist, wissen wir. Aber der Dualismus von Gut und Göse, von Jenseits und Diesseits, Geist und Macht muß, wenn das Reich kommen soll, vorübergehend aufgehoben werden in einem Prinzip, das Askese und Herrschaft vereinigt.* (ibid.: 607).

17 *das heute die Humanität und die Kriterien des Gottesstaates der bürgerlich-kapitalistischen Verrottung entgegenstellt* (ibid.: 608).

18 *seine Aufgabe ist der Schrecken zum Heile der Welt und zur Gewinnung des Erlösungsziels, der staats- und klassenlosen Gotteskindschaft* (ibid.: 609).

19 *daß die Versuchung groß war, sich kopfüber in Naphtas 'sittlich ungeordnetes All' zu stürzen* (ibid.: 705).

20 *Du bist zwar ein Windbeutel und Drehorgelmann, aber du meinst es gut, meinst es besser und bist mir lieber als der scharfe kleine Jesuit und Terrorist, der spanische Folter- und Prügelknecht mit seiner Blitzbrille, obgleich er fast immer recht hat, wenn ihr euch zankt ... euch pädagogisch um meine arme Seele rauft, wie Gott und Teufel um den Menschen im Mittelalter...* (ibid.: 719).

21 *die Knie wollten dem Armen brechen vor dem, was er mit Starren erblickte. Zwei graue Weiber, halbnackt, zottenhaarig, mit hängenden Hexenbrüsten und finger-langen Zitzen, hantierten dort drinnen zwischen flackernden Feuerpfannen aufs gräßlichste. Über einem Becken zerrissen sie ein kleines Kind* (ibid.: 745).

22 These lines are from *Macbeth* (4.1.20–1, 4.1.30–1) when the titular hero visits the witches in their kitchen.

23 *das Wesen der Persönlichkeit* (GKFA 5: 869).

24 *'Der Mensch ist göttlich, sofern er fühlt. Er ist das Gefühl Gottes. Gott schuf ihn, um durch ihn zu fühlen. Der Mensch ist nichts als das Organ, durch das Gott seine Hochzeit mit dem erweckten und berauschten Leben vollzieht. Versagt er im Gefühl, so bricht Gottesschande herein, es ist die Niederlage von Gottes Manneskraft, eine kosmische Katastrophe, ein unausdenkbares Entsetzen –' Er trank* (ibid.: 913).

25 *eine königliche Narretei... Wenn man ergriffen ist, hat man den Mut zu Ausdrücken, die kraß und pietätlos klingen, aber feierlicher sind als konzessio-nierte Andachtsworte* (ibid.: 946–7). This clearly relates to Mann's approving quotation of Schopenhauer's view that Shakespeare's exemplary art forswears finger-wagging moral judgement in favour of a sympathetic and revelatory identification with his characters whoever they are and whatever they do; see his *Reflections of a Nonpolitical Man* (Mann 1983: 163).

26 See Adorno (1983: 34).

27 *Das Shakespeare-Stück gehört zur 'Sache'. Es fällt in den Kreis* (Mann: 2009: 428).

28 The notable exceptions, apart from Fernie's seminal chapter (2012: 115–41), are the pioneering but mostly rather short essays by Puknat & Puknat (1967), Meyers (1973), Szudra (1979), Peres (2009), Cerf (1981; 1985) and Gremler (2005)); they all focus on *Doktor Faustus*.

29 Most comprehensively, if somewhat idiosyncratically (see Höfele 2005), by Roger Paulin (2003), as credited above.

30   For a history of the German Shakespeare Society, with special emphasis on
     the first half of the twentieth century, see Ledebur (2002); for a present-day
     review of its foundation, see the contributions to the 150th anniversary
     convention in Weimar, published in *Shakespeare Jahrbuch* 151 (Bochum:
     Kamp 2015).
31   *Im Hintergrund von Hamlets Seele steht ja durchaus nicht die Frage, auf welche
     Weise er vom König Rache erhalten soll. In seinem tiefsten Innern leidet er unter
     dem Zusammensturze der lichten Lebensanschauung seiner Jugend. Er selbst
     steht in dem kritischen Stadium eines Menschenlebens: dem Übergang von der
     Begeisterung und dem Vertrauen der Jugend zu der dunkleren Weltanschauung
     des reiferen Mannesalters. Sein Glaube und sein Vertrauen zu den Menschen ist
     gesprengt. Das ist das Trauerspiel, das ist [es] in erster Linie. (Georg Brandes)*
     (Mann 1991: 27, English version TD); this is an excerpt from Brandes,
     William Shakespeare (München: Langen 1895). Sandberg (1972: 126) dates
     the entry 1893, but this would be before the publication of Brandes's
     study.
32   On 'The Personal Element in Hamlet', Brandes has this to say: 'The
     experience with shook Hamlet's nature was no other than that which every
     nobly disposed youth, on first seeing the world as it is, concentrates in the
     words: "Alas! Life is not what I thought it was." The father's murder, the
     mother's possible complicity, and her indecent haste in entering upon a
     new wedlock, were only symptoms in the young man's eyes of the worth-
     lessness of human nature and the injustice of life – only the individual
     instances from which, by instinctive generalization, he inferred the dire
     disillusions and terrible possibilities of existence – only the chance occasion
     for the sudden vanishing of that rosy light in which everything had hitherto
     been steeped for him, and in the absence of which the earth seemed to him
     a sterile promontory, and the heavens a pestilent congregation of vapours.
     Just such a crisis, bringing with it the "loss of all his mirth", Shakespeare
     himself had recently undergone' (Brandes 1917: 302–3).
33   Franziska Stürmer (2014) argues that Mann used Harris's narrative of
     Shakespeare's life as a template for Zeitblom's narrative of Leverkühn's
     life. Stürmer's monograph became available just as the present manuscript
     went into press; regrettably, therefore, it was not possible to appreciate her
     argument more fully.
34   *Was uns fast allen fehlt, ist die Kraft zur Wirklichkeit. Und sehen wir uns
     da nach einem Meister um der zugleich alle Wirklichkeit gebe und die Kraft
     sie zu ertragen, so ist es abermals Shakespeare. Seine Wirklichkeit für unser
     Lebensgefühl zu erobern und zu gestalten ist eine der Aufgaben des neuen
     deutschen Geistes* (Gundolf 1920: 358, English version TD).

Works Cited

Adorno, Theodor W., 1983. *Prisms*, trans. Samuel Weber. Boston: MIT Press.
Blond, Philip, 1998. 'Emmanuel Levinas: God and Phenomenology', in *Post-Secular
     Philosophy: between Philosophy and Theology*, ed. Philip Blond. London, New York:
     Routledge, pp. 195–229.

Brandes, Georg, 1917 [1898]. *William Shakespeare: A Critical Study*, trans. William Archer and Mary Morison. London: Heinemann.

Cerf, Steven, 1981. 'Love in Thomas Mann's *Doktor Faustus* as an Imitatio Shakespeari', in *Comparative Literature Studies* 18, pp. 475–86.

Cerf, Steve, 1985. 'The Shakespearean Element in Thomas Mann's *Doktor Faustus*-Montage', in *Revue de Littérature Comparée* 59, pp. 427–41.

Cruttwell, Patrick, 1954. *The Shakespearean Moment and Its Place in the Poetry of the Seventeenth Century*. London: Chatto & Windus.

Fernie, Ewan, 2012. *The Demonic: Literature and Experience*. London, New York: Routledge, 2012.

Grady, Hugh, 1994. *The Modernist Shakespeare: Critical Texts in a Material World*. Oxford: Oxford University Press.

Greenblatt, Stephen, 1980. *Renaissance Self-Fashioning: from More to Shakespeare*. Chicago: University of Chicago Press.

Gremler, Claudia, 2005. '"Die unvermeidlichen Sonette": Thomas Mann and Shakespeare', in *Oxford German Studies* 34, pp. 180–8.

Gundolf, Friedrich, 1920 [1911]. *Shakesepare und der deutsche Geist*. Berlin: Georg Bondi.

Halpern, Richard, 1997. *Shakespeare among the Moderns*. Ithaca: Cornell University Press.

Harris, Frank, 1904. *Shakespeare and His Love. A Play in Four Acts and an Epilogue*. London: Frank Palmer.

Harris, Frank, 1909. *The Man Shakespeare and His Tragic Life Story*. London: Frank Palmer.

Harris, Frank, 1928 [1909]. *Shakespeare der Mensch und seine tragische Lebensgeschichte*, trans. Antonina Vallentin. Berlin: S. Fischer.

Heller, Erich, 1979. *Thomas Mann: The Ironic German*. South Bend, Indiana: Regenery/Gateway.

Höfele, Andreas, 2005. 'Review of Roger Paulin's *The Critical Reception of Shakespeare in Germany, 1682–1914*', in *Shakespeare Quarterly* 56: 4, pp. 489–91.

Karlauf, Thomas, 2007. *Stefan George. Die Entdeckung des Charisma*. München: Blessing.

Lacan, Jacques, 1999. *The Ethics of Psychoanalysis 1959–60: The Seminar of Jacques Lacan*, ed. Jacques-Alain Miller, trans. Dennis Porter. London, New York: Routledge.

Ledebur, Ruth Freifrau von, 2002. *Der Mythos vom deutsche Shakespeare: Die Deutsche Shakespeare-Gesellschaft zwischen Politik und Wissenschaft 1918–1945*. Köln: Böhlau.

Lyotard, Jean François, 1985 [1979]. *Just Gaming*, trans. Wlad Godzich. Minneapolis: University of Minnesota Press.

Mann, Thomas, 1936. *Stories of Three Decades*, trans. H. T. Lowe-Porter. London: Secker and Warburg.

Mann, Thomas, 1951 [1951]. *The Holy Sinner*, trans. H. T. Lowe-Porter. New York: Alfred A Knopf.

Mann, Thomas, 1960 [1951]. *Der Erwählte. Bekenntnisse des Hochstaplers Felix Krull*. Gesammelte Werke, vol. 7. Frankfurt am Main: S. Fischer.

Mann, Thomas, 1961 [1949]. *The Genesis of a Novel*, trans. Richard and Clara Winston. London: Secker and Warburg.

Mann, Thomas, 1968 [1947]. *Doctor Faustus: The Life of the German Composer Adrian Leverkühn as Told by a Friend*, trans. H. T. Lowe-Porter. Harmondsworth: Penguin.

Mann, Thomas, 1982. *Tagebücher 1940–1943*, ed. Peter de Mendelssohn. Frankfurt am Main: S. Fischer.

Mann, Thomas, 1983 [1918]. *Reflections of a Nonpolitical Man*, trans. Walter D. Morris. New York: Frederick Ungar Publishing Co.

Mann, Thomas, 1985 [1924]. *The Magic Mountain*, trans. H. T. Lowe-Porter. Harmondsworth: Penguin. [*MM*]

Mann, Thomas 1986. *Tagebücher 1944–1946*, ed. Inge Jens. Frankfurt am Main: S. Fischer.

Mann, Thomas, 1991. *Notizbücher 1–6*, eds Hans Wysling, Yvonne Schmidlin. Frankfurt am Main: S. Fischer.

Mann, Thomas, 1994 [1901]. *Buddenbrooks*, trans. John E. Woods. London: Vintage.

Mann, Thomas, 2002a [1901]. *Buddenbrooks. Verfall einer Familie*, eds Eckhard Heftrich, Stephan Stachorski, Herbert Lehnert. Große Kommentierte Frankfurter Ausgabe, vol. 1.1. Frankfurt am Main: S. Fischer.

Mann, Thomas, 2002b [1924]. *Der Zauberberg*, ed. Michael Neumann. Große Kommentierte Frankfurter Ausgabe, vol. 5.1. Frankfurt am Main: S. Fischer. [GKFA 5]

Mann, Thomas, 2007 [1924]. *Doktor Faustus. Das Leben des deutschen Tonsetzers Adrian Leverkühn erzählt von einem Freunde*, eds Ruprecht Wimmer, Stephan Stachorski. Große Kommentierte Frankfurter Ausgabe, vol. 10.1. Frankfurt am Main: S. Fischer.

Mann, Thomas, 2009 [1949]. 'Die Entstehung des Doktor Faustus', in: *Essays VI: 1945–1950*, ed. Herbert Lehnert. Große Kommentierte Frankfurter Ausgabe, vol. 19.1. Frankfurt am Main: S. Fischer, pp. 409–510.

Marx, Friedhelm, 2006/2007. 'Der Heilige Stefan: Thomas Mann und Stefan George', in: *George-Jahrbuch* 6, pp. 80–99.

Meyers, Jeffrey, 1973. 'Shakespeare and Mann's *Doktor Faustus*', in *Modern Fiction Studies* 19, pp. 541–5.

Paulin, Roger, 2003. *The Critical Reception of Shakespeare in Germany, 1682–1914: Native Literature and Foreign Genius*. Hildesheim, Zürich, New York: Olms.

Peres, Anna, 2009. 'Shakespeare in Thomas Manns *Doktor Faustus* oder Die Einheit von Wort und Ton bei Adrian Leverkühn. Bemerkungen zu der intertextuellen Strukturierungsmethode Thomas Manns' in *Konnte Rilke radfahren? Die Faszination des Biographischen in der deutschen Literatur. Gedenkschrift für Ferenc Szász*, ed. Imre Kurdi. Frankfurt am Main etc: Lang, pp, 139–47.

Puknat, Elisabeth M., and Siegfried B. Puknat, 1967. 'Mann's *Doctor Faustus* and Shakespeare', in *Research Studies* 35, pp. 148–54.

Rabkin, Norman, 1981. *Shakespeare and the Problem of Meaning*. Chicago: University of Chicago Press.

Sandberg, Hans-Joachim, 1972. 'Suggestibilität und Widerspruch: Thomas Manns Auseinandersetzung mit Brandes', in *Nerthus: Nordisch-deutsche Beiträge* 3, pp. 119–63.

Shakespeare, William, 2008. *The Norton Shakespeare*. Based on the Oxford Edition, eds Stephen Greenblatt et al. New York: Norton.

Stürmer, Franziska, 2014. '*Leverkühn der Mensch und seine tragische Lebensgeschichte*': *Thomas Manns* Doktor Faustus *und die Shakespeare-Biographie von Frank Harris*. Würzburg: Königshausen & Neumann.

Szudra, Klaus Udo, 1979. 'Shakespeare-Reminiszenzen in Thomas Manns *Doktor Faustus*: Quellendeutung als rezeptionsästhetischer Testfall humanistischen Weltverständnisses', in *Kwartalnik Neofilologiczny* 26, pp. 259–78.

Žižek, Slavoj, 1999. *The Ticklish Subject: The Absent Centre of Political Ontology*. London: Verso.

One   The Violence of Desire: Shakespeare, Nietzsche, Mann

Jonathan Dollimore

Thomas Mann compared Nietzsche to Hamlet, both being 'called to knowledge ... and ... shattered by it' (1959: 142).[1] It's an intriguing comparison in the light of Nietzsche's own reading of Hamlet as someone who doesn't think undecisively, but rather knows too much: 'knowledge kills action; action requires the veils of illusion: that is the doctrine of Hamlet. ... true knowledge, an insight into the horrible truth, outweighs any motive for action, both in Hamlet and in the Dionysian man' (1956: 50–2).[2]

This idea is central to Nietzsche's philosophy and Mann's novels, namely that intelligence, rationality, self-reflexiveness, perhaps consciousness itself – those things which make us distinctively human – may also be pathological: they make us sick. Conversely, healthy praxis, a vital engagement with the world, may require illusion and myopia. They found a precedent in the early modern condition of melancholy, and in Hamlet most famously. In fact, Mann observed that Nietzsche's great essay on this very topic, 'Vom Nutzen und Nachteil der Historie für das Leben' ('On the Uses and Abuses of History for Life') was 'a fugue taking for its theme' (1959: 154)[3] the following passage from *Hamlet*:

> ... conscience does make cowards of us all,
> And ... the native hue of resolution
> Is sicklied o'er with the pale cast of thought,
> And enterprises of great pith and moment
> With this regard their currents turn awry,
> And lose the name of action.
> (3.1.85–90)

I'm reminded too of those lines from *Henry IV, Part 2* where time and mutability, seen from an omniscient viewpoint, becomes a kind of entropy:

> O God, that one might read the book of fate,
> And see the revolution of the times
> Make mountains level, and the continent,
> Weary of solid firmness, melt itself
> Into the sea! ...
> ... O, if this were seen,
> The happiest youth ...
> Would shut the book, and sit him down and die.
> (3.1.44–52.4)

Living, surviving, praxis, is conditional on *not* knowing. But of course Nietzsche and Mann went further than this. They were thinking of a knowledge which shatters because it's a dangerous knowledge, undermining of psychic, social and political well-being in the present. And yet this too has an early modern precedent in the subversive thinking of the malcontent – Shakespeare's Edmund in *King Lear* being only the most famous case in point. That was, after all, a time when it was self-evident that thinking outside the doxa could be dangerous. It's why some people paid with their liberty, parts of their body and sometimes with their life for voicing the wrong idea in the wrong place at the wrong time. And when a character in *Mustapha*, a play by Shakespeare's contemporary Fulke Greville, can speak of 'knowledge' as 'the endless hell of thought' (1973: 119), it suggests that then too this dangerous knowing could also be more fundamentally a crisis of consciousness, of being too conscious. Too human.

But it is indeed in modernity that the idea is most familiar to us. Of knowing, for example, that all knowing is illusory, or that all values are debilitatingly relative; or that ethical truths are in fact lies or necessary fictions; or knowing enough to know that we know nothing in the larger scheme of things; or knowing enough to become vulnerable to that disabling existential angst which leads some to surrender to the delusions of religion, fanaticism or the charismatic leader, some to a nihilistic destruction of others and of self, muttering as they do something about the horror, the horror. There's no consolation in this kind of knowing; it's not the cognition of revelation, of the blinding insight, or that very different and precious cognition which leads to a mystical comprehension of the oneness of being. All the more remarkable then that this painful, disturbing cognition is the prerequisite of so much modern philosophy and creativity; and it means that modern art which matters is crucially cognitive.

It might be said that for Shakespeare at his most tragic, the real pathology was not knowledge but desire, the state of being 'blasted with ecstasy', understood in its deepest and most extensive sense, which is to say a desire which is always more than sexual, although it is perhaps expressed most revealingly as sexual desire, as in sonnet 129, 'Th' expense of spirit in a waste of shame' or 147, 'My love is as a fever'. And yet precisely because this was desire in its broadest sense it was, for the Shakespearean protagonist, also deeply cognitive – one only has to regard for a moment the depth of reflection on desire in the period to see that. In a sense it was a theological given: the Fall narrates the desire to eat from the tree of knowledge. Transgressive desire and forbidden knowledge go together.

In *Der Tod in Venedig* (*Death in Venice*) Aschenbach is wrecked by a desire which erupts as much from a cognitive crisis as a sexual one. He too has been called to knowledge and shattered by it. That's to say, he has sought an affirmation not by disavowing the dangerous knowledge but by both confronting and trying to contain it. Affirmation is fraudulent unless it first – in the words of Thomas Hardy – 'exacts a full look at the Worst' (1930: 154). This is what Aschenbach has done in writing 'that powerful tale entitled *A Study in Abjection,* which earned the gratitude of a whole younger generation by pointing to the possibility of moral resolution even for those who have plumbed the depths of knowledge'[4] (David Luke translation of *Death in Venice,* hereafter referred to as *Luke,* 202).[5] Much hangs on that word 'even': moral resolution is possible even – not especially – with knowledge. Knowledge and ethics conflict and it's an ethical/cognitive affirmation which has cost him dear. It has made him spiritually sick, burnt out, ripe for desire as insurrection and self-destruction.

I want to concentrate on three aspects to this knowledge/desire convergence as it involved Thomas Mann, especially in the writing of *Doktor Faustus.* In that these three aspects are inseparable they are really only one, but I distinguish them in what follows for the sake of elucidation. First, the realization that barbarism is not the opposite of the civilization it destroys, but its creation, second (and consequently) the realization that the self-destructive barbarism generated by civilization has a uniquely virulent intensity typically manifested as violation, and thirdly the realization that art, even or especially in its highest manifestations, can be complicit with that barbarism. I use the term barbarism because it's the one generally used as the translation of the German *Barbarei,* but I've come to feel it misses something crucial in Mann's usage, something conveyed most famously perhaps in Walter Benjamin's thesis that there is no document of civilization which is not also a document of barbarism.[6]

Doktor Faustus is a novel which finds the precedent of this dangerous knowledge in the early modern period, in Shakespeare's time. Its use of Shakespearean comedy is well known, not least because Mann himself later documented it.[7] My concern here is with the darker side of the Renaissance, to which Mann's choice of the Faustus myth inevitably led him. It's a myth which leads us back into western theology where the dilemma of the terrible proximity of good and evil, of civilization and barbarism, is faced full on. And of course there is a branch of theology, called theodicy, which addresses exactly this dilemma, and Mann devotes the whole of Chapter 13 of his novel to it. Essentially, the dangerous knowledge which preoccupies Mann is inseparable from a radical theodicy. The word itself originates with Leibniz, but the dilemma it articulates is much older: if God is indeed all-powerful it means He created evil. Orthodox theodicy tries to vindicate God in the face of this dilemma; a radical theodicy tracks evil back to its source in God, thereby offering 'a daemonic conception of God' (H. T. Lowe-Porter translation of *Doctor Faustus*, hereafter referred to as *L-P*, 98)[8] – and sometimes responds rebelliously as in Fulke Greville's famous Chorus Sacerdotum from *Mustapha*:

> Oh wearisome condition of humanity!
> Born under one law, to another bound:
> Vainly begot yet forbidden vanity
> Created sick, commanded to be sound:
> What meaneth nature by these diverse laws?
> Passion and reason self-division cause:
> Is it the mark or majesty of power
> To make offences that it may forgive?
> (1973: 138)

Or, as Zeitblom puts it, paraphrasing the Hegelian teaching of Schleppfuß, '[he] declared the vicious to be a necessary and inseparable concomitant of the holy, and the holy a constant satanic temptation, an almost irresistible challenge to violation' (*L-P* 98).[9] If he is to be believed, Nietzsche was only thirteen when he decided that God was 'the father of evil' (1956: 151).[10] In secular thought the theodical insight becomes the primal drama of evil originating within the good, of evil as violation, of what we hold most precious mutating into its opposite, its negation.

Of course for Mann this was not, most immediately, a philosophical or theological issue but a political one. *Doktor Faustus* was written during, and is partly about, the Second World War, about fascism. Mann called it various things – Nazism, Hitlerism, National Socialism, Fascism. If I use the one term, fascism, it's only for the sake of brevity and not with the intention of collapsing these things into each other.

That Mann's analysis of fascism was deeply theodical can be seen in the way he refused the idea that there were two distinct Germanies, a good one and a bad one. No, there was only the one, and, controversially, he insisted that 'everything German, German history [and] the German spirit' was involved in the catastrophe of Nazism. Indeed, he was even reluctant to draw a distinction between Nazism and the people; Hitler could never have happened but for certain psychological prerequisites that must be sought 'deeper down than in inflation, unemployment, capitalist speculation and political intrigue'. More generally, 'Hitlerism' emerges from 'the bourgeois humanist epoch', which means that the problem cannot even be confined to German culture (Mann 2013: 546).[11]

It's one of the self-serving myths of Western civilization that the repeated eruptions of barbarism in its history, fascist or otherwise, are due to a regressive, primitive brutality which can only be defeated by a redoubling of civilized effort. A theodical vision knows otherwise, knows barbarism as sometimes a viciously civilized affair. It's this which is so intensely dramatized throughout *Doktor Faustus*. It has been said that discrimination is the essence of culture, and theodicy knows that this is true in more ways than one, and that the pejorative and the commendable senses of the word share a common origin.

In Chapter 25 of *Faustus* Adrian gets to talk to the devil, or it may be to himself, since he tells the devil 'you say nothing save things that are in me' (*L-P* 218).[12] Whichever, the dialogue reveals perhaps the most dangerous truth of all, namely that things supposedly antithetical are not only interrelated, but terrifyingly identical. But it's not simply that the terms of a fundamental opposition are really the same thing; it's rather that because of a shared origin they can track back and across into each other. If culture is indeed an effort of discrimination – that is, the necessary, commendable yet precariously artificial assertion of distinction and difference – then the barbaric can be seen as their reduction. And that makes the barbaric a kind of truth, a kind of insight into the origins of civilization. For humanists, reduction is a pejorative; for scientists it's a fundamental objective. So if one were wickedly inclined, it might be said that the devil's work is only a reduction of civilization to first principles and barbarism itself a form of theodicy.

Anyhow, in Adrian's dialogue with the devil and/or the self, oppositions which are the necessary grounds of ethics and even civilization, are found to be paradoxically intimate with each other and, via osmosis, to actually mutate into each other. Osmosis is the enemy of difference and discrimination. As the devil says, 'Everything comes from osmosis' (*L-P* 228–9).[13] Thus the artist becomes the brother of the criminal and the madman; life at its most intense feeds off disease; life 'joyously' embraces 'death and sickness'[14] (John E. Woods translation of *Doctor Faustus*, hereafter referred to as *Woods*, 251), as does genius and intense creativity (*L-P* 236) – this being of course the condition of Adrian as syphilitic artist. It is also what Mann believed to be the condition of Nietzsche, on whom Adrian is extensively based, although this is of course disputed. The Devil further tells Adrian that he will create a barbarism which will be the culmination of present civilization, not a reversion to the pre-civilized. As such it will be what he calls '*a double barbarism* (my italics), because it comes after humanitarianism, after every ... bourgeois refinement', an ultra-refined barbarism having 'a better understanding even of theology than does a culture that has fallen off from the cult, which even in things religious saw only culture, only humanitarianism, but not excess, not the paradox, the mystical passion, the ordeal so utterly outside bourgeois experience' (*Woods* 259).[15]

This is something which the novel reiterates in different ways. At one level it's a question of ignorance and repression; for instance, modern liberal theology may be scientifically superior to the old, but its

> moralism and humanism lack insight into the daemonic character of human existence. Cultured indeed it is, but shallow; of true understanding of human nature and the tragic nature of life the conservative tradition has at bottom preserved far more.
> (*L-P* 89–90)[16]

And what Mann suggests is that such cognitive repression isn't an error so much as a necessity. In other words, it's a paradox of humanism and the humane that it involves a repression of what it is to be fully human. But it is this same repression which, rather than preventing barbarism, becomes its breeding ground. So at one level modern culture has indeed repressed the daemonic, but at another it has actually produced the conditions for it to evolve effortlessly from itself. Crucially then, there is, and there is not, repression. I'll return to this.

In trying to defend Adrian's daemonic compositions against the charge of barbarism, Zeitblom several times returns to a rationalizing metaphor: in that it must inevitably arrive back at its starting point, progression around a sphere is also a regression. So Adrian's creative fusion of the very new and the very old actually derives from 'the nature of things: it rests, I might say, on the curvature of the world, which makes the last return unto the first' (*L-P* 362).[17] Typically with Mann, an evasive rationalization is shown to contain a degree of truth. Adrian's composition, *The Apocalypse*, expresses musically what cannot be said in words; it is at once utterly beautiful and utterly terrifying. Of course this composition doesn't actually exist. More to the point, it could never exist: it's not just a fictional creation but an impossible one as well. But this is how I imagine it, the only way I can imagine it: *the sublime as itself a shattering desublimation.*

How could this impossible, sublime, non-existent composition achieve such an effect? Well, to begin with, it inverts both the natural and musical orders. It uses dissonance to express 'everything lofty, solemn, pious, everything of the spirit; while consonance and firm tonality are reserved for the world of hell' (*L-P* 361).[18] But for Zeitblom, much more disturbing than such inversion, much more radical, is the relationship between two pivotal sections of the composition. The first is a long passage of extreme dissonance, sweeping through fifty bars: 'an overwhelming, sardonically yelling, screeching, bawling ... mocking, exulting laughter of the Pit' (*L-P* 364).[19] And then there follows a passage by a chorus of children which expresses an 'unearthly and alien beauty of sound, filling the heart with longing without hope' (*L-P* 364).[20] And it's terrifying too, the reason being that on the one hand this children's chorus 'touched, and ravished even the reluctant' (ibid.),[21] and on the other, it was actually the earlier passage, the devil's laughter all over again, because in it *'there is not one note which does not occur, with rigid correspondence, in the hellish laughter'* (*L-P* 364, my emphasis).[22] So a radical theodical vision is expressed in musical form. And this, for Zeitblom, is the 'truth' of the music, what he calls its revelation of the profound 'mystery of identity' (*Woods* 397),[23] that is, the 'inner unity', the 'substantial identity of the most blest with the most accurst' (*L-P* 467).[24] It is, he says, a music which expresses 'how close aestheticism and barbarism are to each other' and which 'prepares the way for barbarism in one's own soul' (*Woods* 392).[25]

Now, we know that when he finally read Freud, Thomas Mann was profoundly taken with him, and this for many reasons, two of the most important of which are that he told the disturbing truth, and recognized the importance of disease as an enabler of knowledge. In such respects psychoanalysis was also a kind of dangerous knowledge. And in this regard Freud actually reworks the theodical insight in psychoanalytic terms, as in the following remarkable passage from his article on repression:

> the objects to which men give most preference, their ideals, proceed from the same perceptions and experiences as the objects which they most abhor, and ... they were originally only distinguished from one another through slight modifications ... Indeed ... it is possible for the original instinctual representative to be split in two, one part undergoing repression, while the remainder, *precisely on account of this intimate connection undergoes idealization.*
>
> (Freud 1984: 150, my emphasis)[26]

I'll return to Freud and the question of repression because I think that a theodical sense of life suggests, again, how there is and there is not repression.

We find the theodical sense of life everywhere in the early modern period but in the literature it's perhaps especially visible in its second aspect as discussed here, namely that barbarism is not only intimate with civilization but intensified by it – Mann's 'double barbarism'. And Mann finds his way back to the early modern version of this idea in those twice quoted lines from *Love's Labour's Lost*: 'The blood of youth burns not with such excess / As gravity's revolt to wantonness' (5.2.73–4). Gravity, that which should preclude wantonness, not only succumbs to it, but becomes the agent of its excess, its intensification.

Now, as Zeitblom remarks, these lines are hardly applicable to the person in the play to whom they are applied, the youthful Biron, and he goes on to make it clear that Adrian believes they are actually applicable to Shakespeare, and especially the Shakespeare of the late sonnets, with Rosaline being an understudy for the Dark Lady. So, for Adrian, this is a Shakespeare wrecked by a desire which, as in sonnet 147, is a kind of self-violation so extreme that 'I desperate now approve / Desire is death'; it's a fever longing for that which intensifies the disease, 'feeding on that which doth preserve the ill'. The language here might remind us of those lines of Claudio's in *Measure for Measure*:

> Our natures do pursue,
> Like rats that raven down their proper bane,
> A thirsty evil; and when we drink, we die.
> (1.2.108–10)

Truly then desire as pathology: intensely conflicted, intensely self-conscious, intensely self-destructive. But also intensely cultured. As in sonnet 129, the expense of spirit in a waste of shame, it's about the violation of reason by lust – 'past reason hunted, and no sooner had, / Past reason hated' – but this is no simply lust/reason binary, and nor is the lust in question the same as unbridled instinct; lust here has a level of concentration, an intensity, a kind of sophisticated Machiavellian malevolence – it's 'perjured, murd'rous, bloody, full of blame, / Savage, extreme, rude, cruel, not to trust' (sonnet 129). Lust is not the opposite of civility but its inverted intensification. The idea is pivotal in Jacobean tragedy, especially in its representation of the court, and nicely concentrated in a couple of lines from Flamineo in John Webster's *The White Devil*: 'I visited the court, whence I return'd / More courteous, more lecherous by far' (1983: 26). The difference between this remark of Flamineo's, and the speaker in Shakespeare's sonnet, is that in the one case (Flamineo's) he thinks he's in control whereas in the other he knows he isn't. It's a minor difference because actually, as the play so savagely demonstrates, Flamineo is not in control at all. But theodically speaking the important precedent here is the dramatic realization of the court as both the height of cultural sophistication, and as such, the source of refined barbarism.

Because today we are obsessed with gender, sexual difference and sexual orientation, we interpret the utterly different kinds of desire expressed in the earlier as distinct from the last of Shakespeare's sonnets as occasioned entirely by a difference of object, the young man as distinct from the dark lady. But early modern readers wouldn't have needed to rationalize the difference in this way. Nor would they necessarily assume that the tormented sonnets 129 and 147 were written to the dark lady as distinct from the young man, or indeed another man or another woman – after all, neither of these sonnets has a gendered addressee. Nor would they be surprised that the humane, civilizing love of the early sonnets could mutate into the destructive, intensely conflicted desire of the later ones. And why should we be surprised? After all, most if not all embittered divorcees can produce photos of themselves and their former partners in a smiling embrace on the wedding day, and not a few victims of domestic violence as well. Speaking of which, Othello's sexual jealousy would have been seen as a mutation of his love, not its antithesis. That's precisely why he can say at the end that he 'loved not wisely but too well' (*Othello*, 5.2.353). And when we recall that although *wanton* could mean 'lascivious', more fundamentally it meant 'undisciplined', 'lawless', Othello becomes a most compelling instance of gravity revolting to wantonness. And theodically speaking, it is eminently reasonable to assume that Iago was once genuinely the honest and loyal person he now only pretends to be; in other words – and this is as tragic as the fate of Othello and Desdemona – he was once genuinely that which now makes his evil possible. Which, of course, is exactly the condition of Macbeth. At the outset he really is the loyal subject who has put his life on the line for the King. Like Satan, he begins as the sovereign's loyal ally. And then he kills him. The loyal subject turned regicide. And what makes Macbeth so compelling is the nihilistic integrity with which he sees through his freely chosen barbarism: it's the inversion of his former loyalty and gives a virulent intensity to his violence.

The theodical idea of the most savage kind of wantonness emerging from, and being intensified by, gravity is also dramatized in *Measure for Measure*. Angelo, the puritan upholder of religion and law suddenly becomes wrecked by illicit sexual desire for the chaste Isabella, who aspires to a nunnery. In order to possess her, Angelo embarks upon a reckless course of blackmail, betrayal and would-be murder. It's not just that the man who was immune to the overt licentiousness of the prostitute becomes sexually obsessed with the passionately virtuous Isabella; it's that the man who has spent his life being virtuous now desires to violate the virtuous Isabella. Here is part of Angelo's tortured soliloquy:

> Having waste ground enough,
> Shall we desire to raze the sanctuary
> And pitch our evils there? ...
> Dost thou desire her foully for those things
> That make her good?
> (2.2.174–80)

The idea has also been expressed as proverbial wisdom. In, for instance, the notion that it's the saint who is most susceptible to sin, or the ancient Latin saying that the corruption of the best is the worst, or Shakespeare's own 'Lilies that fester smell far worse than weeds' (sonnet 94). And this wouldn't be the first time that quite profound and complex ideas have been concentrated in proverbial form. Anyway, the point is this: corruption of the best is the worst – this could be a kind of theodical epitaph for the early modern tragic protagonist, who begins as a paragon of excellence and mutates into its negation. We could call it the vicious dialectical intensification of evil by good: evil erupting from within the good, and taking from it a certain intensity which in turn invests evil with a virulence it does not intrinsically have. In that sense it's Augustinian. Yeats famously wrote that 'the best lack all conviction, while the worst / Are full of passionate intensity' (1997: 189). But the theodical sense of this is darker still: the best, *in virtue* of their own passionate intensity become the worst. For Mann this isn't just the condition of the protagonist but the condition of German culture – and beyond that bourgeois humanist culture – in the twentieth century.

There's one further aspect of this that I want to remark and it concerns the early modern obsession with mutability. I quoted earlier those lines from *Henry IV, Part 2* where mutability is imagined as a kind of entropy: an omniscient viewpoint sees everything melt into oblivion. Traumatic enough to make the young man want to die, it's nevertheless still a natural process. But there was another early modern sense of mutability, also deriving from the severer forms of protestant theology, and focused in the late sixteenth-century debate on the decay of nature. The fall, as that fatal complex of knowledge, desire and death, has infected the nature of things as well as the nature of man. Because they eat from the tree of knowledge our first parents bring death into the world, which means that it is shot through with a human guilt at work in everything as an inversion of the life force, ceaselessly transforming things into what they should not be. Contra Wittgenstein, in this theology, death very much *is* an event in life. What recurs in early modern writing is a sense of death not simply as the end of life but shockingly, perversely, its inner dynamic. It's captured in a brilliant image of George Herbert's; he perhaps has in mind the way that dust or leaves collect in a corner, blown there by the eddying of the wind: 'this heap of dust; / To which the blast of death's incessant motion, / ... / Drives all at last' (2005: 58).[27] Here, energy and movement – ostensibly the essence of life – become more truly the dynamic of its dissolution, the incessant motion, the *driving* force of death.

For these writers, death does not merely end life but disorders and decays it from within, its force indistinguishable from the life force. Not merely an ending but an internal undoing. As such, the most cosmic, most culturally necessary of all binary oppositions, life versus death, is subjected to collapse; the absolutely different is inseparable from what it is not, what it cannot be. The absolutely other is found to inhere within the selfsame as nothing less than the dynamic of its dissolution. *Media in vita in morte.* That is why life is experienced as a living death; as Donne puts it in *Deaths Duell*, 'how much worse a death than death, is this life' (1967: 379). And all of this was already in a sense popular in that the sense of death as paradoxically vital, of evil somehow being more alive than good – wickedly alive – had been reflected in the antics of the vice figure of medieval drama, and of course in the dance of death.[28]

Well, we may have forgotten the theology but the idea haunts us still – in, for instance, that melancholy sense of a perpetual falling away in everything, of which failure is the least of it. Before and beyond failure is the repeated trauma of witnessing what we hold most precious mutating into its own negation, and doing so because of some mysterious intrinsic connection within itself with that which it is not. Most memorably perhaps – and commonly – love turning into hate. This idea – idea as experience – also survives into our time, now with a dark romantic inflection, as throughout *Doktor Faustus* (quite literally in the case of the character of Ines Institoris), more generally in our culture as the sense of disease and illness being the breeding grounds for creative genius, or the experience of being most alive in relation to what destroys us, be it narcotics or sex or other kinds of risk, or the sense of art's intimate relation to death.

It survives too in that realization already alluded to, that humanism and the humane involve a repression of what is is to be fully human. Here the role of art is crucial. In Chapter 27 of *Doktor Faustus* Adrian, in a discussion with Zeitblom, rehearses what is known of the immensity and origin of the universe. It puts Zeitblom on the defensive; he recognizes that even a limited apprehension of the full extent of cosmic time and space, not to mention ideas like that of an expanding universe, put the humanist project in question:

> What ... civilizing process born of reverence can come from the picture of vast impropriety like this of the exploding universe? Absolutely none. Piety, reverence, intellectual decency, religious feeling, are only possible about men and through men, and by limitation to the earthly and human ... In this pathos, this obligation, this reverence of man for himself, is God; in a hundred milliards of Milky Ways I cannot find him.
>
> *(L-P 264)*[29]

Precisely: you can't find him. As Zeitblom realizes, these are 'orders of greatness with which the human spirit has no longer any relation' *(L-P 257–8)*.[30] Adrian replies that Zeitblom's humanism, and probably all humanism, inclines to the self-referentiality of the geocentric and anthropocentric ideas of the Middle Ages. For his part Zeitblom finds Adrian's preoccupation with the 'extra-human', as subsequently expressed in a one-movement symphony called 'The Marvels of the Universe', chillingly inhuman. It is such music which contributes to the composer's reputation for 'blasphemy', and 'nihilistic sacrilege' *(L-P 266)*.[31] A profound question is posed here: at what point does cosmic knowledge cease to be containable by, or be rendered compatible with, a conventionally religious awe, and thereby transferable to a religious humanism, and begin to threaten both religion and humanism? One thing is sure: Adrian's artistic compositions have gone way beyond that point. In so many ways of course Adrian *is* Nietzsche: called to art and shattered by it (Mann 1961: 30).[32]

Mann's understanding of the inhumane potential of art – art as dangerous knowledge – is important. The ignoring of such understanding, along with the belief that great art is always and necessarily a profoundly humanizing force, always on the side of the humanitarian project, is one reason why much of our aesthetic philosophy and criticism in the second half of the twentieth century is largely worthless. The claim is that great art is always the most exalted expression of civilized life; that such art and the high culture it serves can only enhance the lives of those who truly appreciate it; that unlike say, propaganda, pornography or popular culture, great art is incapable of damaging or 'corrupting' us. Such an attitude not only fails to take art seriously enough, but rests on a prior process of pro-art censorship more effective than anti-art state censorship. It is a defence *of* art which is more fundamentally a defence *against* art; an exaggerated respect for it becomes a way of not engaging with it. Those who love art the most also censor it the most, smothering it with humanist pieties; they make the aesthetic into a kind of anaesthetic: art becomes a consoling balm applied to the wound of life. To be sure there are some intelligent and insightful versions of this idea – for instance, the claim that great art is characterized by a profound alignment of the ethical conscience and the creative imagination. But this too is to repress the truth explored so relentlessly in *Faustus*, that some of the most compelling art is not just about the tension between these two things (that much being conceded) but their incompatibility. Art has always been a potential vehicle of dissident ideas, desires and knowledges. In their own stupid way censors have known this even as the humanistic critic has not.[33]

In November 1939 Mann published an insightful letter on the 'intricate and painful' relationship between the music of Wagner and National Socialism: 'I find an element of Nazism not only in Wagner's questionable literature; I find it also in his music – albeit I have so loved that work.' He realized that to posit such a relationship would upset many music-lovers, but also insisted that they had to abandon their 'sentimental innocence' about art in the service of this painful truth. For me, the crucial point about this letter is that Mann had the courage to admit that something which spoke so deeply to him aesthetically could also be 'the most profound challenge to one's conscience'. And that, says Mann, is why Wagner 'is one of the most complex phenomena in the history of art and intellect – and one of the most fascinating' (Mann 2013: 543–7; 1985: 196–202).[34] Precisely. It's a letter which takes art more seriously than any anodyne humanist apology for it ever could.

This letter on Wagner, and much else of what he wrote, recognizes that art can be most compelling not when in the service of humane values, but when it is transgressing them; that the aesthetic vision can be most captivating precisely when it exceeds and maybe violates the humanitarian one. This is the dilemma Zeitblom struggles with in relation to Adrian's music. Captivating, and by the same token, potentially dangerous: there can be no guarantee that (for instance) the imaginative exploration of the return of the repressed will be conducive to the health of either the individual or the society; only the stupid or naive can believe that all repression/suppression is bad. Arguably everything that distinguishes us as humane is necessarily steeped in repression, suppression and exclusion. So, obviously the subversion of restraint is compelling. For some we are most human when in a destructive, dangerous and suffering state of freedom, violating the restraints of the very history which has produced us. Mann's Adrian is a version of this idea, albeit a highly ascetic one, and it was most powerfully articulated by Nietzsche, who also believed it was shared by Shakespeare: he argued that whereas Shakespeare dramatized the dangerous truths of human desire, the playwright's critical guardians have disavowed them and censored him in the process. Thus Shakespeare and his guardians fall on opposite sides of Nietzsche's great divide between those who affirm the life force and those who turn away from it, between, in other words, the daemonic and the humanitarian. In *Die Fröhliche Wissenschaft* (*The Gay Science*) this distinction is expressed in terms of two distinct kinds of sufferer: those who suffer from a superabundance of life, and those who suffer from an impoverishment of life. The former 'want a Dionysian art as well as a tragic outlook and insight into life', and willingly confront 'the terrible and questionable ... every luxury of destruction, decomposition, negation'; while the latter needs 'mildness, peacefulness, goodness in thought and in deed. ... a certain warm, fear-averting confinement and enclosure within optimistic horizons' (2001: 234).[35]

Just as with Wagner, Mann identifies significant fascistic strains in Nietzsche. In fact, in that remarkable essay on him, begun immediately after finishing *Doktor Faustus*, Mann denies that Nietzsche was responsible for fascism, suggesting rather that he was created by it. He also describes as 'utterly false' Nietzsche's view that morality was anti-life. Actually, says Mann, what is truly anti-life is aesthetics; it is art and beauty which are 'allied to death' not morality. Moreover – and here Mann's essay clearly crosses with *Faustus* – the aesthetic response to life has a deep affinity with barbarism. It's startling to read, in this nuanced essay, the following assertion: 'In the final analysis there are only two basic attitudes, two points of view: the aesthetic and the moral. Socialism is a strictly moral world-view. Nietzsche on the other hand is the most uncompromisingly perfect aesthete in the history of thought' (Mann 1959: 172). Moreover, his 'glorification of barbarism' (ibid.), his 'raging denial of intellect in favor of the beauty, strength and wickedness of life' is the pure manifestation of aestheticism (ibid.: 173).[36]

But why is the barbarism of the civilized so often about violation? Again, the answer was suggested by Nietzsche. At first sight it seems strange that he compared Hamlet with Dionysian man, especially if we think of Dionysus as the God of a vital, spontaneous, albeit amoral, life force, of pure libidinal freedom. Actually, in both Nietzsche and Mann, he's more the God of calculated violation. Indeed this may be true of the Dionysus myth more generally and in this regard it has been misunderstood or misappropriated in recent times. Dionysus was the god of forces which, although they wreaked havoc upon civilization, neither originate outside of it, nor move beyond it. Like Shakespeare's desire, they originate from within the civilized consciousness, which is where they have always been. There's evidence that in the ancient world Dionysus was the God favoured by the poor and the dispossessed. If so the impetus of Dionysus might be less about breaking free of civilization, and more about violating it from within – or below. This, anyway, is the impetus for Eurpides *The Bacchae*. The play tells of how Pentheus, King of Thebes, tries to suppress the Dionsyiac cult. In response Dionysus behaves like a brutal, vengeful but highly intelligent tyrant, uttering lines like 'Wise men know constraint: our passions are controlled'. As such, he has Pentheus's mother in Dionysiac ecstasy destroy her son. Pentheus pleads for mercy: '"Mother", he cried, / Touching her cheek, "It is I, your own son Pentheus."' In response she literally tears him limb from limb (1960: 220, 242). The virulence of the frenzy, of the orgy, not only presupposes civilized repression but is perversely energized by it. It expresses a sadistic cruelty, a shocking violation of the humane which makes little sense outside of human culture, and is hardly the stuff of instinctual innocence; it is brutal, for sure, but not at all to be confused with unbridled animal instinct.

Likewise with the fearful dream which grips Aschenbach towards the end of *Der Tod in Venedig*. It is actually a dream about a dionysiac orgy, in which the dreamer is both violator and violated. Initially the orgy is a violation from without:

> The scene of the events was his own soul, and they irrupted into it from outside, violently defeating his resistance – a profound intel-lectual resistance – as they passed through him, and leaving his whole being, the culture of a lifetime, devastated and destroyed.
>
> (*Luke* 259)[37]

But it also and crucially leaves him anticipating 'the uttermost surrender', and through that terrifying but liberating radicalism of the dream work, in being violated he becomes one of the violators: 'they were himself as an orgy of limitless coupling, in homage to the god … And his very soul savoured the lascivious delirium of annihi-lation' (*Luke* 260–2).[38] The invasion mutates into an insurgence, an insurrection; masochism and sadism violently dissolve each other into something else, something that can only exist when the ego is truly annihilated, and which reveals in passing that both sadism and masochism, far from being threats to the ego, are actually little more than ego charades.

It is difficult to even think about a dream like Aschenbach's without recourse to the Freudian idea of the return of the repressed. But a theodical perspective requires us to rethink repression itself. And in doing so I want to risk the following transhistorical comparison: in Shakespeare and Mann when the repressed returns it never does so in its 'original' form (but then does it ever?); one might say that it comes back *with a vengeance:* in other words, it comes back intensified by the very process of repression it is breaking through. Repression mutates into violation. So, thinking back to Angelo, we see how desublimated desire has a virulence which is not the opposite of civilization but something more like its intensified expression. That's to say, this is not unfettered pre-social libido indifferent to the civilizing restraint it has escaped, but desire returning via the 'civilizing' mechanisms of its repression, and being intensified by them even as it violates them. Put another way, there is an intensity in the return of the repressed which suggests that, after repression, we can never again access the pure drive or instinct prior to its repression, and so perhaps calls into question the very existence of such a drive. More generally: whether or not the drive exists in a primal, pre-civilized form – and *after all*, how would or could we ever know of its existence *as such*? – the fact remains that whatever is repressed returns with a virulence inseparable from the process of its repression: the repressed comes back mysteriously contaminated and intensified by its history – which is nothing other than the history of civilization. This is what I mean in suggesting that there is and is not repression, and why this is so important for understanding human history.

So in crucial respects Nietzsche is more suggestive here than Freud. Typically Nietzsche claimed that civilization had become less a repression of instincts, than a pathological mutation of them. As such civilization was in certain respects even more destructive than those instincts because, unlike them, it had become anti-life. So civilization does not repress the cruelty and destructiveness of the instincts so much as evolve them to a higher 'spiritual' level. That's why he could say that both Christianity and morality more generally involve a will to deny life, a secret instinct of destruction. At other times he writes as if the pathology is a form of sublimation: 'Almost everything we call "higher culture" is itself based on the spiritualizing and intensifi-cation of cruelty' (Nietzsche 1989: 140).[39] And such sublimation derives from 'the most profound transformation' man has ever undergone: '*conscience* ... is *not* as is no doubt believed, "the voice of God in man" – it is the instinct of cruelty turned backwards [against the self] after it can no longer discharge itself outwards. Cruelty [is] here brought to light for the first time as one of the oldest substrata of culture and one that can least be thought away.' The point here is that instincts denied free play externally turn inward: 'This is what I call man's interiorization; it alone provides the soil for the growth of what is later called man's *soul*' (Nietzsche 1956: 217; Nietzsche 1979: 84).[40] So conscience, morality, the soul – the most cherished constituents of human civilization, derive from a pathology of the instincts rather than their repression: life turned against itself. It's why Mann thought that Nietzsche's insistence that 'that there is no deeper knowledge without experience of disease' (Mann 1947: 414)[41] was not only an important anticipation of Freud but a profound insight into human culture.

In *Doktor Faustus* Mann takes on these ideas, testing them against the 'recent history', which figures in the title and text of his essay on Nietzsche. He rejects Nietzsche's fantasies of a life-affirming barbarism and its corollory, the aesthetics of energy and amoral vitalism. And as Mann rather wickedly observes in relation to the character of Institoris in *Faustus*, it's often the weak who most fantasize this aesthetic:

> Institoris ... was not a strong man ... and behind the gold-rimmed glasses the blue eyes wore a gentle, high minded expression, which made it hard to understand – or perhaps precisely did make one understand – that he respected and revered brute force, but of course only when it was beautiful.
>
> (L-P 278)[42]

In his essay Mann is more direct: recent history has made Nietzsche's 'romantic' celebration of violence now seem like 'the fantasies of an inexperienced child, offspring of a long era of peace and blue-chip security which was beginning to bore' (Mann 1959: 165).[43] So yes – Mann as public intellectual resolutely rejects this aspect of Nietzsche while remaining deeply indebted to the philosopher's cultural diagnosis. Mann gives his own vision of a human civilization which is pathological in its nature, precarious, artificial and deeply flawed, so much so that its survival is sometimes a question of embracing delusions: 'Clearly there is a vast difference whether one assents to a lie out of sheer hatred of the truth and the spirit, or for the sake of that spirit, in bitter irony and anguished pessimism!' (1947: 415).[44] And when barbarism is discovered close to civilization's surface, this is not because it has just irrupted from the depths of the cultural unconscious, but because it never got banished there in the first place. This isn't civilization being shattered by the return of its repressed, but by the intensification of some of its intrinsic, animating forces. The difference between barbarism and civilization matters terribly not because it's great or self-evident, not because it's absolute or metaphysically underwritten, but precisely because it isn't. If this analysis seems pessimistic, it's worth remembering that the conviction that this difference is indeed absolute has played its part in some of the worst atrocities of both earlier and modern times. That's to say, this conviction, paradoxically and tragically, has made some of those who hold it, deeply susceptible to the irruption of barbarism from within the civilized; in other words, in affirming the absolute difference in theory, they exemplify something like its opposite in practice.

The dilemma of the intellectually, morally and *aesthetically* aware humanist like Mann had become one of how to negotiate that potentially shattering nexus between dangerous knowledge and daemonic desire, both in history, and in the self – the very thing which Mann believed had destroyed Nietzsche. Aschenbach thinks he has negotiated it by writing a book called *A Study in Abjection*, but of course he hasn't. Or rather, as intellectual, the negotiation of the dilemma has been at the price of half-dying inwardly – only to then erupt back into life quite disastrously. This resurgence of desire is still under the sway of death and heads for it unerringly. But then life after culture is always problematic and often involves a spiralling downwards – or if you are a romantic – upwards, into self-destruction. As for Mann himself, the writing of *Doktor Faustus* nearly killed him, not least because of its confessional core: 'how much *Faustus* contains of the atmosphere of my life! A radical confession at bottom. From the very beginning that has been the shattering thing about the book' (1961: 124, 132, 144–5, 182).[45] But it was also because, although Aschenbach had been dead for more than 35 years, this novel is about the same dilemma as the early one (1961: 115),[46] only now terribly intensified by recent history.

Nowhere in Mann's work do I find an answer to that dilemma and nor would I expect to. To return to my point of departure: Nietzsche, says Mann, went to 'a martyr's death on the cross of thought', became Hamlet-like in a 'tragedy of insight exceeding strength' (1959: 143, 166),[47] because his was a philosophy involving the double pursuit of truth and of liberation in which the conflict between those two objectives eventually became just too great. The usual alternative to a philosophy of liberation is a religion of redemption, and it was just this which Nietzsche had initially found in Schopenhauer, but then vehemently rejected. For those like Mann, coming after Schopenhauer and Nietzsche, and bearing witness to recent history, neither liberation nor redemption is an option. Instead you endure the dilemma. Post the barbarism of recent history that's part of what it now means to be deeply cultured in the European tradition. And, as *Faustus* testifies, it's when the metaphysical consolations of religion become untenable, that we might learn most from its existential insights: call it spiritual cognition without redemption. Maybe we only really understand what it is to be fallen when we no longer believe in the possibility of redemption.[48] Whatever, a humanism ignorant of this dilemma is shallow and destined eventually to be overwhelmed by its own repressions. Theodically speaking, it's about experiencing that dilemma in and as one's very being, of containing (living) it as a heightened consciousness of self and history, history in the self, and in ways which don't destroy you or others (the risk being ever-present), or lead you to strategies of survival based in renunciation and an inward dying (staying alive by dying to life). It's a containment haunted by so many versions of its possible, perhaps inevitable failure, and if it's true that those who *can* live do so, while those who can't write about doing so, the pursuit of art is itself already a kind of failure, and one which can be ameliorated only to a degree by public success.[49] In almost any late photograph of Mann we sense something of all this. Of course we see what we are meant to see: the urbane gravitas of the world renowned author. But search the gaze more closely and glimpse how much more it intimates – or conceals: secrecy, pain, insularity, an enigmatic coldness. Cruelty?

Notes

1 *zum Wissen nur berufen … daran zerbrach* ('Nietzsches Philosophie im Lichte unserer Erfahrung', hereafter referred to as GKFA 19a: 186).

2 *Die Erkenntnis tödtet das Handeln, zum Handeln gehört das Umschleiertsein durch die Illusion – das ist die Hamletlehre […] die wahre Erkenntniss, der Einblick in die grauenhafte Wahrheit überwiegt jedes zum Handeln antreibende Motiv, bei Hamlet sowohl als bei dem dionysischen Menschen* (Nietzsche 1988c: 57)

3 *eine große Variation des Hamlet-Wortes* (GKFA 19a: 199).

4 *jener starken Erzählung, die,Ein Elender' überschrieben ist und einer ganzen dankbaren Jugend die Möglichkeit sittlicher Entschlossenheit jenseits der tiefsten Erkenntnis zeigte* ('Der Tod in Venedig', hereafter referred to as GKFA 2: 507–8).

5 Quotations from Mann's fiction are variously from the translations by Lowe-Porter, Luke and Woods. Because quotations from the same work may be from different translators, the latter are indicated in the text.

6 *Es ist niemals ein Dokument der Kultur, ohne zugleich ein solches der Barbarei zu sein* (Benjamin 1977: 254). I am grateful to Tobias Döring for help on this point.

7 See Mann (1961), *Genesis*, especially pp. 31–2, resp. *Entstehung* ('Die Entstehung des Doktor Faustus. Roman eines Romans', hereafter referred to as GKFA 19b), especially pp. 432–3; cf. also Alexander Honold's contribution to this volume.

8 *dämonische … Gottesauffassung* (*Doktor Faustus*, hereafter referred to as GKFA 10: 147).

9 *[er] erklärte das Verruchte für ein notwendiges und mitgeborenes Korrelat des Heiligen und dieses für eine beständige satanische Versuchung, eine fast unwiderstehliche Herausforderung zur Schändung* (ibid.: 148).

10 *In der That ging mir bereits als dreizehnjährigen* [sic] *Knaben das Problem vom Ursprung des Bösen nach: ihm widmete ich, in einem Alter, wo man, halb Kinderspiele, halb Gott im Herzen' hat, mein erstes litterarisches Kinderspiel, meine erste philosophische Schreibübung – und was meine damalige,Lösung' des Problems anbetrifft, nun, so gab ich, wie es billig ist, Gott die Ehre und machte ihn zum Vater des Bösen…* This is, in fact, from a Preface ('Vorrede') to *The Genealogy of Morals*, reprinted in: Montinari (1982: 37).

11 This statement from a letter to the editor of *Common Sense* was written by Mann in English. I owe this reference to Dave Paxton.

12   *Ihr sagt lauter Dinge, die in mir sind ...* (GKFA 10: 328).

13   *Es kommt alles von der Osmose ...* (ibid.: 343).

14   *Was auf dem Todes-, dem Krankheitswege entstanden, danach hat das Leben schon manches Mal mit Freuden gegriffen ...* (ibid.: 344).

15   *dich der Barbarei erdreisten, die's zweimal ist, weil sie nach der Humanität ... und bürgerlichen Verfeinerung kommt. ... sogar auf Theologie versteht sie sich besser, als eine vom Kultus abgefallene Kultur, die auch im Religiösen nur eben Kultur sah, nur Humanität, nicht den Exzeß, das Paradox, die mystische Leidenschaft, die völlig unbürgerliche Aventüre* (ibid.: 355).

16   *denn ihrem Moralismus und Humanismus mangle die Einsicht in den dämonischen Charakter der menschlichen Existenz. Sie sei zwar gebildet, aber seicht, und von dem wahren Verständnis der menschlichen Natur und der Tragik des Lebens habe die konservative Tradition sich im Grunde weit mehr bewahrt ...* (ibid.: 135).

17   *sondern in der Natur der Dinge liegt: sie beruht, so möchte ich sagen, auf der Krümmung der Welt, die im Spätesten das Früheste wiederkehren läßt* (ibid.: 545).

18   *daß die Dissonanz darin für den Ausdruck alles Hohen, Ernsten, Frommen, Geistigen steht, während das Harmonische und Tonale der Welt der Hölle ... vorbehalten ist* (ibid.: 544).

19   *grauenhaft anschwellenden, überbordenden, sardonischen Gaudium Gehennas, dieser aus Johlen, Kläffen, Kreischen, Meckern, Röhren, Heulen und Wiehern schauderhaft gemischten Salven von Hohn- und Triumphgelächter der Hölle* (ibid.: 548).

20   *fremden, das Herz mit Sehnsucht* ohne Hoffnung *erfüllenden Lieblichkeit des Klanges* (ibid.: 549).

21   *das auch Widerstrebende gewonnen, gerührt und entrückt hat* (ibid.).

22   *keine Note, die nicht, streng korrespondierend, auch in dem Höllengelächter vorkäme* (ibid.).

23   *Geheimnis der Identität* (ibid.).

24   *die innere Einerleiheit* (ibid.: 705); *die substantielle Identität des Seligsten mit dem Gräßlichsten* (ibid.).

25   *die Nachbarschaft von Ästhetizismus und Barbarei, den Ästhetizismus als Wegbereiter der Barbarei in eigener Seele* (ibid.: 541).

26   *...daß die bevorzugten Objekte der Menschen, ihre Ideale, aus denselben Wahrnehmungen und Erlebnissen stammen wie die von ihnen am meisten verabscheuten, und sich ursprünglich nur durch geringe Modifikationen voneinander unterscheiden. Ja, es kann, wie wir's bei der Entstehung des Fetisch gefunden haben, die ursprüngliche Triebrepräsentanz in zwei Stücke zerlegt worden sein, von denen das eine der Verdrängung verfiel, während der Rest, gerade wegen dieser innigen Verknüpftheit, das Schicksal der Idealisierung erfuhr* (Freud 1969: 252–3).

27   *blast*: to wither, shrivel, blight; 'blasting withers up the brightness, freshness, beauty, vitality, and promise of living things' *Oxford English Dictionary*.

28   Mann remarks as much (1961: 150), after reading Benjamin's *Ursprung des deutschen Trauerspiels* (*The Origin of German Tragic Drama*).

29   *Welche ... der Ehrfurcht entstammende Sittigung des Gemüts kann ausgehen von der Vorstellung eines unermeßlichen Unfugs, wie des explodierenden*

Weltalls? Absolut keine. Frömmigkeit, Ehrfurcht, seelischer Anstand, Religiosität sind nur über den Menschen und durch den Menschen, in der Beschränkung auf das Irdisch-Menschliche möglich. … In diesem Pathos, dieser Verpflichtung, dieser Ehrfurcht des Menschen vor sich selbst ist Gott; in hundert Milliarden Milchstraßen kann ich ihn nicht finden (GKFA 10: 397–8).

30 *Größenordnungen, zu denen der Menschengeist gar kein Verhältnis mehr hat* (ibid.: 387).

31 *dem Maßlos-Außermenschlichen;,Die Wunder des Alls'; Lästerung; des nihilistischen Frevels* (ibid.: 401).

32 cf. *Genesis* pp. 30ff., resp. *Entstehung*, pp. 429ff.

33 I argue this more fully in *Sex, Literature and Censorship* (2001).

34 *diese verzwickten und peinlichen Verhältnisse … Ich finde das nazistische Element nicht nur in Wagners fragwürdiger ,Literatur', ich finde es auch in seiner ,Musik' – ob ich es gleich so geliebt habe … sentimentalen Ahnungslosigkeit … Wagner ist eines der schwierigsten, das psychologische Gewissen am tiefsten herausfordernden, darum aber auch eines der faszinierendsten Vorkommnisse der Kunst- und Geistesgeschichte* (Vaget 2005: 182, 187, 182, 183). This letter to the editor of the American journal *Common Sense* was written in response to an article by Peter Viereck, 'Hitler and Richard Wagner'.

35 *Es gibt zweierlei Leidende, einmal die an der Ueberfülle des Lebens Leidenden, welche eine dionysische Kunst wollen und ebenso eine tragische Ansicht und Einsicht in das Leben, – und sodann die an der Verarmung des Lebens Leidenden, die Ruhe, Stille, glattes Meer, Erlösung von sich durch die Kunst und Erkenntniss suchen, oder aber den Rausch, den Krampf, die Betäubung, den Wahnsinn. … Der Reichste an Lebensfülle, der dionysische Gott und Mensch, kann sich nicht nur den Anblick des Fürchterlichen und Fragwürdigen gönnen, sondern selbst die fürchterliche That und jeden Luxus von Zerstörung, Zersetzung, Verneinung …. Umgekehrt würde der Leidendste, Lebensärmste am meisten die Milde, Friedlichkeit, Güte nöthig haben, im Denken und im Handeln, womöglich einen Gott, der ganz eigentlich ein Gott für Kranke, ein „Heiland" wäre …, kurz eine gewisse warme furchtabwehrende Enge und Einschliessung in optimistische Horizonte* (Nietzsche 1988b: 620–1).

36 *Es gibt zuletzt nur zwei Gesinnungen und innere Haltungen: die ästhetische und die moralistische; und der Sozialismus ist streng moralische Weltansicht. Nietzsche dagegen ist der vollkommenste und rettungsloseste Ästhet, den die Geschichte des Geistes kennt* (GKFA 19a: 220); *Verherrlichung des Barbarischen* (ibid.: 221); *eine rasende Verleugnung des Geistes … zugunsten des schönen, starken, ruchlosen Lebens* (ibid.).

37 *sondern ihr Schauplatz war vielmehr seine Seele selbst, und sie brachen von außen herein, seinen Widerstand – einen tiefen und geistigen Widerstand – gewalttätig niederwerfend, gingen hindurch und ließen seine Existenz, ließen die Kultur seines Lebens verheert, vernichtet zurück* (GKFA 2: 582).

38 *des äußersten Opfers* (ibid.: 583); *als auf zerwühltem Moosgrund grenzenlose Vermischung begann, dem Gotte zum Opfer. Und seine Seele kostete Unzucht und Raserei des Unterganges* (ibid.: 584).

39 *Fast Alles, was wir 'höhere Cultur' nennen, beruht auf der Vergeistigung und Vertiefung der Grausamkeit …* (Nietzsche 1988a: 166).

40 *[D]ies ist das, was ich die Verinnerlichung des Menschen nenne: damit*
    wächst erst das an den Menschen heran, was man später seine "Seele" nennt.
    (Nietzsche 1987: 322); *Die zweite Abhandlung giebt die Psychologie des*
    Gewissens: dasselbe ist nicht, wie wohl geglaubt wird, "die Stimme Gottes im
    Menschen" – es ist der Instinkt der Grausamkeit, der sich rückwärts wendet,
    nachdem er nicht mehr nach aussen hin sich entladen kann. Die Grausamkeit als
    einer der ältesten und unwegdenkbarsten Cultur-Hintergründe hier zum ersten
    Male ans Licht gebracht (Nietzsche 1989: 352).

41 *daß es kein tieferes Wissen ohne Krankheitserfahrung gibt* ... (Mann 1936: 260).

42 *Institoris war in der Tat kein starker Mann,* ... *und hinter der goldenen*
    Brille blickten die blauen Augen mit zartem, edlem Ausdruck, der es schwer
    verständlich – oder eben vielleicht gerade verständlich – machte, daß er die
    Brutalität verehrte, natürlich nur, wenn sie schön war (GKFA 10: 417).

43 *so erscheinen einem Nietzsches Rodomontaden von der kulturerhaltenden*
    und selektiven Funktion des Krieges als die Phantasien eines Unerfahrenen,
    des Sohnes einer langen Friedens- und Sekuritätsepoche mit ,mündelsicheren
    Anlagen', welche sich an sich zu langweilen beginnt (GKFA 19a: 212).

44 *und man sieht wohl: es ist ein großer Unterschied, ob man aus schmerzlichem*
    Pessimismus und bitterer Ironie, von Geistes wegen, die Lüge bejah toder aus
    Haß auf den Geist und die Wahrheit (Mann 1936: 261).

45 *Wieviel enthält der* Faustus *von meiner Lebensstimmung! Ein radikales*
    Bekenntnis im Grunde. Das war das Aufwühlende, von Anbeginn, an dem Buch
    (GKFA 19b: 522).

46 '*Denn Heinrich Manns* Untertan *und Thomas Manns* Tod in Venedig *kann*
    man bereits als große Vorläufer jener Tendenz betrachten, die die Gefahr einer
    barbarischen Unterwelt innerhalb der modernen deutschen Zivilisation, als ihr
    notwendiges Komplementärprodukt, signalisiert haben.' Damit ist sogar auf die
    Beziehungen zwischen der venezianischen Novelle und dem Faustus *schon im*
    voraus hingewiesen (GKFA 19b: 513).

47 *Martertod am Kreuz des Gedankens* (ibid.: 188); *ein tragisches Schicksal über die*
    Kraft gehender Erkenntnis (ibid.: 214).

48 It's not surprising then to read that in the last years of his life Mann
    increasingly thought of himself as a religious author, see Beddow
    (1994: 67).

49 According to Heilbut (1996: 124–5), Mann writes to his brother in 1901: '...
    these highly unliterary ... and vital experiences have proved ... that there
    is something sincere, warm and good in me after all, and not just "irony",
    that after all everything in me is not blasted, overrefined, and corroded
    by the accursed scribbling.' In his diary of the same year: 'Ah, literature
    is death! I shall never understand how anyone can be dominated by it
    without bitterly hating it.' As Heilbut goes on to argue, echoing Nietzsche:
    'literature is death, and [only] the mindless embody life' (ibid.: 135).

Works Cited

Beddow, Michael, 1994. *Thoman Mann: Doctor Faustus*. Cambridge: Cambridge University Press.

Benjamin, Walter, 1977. 'Über den Begriff der Geschichte', in *Illuminationen. Ausgewählte Schriften 1*. Frankfurt am Main: Suhrkamp, pp. 251–61.

Dollimore, Jonathan, 2001. *Sex, Literature and Censorship*. Cambridge: Polity.

Donne, John, 1967. *Selected Prose*, eds Helen Gardner and Timothy Healy. Oxford: Clarendon.

Euripides, 1960. *The Bacchae*, trans. William Arrowsmith, in *Greek Tragedies*, vol. 3, David Grene and Richmond Lattimore. Chicago: University of Chicago Press.

Freud, ~~~~~~nd, 1969 [1915]. 'Die Verdrängung', in *Gesammelte Werke*, eds Anna Freud et al., ~~~10 Werke aus den Jahren 1913–1917*. Frankfurt am Main: S. Fischer, pp. 248–

Freud, Sigmund, 1984 [1~~. ~~n Repression', trans. James Strachey, in *On Metapsychology. The Theory o~ ~ ~hoanalysis*, Pelican Freud Library, vol. 11. Harmondsworth: Penguin, pp. 139–58.

Greville, Fulke, 1973. *Selected Writings*, ed. Joan Rees. London: Athlone.

Hardy, Thomas, 1930. *Collected Poems*. London: Macmillan.

Heilbut, Anthony, 1996. *Thomas Mann: Eros and Literature*. New York: Alfred A. Knopf.

Herbert, George, 2005. 'Church-monuments', in *The Complete English Poems*, ed. John Tobin. London: Penguin, p. 58.

Mann, Thomas, 1936. 'Freud und die Zukunft', in *Imago. Zeitschrift für psychoanalytische Psychologie, ihre Grenzgebiete und Anwendungen* 22: 3, pp. 257–74.

Mann, Thomas, 1947. *Essays of Three Decades*, trans. H. T. Lowe-Porter. London: Secker and Warburg.

Mann, Thomas, 1959. *Last Essays*, trans. Richard and Clara Winston, Tania and James Stern. London: Secker and Warburg.

Mann, Thomas, 1961 [1949]. *The Genesis of a Novel*, trans. Richard and Clara Winston. London: Secker and Warburg.

Mann, Thomas, 1968 [1947]. *Doctor Faustus. The Life of the German Composer Adrian Leverkühn as told by a friend*, trans. H. T. Lowe-Porter. Harmondsworth: Penguin. [*L-P*]

Mann, Thomas, 1985. *Pro and Contra Wagner*, trans. Alan Blunden. London: Faber.

Mann, Thomas, 1993 [1912]. 'Death in Venice', in *Selected Stories*, trans David Luke. London: Penguin. [*Luke*]

Mann, Thomas, 1997 [1947]. *Doctor Faustus. The Life of the German Composer Adrian Leverkuhn as told by a friend*, trans John E. Woods. New York: Vintage. [*Woods*]

Mann, Thomas, 2004 [1912]. 'Der Tod in Venedig', in *Frühe Erzählungen*, ed. Terence J. Reed. Große Kommentierte Frankfurter Ausgabe, vol. 2.1. Frankfurt am Main: S. Fischer, pp. 501–92. [GKFA 2]

Mann, Thomas, 2007 [1947]. *Doktor Faustus*, ed. Ruprecht Wimmer. Große Kommentierte Frankfurter Ausgabe, vol. 10.1. Frankfurt am Main: S. Fischer. [GKFA 10]

Mann, Thomas, 2009a. 'Nietzsches Philosophie im Lichte unserer Erfahrung', in *Essays VI. 1945 –1950*, ed. Herbert Lehnert. Große Kommentierte Frankfurter Ausgabe, vol. 19.1. Frankfurt am Main: S. Fischer, pp. 185-226. [GKFA 19a]

Mann, Thomas, 2009b [1949]. 'Die Entstehung des Doktor Faustus. Roman eines Romans', in *Essays VI. 1945–1950*, ed. Herbert Lehhert. Große Kommentierte

Frankfurter Ausgabe, vol. 19.1. Frankfurt am Main: S. Fischer, pp. 409–510. [GKFA 19b]

Mann, Thomas, 2013 [1939]. 'Letter to the Editor of Common Sense', in *The Third Reich Source Book*, eds Anson Rabinbach, Sander L. Gilman. Irvine: University of California Press, pp. 543–7.

Montinari, Mazzino (ed.), 1982. *Nietzsche lesen*. Berlin: de Gruyter.

Nietzsche, Friedrich, 1956. *The Birth of Tragedy and the Genealogy of Morals*, trans. F. Golffing. New York: Doubleday.

Nietzsche, Friedrich, 1973. *Beyond Good and Evil*, trans. R. J. Hollingdale. Harmondsworth: Penguin.

Nietzsche, Friedrich, 1979. *Ecce Homo*, trans. R. J. Hollingdale. Harmondsworth: Penguin.

Nietzsche, Friedrich, 1987 [1886]. 'Zur Genealogie der Moral', in *Jenseits von Gut und Böse. Zur Genealogie der Moral*, Kritische Studienausgabe, eds Giorgio Colli and Mazzino Montinari, vol 5. München: dtv, pp. 245–412.

Nietzsche, Friedrich, 1988a [1886]. 'Jenseits von Gut und Böse', in *Jenseits von Gut und Böse. Zur Genealogie der Moral*, Kritische Studienausgabe, eds Giorgio Colli and Mazzino Montinari, vol 5. München: dtv, pp. 9–243.

Nietzsche, Friedrich, 1988b [1882]. 'Die fröhliche Wissenschaft', in *Morgenröte, Idyllen aus Messina. Die Fröhliche Wissenschaft*, Kritische Studienausgabe, eds Giorgio Colli and Mazzino Montinari, vol 3. München: dtv, pp. 343–651.

Nietzsche, Friedrich, 1988c [1878]. 'Die Geburt der Tragödie', in *Die Geburt der Tragödie. Unzeitgemäße Betrachtungen I-IV. Nachgelassene Schriften 1870–1873*, Kritische Studienausgabe, eds Giorgio Colli and Mazzino Montinari, vol 1, pp. 9–156.

Nietzsche, Friedrich, 1989 [1886]. 'Ecce Homo', in *Der Fall Wagner. Götzen-Dämmerung. Der Antichrist. Ecce Homo. Dionysos-Dithyramben. Nietzsche contra Wagner*, Kritische Studienausgabe, eds Giorgio Colli and Mazzino Montinari, vol. 6. München: dtv, pp. 255–374.

Nietzsche, Friedrich, 2001 [1882/1897]. *The Gay Science*, ed. B. Williams, trans. J. Nauckhoff. Cambridge: Cambridge University Press.

Prater, Donald, 1995. *Thomas Mann: A Life*. Oxford: Oxford University Press.

Shakespeare, William, 2008. *The Norton Shakespeare*. Based on the Oxford edition, eds Stephen Greenblatt et al., 2nd edition. New York: Norton.

Vaget, Hans Rudolf (ed.), 2005. *Im Schatten Wagners: Thomas Mann über Richard Wagner. Texte und Zeugnisse 1895–1955*, revised edition. Frankfurt am Main: Fischer Taschenbuchverlag.

Webster, John, 1983. 'The White Devil', in *The Selected Plays of John Webster*, eds Jonathan Dollimore and Alan Sinfield. Cambridge: Cambridge University Press.

Yeats, W.B., 1997. 'The Second Coming', in *The Poems*, ed. Richard J. Finneran. The Collected Works of W. B. Yeats, vol. 1, 2nd edition. New York: Scribner, p. 189–90.

Two

Laughter in the Throat of Death:
Thomas Mann's Shakespearean
Sprachkrise
Richard Wilson

To enforce the painèd impotent to smile

'It cannot be, it is impossible. / Mirth cannot move a soul in agony'
(*Love's* 5.2.833–4), the first words of Shakespearean drama quoted in
Thomas Mann's *Doktor Faustus* (*Faustus* 175)[1] come from the end of the
play its anti-hero Leverkühn will transpose into his operatic debut, and
they help to explain not only why the fictional composer is obsessed
by *Love's Labour's Lost*, but also why the real author chose this text as
a 'surprising, if not bizarre' source for his demonic novel (Fernie 2012:
119). Biron's denial of the possibility of laughter is his riposte to the
penance imposed by Rosaline, to visit for 'this twelvemonth term from
day to day / ... the speechless sick and still converse / With groaning
wretches, and your task shall be / With all the fierce endeavour of
your wit / To enforce the painèd impotent to smile' (*Love's* 5.2.827–31);
and it is preceded by a line that, like so much left unspoken in *Doktor
Faustus*, resonates silently with the very first Shakespearean words
cited, 'To hear with eyes belongs to love's fine wit', from sonnet 23, to
become a Pythagorean subtext, 'meant more for the reading eye than
for the ear' (*Faustus* 67),[2] of the entire work. 'To move wild laughter in
the throat of death?', Biron protests incredulously, 'It cannot be, it is
impossible' (*Love's* 5.2.832–3). The novelist was deep into discussions
with Theodor Adorno when in the spring of 1944 he wove into his
Faust story the exchanges about *Love's Labour's Lost* between Adrian
and Serenus Zeitblom, the narrator who becomes the opera's librettist;
but he was also in what he called the 'false and intolerable position' of
being pressed to speak about the fate of Nazi Germany: 'the country
whose language you write' (quoted in Prater 1995: 360).[3] Shakespeare's

line about the impossibility of moving 'laughter in the throat of death' therefore became, in this paralysing context, a pre-echo of Adorno's gravest *obiter dictum*, itself a reverberation of Karl Kraus's notorious confession[4] that 'on the subject of Hitler I have nothing to say':

> Traditional culture has become worthless today … Even the most extreme consciousness of doom threatens to degenerate into idle chatter. Cultural criticism finds itself faced with the final stage of the dialectic of culture and barbarism. To write poetry after Auschwitz is barbaric. And this corrodes even the knowledge of why it has become impossible to write poetry. Critical intelligence cannot be equal to this challenge so long as it confines itself to self-satisfied contemplation.
>
> (Adorno 1983: 34)[5]

'The words of Mercury are harsh after the songs of Apollo. You that way, we this way' (*Love's* 5.2.903–4): what Mann identified in Shakespeare, his choice of *Love's Labour's Lost* suggests, was a pretext of modernity's *Sprachkrise*, the speechlessness that Hugo von Hofmannsthal also dated to the Shakespearean moment with his *Letter of Lord Chandos*, and that the poet Rilke inaugurated in 1899, when he quavered that 'I am so afraid of people's words' (2011: 7).[6] In fact, Shakespeareans have long perceived how the coda of the comedy confirms the chasm between sign and referent that has been threatening as a result of the play's iconoclastic deconstruction of euphuistic 'Taffeta phrases, silken terms precise, / Three-piled hyperboles, spruce affectation, / Figures pedantical' (*Love's* 5.2.406–8); and that this verbal frenzy, during which, as Stanley Wells remarks, words 'run counter to the intention of the speaker' by enacting 'what has been repressed' (1982: 137–47), heralds a representational impasse for the 'great feast of languages' (*Love's* 5.1.34–5) that has constituted the humanist tradition. But it was left to a novelist transfixed by the specifically German shock about the twentieth-century crisis of language to unlock the catastrophic implications of a play that by 'a repeated quibble on *light*' anticipates Freud's assault on the meaning of meaning, and on the project of Enlightenment itself (Mahood 1968: 29, 175).

By intruding *Love's Labour's Lost* into his *Doktor Faustus*, Mann was insisting on a dark intertext often overlooked by Shakespeareans, namely the terroristic linguistic destructiveness it shares with the theatre of Christopher Marlowe.[7] For though the comedy was written in the bloody wake of the St Bartholomew's Day holocaust, with exactly the same cast as *The Massacre at Paris*, Marlowe's savage docudrama on the atrocity, critics are loth to locate a historical determinant for the return of the repressed from the unconscious of the text in this spewing of unintended consequences out of good intentions. Still less are they ready to identify in the macabre messenger Mercade, who appears at the close of the comedy, 'the agent of England' codenamed Mercury – the dead poet Marlowe himself – who at the end of his last tragedy gave himself a Hitchcockian cameo role to tell the world the news of the assassination of the King of France that will lead to the succession of the King of Navarre, and the cruel illusion of ending Europe's religious wars. Yet Marlowe had himself been assassinated, the victim of those wars, a year before *Love's Labour's Lost*. When Shakespeare brings the ghost of the dead man back from his own play, to fulfil his last orders, and tell the heedless lovers 'the news / I bring is heavy on my tongue' (5.2.701–2), the great survivor is therefore flirting not only with his rival's demonic conception of theatrical spectrality, but confusing fact with fiction so uncannily as to compel us to ask what it is that lies so heavy on the tongue that even the Bard cannot spit out.

Editors are puzzled that the dramatist seems to choke on Mercade's news at the end of *Love's Labour's Lost* by repeating variants of the same lines about peacetime reconstruction twice, a unique textual stutter which reveals Shakespeare himself struggling to express the truth. The reality of religious terror is the hate that dares not speak its name in Shakespeare's post-war comedy; and so successful has been the displacement of this violence onto the erotics of those who battle instead 'against (their) own affections / And the huge army of the world's desires' (1.1.9–10), that critics still collude in the repression. But the traumatic context highlights the theme of the inexpressible that links this unlikely play with Mann's own post-war story, and its similar interplay of war with art. So Adorno's interdiction on 'the songs of Apollo' after the news of the camps suggests that when he advised him on musicology in *Doktor Faustus* the philosopher might also have been the person who nudged the novelist into recognizing in what Zeitblom terms Shakespeare's 'twisted ordering of ideas' (*Faustus* 232) a surprising prefiguration of 'the final stage of the dialectic of culture and barbarism', and a shadowing of the more obvious Elizabethan drama about the 'breakneck game played by art at the very edge of impossibility' (*Faustus* 233),[8] Marlowe's *Doctor Faustus*. With a comparable focus on the self-defeating quest for knowledge to 'make us heirs of all eternity' (*Love's* 1.1.7), yet a Pageant of Nine Worthies to sublimate the masque of Seven Deadly Sins, *Love's Labour's Lost* 'performs an exorcism on *Doctor Faustus*', it has been said (Brown 2003: 21). But Adorno's bar on poetry makes one suspect that Shakespeare's scepticism about whether the world is ready for a 'world-without-end bargain' (*Love's* 5.2.771), or whether 'sickly ears, / Deafed with the clamours of their own dear groans, / Will hear your idle scorns' (*Love's* 5.2.840–2), casts an even deeper pall than the Faust legend over the hitherto unstoppable ironist who was just then being begged to return, like Biron, from Los Angeles to Munich, to accomplish his 'historic work':

> Please, do come soon; look into the faces furrowed with grief; see the unspeakable suffering ... Come soon like a good doctor who sees not only the symptoms but seeks the cause of the sickness and endeavours to remedy this, who however knows that surgical interventions are necessary, above all with the many who once placed value on being called intellectual.
>
> (Walter von Molo, quoted in Kurzke 2002: 498)[9]

The medical metaphor with which Mann was implored to return to Germany by Walter von Molo, pre-war President of Prussia's *Dichterakademie*, was not persuasive, considering the theme he was working into his story about a 'genius whom disease has made a genius' (*Faustus* 258), that the health dispensed by 'the good family doctor' has 'little to do with intellect or art' (*Faustus* 80).[10] As Jonathan Dollimore comments, in *Doktor Faustus* the syphilitic composer personifies his creator's belief that sickness is 'life manifested in its most vigorous form' (Dollimore 1998: 276). Yet, by now reconsidering the Nietzschean image of illness 'springing in drunken boldness from rock to rock' (*Faustus* 258) as a form of diabolism, when at the dead centre of the tale the Devil offers the poison of 'genius-bestowing disease' (ibid.)[11] to Adrian, Mann was ironizing both his own intellectual formation and one of the most politically charged issues in modern philosophy. For the idea that Nietzsche's 'magnificent interpretation' of his own syphilis, that 'sickness brought me to my senses', was *correct*; and that this infection, or another 'unknown biological factor', made possible his convulsive thinking and 'spiritual greatness', had been the argument of the 1935 book that the über-humanist philosopher Karl Jaspers wrote to reclaim Nietzsche from the Nazi will to power. Jaspers admitted how 'confusing it is for us to consider sickness' (Jaspers 1997: 107) an index of health in cases like those of Nietzsche or Hölderlin, and 'health in the medical sense a sign of illness' (ibid.: 111), for such apparent nihilism left ethics speechless with indecision in 'the task of overcoming it' (Jaspers 1975: 164).[12] And from the Nietzsche archive, Heidegger shot back that such a muddying of categories indeed made it sound as if 'the whole of philosophy is not to be taken seriously', when it concerns 'our western existence and our future' (quoted in Kirkbright 2004: 161).[13] Thus, with *Doktor Faustus*, Mann – who had made his decision to go into actual, and not imaginary exile – found himself in ironic accord with Hitler's thinker, for Jasper's sophistry that 'Nietzsche asks of all philosophizing whether it was not illness that brought it forth' (Jaspers 1997: 114),[14] was there ascribed to the forked tongue of the Devil.

A light for Monsieur Judas

It is in the context of the decisionist turn of German philosophy at what, in his 1934 lectures on Hölderlin, Heidegger hailed as the advent of 'a different history' (1989: 1)[15] with the Nazi seizure of power, and of liberal hand-wringing before existentialism's bullying jargon of authenticity, cleansing, health, resoluteness and strength, that the fastidious quibbling pursued by the lofty likes of Jaspers in their diagnosis of Nietzsche's sickness emerges for Mann, as it did for Adorno, as criminally collusive in its own defeat. That self-defeat is written into the pusillanimity of Zeitblom, whose humanistic belief in 'the free and beautiful human being' (*Faustus* 41) is reduced at the end to fretting whether Germany 'can so much as open its mouth' (*Faustus* 506).[16] This unreliable narrator is thought to be based on Mann's erstwhile intimate, the aesthete and Nazi fellow-traveller Ernst Bertram, whose biography of Nietzsche called the philosopher a 'Judas' for satirizing Germany.[17] And with its warning that 'Light seeking light doth light of light beguile' (*Love's* 1.1.77), so 'By light we lose light' (*Love's* 5.2.376), the *malocchia* of *Love's Labour's Lost* strangely presages this critique of Enlightenment, Ewan Fernie reminds us, as an anxiously self-subverting epistemology, 'sicklied o'er with the pale cast of thought' (*Hamlet* 3.1.30), that 'culminates in terrible darkness' (Fernie 2012: 120). When it bids adieu to the discredited professor – 'A light for Monsieur Judas. It grows dark, he may stumble' (*Love's* 5.2.618) – this twilight comedy, which moves inexorably towards the scene at dusk when the 'learned men' (*Love's* 5.2.875) are gently ordered to depart, because 'The scene begins to cloud' (*Love's* 5.2.718), would therefore surely have seemed unhappily timely to the author who was prefacing his novel about the fall of men and treason of the clerks with nocturnal lines from Dante: 'The day was ending, and the brown air / Released the animals of the earth from their fatigue' (Dante 2006: 13).

'Worthies, away!' (*Love's* 5.2.718): in its bleak dismissal of the disgraced 'book men' (*Love's* 2.1.227), the darkening world of *Love's Labour's Lost* must have looked hauntingly suggestive to Mann of the moral night that descended on Weimar culture after 1933, with the capitulation of the universities to the Nazis and the 'inner exile' of Germany's liberal intellectuals. With his own formal drive to 'combine the elements of restoration, indeed of the archaic, with revolution' (*Faustus* 202), the novelist had long been alert to the 'Janus face' (*Faustus* 207)[18] of Germany's conservative revolution, which fused a hunger for modernity, he perceived, with a lust for ruins and 'dreams of the past: a highly technological romanticism' (Mann trans. and quoted in Hert 1984: 2).[19] So Shakespeare could almost have been predicting the turn towards this 'archaic-revolutionary' (*Faustus* 203)[20] or reactionary modernism in the oxymoronic idea he stages in the play, and which is cited conspicuously in Mann's text (*Faustus* 175), of the intellectual scandal that 'The blood of youth burns not with such excess / As gravity's revolt to wantonness' (*Love's* 5.2.73–4). The appeal of this comedy to the author of *Faustus* might, then, have been its anti-cathartic message, that the 'way to choke a gibing spirit' is to jest 'a twelvemonth in an hospital' in vain (*Love's* 5.2.835–48). With its laborious unfunny jokes, and disgust at the 'maggot ostentation' (*Love's* 5.2.409) of the 'apt and gracious words' in Biron's most 'mirth-moving jest' (*Love's* 2.1.71–3), *Love's Labour's Lost* offers an uncanny premonition, in any case, of the crisis of literary expression which became the general 'retreat from the word' that George Steiner described in *Language and Silence* as the collective writers' block resulting from doubt as to whether 'our civilization, by virtue of the inhumanity it has carried out and condoned [has] forfeited claims to that indispensable luxury we call literature' (Steiner 1969: 75).

No poetry after Auschwitz; and 'no more Goethean *Fausts* either' (Fetzer 1996: 89). Mann's intolerably verbose *Faustus* would therefore be constructed as one enormous seizure of stammering, or set of stuttering variations on what cannot be said; in particular, the impossibility of signifying hell: an actuality, so its Devil loquaciously avers, whereof we cannot speak, since it lies so far outside language that words 'can make no claim to designate that which can never ever be designated or denounced in words' (*Faustus* 260).[21] So the screams of lamentation from within the country about the barbarism that had overtaken Germany were said in the novel to be like King Claudius's attempt to pray in *Hamlet*, words that stick in the throat, and 'never to heaven go' (*Hamlet* 3.3.98; *Faustus* 184).[22] And at its centre would be a lecture by Old Nick which begins in the assumed 'voice, the enunciation of a player' (*Faustus* 240), before turning into a wicked parody of none other than Adorno himself, intoning on the 'prohibitive difficulties' of modern art, which 'scorns extension', and 'leaves time standing vacant' (*Faustus* 256), by going nowhere ceaselessly, as if walking 'upon a road of peas' (*Faustus* 254).[23] Thus it was the Elizabethan comedy's premature alertness to how 'composition itself has grown too difficult, desperately difficult' (*Faustus* 254),[24] that Mann recorded in his notes; as when his self-conscious sententiousness at an election rally for Roosevelt, in contrast to the vivacious young ventriloquist with her 'pop-eyed doll', which hilariously upstaged him, sent the smiling public man back with gritted teeth to the scene where the Lords' ridiculously 'disguised' and 'vilely penned' (*Love's* 5.2.301–5) Muscovite embassy is dashed by 'some slight zany', like 'a Christmas comedy' (*Love's* 5.2.462–3), for the moral of his own love's labour's lost:

I was still laughing when I went up to the platform to make my speech – one obviously far too earnest for these circumstances ... More comedy followed it, and in the end everyone had so thoroughly amused himself that no one had the slightest lingering doubt of F.D.R.'s re-election. How strangely it touched me to read the brief diary note of the day immediately thereafter. I had once more returned to *Love's Labour's Lost* and copied out a couplet from the play:

There form confounded makes most form in mirth,

When great things labouring perish in their birth. [5.2.516–7]

My notation was: 'The first line may apply to *Joseph*, the second to *Faustus*.'

(Mann 1961: 82)[25]

On the stump in Bel Air, the Nobel Laureate is drowned out by a ventriloquist's dummy; and though he could not help laughing, this literal loss of face in his personal *Sprachkrise* cues an appalled realization of how 'That sport best pleases that doth least know how', because of its unselfconsciousness, as the Princess theorizes in the play, whereas when 'zeal strives to content ... the contents / Dies in the zeal of that which it presents' (*Love's* 5.2.513–5). 'You have put me out of countenance', the humiliated schoolmaster indeed complains, after the audience pokes fun at him during the over-rehearsed play-within-the-play (*Love's* 5.2.609). And Mann's recall of how his own symbolic castration by a puppet confirmed his 'scruples and doubts' about *Faustus*, or rather, 'how disposed I was to believe in its failure', is connected in his memoir on the forty-year genesis of his text to the anxieties that increased in proportion to his psychosomatic migraines (Mann 1961: 82).[26] So he punctuated his interminable fiction with 'uneasiness, a labored breathing' (*Faustus* 5), like the inhalations of a stutterer, signalling that 'I am actually seeking out delays and digressions' (*Faustus* 34) to register 'a state of mind that is the most onerous combination of a heart-pounding need to speak and a deep reticence before my own inadequacy' (*Faustus* 6).[27] Clearly, there was an elective affinity in Mann's mind between his complex about completing this endlessly retarded narrative, his worry about whether 'perhaps it was too late to start a thing like this' (Mann to Helen Lowe-Porter, as quoted in Prater 1995: 368), and Shakespeare's poetic persona as 'an unperfect actor' (sonnet 23) struck dumb in incapacitating embarrassment: 'a foolish mild man, an honest man', but 'soon dashed ... a marvelous good neighbor, faith, and a very good bowler, but ... alas, you see how it is – a little o'erparted' (*Love's* 5.2.571–4).

In a fiction where we are told the German problem is to escape suffocation, and breathe in the *Lebensraum* of 'free and open air' (*Faustus*

325); but in which the geopolitics of this 'last chapter of world history' (ibid.)[28] are filtered via the dialogue *On the Marionette Theatre* which inspires Adrian to write a puppet opera, where the stuttering poet Kleist struggles to break through his paralysing self-consciousness to attain the unselfconscious expressiveness of a dummy, it is telling that Shakespeare is initially heard on the lips, 'first shaped around the English language' (*Faustus* 55), of stammering Wendell Kretzschmar, whose career is blighted by 'the model of a particularly heavy and well-developed stutter' (*Faustus* 54).[29] The lectures on Beethoven and the Bard the afflicted organist coughs up are marred by his distracting impediment, 'because this unfortunate stutter made listening a hair-raising journey, producing both terror and laughter' (ibid.); like that provoked by the frustrated Beethoven himself, staring at his uncomprehending public in 'mad abstraction' (*Faustus* 63).[30] What 'the stutterer taught us', Zeitblom reflects, was art's subjection to 'its elemental forces' (*Faustus* 193).[31] The sufferer's 'red and swollen face' (*Faustus* 54),[32] and the titters it incites, thus prompt one of the key questions of the novel, lately posed in Marc Shell's brilliant study *Stutter*: 'do people laugh in a way that duplicates the involuntariness' of the suffering, and if so, what does this mimesis tell us about intentionality and agency, or 'the gap between the involuntary and the voluntary so fundamental to twentieth-century aesthetics?' (Shell 2005: 3). For the effect of this performative crisis, with its 'anxious, tense waiting for the next convulsive impasse' (*Faustus* 54), as the stammerer enacts his own thesis on the liberation of cultural creation, is to make 'his constantly imperiled speech' (*Faustus* 61) a paradigm of the modern artwork as an 'expression of suffering in its real moment' (*Faustus* 256),[33] and in its adversarial problematic with its audience, a filmic prologue to the novel:

> – how tragic, since he was a man with a great wealth of urgent ideas and a passionate desire to communicate them in speech … whether he was impeded by a sibilant, which, with his mouth tugged wide, he would extend as the sound of a locomotive letting off steam; whether in his struggles with a labial his cheeks would puff out, his lips given over to the popping rapid-fire of short, soundless explosions; or whether, finally and simply, his breath would end up in hopeless stammering disarray, his funnel-shaped mouth snapping for air like a fish out of water. It is true that his moist eyes were laughing all the while, and apparently he saw the situation from the humorous side, but that was no consolation for everyone else, and ultimately one could not blame the public for avoiding these lectures.
>
> (*Faustus* 54)[34]

Mann was clearly fascinated by the stutter as a paroxysm of blocked self-consciousness that dehumanizes by taking away the speech that defines the human, along with intention and volition. So, no wonder that Adrian's *pièce de resistance* is a puppet show starring a weeping dog (*Faustus* 333); nor that his setting of *The Tempest* zooms in on the place where the dog goes 'bow wow' and the chanticleer cries 'cock-a-diddle-dow'(*Tempest* 1.2.385, 390); for such scenes of suspended animation remind us not only how the novelist had appropriated his brother Heinrich's marionette theatre as a child, but how enchanted he became with the 'trick world' of *Bambi*, so that nothing thrilled him more than receiving a Yale doctorate beside Walt Disney (cf. Prater 1995: 5, 281, 284, 292; Kurzke 2002: 528). As Gertrude Stein said in 1935, 'Funnily enough the cinema offered a solution' (1935: 176) to the modern crisis of meaning, by making a continuous present of repeated beginning, like the freeze-frame of her own palilalia. So, funnily enough, it is no accident that Mann's stuttering pedagogue, whose spasms of '*dim – dada!*' (*Faustus* 59) foretell art coming to 'a total standstill' (*Faustus* 88), should adore the Shakespeare 'he knew intimately and admired passionately' (*Faustus* 79) for its animality and 'barbarism' (*Faustus* 66);[35] nor that it is this stammerer who plants the idea that *Love's Labour's Lost* scorns humanism out of hatred of its *barbarous* repetitiveness. Later his pupil will insist on setting hiccupping lines from the play, like 'hit it ... Thou canst not hit it, hit it, hit it, / Thou canst not hit it ... An I cannot, cannot, cannot, / An I cannot' (*Love's* 4.1.121), as if enthralled that a comedy which ends with an owl and a cuckoo parroting human language, in onomatopoeic avian wisdom that to wit to woo is cuckoo for a cuckold, predicts the mockery of romantic dreams in the wise quacks of Donald Duck, or the titubating lyrics of the bird-man Papageno. For Mann seems to have intuited what postmodern critics such as Jonathan Goldberg discover in the Shakespearean text, 'a space of endless *copia*' animated by stammering perseverative punning as an egotistical function of 'the fact that there is no reason to stop', and by the cruel animus of this hostile act of revengeful authorial ventriloquy (Goldberg 1986: 7, 99–100, quoting Roland Barthes on repetition 1974: 176–7).

A man replete with mocks

Ever since his father cruelly challenged the infant Tommy to eat as many of the chocolates called 'Othellos' as he desired, Mann had associated Shakespeare with the performance of *pretended* feeling (Kurzke 2002: 9–10). But the linguistic scepticism of a comedy which opens with such a stark staging of Shakespeare's primal scene of a loyalty test, when Biron hesitates as the other 'brave conquerors' who 'war against ... the huge army of the world's desires' queue to subscribe to King

Ferdinand's 'schedule', pledging to obey his 'late edict' to reconstruct a peacetime Navarre as 'the wonder of the world', with its court 'a little academe, / Still and contemplative in living art' (*Love's* 1.1.7–18), must have had particular bite for Mann at a time when he too was preparing to take an oath of allegiance. For it was while thinking about a Shakespeare who was 'tongue-tied by authority' (sonnet 66) that the novelist was himself examined for over an hour in January 1944 on the constitution and history of the United States, when he merely exposed his ignorance, before finally signing his own 'schedule' on June 23, and swearing to 'absolutely and entirely renounce and abjure fidelity to any foreign prince, potentate, or State', to 'support and defend the Constitution and laws of the United States', and to take 'this obligation freely and without any mental reservation or purpose of evasion. So help me God. In acknowledgment whereof I have hereunto affixed my signature'.[36]

Before affixing his signature endorsing his 'deep oaths', as required by the mad legalistic constitutionalism of Navarre, Biron points out that he has 'already sworn' his loyalty once, albeit 'By yea and nay, sir, (for) then I swore in jest' (*Love's* 1.1.23; 34; 54). And in a tricky parallel, Mann had to write instantly to Edward Beneš, President of the Czech government in exile (cf. Prater 1995: 257), excusing himself for enlisting in America's 'cosmopolitan universum' (ibid.: 365), when just eight years earlier he had been overwhelmed by congratulations on taking the oath to become a citizen of Czechoslovakia. During the Munich betrayal of 1938, the novelist had pledged before a rally of twenty thousand in New York's Madison Square Garden to fight for Czech democracy, as it stood alone 'in one of the filthiest dramas ever performed' (ibid.: 289); and he had since tried to hoodwink the Free Czechs that becoming an American did not require him to surrender his Czech nationality. He was reacting to bitter accusations of 'disloyalty to Europe' (Prater 1995: 283). But if this new citizen of the United States experienced pangs of conscience about deserting the Czechs, he was not much freer of 'mental reservation or purpose of evasion' than Biron, about what he called 'the demands this country makes on me in its naïve eagerness', having confided in his diary that the 'democratic idealism' he was mugging up, like a conscientious student, was perhaps only another hypocritical act: 'Do I believe in it? Don't I just try to understand it as if it were a role?':

> Faithfully, I am developing here the intellectual world of democratic idealism – I believe, fairly correctly; I have never studied it, but things do have their own inner logic – and a kind of political Sunday sermon comes into being, in which it would be better for me if I could have it given by a fictional character

instead of giving it on my own in a dreamlike fashion. Do I believe in it? Largely! But probably not so much that I should give it in my own name – just between us, it is a role – with which I identify myself as much as a good actor identifies with his. And why am I playing it? Out of hatred for fascism and Hitler. But should one let one's role be played before such an idiot?

(quoted in Kurzke 2002: 420)[37]

As his biographer Hermann Kurzke dryly remarks, '"I am an American": Thomas Mann is pleased to say in a radio interview' (Kurzke 2002: 419); whereas, or so he now claims, he had never tried to seem a Czech. For in the Land of the Free, and all thanks to Mr Hitler, he declares, 'of a sudden there is no more talk of "tact"' (quoted in Kurzke 2002: 422).[38] Thus, the Nobel Prize-winner advertises Virginia cigarettes on air, or chews pancakes with maple syrup, as his contributions to the war effort; though when he pretends his desert island disc is Noel Coward's 'Don't put your daughter on the stage, Mrs Worthington' (ibid.: 419), his choice of lyrics sounds slyly self-ironic. Likewise, Shakespeare's Biron will announce that because 'Honest plain words best pierce the ear of grief' (Love's 5.2.735), the time of austerity demands he expresses himself only 'In russet yeas and honest kersey noes … so God help me, law!' (Love's 5.2.412–4); while all the time opening himself to Rosaline's silencing objection that the articulacy of 'the world's large tongue / Proclaims you for a man replete with mocks, / Full of comparisons and wounding flouts, / Which you on all estates will execute / That lie within the mercy of your wit' (Love's 5.2.819–23).

Some fierce thing replete with too much rage

On Adrian's desk, his Kleist, 'with a bookmark inserted at the essay on marionettes', is propped against 'the inevitable sonnets of Shakespeare' and editions of *Twelfth Night, Much Ado About Nothing,* and *The Two Gentlemen of Verona (Faustus* 322).[39] The choice of texts flags Mann's musing on Frank Harris's fantasia *The Man Shakespeare,* with its decoding of the triangular love stories in the three plays as reflections of the poet's supposed betrayal by his noble friend William Herbert, whom he sent to court Mary Fitton, who 'wooed and won' the messenger instead (Harris 2008: 162).[40] What would surely have irked Mann about this book, however, was its obtuseness that a heterosexual Will felt desire exclusively for Mary, 'never loved the youth', and must be cleared of any 'guilty intimacy' (ibid.: 185–6). By 'vigorously rejecting the view that Shakespeare had homosexual tendencies', Harris, ever 'the confirmed heterosexual' (Stape 2008: 17), was 'clearing the air of some fumes', as the scholar Samuel Schoenbaum unhappily put it (1991: 487), in the wake of Oscar Wilde's mobilization of the sonnets in his defence at his trials in 1895. But Mann would have known how loudly Stefan George had claimed these poems for peder-astic 'Uranian' love with his 1909 translation; and how scornfully the other Shakespearean he consulted, the great Dane Georg Brandes, had 'lashed out at Harris's arguments' (Stape 2008: 10), at a high-profile lecture in New York.[41] And, above all, he would remember how the 'brilliant' theory of 'Mr Frank Harris' had been mercilessly spoofed by James Joyce in *Ulysses*, where its recital in the National Library is aborted after John Eglinton objects:[42]

> – You have brought us all this way to show us a French triangle.
>   Do you believe your own theory?
> – No, Stephen said promptly.
> – Are you going to write it? Mr Best asked. You ought to make it
>   a dialogue, don't you know, like the Platonic dialogues Wilde
>   wrote.
> John Eclecticon doubly smiled.
>
> (Joyce 1969: 213)

Joyce's eclectic librarian smiles doubly at the idea of setting Harris's normalizing theory about Shakespeare's 'Dark Lady' as a Platonic dialogue in the style of Wilde's, because its entire purpose had been to purge the sonnets of Platonized sodomy; and in his own dialogue we can detect the Uranian author of *Der Tod in Venedig* smiling just as knowingly. For in *Faustus*, the banal biographical thesis about the poet's passion for a Waiting Lady serves as an apt frame not only for Zeitblom's naïve relief when Adrian announces the improbable intention to marry another Marie, but also for the gullible schoolmas-ter's untrustworthy narration of German history. From Harris the pedagogue absorbs the myth of Shakespeare as an abyss of inhuman coldness, 'into which the feelings others expressed for him vanished' (*Faustus* 8),[43] the empty husk of impersonality admired by modernists like T. S. Eliot or Borges, who kills by omission because he cannot love. Such is the asceticism mocked, however, in *Love's Labour's Lost*. And the novel reads something deeper in the 'tendency at work' in these plays, the 'preference' they dramatize 'for sending someone else' to speak of love (*Faustus* 446)[44] by using a voyeuristic wit to woo. What Mann thereby traces in the pattern of these 'French triangles' is something far more disturbing about the tension between author's pen and actor's voice, and closer to his own psychomachia, the inference that each man kills the thing he loves in order to possess it wholly:

> In *Faustus* it takes a peculiar form of montage. Adrian, governed
> by his special relationship with the 'wooer' Rudi Schwerdtfeger,

deliberately and with sinister playfulness repeats a cliche, or myth, with dread purpose. On the devil's instigation, with malice aforethought, he is bringing Rudi to his death – and Zeitblom knows it.

(Mann 1961: 32)[45]

Read as a work about agency and possession, *Faustus* strikingly foretells recent criticism that finds what Dollimore terms 'two concepts of mimesis' in Renaissance theatre, and a fight to death between authors' designs and actors' bodies (1984: 70–82).[46] Thus, underlining episodes in the *Works* that Harris italicized, like Orsino's scheme to woo Olivia through the pageboy Cesario, rather than a 'nuncio of more grave aspect' (*Twelfth* 1.4.27), the novelist responded to the meta-dramatist who strings his plots on the excruciating suspense of breathing seizures, like the pregnant pause of Pyrrhus, when actors 'shiver and look pale, / And throttle their practised accents in their fears' (*Dream* 5.1.102); a speechlessness that seems rich coming from such a windbag, who in films like *Shakespeare in Love* or *The King's Speech* fills our stammerers with words. For though Shell speculates the poet may have suffered a speech impediment, such as cluttering, or tachyphemia – rapid irregular speech – there is something deeply suspect about his pretence, in scorn of 'the rattling tongue / Of saucy and audacious eloquence' (*Dream* 5.1.102), that 'silence shall be most my glory, / Being dumb' (sonnet 83; Shell 2005: 169, 216). And Mann's reading of the plays suggests he had heard something more than organic hesitancy in the truly tongue-twisting Shakespearean injunction to 'Speak the speech, I pray you, as I pronounced it to you – trippingly on the tongue' (*Hamlet* 3.2.1–2).

In *The Anatomy of Influence* Harold Bloom has argued that Shakespeare was *dumbstruck* by *Doctor Faustus*, and became 'the major master of ellipsis', with 'dumb thoughts speaking in effect' (sonnet 85), as Marlowe exerted 'all his might to make [him] tongue-tied' (sonnet 80; Bloom 2011: 49–55). But Mann saw how the very title of *Love's Labour's Lost* revealed the equally uncanny revenge of a palilaliating player. Thus the Shakespearean stutter acquires a diabolical animus in *Faustus*, when Mann adopts it as a master trope not only for his own 'ironical juxtaposition of manner and substance', but for modernism's passive aggressive anti-aesthetic, when the composer reprises the story of the sonnets by projecting what he calls 'the most secret pages in the book of my heart' (*Faustus* 460)[47] through the inanity of his own dumb blond, the violinist Rudi. Many stammerers cease to stumble over words when they assume the ventriloquy of a mask or persona, Shell, himself a stutterer, testifies (2005: 196). A prime instance would be the author of *Confessions of a Mask*, Yukio Mishima, who conquered a crippling stutter by reciting aloud the 'epic flow of conversation' in Mann's books (Scott-Stokes 1974: 142).[48] Likewise, the 'tongue-tied muse' of the sonnets looks 'for recompense' through his beautiful 'dumb presager', 'More than that tongue that more hath more expressed' (sonnet 85). Shakespeare, if his poetry is believed, was one of those only able to overcome his own dumbness through a dummy, like the Fair Youth. But it took the author of *Doktor Faustus* to perceive the devilry of this act of human puppetry (Heller 1958: 24):

> As an unperfect actor on the stage
> Who with his fear is put besides his part,
> Or some fierce thing replete with too much rage
> Whose strength's abundance weakens his own heart,
> So I, for fear of trust, forget to say
> The perfect ceremony of love's rite,
> And in mine own love's strength seem to decay,
> O'er-charged with burden of mine own love's might.
> (sonnet 23)

'I cannot heave / My heart into my mouth' (*King Lear* 1.1.89–90): whether or not he stuttered, Shakespeare was all too familiar, we can infer, with the stage-fright that throws the page Moth in *Love's Labour's Lost*: 'They do not mark me, and that brings me out' (5.2.172). But the dramatist who hangs play after play on the apparently involuntary caesura of the 'spell-stopped' (*Tempest* 5.1.61) actor drying 'Between the acting of a dreadful thing / And the first motion' (*Julius* 2.1.63–4), and whose most cluttering character puts a stop to all 'stops' (*Hamlet* 3.2.336) when 'The rest is silence' (*Hamlet* 5.2.300), is equally aware, his sonnet about dumb waiting implies, that these 'trips of the tongue' may also constitute a playing for time, an artful strategy for keeping mum, or the passive aggression of 'some fierce thing replete with too much rage', like the historical Claudius's prevaricating stutter, or Antony's 'pause till it come back', on pretending to be lost for words (*Julius* 3.2.104). Thus, 'there is much music, excellent voice in this little organ, yet cannot you make it speak' (*Hamlet* 3.2.338), Hamlet stalls; and Iago: 'From this time forth I never will speak word' (*Othello* 5.2.310). If all speech dysfunctions raise 'questions about the distinction between voluntary and involuntary action', what the Prince of Hesitation calls his 'brute part' (*Hamlet* 3.2.95), after the classic stumbler Brutus, the hiatus or 'interim' (*Hamlet* 5.2.74) that follows the execution gesture to 'cut' the speaker, must therefore truly 'give us pause' (*Hamlet* 3.1.70; Shell 2005: 7). As does Adrian's voicelessness in *Doktor Faustus*, when, having never before lacked words, he suddenly clams up, and making the airhead Rudi his 'mediator', 'interpreter' and 'intercessor', announces that 'I don't have at my command the means to express, to drive home my feelings and my wishes – particularly not in the company of others, before whom I really am embarrassed' (*Faustus* 458–9).[49]

Since Adorno would symptomatize the circular repetition compulsion in the syllables 'da da', along with the suspended animation of walking on the spot, as the 'paradoxical dynamic at a standstill' which was the syncopated Chaplinesque 'artfulness of all anti-art' on the Fordist conveyor-belt of mechanical mass reproduction (Adorno 2004: 39),[50] it is appropriate that the first to associate Shakespeare with the disfluency of such an aggressive form of speechlessness should be the arch-modernist Joyce, who has the Bard loom up in umbrage at Stephen's triangulating theory, 'rigid in facial paralysis'. Joyce's apoplectic Shakespeare materializes to bemoan 'in dignified ventriloquy' that ''Tis the loudest laugh bespeaks the vacant mind'; but chokes in a paroxysm of aphasia, like the Moor's, on unbidden thoughts of cuckoldry: 'Iagogo! ... Iagogogo! ... Weda seca whokilla first.' So, as the tragicomic cuckold Bloom asks, 'When will I hear the joke?' (Joyce 1969: 508–9) it is not fanciful for *us* to hear in this disingenuous question, not only a critique of *Hamlet* or *Othello*, but an echo of the adversarial relationship with its public of a modernism that sounds in its avian ejaculation like '"Jug jug" to dirty ears' (Eliot 1952: 1.103).

'What's so funny?' At the time of *Faustus*, Mann was studying *Finnegans Wake* in an effort to answer this question, given that art 'cannot survive with just James Joyce, Picasso, Ezra Pound and the Duchess of Clermont-Tonnère in the audience' (*Faustus* 421).[51] But when 'someone' said that 'under the cover of a conventional use of language, he has been as adventurous an innovator as Joyce', he balked at the comparison: if they had been so similar, Joyce would have written 'much better, more boldly, more splendidly' (cf. Prater 1995: 366). 'Stylistically,' however, he confided to his diary, 'I now really know only parody. In this close to Joyce' (ibid);[52] and viewed in light of the aim to 'move wild laughter in the throat of death', it is hard not to see Mann's over-determined magnum opus, with its counterpoint between narrative time, clocking his 1904 love affair with Paul Ehrenburg, and the last hours of the Thousand Year Reich, as a move in his *agôn* with the English-speaking world, an attempt to surpass *Ulysses* with a yet funnier send-up of Shakespeare scholarship than the Irishman's, or even than Oscar Wilde's 'Portrait of Mr W. H.' (Prater 1995: 366). As Michael Wood has argued, the unlikely image of the starched Thomas Mann as 'Joyce in disguise, a Joyce masquerading as a Galsworthy', is boosted by the exchange at the magic-realist heart of *Faustus* between the composer and the Devil about mimetic desire as rivalry, like the pastiche of the ice flowers young Adrian cultivates, the fiendish simulacra of his syphilis virus, or the kitsch concerto he composes for Rudi as their love-child (Wood 2003: 3-6), to 'raise the game to a yet higher power by playing with forms from which ... life has vanished' (*Faustus* 257). For lecturing with the owlishness of Adorno, the Devil promises that by such parodic parasitism the artist will break through 'the laming difficulties of the age' to reach a 'barbarism' that is repetitiously 'double', because it impersonates 'every bourgeois refinement' (*Faustus* 259),[53] while going nowhere fast.

In tuning his *roman à clef* to *Love's Labour's Lost*, Fernie points out, Mann saw how the comedy 'entails a double mockery ... of both world-transcending aspiration and of sentimental revulsion from it', but that as there is 'no haven from mockery here, this truly entails laughter in the dark' (Fernie 2012: 121). There is hardly a page of *Faustus* that does not indeed record some sinister hilarity in Adrian, from the sardonic smirk with which he observes the cannibalism of chemical osmosis (*Faustus* 22), to the 'sort of smile' with which he recites Prospero's farewell to Ariel after the agonizing death of his 'last love' Echo (*Faustus* 503),[54] the child based on the novelist's own grandson. 'Even though they're dead', as his father observes of the creatures transfixed in the 'still and contemplative' aesthesis of (*Love's* 1.1.15) the laboratory, Adrian 'was shaking with suppressed laughter' (*Faustus* 23). 'It is all a matter of osmosis ... in whose sportive tricks you took such delight', the Devil winks, after Adrian grins that 'Their misery made me laugh' (*Faustus* 251). And the collusive narrator is himself duly hypnotized by this 'sense of the comic, his craving for it, his habit of laughing, laughing to the point of tears' (*Faustus* 94), while leaving it to the reader to decide 'whether such things deserve tears or laughter' (*Faustus* 23).[55] Post-war German readers certainly took this maniacal laughter to be the novelist's own response to their pathetic pleading. But as Wood winces, if this is meant to be funny, Mann is 'smiling when there doesn't seem to be anything to smile about', while, if we smile at all, our own rictus is 'an expression of uncertainty. I don't know whether it helps to remember that his favourite comedian was Jack Benny' (Wood 2003: 6).

Mann was always 'laughing himself silly' (Heilbut 1995: 53) at his Hollywood neighbour Charlie Chaplin. But laughter in the dark is much more difficult to place. Of course, the author of the *Reflections of a Non-Political Man* is laughing at himself in *Faustus* as a Hamlet-like procrastinator. No one who studies the novel as a *paragone* between the words of Mercury and the songs of Apollo can miss the twist, however, that given the displacement of guilt for Auschwitz onto music, it is the writer who laughs last. That was certainly how Schoenberg read the story, which outraged him not only because of his identification with Leverkühn, as inventor of twelve-tone composition, but due to its imputation of culpability for the Holocaust. Ingenuously, the *avant-garde* composer protested he had always been an ardent monarchist (Schoenberg 1977: 551–2). Likewise, a heartbroken Adorno bewailed that 'it was as if T. M. had slandered him from beyond the grave' (Adorno to B. Bräutigam, 18 March 1968, quoted in Claussen 2008: 117), when publication of the notes told the world how the novelist mimicked his voice to 'make him swell up in a not very pleasant way, so it sounds as if it was actually he who wrote *Faustus*' (Mann to Jonas Lesser, 15 October 1951, quoted ibid.).[56] The philosopher once praised Mann's po-faced comic impressions as masks to efface the Romantic cult of genius (quoted ibid.: 36). But in its confusion of autobiography with history, its Shakespearean mix of 'spontaneous oafishness side by side with the comically sublime' (*Faustus* 174), and its self-proliferating paratexts, *Faustus* seems to revert to the impure aesthetics of an older form of theatrical personation, one that toys with life and death, as studied by Walter Benjamin in *Ursprung des deutschen Trauerspiels* (*The Origin of German Tragic Drama*), which the novelist read for its analysis of demonic laughter and the 'obscenely comic figure of the devil' (*Faustus* 106; Grady 2009: 26–8 et passim.).[57] 'Murder' is what Mann himself called his killing imitation of actual persons in this 'living art' (*Love's* 1.1.14): 'Bad, bad' (Thomas Mann to Katia Mann, 18 July 1947, quoted in Kurzke 2002: 509).[58] His narrator is in no doubt where such mimetic homicide originated: 'The party guilty of this caricature … was not Adrian, but Shakespeare' (*Faustus* 232).[59] But whether complicit or not in the horror that it presents to us for laughs, the ventriloquism with which 'the Magician' manipulated his historical models like inert dummies was surely moving 'wild laughter in the throat of death'.

Notes

1   All Shakespeare quotations are from the Norton edition, based on the Oxford text, edited by Stephen Greenblatt, Walter Cohen, Jean Howard and Katherine Eisaman Maus (New York: 2008); and all quotations from Thomas Mann's *Doctor Faustus: The Life of the German Composer Adrian Leverkühn As Told by a Friend* are from the translation by John E. Woods (New York: Vintage 1997).

2   *was mehr für das lesende Auge, als für das Ohr bestimmt gewesen* (*Doktor Faustus*, hereafter referred to as GKFA 10: 93).

3   *eine schiefe und unzuträgliche Stellung zu dem Land, dessen Sprache man schreibt* (Mann 1970: 27).

4   *Mir fällt zu Hitler nichts ein*: with this confession, Karl Kraus famously opened his *Dritte Walpurgisnacht* (written in 1933, published in 1952).

5   *Als neutralisierte und zugerichtete aber wird heute die gesamte traditionelle Kultur nichtig … Noch das äußerste Bewußtsein vom Verhängnis droht zum*

Geschwätz zu entarten. Kulturkritik findet sich der letzten Stufe der Dialektik von Kultur und Barbarei gegenüber: nach Auschwitz ein Gedicht zu schreiben, ist barbarisch, und das frißt auch die Erkenntnis an, die ausspricht, warum es unmöglich ward, heute Gedichte zu schreiben. Der absoluten Verdinglichung, die den Fortschritt des Geistes als eines ihrer Elemente voraussetzte und die ihn heute gänzlich aufzusaugen sich anschickt, ist der kritische Geist nicht gewachsen, solange er bei sich bleibt in selbstgenügsamer Kontemplation (Adorno 1955: 30-1).

6   *Ich fürchte mich so vor der Menschen Wort* (Rilke 1955: 194).

7   But see Meyers (1973), and Brown (2003).

8   *verschrobene Ideenordnung* (GKFA 10: 317); *halsbrecherisches Spielen der Kunst am Rande der Unmöglichkeit* (ibid.: 318).

9   *Bitte, kommen Sie bald, sehen Sie in die von Gram durchfurchten Gesichter, sehen Sie das unsagbare Leid … Kommen Sie bald wie ein guter Arzt, der nicht nur die Wirkung sieht, sondern die Ursache der Krankheit sucht und diese vornehmlich zu beheben bemüht ist, der allerdings auch weiß, daß chirurgische Eingriffe nötig sind, vor allem bei den zahlreichen, die einmal Wert darauf gelegt haben, geistig genannt zu werden …* (Walter von Molo zu Thomas Mann, in Kurzke 1999: 529).

10   *des von Krankheit Genialisierten* (GKFA 10: 354); *mit Geist und Kunst hat die denn wohl freilich nicht viel zu tun* (ibid.: 109).

11   *in kühnem Rausch von Fels zu Felsen sprengt* (ibid.: 354); *Genie spendende Krankheit* (ibid.).

12   *Es ist für uns verwirrend, wenn dasselbe … nun plötzlich Krankheit … sein soll* (Jaspers 1974: 107–8); *Gesundheit im medizinischen Sinne, … wird zum Zeichen eigentlichen Krankseins* (ibid.: 112); *Nihilismus und der Aufgabe, durch ihn hindurchzukommen* (Jaspers 1951: 339).

13   The reference is to Martin Heidegger's *Nietzsche: Der Wille zur Macht als Kunst*, his Freiburg lectures 1936/37. Heidegger Gesamtausgabe (Frankfurt am Main: Vittorio Klostermann), vol. 43.

14   *Nietzsche stellt daher die Frage an a l l e s Philosophieren, ob nicht Krankheit gewesen ist, was diese Gedanken hervorgebracht hat* (Jaspers 1974: 115).

15   *den Anfang einer anderen Geschichte* (Heidegger 1989: 1). See also Theodor Adorno, *The Jargon of Authenticity*, trans. Knut Tarnowski and Frederic Will (London: 2003), pp. 3–4 *et passim*.

16   *das Ideal des freien und schönen Menschen* (GKFA 10: 60); *in menschlichen Angelegenheiten den Mund aufzutun* (ibid.: 697).

17   For Bertram as a model for Zeitblom, see Frances Lee (2007: 283–5 *et passim*).

18   *das Wiederherstellende, ja, das Archaische mit dem Revolutionären zu verbinden* (GKFA 10: 276); *Doppelgesicht* (ibid.: 282).

19   *Vergangenheitstraum, der hochtechnisierte Romantizismus* (Mann 1996: 277).

20   *archaisch-revolutionären* (GKFA 10: 277).

21   *können nicht den Anspruch erheben, das zu bezeichnen, was nimmermehr zu bezeichnen und in Worten zu denunzieren ist* (ibid.: 357).

22   *nicht zum Himmel dringen* (ibid.: 253).

23   *mit der Stimme, der Artikulation eines Schauspielers* (ibid.: 327); *prohibitiven Schwierigkeiten* (ibid.: 351); *es verschmäht die Ausdehnung* (ibid.); *und läßt ihn leer stehen* (ibid.); *Eine Wallfahrt auf Erbsen* (ibid.: 348);

24 *Das Komponieren selbst ist zu schwer geworden, verzweifelt schwer* (ibid.: 349).

25 *daß ich noch lachte, als ich zu meiner unter diesen Umständen offenbar viel zu ernsten Rede aufs Podium stieg ... Neue Komik folgte darauf, und schließlich hatte jedermann sich so glänzend unterhalten, daß keinem die Wiederwahl F.D.R.'s zweifelhaft war.*
Wie sonderbar berührt es mich, die kurze Aufzeichnung des nächstfolgenden Tages zu lesen! Sie betrifft eine wiederholte Beschäftigung mit Loves' Labour Lost *und hält eine ominöse Sentenz des Stückes fest, die Verse:*
'There form confounded makes most form in morth;
When great things labouring perish in their mirth.'
Ich fügte hinzu: 'Der erste Vers mag auf Joseph, *der zweite auf* Faustus *zutreffen'* ('Die Entstehung des Doktor Faustus. Roman eines Romans', hereafter referred to as GKFA 19: 480–1).

26 *mit welchen Skrupeln und Zweifeln* (ibid.: 481); *wie sehr ich geneigt war, an sein Verderben zu glauben* (ibid.).

27 *Unruhe und Beschwertheit des Atemzugs* (GKFA 10: 11); *daß ich nach Verzögerungen und Umschweifen geradezu suche* (ibid.: 51); *einen Gemütszustand, worin herzpochendes Mitteilungsbedürfnis und tiefe Scheu vor dem Unzukömmlichen sich auf die bedrängendste Weise vermischen* (ibid.: 12).

28 *Wie kommt man ins Freie?* (ibid.: 449); *das letzte Kapitel von der Geschichte der Welt* (ibid.).

29 *zuerst von der englischen Sprache geformt[en]* (ibid.: 78). *ein besonders schwer und exemplarisch ausgebildetes Stottern* (ibid.: 77);

30 *weil sein Stotterleiden das Zuhören zu einer aufregenden und klippenvollen Fahrt machte, beängstigend teils, teils zum Lachen reizend* (ibid.: 76); *wirrer Abwesenheit* (90).

31 *Mich erinnerten sie stets daran, was uns der Stotterer einst über die Neigung der Musik gelehrt hatte, ihre Elemente zu zelebrieren* (Mann 2007b: 971). Woods's translation is based on the first publication of *Doktor Faustus* in 1947. The standard edition cited in this volume refers to the second edition in 1948. The passage has been removed from the second edition by Thomas Mann and is thus cited here in German from the commentary in the *Große Kommentierte Frankfurter Ausgabe*, vol. 10.2.

32 *mit rot anschwellendem Gesicht* (GKFA 10: 77).

33 *ängstlich gespanntes Warten auf das nächste konvulsivische Festsitzen* (ibid.: 76); *sein immerfort gefährdetes Sprechen* (ibid.: 87); *Ausdruck des Leidens in seinem realen Augenblick* (ibid.: 351).

34 *– tragisch, weil er ein Mann von großem, drängendem Gedankenreichtum war, der mitteilenden Rede leidenschaftlich zugetan ... sei es, daß ein Zischlaut ihn hemmte, den er mit in die Breite gezerrtem Munde, das Geräusch einer dampflassenden Lokomotive nachahmend, aushielt, oder daß im Ringen mit einem Labiallaut seine Wangen sich aufblähten, seine Lippen sich im platzenden Schnellfeuer kurzer, lautloser Explosionen ergingen; oder endlich auch einfach, daß plötzlich seine Atmung in heillos hapernde Unordnung geriet und er trichterförmigen Mundes nach Luft schnappte wie ein Fisch auf dem Trockenen – mit den gefeuchteten Augen dazu lachend, das ist wahr, er selbst schien die Sache heiter zu nehmen, aber nicht für jedermann war das ein Trost, und im Grunde war es dem Publikum nicht zu verargen, daß es diese Vorlesungen mied* (ibid.: 77).

35 *Dim – dada!* (ibid.: 84); *völlig zum Stillstand zu kommen* (ibid.: 120); *ein intimer Kenner und leidenschaftlicher Verehrer* (ibid.: 107); *Barbarei* (ibid.: 91).
36 This is the Naturalization Oath of Allegiance to the United States of America.
37 *Treulich entwickle ich da die Gedankenwelt des demokratischen Idealismus – ich glaube, ziemlich richtig; studiert habe ich sie nie, aber die Dinge haben ja ihre innere Logik –, und es kommt eine Art von politischer Sonntagspredigt zustande, bei der mir wohler wäre, wenn ich sie von einer Romanfigur halten lassen könnte, statt sie extemporischer und traumhafterweise so ganz auf eigener Hand zu halten. Glaube ich denn daran? Weitgehend! Aber doch wohl nicht so, daß ich sie ganz im eigenen Namen halten dürfte. Unter uns gesagt, ist es eine Rolle, – mit der ich mich so weit identifiziere, wie ein guter Schauspieler sich mit der seinen identifiziert. Und warum spiele ich sie? Aus Haß auf den Faschismus und auf Hitler. Aber sollte man sich von solchem Idioten seine Gedanken und seine Rolle vorspielen lassen?* (in Kurzke 1999: 448–9).
38 *I am an American: Das zu sagen gefällt Thomas Mann in einem Radio-Interview des Jahres 1940* (Kurzke 1999: 447); *und auf einmal … war nicht die Rede mehr von 'Takt'* (ibid.: 450).
39 *worin das Lesezeichen bei dem Aufsatz über die Marionetten eingelegt war, ferner die unvermeidlichen Sonette Shakespeares* (GKFA 10: 445).
40 See Steven Cerf (1981: 480–2).
41 For Stefan George's pederastic interpretation of the sonnets, see especially Marita Keilson-Lauritz (2005).
42 See Philip Kitcher (2013: 189–94).
43 *in welchem Gefühle, die man ihm entgegenbrachte, untergingen* (GKFA 10: 15).
44 *eine Tendenz* (ibid.: 617); *die Neigung* (ibid.); *zu schicken, einen anderen …* (ibid.).
45 *Dem Faustus ist es aufmontiert in der Weise, daß Adrian, durch sein beson- deres Verhältnis zu dem "Werber" Schwerdtfeger bestimmt, es in Aktion setzt, bewußt und düster spielerisch ein Klischee oder einen Mythos wiederholend, zu unheimlichstmn Zweck. Was er an Rudi verübt, ist ein prämeditierter, vom Teufel verlangter Mord – und Zeitblom weiß es.* (GKFA 19: 433).
46 See also Robert Weimann (2000).
47 *die geheimsten Blätter im Buche meines Herzens* (GKFA 10: 635).
48 Mishima worked his humiliation as a stutterer into the ordeal of the seminarian Mizoguchi in his novel *The Temple of the Golden Dawn*; see Christopher Eagle (2011).
49 *Mittler; Dolmetsch; Fürsprecher* (GKFA 10: 635); *ich verfüge nicht über die Ausdrucksmittel, ihr meine Gefühle und Wünsche nahezubringen, – besonders nicht in Gesellschaft anderer, vor denen den Kurschneider und Seladon zu spielen, mich denn doch etwas geniert* (ibid.: 633).
50 *zu einer paradoxen Dynamik im Einstand* (Adorno 1970: 52); *das Kunsthafte an der Antikunst* (ibid.: 53).
51 *Mit James Joyce, Picasso, Ezra Pound und der Duchesse de Clermont-Tonnère als Publikum allein kommt man nicht aus* (GKFA 10: 580).
52 *Ich kenne im Stilistischen eigentlich nur noch Parodie, stehen darin Joyce nahe*: diary entry 19 September 1943 (Mann 1982: 627).
53 *Man könnte das Spiel potenzieren, indem man mit Formen spielt, aus denen, …*

das Leben geschwunden ist (GKFA 10: 353); *die lähmenden Schwierigkeiten der Zeit; Barbarei; zweimal; bürgerliche[n] Verfeinerung* (ibid.: 355).

54   *einer Art von Lächeln; letzte Liebe* (ibid.: 694).

55   *von unterdrücktem Lachen geschüttelt* (ibid.: 36); *Ihr Elend macht mich lachen* (ibid.: 343); *Seinen Sinn für das Komische, sein Verlangen danach und seine Neigung zum Lachen, ja zum Tränen-Lachen ...* (ibid.: 127); *ob dergleichen zum Lachen oder zum Weinen ist* (ibid.: 36).

56   *T.M. habe ihn gleichsam aus dem Grab verleumdet* (Adorno an B. Bräutigam, 18. März 1968, Adorno 1992: 31; in Claussen 2003: 146); *er sich in nicht ganz angenehmer Weise bläht, sodaß es bei ihm nachgerade ein wenig so herauskommt, als habe eigentlich er den 'Faustus' geschrieben* (Mann an Jonas Lesser, 15. Oktober 1951, in Mann, 1965: 226; in Claussen 2003: 146).

57   *das Naturwüchsig-Tölpelhafte neben das Komisch-Sublime zu stellen* (GKFA 10: 239); *obszön, humoristische Figur des Teufels* (ibid.: 144).

58   *Schlimm, schlimm* (Thomas Mann an Katia Mann, 18 Juli 1947, in Kurzke 1999: 538)

59   *An der Karikatur ... war nicht Adrian schuld, sondern Shakespeare* (GKFA 10: 317).

Works Cited

Adorno, Theodor W., 1970. *Ästhetische Theorie*, in *Gesammelte Schriften*, vol. 7. Frankfurt am Main: Suhrkamp.

Adorno, Theodor W., 1955. *Prismen. Kulturkritik und Gesellschaft*. Frankfurt am Main: Suhrkamp.

Adorno, Theodor W., 1983. *Prisms*, trans. Samuel Weber. Boston: MIT Press.

Adorno, Theodor W., 1992. *Frankfurter Adorno Blätter*, ed. Rolf Tiedemann, vol. 1. München: edition text + kritik.

Adorno, Theodor, 2004. *Aesthetic Theory*, trans. Robert Hullot-Kentor. London: Continuum.

Barthes, Roland, 1974. *S/Z*, trans. Richard Miller. New York: Hill and Wang.

Benjamin, Walter, 1998. *The Origin of German Tragic Drama*, trans. John Osborne. London: Verso.

Bloom, Harold, 2011. *The Anatomy of Influence*. New Haven: Yale University Press.

Brown, Eric, 2003. 'Shakespeare's Anxious Epistemology: *Love's Labour's Lost* and Marlowe's *Doctor Faustus*', in *Texas Studies in Literature and Language*, 45:1, pp. 20–41.

Cerf, Steven, 1981. 'Love in Thomas Mann's *Doktor Faustus* as an Imitatio Shakespeari', in *Comparative Literary Studies*, 18:4, pp. 475–86.

Claussen, Detlev, 2003. *Theodor W. Adorno: Ein letztes Genie*. Frankfurt am Main: S. Fischer.

Claussen, Detlev, 2008. *Theodor W. Adorno: One Last Genius*, trans. Rodney Livingstone. Cambridge MA.: Harvard University Press.

Dante, 2006. *Inferno*, trans. Robin Kirkpatrick. Harmondsworth: Penguin.

Dollimore, Jonathan, 1984. *Radical Tragedy: Religion, Ideology and Power in the Drama of Shakespeare and his Contemporaries*. Brighton: Harvester Press.

Dollimore, Jonathan, 1998. *Death, Desire and Loss in Western Culture*. London: Penguin.

Eagle, Christopher, 2011. 'Organic Hesitancies: Stuttering and Sexuality in Melville, Kesey, and Mishima', in *Comparative Literature Studies*, 48:2, pp. 200–18.

Eliot, T. S., 1952 [1922]. 'The Waste Land', in *The Complete Poems and Plays. 1909–1950*. New York: Harcourt, Brace and Company.

Fernie, Ewan, 2012. *The Demonic: Literature and Experience*. London: Routledge.

Fetzer, John F., 1996. *Changing Perceptions of Thomas Mann's 'Doctor Faustus': Criticism 1947–1992*. Columbia, S.C.: Camden House.

Goldberg, Jonathan, 1986. *Voice Terminal Echo: Postmodernism and English Renaissance Texts*. London: Methuen.

Grady, Hugh, 2009. *Shakespeare and Impure Aesthetics*. Cambridge: Cambridge University Press.

Harris, Frank, 2008 [1909]. *The Man Shakespeare and His Tragic Life*, ed. J. H. Stape. Ware: Wordsworth.

Heidegger, Martin, 1989. 'Hölderlins Hymnen "Germanien" und "Der Rhein"', in *Heidegger Gesamtausgabe*, ed. Suzanne Ziegler, vol. 39. Frankfurt am Main: Vittorio Klostermann.

Heilbut, Anthony,1995. *Thomas Mann: Eros and Literature*. New York: Alfred A. Knopf.

Heller, Eric, 1958. *Thomas Mann: The Ironic German*. London: Secker & Warburg.

Hert, Jeffrey, 1984. *Reactionary Modernism: Technology, Culture, and Politics in Weimar and the Third Reich*. Cambridge: Cambridge University Press.

Hofmannstahl, Hugo von, 2005. *The Lord Chandos Letter*, ed. Joel Rotenberg. New York: New York Review of Books.

Jaspers, Karl, 1951. *Rechenschaft und Ausblick*. München: Piper.

Jaspers, Karl, 1974 [1935]. *Nietzsche. Einführung in das Verständnis seines Philosophierens*. Berlin, New York: Walter de Gruyter.

Jaspers, Karl, 1975. 'On My Philosophy', in *Existentialism from Dostoevsky to Sartre*, ed. Walter Kaufmann. London: Penguin.

Jaspers, Karl, 1997 [1935]. *Nietzsche: An Introduction to the Understanding of His Philosophical Activity*, trans. Charles Wallraff and Frederick Schmitz. Baltimore: Johns Hopkins University Press.

Joyce, James, 1969 [1922]. *Ulysses*. Harmondsworth: Penguin.

Keilson-Lauritz, Marita, 2005. ' Stefan George's Concept of Love and the Gay Emancipation Movement', in *A Companion to the Works of Stefan George*, ed. Jens Rieckmann. Rochester, NY: Camden House, pp. 207–29.

Kirkbright, Suzanne, 2004. *Karl Jaspers: A Biography: Navigations in Truth*. New Haven: Yale University Press.

Kitcher, Philip, 2013. *Deaths in Venice: The Cases of Gustav von Aschenbach*. New York: Columbia University Press.

Kurzke, Hermann, 1999. *Thomas Mann. Das Leben als Kunstwerk*. München: C. H. Beck.

Kurzke, Hermann, 2002. *Thomas Mann: A Biography*, trans. Leslie Wilson. London: Allen Lane.

Lee, Frances, 2007. *Overturning 'Doctor Faustus': Rereading Thomas Mann's Novel in Light of 'Observations of a Non-Political Man'*. Rochester, NY: Camden House.

Mahood, M. M., 1968. *Shakespeare's Wordplay*. London: Routledge & Kegan Paul.

Mann, Thomas, 1961 [1949]. *Genesis of a Novel*, trans. Clara and Richard Winston. New York: Alfred A. Knopf.

Mann, Thomas, 1965. *Briefe 1948–1955*, ed. Erika Mann. Thomas Mann Briefe, vol. 3. Frankfurt am Main: S. Fischer.

Mann, Thomas, 1970. 'Thomas Mann – Erich von Kahler. Briefwechsel im Exil', hg. Hans Wysling. *Blätter der Thomas-Mann-Gesellschaft Zürich*, Nummer 10.

Mann, Thomas, 1982. *Tagebücher 1940–1943*, ed. Peter de Mendelsohn. Frankfurt am Main: S. Fischer.

Mann, Thomas, 1996 [1945]. 'Deutschland und die Deutschen', in *Deutschland und die Deutschen. 1938–1945*, eds Hermann Kurzke, Stephan Stachorski. Thomas Mann Essays, vol. 5. Frankfurt am Main: S. Fischer, pp. 260–81.

Mann, Thomas, 1997 [1947]. *Doctor Faustus: The Life of the German Composer Adrian Leverkühn As Told by a Friend*, trans. John E. Woods. New York: Vintage.

Mann, Thomas, 2007a [1947]. *Doktor Faustus*, ed. Ruprecht Wimmer. Große Kommentierte Frankfurter Ausgabe, vol. 10.1. Frankfurt am Main: S. Fischer. [GKFA 10]

Mann, Thomas, 2007b. *Doktor Faustus. Kommentar*, eds Ruprecht Wimmer and Stephan Stachorski. Große Kommentierte Frankfurter Ausgabe, vol. 10.2. Frankfurt am Main: S. Fischer.

Mann, Thomas, 2009 [1949]. 'Die Entstehung des Doktor Faustus. Roman eines Romans', in *Essays IV. 1945–1950*, ed. Herbert Lehnert. Große Kommentierte Frankfurter Ausgabe, vol. 19. Frankfurt am Main: S. Fischer. [GKFA 19]

Meyers, Jeffrey, 1973. 'Shakespeare and Mann's *Doctor Faustus*', in *Modern Fiction Studies* 19, pp. 541–5.

Prater, Donald, 1995. *Thomas Mann: A Life*. Oxford: Oxford University Press.

Rilke, Rainer Maria, 1955. *Sämtliche Werke*, eds Ruth Sieber-Rilke and Ernst Zinn. Wiesbaden: Insel Verlag.

Rilke, Rainer Maria, 2011. *Selected Poems*, eds Susan Ranson and Marielle Sutherland. Oxford: Oxford University Press.

Schoenbaum, Samuel, 1991. *Shakespeare's Lives*. Oxford: Oxford University Press.

Schoenberg, Arnold, 1977. 'My Attitude to Politics', repr. in H. H. Stuckenschmidt, *Arnold Schoenberg: his life, world and work*. London: John Calder, pp. 551–2.

Scott-Stokes, Henry, 1974. *The Life and Death of Yukio Mishima*. New York: Farrar, Straus & Giroux.

Shakespeare, William, 2008. *The Norton Shakespeare*. Based on the Oxford Edition, eds Stephen Greenblatt et al. New York: Norton.

Shell, Marc, 2005. *Stutter*. Cambridge, MA.: Harvard University Press.

Stape, J. H., 2008. 'Introduction', in Frank Harris, *The Man Shakespeare and His Tragic Life*, ed. J. H. Stape. Ware: Wordsworth.

Stein, Gertrude, 1935. 'Portraits and Repetition', in *Lectures in America*. Boston: Beacon, pp. 165–208.

Steiner, George, 1969. *Language and Silence: Essays 1958–1966*. Harmondsworth: Penguin.

Weimann, Robert, 2000. *Author's Pen and Actor's Voice: Playing and Writing in Shakespeare's Theatre*. Cambridge: Cambridge University Press.

Wells, Stanley, 1982. 'The Copy for the Folio text of *Love's Labour's Lost*', in *Review of English Studies* 33, pp. 137–47.

Wood, Michael, 2003. 'Impossible Wishes', *London Review of Books* 25:3, 6 February, pp. 3–6.

Three   Masquerades of Love: *Love's Labour's Lost* and the Musical Development of Shakespeare's Comedy in Mann's *Doktor Faustus*
Alexander Honold

Shakespeare and the theatricality of the Faustus novel

Thomas Mann did not write a single comedy – why? The short answer: because he knew how to use Shakespeare's comedies and transferred them to his favourite form, the novel. And why does the artist's pact with the devil impose on Leverkühn the sacrifice to ban all love? Again, for now, just a suggestion: because love, in an existential perspective, is a mode of bending and relativizing the self. This is what comedy, among dramatic genres, brings about. Whereas tragedy works by generalizing pity, comedy makes a claim for mutual emotional inclination; whoever yields to such a claim acknowledges his or her own deficiency or weakness. Music,[1] on the other hand, emerges in this novel about the 'German composer' as a medium to negotiate dramatic forms, especially those concerned with emotional confusion and comedy. In this way, the protagonist's resistance to love as well as his disposition to be a tragicomic hero are part of a formal aesthetic approach that makes music a weapon of mockery. The mask of the mocker enables the composer in turn to distance himself, as a figure, from his own artistic ambition and the demands of communicative action. With his devilish pact of creation Leverkühn learns to put the unheard into music, beyond the point where all conventional means of composition are exhausted (that is, beyond the *Kunstperiode*) – in fact mocking himself, even mocking his own mocking. Thus, everything is interrelated and over-determined and constitutes a rich texture of circular cross-references. Mann's novel makes Shakespeare's play and its fictional operatic version the driving force to compose a quartet of love, art, music and comedy. The present chapter sets out to trace these entanglements.

The plot structure of comedy makes its figures undergo a stress test that deforms them and lays bare their substance, in functional terms corresponding closely to the work of musical variation, modulation and dissociation known as the 'development', i.e. the middle part of the classical sonata form. Development and comedy both operate by way of constant transformations.

Comedy is governed by chance, while tragedy acts out fate. No other work by Thomas Mann presents the counterpoint and play of these two forces more powerfully than *Doktor Faustus*,[2] his late *Künstlerroman* continuing the great tradition of Faustus versions since the Renaissance[3] and, at the same time, paying homage arguably also to Shakespeare. For it is through Shakespearean echoes that this musical novel gains its sense of the theatrical, of performance and of stage effect.

In Leverkühn's list of works, *Love's Labour's Lost*[4] holds special place and so offers good reason to discuss the relevance of this subject. Moreover, the choice of this particular play and its function in the narrative development encourage us also to explore the role of Shakespeare and the comic, more generally, in this novel. For this purpose, I shall focus on three aspects: first, why and in what way comedy here figures as a narrative analogy to the art of music; we can trace these interrelations in Leverkühn's musical education, presented at some length in the early chapters, especially the art of counterpoint which soon becomes the mode he favours, bringing it to new accomplishments. Contrapuntal techniques, I suggest, correspond remarkably well to the structural modes of Shakespearean comedy, especially dramatic techniques of parallel plotting, mirroring and inversion. And in the same way that love functions as the linking principle for comedy's dramatis personae, we find in music a principle of general relatedness, realizing the same degree of compositional interweaving and joining.

Secondly, and in connection with the first aspect, I look at the life and circumstances of the central figure, the composer Adrian Leverkühn. Mann did not write a musicological thesis novel, but integrated Leverkühn's aesthetic notions and artistic endeavours, for all their professional technicalities, into a fully realized biographical narrative providing a portrait of the artist as a young and developing man. As with earlier artist figures in Mann's work, art and life are here presented as a principal antithesis. As before, the artist hero must therefore subject his entire life to the demands of his art, in consequence risking ever more serious personal problems. These emerge, in particular, through his negative imprint, as it were, on his social surroundings and may, for participant observers, have bizarre or even comic effects. The artist figure appears distant and absurd. Depending on context, he seems either cold or inflamed and, in the eyes of others, simply odd. In the case of *Doktor Faustus*, this social separation and the ensuing conflicts are inherent already in the tradition and the motif of the devil's pact. The seducer promises the artist two dozen creative years, highly successful and productive; in return he imposes the commandment: 'You may not love' (*Doctor Faustus*, hereafter referred to as *Faustus*, 264).[5] What, however, does this mean: 'not love'? Even Leverkühn, though haunted by the devil, pretends not to know the answer, but he senses it only too well. He is banned from all emotional involvement and from hope for feelings in return. In the biographical strand of the novel, the comic has both an objective and a subjective aspect: in his external relations, it manifests itself as a mode of bending and correction, in the artist's self-relation as constant reservation, inauthenticity and mockery.

Thirdly, we shall look at *Doktor Faustus* as political allegory and 'Deutschland-Roman', i.e. a novel of Germany.[6] Written in the last two years of World War II and written, in a sense, both from the inside and the outside of Hitler's totalitarian power, this is a narrative of ruin, doom and national catastrophe, offering its cultural anamnesis. In the perspective of the novel, Faust's pact with the devil and Leverkühn's liberation of musical art from time-worn conventions have highly political significance: in symbolic terms, anticipating historical developments, they set free the demonic. In this way, the novel is burdened with philosophical and political arguments (and their burden of proof) which requires, for aesthetic just as for ideological reasons, some kind of balance. This is why comedy – in structural terms as a genre of counterpoint, in biographical terms as love negated – is used as a narrative device.

Labour of love and art of disguise: *Love's Labour's Lost*

All in all, four Shakespearean comedies are mentioned in *Doktor Faustus*; apart from *Love's Labour's Lost*, serving as source for the libretto of Leverkühn's opera, these are *Much Ado About Nothing*, *The Two Gentlemen of Verona* and *Twelfth Night*. Written in the early part of his career (with the exception of *Twelfth Night*), they show Shakespeare as a dramatist happy to experiment, trying out various forms of plotting and configuration, employing diverse tricks of language and working with many different settings. In some cases (such as *Two Gentlemen*) we know what models and source texts he used, in others he seems to have followed his own ideas or taken inspiration from prominent contemporaries, like Henry of Navarre, since 1589 King Henry IV of France, in *Love's Labour's Lost*.

In all these plays, rather predictably, vagaries of love form the basic plot pattern. Whatever entanglements these lovers must endure before eventually entering into their unions is the stuff of comedy. For this reason, any simple and straightforward coupling would be rather unproductive; comedy lives by all that hinders love, impedes, disturbs or misleads it. This is what produces thrill and opportunities of entertainment, as well as of ironic distancing. Separations, displacements and mistaken identities are as essential for romantic comedy as are its pairs of friends or siblings torn apart, discrepancies between avowed and actual behaviour, or between conduct and emotional life.

What is more, Shakespeare often highlights language as an artistic-artificial diction and turns the lovers' discourse into genuine theatrical performance, in forms of travesty or masquerade. Emotional inclination is not towards a person *as such*, but to the image that another character has made of him or her. This is why such love affairs are principally and fundamentally comic. In *Love's Labour's Lost*, language goes mad for scenes on end where parody and verbal excess become dominant. More than ever Shakespeare engages with rhyming, punning and a whole array of elaborate poetic patterns. We get sonnets and canzones, stilted rhetoric and French loan words, as English becomes quite suffused with Petrarchan clichés from the fashion of romantic courtship – all set to display cultivated erudition. After all, this entire exercise in stylish ostentation and citation, as ambitious as it is affected, is only meant to make a strong impression. The male protagonists engage in it, ironically, after having withdrawn from the world to the solitude of the court of Navarre where they plan to devote themselves to three years of an ascetic life of contemplation.

Evidently, this is based on Henry of Navarre, later King Henry IV of France, and his idea of philosophical government. In the play, King Ferdinand formulates this notion and inspires his followers Berowne, Longaville and Dumaine, whose names suggest historical figures from the same context. No worldly ado, no idle ambition, no physical pleasure are to distract them from their strictly intellectual pursuits – and above all: no women. Yet the very project of demonstrative austerity, as announced by the King, is full of proud pretension soon revealing itself as a studied pose. Its crux lies in the self-defeating gesture of demonstrating publicly how to forgo public opinion: 'Navarre shall be the wonder of the world, / Our court shall be a little academe, / Still and contemplative in living art' (1.1.12–14). In silent self-sufficiency their small academy of neo-platonic scholarship shall prosper in unequalled glory; even Berowne, known for wit and eloquence and initially hesitant, eventually agrees with the other three courtiers. They all swear strictly to renounce love and the world for three years, but the performative imperative of their resolve already implies failure.

To shake up this curious community of philosophical abstainers, no more is needed than the simple plot device that the Princess of France and three of her ladies, Rosaline, Catherine and Maria, come to visit, thus forming a perfect match for the King, his three nobles and their inevitably budding feelings. One after the other, the courtiers break their vows and give rein to romance. Within this dramatic structure, 'love' stands for the strongest possible dependence on winning others and their recognition. Rather than ignoring all society as planned and promised, the courtiers now proceed to gain attention from their chosen ladies and convince them of their feelings' force. The great verbal investments and witty inventions in the play are motivated by the characters' rhetorical endeavours to this end – in a double way: their ornate speeches are to prove their competence in courtly codes of wooing while also emphasizing the sincerity of their erotic longing. But the weak spot of their protestations lies in the discrepancy between verbal performance and dramatic desire, repeatedly producing comic effects, all the more so since the ladies all attack it with precision. Their passions have not just been diligently put to paper but are themselves induced by paper work (following Petrarchan reading):

> Princess: ...Yes, as much love in rhyme,
> As would be crammed up in a sheet of paper
> Writ o'both sides the leaf, margin and all,
> That he was fain to seal on Cupid's name.

(5.2.6–9)

The comedy of love turns into a contest of poetic genres, followed by theatrical performance in a masque. And like the lords, so the ladies. They respond to the male charade with their female art of masking, as proposed by the Princess: 'For, ladies, we will every one be masked, / And not a man of them shall have the grace, / Despite of suit, to see a lady's face' (5.2.127–9). What we note here is a prominent and pointed reciprocity that can be seen as the basic pattern of all comedy: tit for tat. The ladies even exchange masks so as to trick their suitors into wooing the wrong woman, 'so shall your loves / Woo contrary, deceived by these removes' (5.2.134–5).

But why these constant masquerades and why all the deception? Does the whole bantering not discredit characters and their avowed affections? Or are disavowal and dissimulation perhaps already moves in the game of love? The German version of the title *Verlorne Liebesmüh,* i.e. 'lost labour of love' has become proverbial (even though Wolf

Graf Baudissin's less pertinent *Liebes Leid und Lust* is more canonical).
Should we then take the title to suggest that all love's efforts are in
vain, without effect or consequence? Or should we understand love
always to involve a waste of labour and to encourage great investments without considering returns? It would, however, be a lost cause
to resist the personal urge and drive to love – another point made with
the title.

Neither lust nor labour in love can, it seems, be quite avoided – and
here, precisely, comedy arises from fruitless resistance. Furthermore,
love's labour is by no means unproductive for the arts (as the King and
his lords thought at the beginning); as evident in the Petrarchan and
neo-platonic models implied in the kind of study first attempted here,
art and love in fact go hand in hand.[7] The suitors write letters, sophis-
ticate themselves in secret signs and endeavours, which are then upset
and publicly exposed through the boorish play of subalterns. Each of
the four, having broken his vow, sees and blames the others for having
broken theirs. First Berowne, then the King, then Longaville and finally
Dumaine enter the stage in act four *reading*. This simply signifies (as
is immediately realized by the other characters, who are watching
them) that they are all in love and evidently quite entangled in a ritual
exchange of love letters.

Whenever a nobleman breaks a solemn vow, this is serious and
alarming. If he could plead moral grounds, his behaviour might still
seem pardonable in a given case. Yet the fact that all four nobles, quite
independently, have abandoned their sworn fortress of pious study
and asceticism, defecting to the camp of love and passionate vows
without any resistance, must degrade their individual, incomparable
affections and turn them into figures of a functionally repetitive
mechanism. Hence the general formula of love played out in comedy:
'this is how everyone does it' or *così fan tutti*. Constitutive for the comic
genre are discrepancies between intention and action, semblance and
reality and, most of all, the seriality of the emotional involvement
that the characters, rather soberingly, must go through. To be sure,
the turn from celibacy to amorous adventures is not really surprising
here. Comic effects rather result from the way in which these proud
and self-assured men all turn out to behave quite so predictably and
transparently. Each an echo of the other, they all woo according to
the same song, even while believing they entreat their chosen one in
highly original terms. The ladies are quite capable of witty repartees
and return 'mock for mock' in the masque by letting their lovers swear
false confessions of love, or rather, confessions to the wrong addressee.
As the Princess rejoices, 'There's no such sport as sport by sport
o'ertherown' (5.2.153).

Sex and the fugue – musical lust and musical mock

Central for *Love's Labour's Lost* is the device of *mockery*, i.e. parodistic teasing.[8] It combines, and compresses, the rhetorical strategy of comic *imitatio* with a battle of words in dramatic dialogue, as illustrated in the following example:

> Princess: We are wise girls to mock our lovers so.
> Rosaline: They are worse fools to purchase mocking so.
>
> (5.2.58-9)

Like Berowne, throughout portrayed to be thoughtful and not as easily persuaded to the vow of celibacy as the King and the two others, so Rosaline (his counterpart and love interest) plays a comparable role among the ladies. She moderates their mockery and shows mercy with the suitors (especially her own), pleading for moderation. Her little dialogue with the Princess is paradigmatic for the war of words that Shakespeare's characters continuously engage in. The Princess suggests that the principle of the female faction should be to mock and shame the faithless suitors as much as they can. She sees the plot of love in terms of a war in which 'wise girls' know how to use at strategic advantage so as to humiliate the men with their false protestations. Rosaline, however, counters this declaration with a degree of empathy for such 'worse fools' who have thereby betrayed themselves to mockery. Her remark contradicts the Princess yet replies to her in almost the same verbal form. Statement and reply are constructed here as echoes, the repetition – or rather rejection – clearly emphasizing its similarity with the preceding statement while, however, inversing its meaning. In the two verses, their syntactic parallelism only highlights their semantic opposition, like a mirror image: mockery is dealt or suffered, both 'we' and 'they', the 'wise girls' and the 'worse fools', are designated with anaphoric assonance, thus making their actual difference, in their plot functions, even more striking.

Throughout the play, such strict oppositions worked out in verbal structures of statement and reply, thesis and antithesis, are the currency of all communication. Lords and ladies, just as masters and servants, are constantly engaged in verbal contests and a 'Civil War of Words'. The turning point of comedy, the change of fortune in the Aristotelian sense constitutive for this genre, is realized here right in the rhetorical microstructure of such verbal exchanges and their punning. And when we look for broader relations beyond single lines or verses and their poetic structures, i.e. look at the characters' speeches like sonnets or any of the other stanza forms liberally used throughout, we find ever larger realizations of the formal patterns just observed: rhyme, assonance, alliteration, parallelism and antithesis. In this way, our horizontal, syntagmatic reading of the text is being complemented by a line of vertical connections where paradigmatic similarities find their emphasizing echo. The dramatic text becomes readable as a musical score.

Echoing, mirroring and reversing are formal hallmarks of the rhetoric in Shakespeare's dialogue, where they are amply used. All these are equally musical devices – learned and treasured not least by the piano student and aspiring composer Adrian Leverkühn, as portrayed in the early chapters of Mann's musical *Bildungsroman*. The fact that Mann's protagonist should choose this particular Shakespearean text as the basis for his opera libretto is plausible not only for its plot of failing celibacy; surely we should just as much acknowledge these formal properties and their significance, i.e. the play's imitative use of language and polemic wit. Technically, this opera is Leverkühn's masterpiece, demonstrating his virtuosity in handling contrapuntal composition. Bassoonist Griepenkerl, employed to copy out the score, praises 'the delicate subtlety of its workmanship', the rhythmical smoothness of the work and also its 'technique of orchestration by which the complexity of interweaving voices was often kept perfectly lucid' (*Faustus* 277).[9] All these concern the design, the inner ergonomics of the structure; his praises peak in Leverkühn's 'compositional fantasy' as 'demonstrated by the way a given theme was transformed in manifold variations' (ibid.).[10] These features, suggestively presented to the reader's imagination, show that this composer does not entertain, as might be expected in his day and age, the late romantic notion of music as pure expression, but rather follows the strict compositional technique of earlier centuries and stylistic periods.

Two points in particular differentiate Leverkühn from late romanticism. The first is his obsession with 'strict style' (*Faustus* 202), in which, according to the famous formulation, ideally, '[f]ree notes would no longer exist' (*Faustus* 205) and nothing subjective or contingent can be found.[11] On the other hand, Leverkühn's attitude is characterized by his 'sense of the comic' and his 'habit of laughing' (*Faustus* 94).[12] His musical language takes pleasure in mocking the pathos of expressive music and prefers the parodistic. As shown in narrative retrospect, these two characteristics of Leverkühn's music are hardly, if at all, compatible with the humanist credo and enlightened belief in progress embodied in Zeitblom and desperately upheld by him before becoming crushed in the bombing nights of World War II. This biographer and childhood friend is not too fond of Leverkühn's laughter for which nothing is ever sacrosanct, nor of his relentless formal rigour which resents everything that is just beautiful and discards it for the coherent and the correct. In this respect, Leverkühn's main features are always countered and distorted through the perspective of a sceptical narrator and commentator guarding his own distance from them – a narrative realization, we might say, of the compositional technique with two musical parts in counterpoint.

One of the leading structural concepts for the narrative procedure of the novel, then, is polyphony and its related techniques from the art of fugue, offering a close correspondence between style and subject. Basic principles of counterpoint and polyphonic composition are variously discussed in *Doktor Faustus* at some length, first with the simple rounds sung by the children, later in the learned music lectures on the fugue and Beethoven's alleged negligence of it. The novel manages to treat all such aesthetic issues not as dry academic matter but integrates them fully in the plot and its dramatic potentials, as evidenced with the earliest insights given to the premature yet very young musician on his parents' farm, Buchel. As remembered and reported by the biographer, who was in fact himself involved, the stable-maid Hanne 'arranged little singing lessons' (*Faustus* 31) for the children, especially Adrian and his friend Serenus Zeitblom, thus acquainting them informally with the rudiments of counterpoint. In suitable songs, 'a temporal inter-weaving' and 'imitative entrances' were practised, 'to which one was prodded by a poke in the ribs from barnyard Hanne once the song was already underway' (ibid.).[13] Notably, these early musical instructions appear in the narrative in unmistakably erotic framing: 'And strangely enough, whereas Elsbeth Leverkühn, with her lovely voice, abstained from singing out of some kind of chaste modesty, this creature still smelling of her animals would go at it with abandon' (ibid.). Rather than the chaste and slightly fragile Frau Mama, the coarse 'milk-maid with a wobbly bosom' (*Faustus* 30) is the one to initiate the marvelling boy into the first delights of harmony and consonance – by all means sensual pleasures, and reliably produced by singing 'Are you sleeping' (*Faustus* 31)[14] in several voices together.

And yet, according to the informed narrator, these sensual pleasures of music were governed, like all rounds, by contrapuntal delayed repetition:

> And so, although we were always separated from one another in time, each melodic present kept delightful company with all the others, and what we produced formed a charming weft, an ensemble sound, that 'simultaneous' singing could never form – a structure whose vocal pattern we happily enjoyed without inquiring further about its nature and cause.
>
> (*Faustus* 32)[15]

The sensual thrill of such harmonies offers titillating pleasures to the ear which the singers cannot, in fact, obtain alone but only when they join and sing together, following these regulations. One of the boys turns out to be particularly responsive to the stable-maid's instruction, even initiation: '[a]t age eight or nine' Adrian's 'brief burst of laughter – which he would release, more in mockery than amazement' after the fading of the chords, shows not just 'that he could see through the little song's construct' (ibid.), but also that he would faithfully continue to indulge in its fair beauty. Adrian is thus initiated into the rudiments of 'imitative polyphony' (ibid.), in a manner later mirrored by the existential dilemma imposed on him of sublimating all his sexual needs in music. The division of labour between two female protagonists – mother or wife versus libidinous stable-maid, the spiritual versus the sensual and natural – is evidently modelled on a classic scheme of comedy, whose types the novel uses for its intricate psychological patterning and conditioning. This scheme later re-emerges with Adrian's fixation on *Hetaera Esmeralda*, i.e. the disso-ciation of the feminine between the fatal seductress and, on the other hand, the artist's female worshippers, plain and dull and caricatured with some relish.

Even at an early age, then, Adrian shows signs of an 'initiate's sneer' (ibid.),[16] especially in the mocking laughter that will become his trademark. At the same time, his distancing gestures concern the scene of this initiation just as much as the secrets so revealed. In terms of the female duality between 'a wobbly bosom'[17] and 'chastity', the musical attractions of polyphonic consonance quickly become problematic and lead him into a dilemma. If the 'temporal interweaving' when singing the same melody together in a round produces an aesthetic surplus for the singers, then their singing practice turn them into complementing parts and pairs of different voices – hence also, we may conjecture, into complementing gender roles, such as the buxom stable-maid countered by the delicate young boy. And yet, it seems to little Adrian that the musical pleasure gained from a major third is all too coarse and simple to be quite enjoyed. That is to say, the dramaturgy of 'major' gender difference does not rule out more subtle differences, in this case between tender motherhood and drastic sensuality. Later, in the years of Adrian's manhood, the pitch-black eyes and warm 'mezzo-soprano' voice will be transferred from his mother to Marie Godeau, the woman he woos and only almost marries. The mother's fragility, in turn, will find its revenant in Nepomuk Schneiderwein, the little boy called Echo, so that the hetero- and homosexual lines intersect and intertwine in a generational change.

Leverkühn's original sin is his *coldness*. Already in his school days, his friend and school mate Zeitblom recalls, Adrian never cared much for his talents. With few exceptions, like maths or music, the subjects or the skills acquired literally leave this pupil cold. Even Adrian's first choice of studies, his devotion to theology, reflects the same indifference. With the help of no less power than this first and foremost academic faculty, he may have planned 'to humble' and 'discipline' himself, as he writes to his music teacher, 'to punish the arrogance of my coldness' (*Faustus* 140).[18] But the greatest and most vital challenge for this coldness is again his love life, represented to the young theology student only in terms of sinful sexuality, an image determined by strict moral notions of the fall and punishment. This is the reason why the hero must be cured from simple innocence, rather drastically, when the infernal serving-man in Leipzig uses the city tour to lure him to the brothel. Adrian, quite unprepared for the attractions waiting there, first tries to save the situation by escaping to the piano before making for the exit, but eventually his resistance falters. In one of the prostitutes he recognizes 'Esmeralda', the exotic butterfly from childhood days. He looks for her once more, manages to follow her obsessively to Graz and Preßburg, only to contract, not without knowing, the venereal disease from her that renders his entire artist's life tragically ironic.

Critical discussions of the novel routinely interpret all these points – being, literally, misguided and seduced, the subsequent return of his childhood fantasy of *Hetaera Esmeralda*,[19] and the improbable coincidences leading Leverkühn to give up medical treatment – as necessary steps on his way to the devil's pact, signifying his demonic genius. Doubtless, this precisely is the trail we are supposed to follow in this narrative arrangement: taking it for granted and *inevitable* that he, with the characteristic boldness indicated by the surname Lever*kühn* (i.e. *bold*), must reach out for elemental forces, conjuring the devil, madness and his doom. However, such a reading is never exclusively suggested in the text but complemented by a contrapuntal view. Through his Leipzig adventure, Leverkühn no longer appears to be so fully self-controlled and unapproachable as before, now finding himself in an unexpected situation and losing his bearings. This, in fact, is typical of comedy. The brothel scene as such is not actually tragic but rather embarrassing, humiliating – yet also thoroughly comic. The cold protagonist warms to new prospects, the hard and haughty is being humbled and softened: thus, the comic situation of basic disorientation works as a social corrective.

The devil's pact and ban on love – twelve-tone technique as a *Beziehungstat*

Viewed in this way, like a prelude, the Leipzig experience corresponds to the comic love cure performed in Shakespeare's comedy, soon the subject of Leverkühn's opera. The play demonstrates, as we have seen, how the vehement rejection of love may quickly turn to desperate lovesickness and personal obsession. The composer may well have been aware of this connection when just this play caught his eye. *Love's Labour's Lost*, however, holds an exceptional position in the playwright's oeuvre. Its intricate rhetorical exchange of blows so rich in puns and formal experiments renders the play's aesthetic pattern virtually untranslatable and gives it rather verbal-musical affinities.

In formal terms, the play's characters suggest four different attitudes towards, or uses of, the linguistic sign, evenly distributed among the four main groups of the dramatis personae.[20] The King and lords represent a blatantly instrumental relation to language; they are prepared to use words for disguise or simulation and turn all arguments into their contraries. The French ladies and their Princess, while belonging to the same communicative culture of rational inter-action, represent the opposite position with some force: they insist on sincerity in verbal action and on pragmatic consequences – hence their fury at the suitors' empty vows and their painful punishment for opportunistic verbiage. In the subplot we find animistic language uses, mirrored in the two subgroups: for the three clown figures, Costard, Dull and Moth, words have magical efficacy to change reality; whereas the three figures of fantastic romancing, Don Armado, Holofernes and Nathaniel, simply marvel at all linguistic signs as curious creatures of their own.

In the constellation of the plot, characters are grouped consist-ently both in their social status and their language use. Senders and receivers, serious and parodistic speakers, although changing in their dominance, are symmetrically and evenly distributed, forming a square of functional positions, each one offering its answer to the fundamental question of pragmatics: 'How to do things with words?'[21] The difference in their linguistic attitudes and notions makes them part and parties of the conflict here enacted. The comedy's rhetorical-musical pattern therefore is a fourfold arrangement of two corresponding subgroups, each sharing certain traits while engaging in a contest of antitheses, at the same time as they constitute a reversed difference to one of the two main groups, which are equally in conflict with each other. Together, these four groups and their verbal behaviour represent the quasi-musical pattern of a theme with variations. Each one, as a series of figures, is part of a single composition showing, all in all, the formal principles of similarity and variation, of parallelism and antithesis, of horizontal shifts and vertical consonance.

At this point, with regard to the techniques of composition, we should recall the musicological instructions Mann obtained from Adorno, who willingly, from his philosophical horizon, provided essential information on the contexts of contemporary music and dodecaphony in particular. Adorno even answered Mann's request for sketches and descriptions of the fictional musical works that

Leverkühn composes, such as the violin concerto, the Apocalipsis cum figuris, the ensemble and chamber music and the 'Klage Dr. Fausti' (cf. Mann 2007b: 1153–8). He also sent the novelist a copy of his work in progress Philosophie der neuen Musik, i.e. Philosophy of New Music (1949), where Arnold Schönberg's twelve-tone technique and its historical preconditions receive much attention. In this book Adorno relates the new musical techniques to classical and pre-classical traditions, tracing their continuities and reprises in the development of musical forms. Above all, he points out how Schönberg's innovations in fact renew the contrapuntal arts of Renaissance music while also taking up some tendencies from the classical sonata and its development.

It is this compositional procedure which realizes the memorable principle: 'Each tone [Ton] of the whole composition is determined by this 'row' [Reihe]; there is no 'free' note any more' (cf. Mann 2007b: 488).[22] According to Adorno, Schönberg's central merit is not actually the strict adherence to the tone row in its prime form with twelve distinct notes,[23] but his brilliant idea to subject this row to the full repertoire of 'classical and, even more, archaic techniques of variation' (ibid.: 489),[24] thus relating the most recent music to some old forms indeed. In a passage excerpted by Mann we read: 'For the most part, he [Schönberg] utilizes the rows in four transformations: as the basic row; as its inversion, that is to say, by replacing each interval of the row with the interval in the contrary direction (on the pattern of the "inverted fugue" …); as its retrograde – or "crab" – in the manner of the ancient contrapuntal practice, so that the row begins with the last tone and concludes with the first; and as retrograde of the inversion' (Adorno 2006: 51, cf. Mann 2007b: 489).[25] The techniques Adorno lists here are not just identical with the constructions described in Doktor Faustus and adopted by Leverkühn so as to renew the art of the old masters (which, given the author's source material, is hardly surprising), they are also remarkably fitting to describe the verbal patterns and character constellation that we find in the very Shakespeare comedy he chooses for his opera. As argued earlier, thesis and inversion (i.e. the studied rejection and witty affirmation of love), retrograde and the inversion of the retrograde (i.e. foolish wooing and its satirized rebuff) are performed here, and pitted one against the other, like variations of a row. Rereading Love's Labour's Lost in view of twelve-tone music, we recognize it as a veritable masterpiece of verbal contrapuntal art and as the perfect model for this German composer's vocation.

Since its earliest beginnings, Leverkühn's compositional activity is entirely devoted to developing a single motif and the aesthetic value of its musical material, a theme with variations on the fundamental question: what is 'love'? For an artist, love could mean attachment in the sense of binding his creative sovereignty to a working principle, to some material and mode of aesthetic shaping, which are not governed but which govern him. Even though he knows that it has long determined his creative life, Leverkühn raises this crucial question, in so many words, only in his Palestrina conversation with the devil: 'I (must truly laugh): 'Not love! Poor Devil! Would you attest to your reputed stupidity and bell yourself as a cat, by wanting to found your business and promise on so pliant, so captious a term as – 'love'? Does the Devil propose to prohibit lust? If not, then he must chance sympathy and even *caritas*, else he is betrayed in consummate fashion' (*Faustus* 264).[26] Here Adrian, not without cunning, resorts to reasoning and quibbling as weapons in his contest of strength with the tempter. He hopes to challenge and defeat him by the very means and on the grounds which Satan likes to use himself for his infernal business – a desperate strategy that is as comic as it is consequential. It seems as if, half-knowingly, Leverkühn is pointing to the art of fugue with its four central variants that make up his own life. *Love, lust, sympathy* and *caritas* are variations of a single theme, and just as in the contrapuntal arts we can identify modes of inversion and retrogression, whether isolated or in combination. In this fourfold matrix, two terms connote sexual or erotic meanings, the two others spiritual or moral sublimations. As regards erotic relations, we might distinguish between sending and receiving parts – wooing versus being wooed – that complement each other; as regards the moral sphere, the main distinction lies between hierarchical and non-hierarchical relations. Needless to say, the love matrix includes both genders and two generations.

When Leverkühn seals his deal with the devil, he has gone through no more than one (though formative) love experience and got over it, together with the still progressing syphilitic infection he received from it. Yet in his middle years he is to have three more relationships: his love for a man, his chaste devotion to a woman, and his strong but tender charitable feelings for a child. We may partly correlate the character of these relationships with the four concepts mentioned in his response to the devil. *Caritas* prevails in his relationship to nephew Nepomuk, whereas with Marie Godeau he aspires to a union of like minds and hearts in sympathy. In both cases, however, other kinds of love still interfere. As regards the Leipzig (or, in actual fact, Hungarian) prostitute, clearly sensual pleasure is quite dominant, even though her shy and tender gesture touching his arm at the piano also stimulates much deeper and sincere affection in him. Quite possibly, this personal encounter on the marketplace of lust, for all its bizarre travesty, may well be the love of his life. Adrian, at any rate, pays for it with the highest price and knows what he is doing. In this way, the Hetaera Esmeralda affair seems quite precarious and ambiguous: fateful, lethal, but also an intensification of his creative destiny.

Leverkühn's relationship with Rudolph, aka Rudi, Schwerdtfeger is just as precarious. From the beginning, the violinist is entangled in so many liaisons that he cannot live up to any form of balanced give and take. Homoerotic inclinations are hardly suggested in Leverkühn's earlier life. Now, however, for the first time he can clearly play the lead. Now Adrian is the one to be wooed and grant favours, whereas with Esmeralda he was the sufferer and suitor and receiver. So now, emphatically, we must speak of love. The figure of Rudi Schwerdtfeger, the charming violinist with the slim sound, is modelled on Paul Ehrenberg, the painter and Mann's youthful friend (in poor disguise, hence easily identifiable to all initiates), in fact 'the greatest love of Mann's young years in Munich' (Mann 2007b: 502),[27] in whose honour the novelist – not for the first time and not without nostalgia – has built a personal monument. Is therefore the relationship to Schwerdtfeger from the beginning based on erotic attraction and, more precisely, is Adrian Leverkühn homosexual?

This is what his old friend Zeitblom, plain average citizen, evidently fears and feared already with Rüdiger Schildknapp, Adrian's earlier soul-mate and companion, whom Zeitblom saw as a corrupting rival. With blatant homophobia, the narrator now struggles to deny all forms of physical attachment between Leverkühn and Schwerdtfeger. He interrupts their tender hug – following a flush of excitement on Schwerdtfeger's part – with a harsh 'Enough!' (*Faustus* 337)[28] and an angry gesture. Such homophobic resistance, however, noticeable also on the level of narration, is countered almost inadvertently by increasing evidence, never quite acknowledged by the narrator. In the course of the fatal affair around Ines Institoris and her obvious advances towards Rudi, Zeitblom observes with remarkable resolution that Rudi, the 'young man' and proper gentleman, 'could not help responding' to the longings of the married woman. It would have been 'lovelier still', the narrator adds half-heartedly, 'had [Rudi Schwerdtfeger] not responded' (*Faustus* 348)[29] to these female sexual needs and offers. In this event – and that is what the half-stifled addition suggests – he would have seriously neglected his masculine duty and raised the ire of 'suspicion'.

The narrator's severely moral interference is remarkable but not surprising. Constantly he registers all budding homoerotic developments between Schwerdtfeger and Leverkühn with great discomfort and calls Rudi, somewhat contemptuously, 'a man who, in terms of both psychological makeup and behavior, was still a boyish ladykiller' (ibid.) – thus actually emphasizing his androgyny and flirtatious bisexuality. Later when Adrian, allegedly on Rudi's prompt, plans the winter trip with his best friends including Mlle Godeau and her mother, Zeitblom harbours doubts whether 'that elfin platonist'

(*Faustus* 446)[30] would really be interested in such an act of gallantry. Incidentally, the name of the youthful violinist, favoured by men and women alike, also gives a doubly coded signal and an invitation to flexible readings – not least because of Mann's well-practised art of telling names. The masculine though stiff name 'Rudolph', cultivated by the narrator, yields to the more intimate informal 'Rudi' used in society; the components of his surname, too, allow for various erotic connotations, combining a sword [*Schwert*] with a broom [*Feger*] while also suggesting its idiomatic meaning 'hottie'. Perhaps even the unusual spelling with the idiosyncratic '-dt' might hold significance as a combination of the voiced and unvoiced, soft and hard, which in the form of the dental plosive are placed indistinguishably together.

Adrian's love for this youth is among the painful points which the narrator can only report with great qualms.[31] What is more, this part of his story is skilfully and meaningfully interlaced with war events, situated at the time of telling, leading to the turning fortunes on the Western front and Germany's military defeat. The dreaded invasion in France 'has [since] taken place' (*Faustus* 355)[32] – the author himself, however, notes the coincidence with his own birthday with satisfaction[33] –, there is 'no stopping the foe' (ibid.) on either front, as the narrator and witness reckons rightly, hence his repeated bitter sighs: 'No stopping them! Oh my soul, do not think it through to the end!' (*Faustus* 356).[34] But in part, Zeitblom is here also bracing himself against the fatal amorous bonds variously entangling Rudi Schwerdtfeger with Ines Institoris, Adrian Leverkühn with Rudi Schwerdtfeger, and finally the latter two with Marie Godeau: their fate cannot be stopped.

Enharmonic change: plot patterns of comedy

It all began when Adrian as a pupil, out of boredom and '[i]dleness', 'the root of all vice' (*Faustus* 50), as they say, started experimenting with tones and sounds while playing the harmonium at his uncle's. This made him eventually a musician and composer. Once he happened to surprise his friend Serenus with a curious chord he had struck, 'all black keys' (*Faustus* 51), which initially 'looked like F-sharp major', but was then 'unmasked as belonging to B major' (ibid.). What Adrian was thus demonstrating to the older classmate is his personal discovery of the circle of fifths: '"A chord like this," he proposed, "has no key as such. It's all relationship, and the relations form a circle"' (ibid.).[35] Prophetic words, indeed, that touch the core of the analogy between music and comedy and, at the same time, lay the trace for the protagonist's future love relationships.

Mann's musical example (albeit somewhat inappropriate for this purpose) describes the phenomenon of so-called enharmonic change. As Adrian insists (in rather more general terms): 'It's all relationship.

And if you want to give it a more exact name, then call it "ambiguity"' (ibid.).[36] One could, for instance, understand a given note 'like this or, again, like this', meaning, 'as augmented from below or as diminished from above'. According to the narrator, these explanations show young Leverkühn already 'skilled at enharmonic transpositions' and 'not unskilled at certain tricks for using them to evade a key and recasting them as modulation' (ibid.).[37] So what may be the corresponding tricks, acts of recasting or modulation on the field of love relationships? Here again Shakespearean comedy provides some elementary schooling in the arts of simulation, transfer, transformation and deception.

Indeed, Mann's novel is itself engaged in such a game of enharmonic changes and confusions where 'all is relationship' and part of a system of equally inexhaustible combinations as the circle of fifths and its various keys for the composer. More of this emerges from the draft versions suggesting Mann's initial plans for this part of the plot: Leverkühn was to meet the stage designer Marie Godeau at the premier of his violin concerto (here taking place in Switzerland) and become close to her *before* starting his affair with young Schwerdtfeger. In his diary the author noted problems with the chronology and, even more, causality of these two love stories and their mutual entanglement: 'Worry about plot: has Adrian met Marie G. already in Geneva, occ. violin concerto? But he then travels with Rudi to Hung. estate. All quite confused and complicated: follows R., quite fallen for him, to Tolna's invitation – after meeting Marie. Is this acceptable? It must be defended' (quoted in Mann 2007b: 757).[38]

Would a man like Leverkühn, had he already encountered the ravishingly beautiful Mademoiselle Godeau, embodiment of dark romanesque femininity as well as motherhood reincarnated – would Leverkühn still have been fooled into the escapade with Rudi Schwerdtfeger? That would have been, to speak with biographer Zeitblom, 'lovelier still' – truly precarious and yet deliberately 'defended'. As it happens, the novelist eventually decided to avoid such complex motivations, reshuffling the sequence of events. In the final version, the violin concerto premieres in Vienna (instead of Geneva or Basel),[39] so the Swiss concerts with Leverkühn's opportunity to meet Marie Godeau come later in the course of repeat performances. Now his relationship with Schwerdtfeger appears to be a love affair in fits and starts and more provisional, 'a temporary stopgap' (*Faustus* 458) for the arousal of the cold artist 'to humanness' (ibid.), as Adrian tries to make the youth believe when requesting his help in courtship. But what if it were the other way round? Surely, the novelist found himself in all the trouble of multiple relationships precisely because, had he followed his first impulse, he would have preferred the alternative – even more confusing – plot sequence, letting Leverkühn elope with Schwerdtfeger after his understanding with Mlle Godeau. In this causality, his intention would have been a proper bourgeois marriage so as to warm the lonesome artist 'to humanness' (ibid.)[40] and so make the relationship to Schwerdtfeger he actually desires possible.

However, instead of risking such explicit readings, Mann preferred to keep his novel quite ambiguous. Leverkühn's progress was not to be from lecher cured to husband chastened, nor from closet gay to open homosexual. In fact, the lived relationship with Schwerdtfeger remains in need of a mediating third, i.e. the musical work created for and with the partner. Rudolph clearly says what his desire for a tailor-made concerto means to him: 'I'd make it part of me, so I could play it in my sleep, and cherish and coddle every note like a mother, because I'd be its mother, and you would be the father – it would be like a child between us, a platonic child' (*Faustus* 369).[41] Here the violin 'concerto' lives up to the literal meaning of this term signifying collaboration, contest and joint aspiration. The homoerotic fantasy of procreation includes and parodies the heterosexual gender roles of mother and father, without obligation (or even ability) to decide between biological actuality and cultural travesty.

Still, begetting such a child and giving birth to it in musical performance are rather different things, just as in real pregnancy. The composer leaves his imprint which the performer, in a belated act, interprets. Leverkühn has long planned how to deal with Zeitblom, Schwerdtfeger and with Marie Godeau and thus proves his mettle, literally, as a 'composer'. With his intricate network of various, and variously 'orchestrated', triangular connections the protagonist becomes his own only begetter and manages, for the time being, to become part of his own Shakespearean comedy. In this way, *all* romantic plot options remain open and simultaneously unrealized. The novel's infernal knot is untied neither with a 'break-through' to the homoerotic *amour fou* of two artist figures nor with a conventional return to marriage ever after. Ambiguity remains the key. On second thoughts, the plot sequence initially planned (from Marie Godeau to Rudi Schwerdtfeger) is not actually less plausible than the final story, and the final story, in turn, no less daring than the earlier. Both versions and their proper sequence are unconvincing when – and *because* – the real issue is persisting and confusing simultaneity. The novelist's shuffling with chronology and his transfer of features from one relationship to the other show him in an aporetic situation, trying to combine *at one go* two opposing principles: dramatic coincidence with narrative sequence.

Storytelling needs to reduce alternatives, one by one, in the unfolding of a plot. The process of narration always comes to points of bifurcation, having to choose one and reject the other option. But

Leverkühn's choices are often ambiguous: first theology but later music; a quiet country life but one involved with urban bohemians; the strict solitude of an ascetic artist and the desperate need of reaching out for love. All Leverkühn's matters of the heart are equally ambiguous and never quite resolved: he confides in his old friend telling him not just of his Leipzig adventure but also of some later intimate affairs and yet he puts his serious marriage plan into the untrustworthy hands of Schwerdtfeger, a notorious rake. Leverkühn's marital intentions seem to bear the seed of failure from their very start, placed under the ironic observation of their originator and main actor who does not quite believe in his idea and nevertheless tries it out. There is no clever or premeditated murder plot that we could make out in the text, just a performative contradiction triggered, as if by chance, through various others and their chain reaction of responses. The idea to entrust, of all people, his faithless lover with a task demanding utmost self-denial is as absurd as – at around the same time but in a different literary scene – Franz Kafka's testament, entrusting Max Brod with the obligation to destroy his literary legacy, a task this pious friend could never carry out.[42] As it happens, Zeitblom, too, received the youthful Leipzig confession with the obligation to destroy it after reading and he, too, refused to follow this instruction but decided to regard the letter 'as a document that included as an essential part this order to destroy, which cancelled itself out, so to speak, by its documentary nature' (*Faustus* 154).[43]

In Leverkühn's story, the two friends – the one most fickle, the other most loyal – are balanced in their influence. Is it a comedy? Is it a tragedy? The novel seems to have it both ways, accepting the Faustus story of the early modern *Volksbuch* and Shakespearean comedy as fundamentally different yet equally formative forbears. A biographical novel like this, and one with an intrusive homodiegetic narrator like Zeitblom, surely is the paradigm of a narrative whose discourse highlights the generic contrast between a diegetic mode of representation and, on the other hand, the dramatic mode of scenic-mimetic presentation. And yet, does not Zeitblom's narrative presence constitute another 'stage' on which the novel's representations are being performed in an artistic spectacle of language? Exactly in the middle of the plot, the narrator for once withdraws and lets Adrian's 'document' from Palestrina speak, thus yielding his almost authorial retrospect to a vividly dramatic play-within-the-play between 'Faustus' Leverkühn and his Mephistophelian visitor.

In a later abandoned passage from the drafts, the narrator hesitates to share his biographical authority over this devilish encounter, reluctant, as it were, to clear the stage for its presentation: that is to say, he is clearly jealous. Commenting on Leverkühn's record and the 'other's' role therein, Zeitblom justifies this erotic rivalry by pointing out his own, rather more reliable and less ambiguous, narration. And yet we also find a different statement, possibly a bit of dialogue or dream, deeply puzzling and without superior authority: 'It is bitter for me having to accept the ambiguous. But I cannot do without it when considering the question if the document beside me, cited in the following, is a monologue or dialogue' (Mann 2007b: 989–90).[44] That is to say drama, or the dramatic as a mode of narrative, here depends ultimately on one's own belief in the devil's real presence. Or perhaps the other way round? Perhaps the possibility of witnessing and presencing the diabolic depends on using narrative versus dramatic modes to render it in language?

As for music, we may find similar ways of relating its different styles to narrative versus dramatic modes – this is, at any rate, what the aesthetic and historical excursions in the novel would imply when we read them as poetological suggestions. Leverkühn's style of composition – setting out from late-romanticist beginnings and moving backwards in time, step by step, beyond the classic period to the primal grounds of early modern polyphony and counterpoint and trying to renew their strictly mathematical art forms for writing music in the present age – this emerging style is far from reaching a full synthesis of musical paradigms, but such a synthesis eventually becomes thinkable and desirable: 'The final task is to sublate the antithesis between the polyphonic style of fugues and the homophonic pleasure of sonatas' (ibid.: 981).[45] The sonata shows a tendency for homophonic chords and harmonious structures in developing its various parts and may, for this reason, be seen in analogy to forms of story-telling with manifest and dominant narration. The polyphonic style of fugues, by contrast, may be analogous to types of narrative allowing for more scenic, i.e. dramatic potentials. According to his literary inventor, the onus is on Leverkühn to reconcile these two alternatives in music – a project which may also manifest Thomas Mann's own ideas of integrating diegetic with dramatic forms of narrative.

Translated from German by Johannes Ungelenk and Tobias Döring

Notes

1   On the level of the epic or diegetic presentation, the engagement with musical artefacts can only be conducted in an indirect way, either via the ekphrasis of musical progressions, a technique that Steven Paul Scher has called 'verbal music' (Scher 1968), or via the evocation of well-known compositions that appeal to extratextual experiences (with regard to existing works or composers) or possibilities of referentialization. Music as

a form of art has a need for the vivid, acoustic realization of its notation, for presence and performance, a need even stronger for music than for literature. It is, however, only the text of the notation (especially before audiovisual media of registration came into operation) that allows for the permanent storage of and the intersubjective communication about musical events.

2   Cited henceforth in the translation by John E. Woods (Mann 1999), with the German original provided in notes. All translations of the commentary on *Doktor Faustus* (Mann 2007b) are by Johannes Ungelenk and Tobias Döring, unless otherwise indicated.

3   First of all it is important to note that Thomas Mann's *Faustus* is situated both in the tradition of the so-called *Volksbücher* as well as in the elaborate Faust literature of high culture, from Marlowe to Goethe. In essence, the story of Faust is a duel between a scholar and his diabolic tempter, thereby at the same time a contest of the standards of human knowledge and understanding and the world of elementary natural forces. The abstract plot level of challenging nature's secrets by the urge to know and the will to power on the part of modern man, or Faustian man, is transfigured in the dramatic configuration of the diabolic wager, which promises the elderly Faust a new, young life, if he subscribes to the principle of the antigodly with regard to his end and the metaphysical destiny of his soul.

4   Cited according to the *Arden Shakespeare Third Series* (Shakespeare 1998).

5   *Du darfst nicht lieben* (*Doktor Faustus*, hereafter referred to as GKFA 10: 363).

6   Wimmer's commentary (Mann 2007b: 485–6) notes those 'signals' [*Signale*] in the text that 'suggest a parallelisation, which move Adrian Leverkühn in the proximity of an allegory of Germany'; it emphasizes, however, that the author has countered an all-too direct politicization of Leverkühn's will to form with clear moments of distancing, for example in the discussions of the students' community during their hiking tours.

7   For the Petrarchan concept of the rhetorically elaborated love in this comedy, see Carroll (1976) and Breitenberg (1992).

8   Concerning mockery cf. Carroll (1976) and Parker (1993).

9   *die Feingliedrigkeit der Faktur* (GKFA 10: 381); *die Instrumentationstechnik, durch welche ein oft kompliziertes Stimmengewebe volkommen klar gehalten sei* (ibid.).

10   *kompositorische Phantasie* (ibid.); *in der Abwandlung eines Gegebenen in vielfachen Variationen bekunde* (ibid.).

11   *strengen Satz* (ibid.: 276); *keine freie Note mehr* (ibid.: 280). This is taken verbatim from Adorno's *Zur Philosophie der Neuen Musik* (cf. Mann 2007b: 488).

12   *Sinn für das Komische* (GKFA 10: 127); *Neigung zum Lachen* (ibid.).

13   *kleine Gesangsübungen zu veranstalten pflegte* (ibid.: 46); *eine zeitliche Verschränkung* (ibid.: 47); *nachahmendes Eintreten* (ibid.); *zu dem man im gegebenen Augenblick durch einen Rippenstoß der Stall-Hanne aufgefordert wurde, wenn der Gesang schon im Gange war* (ibid.).

14   *Eigentümlich genug: wessen die schönstimmige Elsbeth Leverkühn aus einer Art von Keuschheit sich enthielt, damit ging dieses tierisch duftende Geschöpf frei*

heraus (ibid.: 46); *Stallmagd mit Waberbusen* (ibid.); *O, wie wohl ist mir am Abend* (ibid.: 48).

15 *So ... waren wir immer in der Zeit auseinander, während doch die melodische Gegenwart eines jeden sich erfreulich zu der des andern verhielt und, was wir hervorbrachten, ein anmutiges Gewebe, einen Klangkörper bildete, wie der‚gleichzeitige‘ Gesang es nicht war; ein Gefüge, dessen Stimmigkeit wir uns gefallen ließen, ohne ihrer Natur und Ursache weiter nachzufragen* (ibid.).

16 *acht- oder neunjährige Adrian* (ibid.); *kurze, mehr spöttische als erstaunte Auflachen; Machart dieser Liedchen durchschaute* (ibid.); *imitatorische Polyphonie* (ibid.: 49); *moquanter Eingeweihtheit* (ibid.).

17 Cf. the deleted notion of 'Schlotterbusen' that had initially been used in this place (cf. Mann 2007b: 213) and is realized later in the novel, in Pfeifferinger's variation of the scheme.

18 *beugen* (GKFA 10: 49); *disziplinieren* (ibid.); *den Dünkel meiner Kälte bestrafen* (ibid.).

19 This fragile-winged creature is part of his father's collection of butterflies, especially singled out for discussion in the report on Adrian's childhood.

20 For the following I draw on Ralph Berry, 'The words of Mercury' (1969).

21 See John L. Austin, *How to do things with words* (1975).

22 *Jeder Ton der gesamten Komposition ist durch diese ‚Reihe‘ determiniert; es gibt keine ‚freie‘ Note mehr* (cf. Mann 2007b: 488).

23 Cf. also Mann (ibid.: 489): 'Independent of Schoenberg the Austrian composer Hauer had already developed a similar procedure [*Verfahren*] (the twelfth-tone row), with poor results. ... Opposed to that Schoenberg includes the classical and, more importantly, the archaical techniques of variation in the twelve tone material' (Thomas Mann highlighted these passages in his copy of Adorno's *Philosophie der Neuen Musik*): *Ein solches Verfahren (der Zwölftonreihe) hat unabhaengig von Schoenberg der oester-reichische Komponist Hauer ausgebildet, und die Resultate sind von oedester Duerftigkeit. ...Dem gegenueber nimmt Schoenberg die klassischen und mehr noch die archaischen Techniken der Variation radikal ins Zwoelftonmaterial auf* (von Thomas Mann hervorgehobene Passagen aus Adornos Manuskript der *Philosophie der Neuen Musik*).

24 *die klassischen und mehr noch die archaischen Techniken der Variation* (ibid.: 489). See an abandoned passage of *Doktor Faustus*: 'The unification of the oldest with the newest is not at all a deed of arbitrariness, as it would seem. It lies in the nature of things, is down to the curvature of the earth, so to speak, that the earliest returns in the latest': *Die Vereinigung des Aeltesten mit dem Neusten ist mitnichten eine solche Tat der Willkuer, wie es scheinen möchte: Es liegt in der Natur der Dinge, liegt an der Kruemmung der Welt, sozusagen, dass im Spaetesten das Frueheste wiederkehrt* (ibid.: 1015–16).

25 *Meist verwendet er* [Schönberg] *die Reihe in vier Modi: als Grundreihe, als deren Umkehrung, also indem jedes Intervall der Reihe durch das in der Gegenrichtung ersetzt wird (nach Art der ‚Umkehrungsfuge‘) ...; als ‚Krebs‘ im Sinne der alten kontrapunktischen Praxis, so dass die Reihe mit dem letzten Ton beginnt und mit dem ersten schliesst; und als Umkehrung des Krebses* (ibid.: 489; Mann underlined the technical terms of the four modes).

26 *Ich (muß wahrlich lachen): 'Nicht lieben! Armer Teufel! Willst Du dem Ruf
    deiner Dummheit Ehre machen ..., daß du Geschäft und Versprechen gründen
    willst auf einen so nachgiebigen, so verfänglichen Begriff wie – Liebe? Will der
    Teufel die Lust prohibieren? Wo nicht, so muß er die Sympathie in Kauf nehmen
    und sogar die Caritas, sonst ist er betrogen wie es im Buche steht'* (GKFA 10:
    363).

27 *Thomas Manns große Liebe in den frühen Münchner Jahren* (Mann 2007b: 502).

28 *Genug* (GKFA 10: 467).

29 *junge Mann* (ibid.: 480); *gar nicht umhinkonnte* (ibid.); *zu gehorchen* (ibid.);
    noch schöner gewesen (ibid.); *nicht gehorcht hätte* (ibid.).

30 *der seelischen Konstitution und selbst dem Gehaben nach knabenhaften
    Frauenliebling* (GKFA 10: 481); *dieser elbische Platoniker* (ibid.: 617).

31 In a passage of the draft that has been cut the narrator responds to the
    nature of this love and the difficulties in describing it in much greater
    detail (cf. Mann 2007b: 1023–4).

32 *hat sich vollzogen* (GKFA 10: 489).

33 Diary entry by Thomas Mann, dated 6 June1944 (Mann 2007b: 675).

34 *kein Halten mehr* (GKFA 10: 490); *Kein Halten mehr! Seele, denk' es nicht aus!*
    (ibid.).

35 *Müßiggang* (ibid.: 72); *aller Laster Anfang* (ibid.); *lauter schwarze Tasten*
    (ibid.: 73); *Fis-Dur ausgesehen* (ibid.); *H-Dur gehörig* (ibid.); *'So ein
    Zusammenklang', meinte er, 'hat an sich keine Tonart. Alles ist Beziehung, und
    die Beziehung bildet den Kreis'* (ibid.).

36 *Beziehung ist alles. Und willst du sie näher beim Namen nennen, so ist ihr Name
    Zweideutigkeit* (ibid.: 73).

37 *so verstehen oder beziehungsweise auch so* (ibid.: 74); *als erhöht ... von
    unten oder als vermindert von oben* (ibid.); *als kundig der enharmonischen
    Verwechslung* (ibid.); *nicht unkundig gewisser Tricks, wie man damit ausweicht
    und die Umdeutung zur Modulation benutzt* (ibid.).

38 *Sorge wegen der Handlung: Hat Adrian schon in Genf, anl. des Violin-Konzerts
    Marie G. kennen gelernt? Aber er reist dann mit Rudi auf das ung. Gut. Etwas
    wirr und kompliziert: Mit R., dem er gerade verfallen, folgt er der Einladung der
    Tolna – nachdem er Marie schon gesehen. Ist das annehmbar? Es will vertreten
    sein* (Diary, 15 July 1946, quoted in Mann 2007b: 757).

39 Both variants can be found in the cut drafts (cf. Mann 2007b: 1020).

40 *ein vorläufiger Notbehelf* (GKFA 10: 633); *fürs Menschliche* (ibid.: 632).

41 *Einverleiben wollt ich es mir, daß ich's im Schlafe spielen könnte und es hegen
    und pflegen in jeder Note wie eine Mutter, denn Mutter wäre ich ihm, und Sie
    wären der Vater, – es wäre zwischen uns wie ein Kind, ein platonisches Kind*
    (ibid.: 510).

42 Cf. Roland Reuß: 'Lesen, was gestrichen wurde. Für eine historisch-
    kritische Kafka-Ausgabe' (1995).

43 *als ein Dokument zu betrachten, von dem der Vernichtungsbefehl ein Bestandteil
    war, so daß er eben durch seinen dokumentarischen Charakter sozusagen sich
    selber aufhob* (GKFA 10: 211).

44 *Mich stimmt es bitter, das Zweideutige anerkennen zu müssen. Dennoch muß ich
    es zuhilfe nehmen angesichts der Frage, ob das, was neben mir liegt und was ich
    nun einrücke, ein Monolog oder eine Zwiesprache ist* (Mann 2007b: 989–90).

45   *Ganz zuletzt geht es um die Aufhebung des Gegensatzes von polyphonem Fugenstil und homophonem Sonatenwesen* (ibid.: 981).

Works Cited

Adorno, Theodor W., 1949. *Philosophie der neuen Musik*. Tübingen: Mohr.

Adorno, Theodor W., 2006 [1949]. *Philosophy of New Music*, trans. Robert Hullot-Kentor. Minneapolis: University of Minnesota Press.

Austin, John Langshaw, 1975. *How to do things with words*, 2nd edn. Cambridge, MA.: Harvard University Press.

Berry, Ralph, 1969. 'The Words of Mercury', in *Shakespeare Survey* 22, pp. 69–77.

Breitenberg, Mark, 1992. 'The Anatomy of Masculine Desire in *Love's Labour's Lost*', in *Shakespeare Quarterly* 43: 4, pp. 430–49.

Carroll, William C., 1976. *The great Feast of Language in Love's Labour's Lost*. Princeton: Princeton University Press.

Mann, Thomas, 1999 [1947]. *Doctor Faustus. The Life of the German Composer Adrian Leverkühn as told by a Friend*, trans. John E. Woods. New York: Vintage. [*Faustus*]

Mann, Thomas, 2007a [1947]. *Doktor Faustus*, ed. Ruprecht Wimmer. Große Kommentierte Frankfurter Ausgabe, vol. 10.1. Frankfurt am Main: S. Fischer. [GKFA 10]

Mann, Thomas, 2007b. *Doktor Faustus. Kommentar*, ed. Ruprecht Wimmer. Große Kommentierte Frankfurter Ausgabe, vol. 10.2. Frankfurt am Main: S. Fischer.

Parker, Patricia, 1993. 'Preposterous Reversals: *Love's Labor's Lost*', in *Modern Language Quarterly* 54: 4, pp. 435–82.

Reuß, Roland, 1995. 'Lesen, was gestrichen wurde. Für eine historisch-kritische Kafka-Ausgabe', in *Franz Kafka. Historisch-kritische Ausgabe sämtlicher Handschriften, Drucke und Typoskripte. Einleitung*, eds Roland Reuß, Peter Staengle. Basel, Frankfurt am Main: Stroemfeld, pp. 9–24.

Scher, Steven Paul, 1968. *Verbal music in German literature*. New Haven: Yale University Press.

Shakespeare, William, 1998. *Love's Labour's Lost*, ed. H. R. Woudhuysen. The Arden Shakespeare. Third Series. Walton-on-Thames: Nelson.

Four   The Magic Fountain:
Shakespeare, Mann and
Modern Authorship
Tobias Döring

Authorship has long been questioned and debated,[1] not least for the impact authors may have on the world. Late in his life, for instance, W. B. Yeats wrote 'Man and the Echo', a poem in which he wondered what effects some of his earlier writing might have had: 'Did that play of mine send out / Certain men the English shot? / Did words of mine put too great strain / On that woman's reeling brain?' (Yeats 1997: 353) What these anxious questions are debating is the key to poetic potency: how can we determine what authors really do and what powers their words ultimately have? If the term *poetry*, derived from *poesis*, signifies a process of making or production, what is actually produced in poetry, or perhaps produced *with* and *by* poetry? Can there be creation that is purely verbal, brought about by means of words? Are we supposed to see authors as makers, making things happen? If not, with what other authority should we credit them?

To raise such questions registers a sense of crisis, the sense that confidence in poetic potency is lost or waning. 'For poetry makes nothing happen', W. H. Auden famously declared in his echo to Yeats's poem: it merely 'survives / In the valley of its making where executives / Would never want to tamper, flows on south / From ranches of isolation' (Auden 1976: 197). Wherever these valleys or ranches may be, and whatever channels of poetic flow they figure, Auden's phrase suggests that sanctuaries of this sort are remote and that their use for us is doubtful. This sober diagnosis is relevant not just for modernism and the modernist distrust of language. It is discernible also in early modern reflections on the poet's art, such as Sidney's *Defence of Poesy*, which – for all its brazen claims – may well be driven by some nagging doubt as to the nature of his verbal acts. According to Sean Keilen (2006: 52), Sidney's most audacious move is to associate poetic speech with God's unique ability to create *ex nihilo*. But such confident associations with divine potency and power would be a problem rather than a promise. To say, as Sidney does (1989: 235), 'Now, for the poet, he nothing affirms, and therefore never lieth' could also be a finer version of what Auden says when he bluntly denies all effect or efficacy to poetry: now, for the poet, he nothing affirms, and therefore makes nothing happen. Yeats concludes his poem with a grand apostrophe, 'O Rocky voice', as if to try out one more time a powerful poetic pose, described by Jonathan Culler as the traditional self-authorizing gesture of poetic discourse where 'the vocative of apostrophe is a device which the poetic voice uses to establish with an object a relationship which helps to constitute him' (1981: 157). Yet precisely this relationship and self-constitution have come under question when the key to poetic potency lies in the hands of believers. How may poets, writing in a modern age of crisis, ever handle or retrieve it?

This is what the present chapter sets out to pursue in a dialogue of modernist and early modern texts, with reference not to Auden, Yeats and Sidney, but to Thomas Mann and Shakespeare. The issue is to gauge their programmatic engagements with the potencies or possibilities of their own art by means of this very art and in the awareness of crisis. For this purpose, I take the term poetry in the wider sense of *poesis* as cultural production, and I take two sample texts which lend themselves to such a project because they encourage us to read them as inquiries into the conditions of poetic making, especially their own making: *The Tempest*, Shakespeare's play with the strongest metadramatic dimension in all his work, and Mann's 'Fragwürdigstes', i.e. 'Highly Questionable', the chapter about occult séances in Dr Krokowski's cabinet near the ending of *Der Zauberberg* (*The Magic Mountain*), offering in many ways the climax of the metapoetic reflections that proceed throughout this novel.

In conjoining these two texts, my point is not to suggest influence. We should rather think of confluence or correspondence, of joined, though different, cultural responses to a problem faced by both and treated, in each case, with symptomatic force: the problem of authorship in the post-auratic modern age. Mann famously said of Shakespeare that he liked to find, not to invent, the substance of his work – 'Er fand viel lieber, als daß er erfand' (in his 1906 essay 'Bilse und ich', Mann 2002b: 100) – an artistic principle that has been identified as Mann's own working method (Kurzke 2001: 20). In this sense, then, of remaking what the writer has found, I suggest that Mann found in *The Tempest* just the stuff his own poetic dreams are made on: a figure like the magus Prospero, highly usable for him because it is so highly questionable. Conversely, we read Shakespeare's *Tempest* and its magic practice differently after having read *Der Zauberberg* with its scenes of conjuring the dead. If Shakespeare must have come to Mann in 'such a questionable shape', as Hamlet says when he confronts the ghost (1.4.24), Shakespearean texts are critically reshaped when they are confronted with Mann's work. My project in this chapter is to explore what happens when we read both of them together, trying to trace such processes of mutual ghosting.

Ghosts are, in fact, crucial to this project – and they are crucially embarrassing to modern readers.[2] In Shakespeare's play, the 'airy spirit' Ariel, agent and medium of the magician's art, finds little favour with enlightened spectators, just as Hans Castorp's steady, if reluctant, descent into the spiritism of Krokowski's circle is resented not only by humanists like Settembrini. As Michael Maar writes in his book-length study of Mann's chapter (1995: 18), critics remain puzzled, sometimes irritated, by this occult episode dealing with the return of the dead, thus scandalously breaking with the expectations of verisimilitude: what may have motivated Mann, close to the ending of his epic narrative, to probe into such murky depths? He is drawing, as is well established, on personal observations of parapsychological adventures centring on the notorious Albert von Schrenck-Notzing, Munich's leading occultist, also described in his 1924 essay 'Okkulte Erlebnisse' (Mann 2002c). And yet, this rather begs the question: if Mann, like Shakespeare, liked to find, not to invent, his literary matter, why should he find these ghostly gambles useful for his purpose? What *does* he find, what do *we* find, in them? Trying to address such questions, I follow Maar's suggestion (1995: 232) that 'Highly Questionable' turns *Der Zauberberg* into a metanovel about the process of producing art – in just the same way, we might add, that Prospero's magic turns *The Tempest* into a metadrama about the powers and conditions of theatrical performance. The ghosts involved – Holger and Ariel – are therefore better taken seriously, as discursive phenomena of a second order: for whenever we receive report on ghosts, we are compelled to observe the observer because the actual object of this observation usually eludes us. As questionable shapes and threshold figures for the claims of realism, ghosts make us reflect on media and mediality, on the conditions of perception and of cultural production (Baßler et al. 2005: 10–11).[3] Thus, the key to under-standing poetic potency may best be found with ghosts.

*

Here is a telling anecdote, a report on an uncanny apparition from early seventeenth-century England. A group of players, touring Exeter, was performing Marlowe's *Doctor Faustus*, complete with the doctor's conjuring and all the devils as required in the cast. But when it came to Faustus's scene of magic incantation, 'on a sudden they were all dasht …, for they were all perswaded, there was one devell too many among them' (Marlowe 2005: 181) – a terrible reminder to the players that their performance may have unforeseen effects because the words they utter in the play could turn out in the world to be of real consequence. This, the report continues, brought their performance to a hasty end, with the spectators leaving the place in panic and the players 'contrarye to their custome spending the night in reading and in prayer' (ibid.). What are we to make of this?

Clearly, in some sense, we are dealing with a piece of propaganda advertising special thrills that Marlowe's *Doctor Faustus* offers to spectators. But in a fundamental sense, we are confronted with a question, not unlike Yeats's self-questioning in 'Man and the Echo', about the force involved in words, a controversial point not least in religious debates of the early modern period – for protestants like King James there 'is no power inherent in the circles, or the holiness of the names of God blasphemouslie vsed: nor in whatsoeuer rites or ceremonies at that time vsed' (1969: 16). At issue is the question under what conditions words can actually do things, such as getting people married or getting devils to appear. In his scene of conjuring, Faustus first congratulates himself on having achieved just this: 'I see there's virtue in my heavenly words' (1.3.27), only anxiously to ask a moment later in response to Mephistopheles' quibbles: 'Did not my conjuring speeches raise thee? Speak' (1.3.27–45, Marlowe 2005: 15). Given such uncertainties about the status of his invocatory acts, we may also understand why the anecdote about the Exeter performance is as appalling as it is appealing: it persuades us to believe in verbal power extending even to infernal realms, a fantasy of magical authority uttering someone into being – 'there was one devell too many among them'.

This belief also extends to Doctor Krokowski's cabinet: 'There was one more person in the room than before' (*The Magic Mountain*, hereafter referred to as *MM*, 680).[4] With the appearance of the late Joachim Ziemßen, Castorp's cousin, who, after a great deal of labour and with the help of both the Danish medium Elly and Castorp himself, is eventually summoned by the spirit Holger, the occult business staged in this chapter comes to its questionable climax and confronts us, as readers, with the crucial question whether we should take this scene for real, i.e. seriously believe in the return of the dead. According to Maar, there lies the scandal for modern sensitivities: necromancy breaks with plausibility – where even Albert von Schrenck-Notzing drew the line – hence with the conventions of realist fiction to which the novel otherwise adheres. Ghosts, however, have long haunted works of literary realism, where they serve as self-reflexive threshold figures marking narrative modalities and testing the conventions or conditions of their medium. In just this way, Maar argues (1995: 254), Mann's occult chapter dramatizes notions of producing fiction through mutual inter-penetration, or imbrication, of life and literature – notions rendered most explicitly in sexual terms:

> The reader knows we speak of our husband- and fatherhood, the act of birth, which Elly's wrestling did so unmistakably resemble that even he must recognize it who had never passed through this experience, even our young Hans Castorp; who, not having shirked life, now came to know, in such a guise, this act, so full of organic mysticism. In what guise! To what an end! Under what circumstances!
>
> (*MM* 676–7)[5]

The various features of the séances described throughout the chapter in great detail – the darkened room, the atmosphere of secrecy, the medium's state of mind half-conscious, half-awake, the frequent mentioning of the writing table – all contribute to the same effect, pointing to a process of poetic composition going on. With Ellen Brand's and Castorp's double act of orgasm and birthing, the narrative here stages acts of literary creativity rendered through a conventional notion by which artistic creation has long been imagined: sexual procreation. The discursive connection thus drawn between artistic production and sexual reproduction indeed forms a topos (cf. Begemann/Wellbery 2002), a favoured way of speaking about artworks and their origin – relevant also, for instance, in speaking of the violin concerto in Mann's *Doktor Faustus*[6] – in a rhetoric of begetting and conception, pregnancy and birth.[7] Drawing on this topos, the séance turns into the traditional scene of writing. We should also recall that, as the crucial means to invoke Joachim's spectral presence, the tragedy of Doctor Faustus forms the soundtrack to this scene, not Marlowe's sixteenth-century version but Gounod's nineteenth-century opera: Valentine's famous aria, Joachim's favourite piece, is playing on the gramophone. The ghosts therefore combine their force. In the sense suggested earlier, the medium of the séance, Elly, and the Gounod record as the medium of music draw attention to the magic mediality which must here be at work producing the sight (Joachim) while reproducing the sound (Valentine) of someone absent and long gone – an act of (musical) reproduction leading on to (visual) production; poesis predicated on mimesis.[8]

In fact, the particular aria that accompanies, and possibly enables, this scenario of literary creation raises even more suggestive points.

In Gounod, the soldier Valentine has been called to war and prays to God that He protect his sister Margarethe in his absence; the brother is, in turn, himself protected by the sacred medal which she gave him, a magic object offering its bearer charm. Yet this aria, known as 'Valentine's prayer', is without equivalent in Goethe's tragedy, on which the libretto otherwise is based. In Goethe's version, Valentine does not *pray* for Gretchen but *curses* her, calling her a harlot and, instead of asking for divine protection, telling her to leave God out of it ('Laß unsern Herrgott aus dem Spaß', line 3733). Gounod's aria and Goethe's scene, that is to say, dramatize a glaring contrast in verbal performance: praying versus cursing. And yet there is a fundamental point they share because these speech acts are two strong examples of the kind of verbal force that Marlowe's Faustus called the 'virtue' in his words. Prayers, just like curses, only work when they make things happen, as pragmatic agents making an impact on, and a difference in, the real world. For this reason they perform the kind of potency that poets must aspire to when they, according to an old, emphatic model of poetic force, are seen as demiurges of literary creation. It is such a model which I think Mann's chapter stages with the occult invocation of Joachim's ghost. Highly questionable though it surely is, this notion of the author as magician – in the sense in which George Eliot opens *Adam Bede*: 'With a single drop of ink for a mirror, the Egyptian sorcerer undertakes to reveal to any chance comer far-reaching visions of the past. This is what I undertake to do for you, reader' (2001: 7) – is being established and explored throughout the séances, the conjuror whose words wield powers ordinary mortals might at best experience in praying or in cursing; a poet who makes something happen.

*

This model is also at play in *The Tempest*. Like all early modern plays on magic and magicians,[9] above all *Doctor Faustus*, Shakespeare's drama stages occult practice so as to explore the possibilities of stagecraft and test the power of the playhouse, a recently established medium, which attracted so much cultural attention because its art seemed to involve enormous forces: 'If by your art, my dearest father, you have / Put the wild waters in this roar, allay them' (1.2.1–2). 'If': Miranda's first words in the second scene of *The Tempest* open this process of inquiry with a conditional, a testing out of possibility. Her deictic phrase 'this roar' points to the storm we have just witnessed in scene one, which is now past and which she now turns into something to observe and question. With her deictic gesture Miranda frames it, placing the 'wild waters' in inverted commas, as it were, at one remove from reality, cited or recited, thereby placing us in a position as self-conscious beholders musing on the magic of the stage. Thus, the titular event of the play is marked off as a spectacle for speculation: if by the art of theatre we have been put in such an anxious state of mind as to believe in storm, our fears are now allayed.

Or perhaps not. For what a potent medium theatre must be if it can do such things and produce such virtual realities! The entire shipwrecked party is eventually saved, no lives are lost and all are happily reunited at the end. But the virtual risk remains and is explored throughout the play: the dangers of theatrical performance, dabbling in potential powers which, like Faustus's incantations when performed in Exeter, may turn out questionable and beyond control. *The Tempest*, to be sure, is routinely read as a great demonstration of metatheatre, with Prospero's art representing the dramatist's, an authority whose power is at stake. Beginning with Miranda's conditional, the play unfolds as a process of showing, proving, testing or contesting his magisterial power. Yet it is crucial, I think, to acknowledge that this is not simply a celebration but also involves anxious questioning, a search for origins now lost and no longer retrievable, ending on a plea for transformation.

Such questions are raised, above all, with the scene that corresponds most closely to the conjuring scene in *Doctor Faustus*, when Prospero draws a magic circle and utters his most famous incantation:

Ye elves of hills, brooks, standing lakes and groves,
And ye that on the sands with printless foot
Do chase the ebbing Neptune, and do fly him
When he comes back; you demi-puppets that
By moonshine do the green sour ringlets make,
Whereof the ewe not bites; and you whose pastime
Is to make midnight-mushrooms, that rejoice
To hear the solemn curfew, by whose aid –
Weak masters though ye be – I have bedimmed
The noontide sun, called for the mutinous winds,
And 'twixt the green sea and the azured vault
Set roaring war; to the dread-rattling thunder
Have I given fire and rifted Jove's stout oak
With his own bolt: the strong-based promontory
Have I made shake, and by the spurs plucked up
The pine and cedar; graves at my command
Have waked their sleepers, ope'd and let 'em forth
By my so potent art. But this rough magic
I here abjure; and when I have required
Some heavenly music (which even now I do)
To work mine end their senses that
This airy charm is for, I'll break my staff,

Bury it certain fathoms in the earth,
And deeper than did ever plummet sound
I'll drown my book.
(5.1.33–57)

This is the only point in the entire play at which we actually witness Prospero conjuring. Significantly, it comes late in the plot; unlike Faustus, Prospero does not *begin* his practice in the occult art but strives to *conclude* it. It is his final magic act to trace this circle where soon his adversaries from Milan, as the Folio stage direction says, all 'stand charmed' (1999: 267) or, as Prospero himself says, stand 'spell-stopped' (5.1.61). Thus he casts a spell to renounce spells forever: the great invocation is not meant to raise any ghosts, but to abjure their power and renounce all magic, to drown the book and break the staff. This may be a reason why this speech is full of contradictions, like the oxymoron 'weak masters' (5.1.41), and ambiguities: the term 'rough magic' (5.1.50) does not really suit the idea of white magic, in opposition to Sycorax and her foul charms otherwise maintained. Most pertinent to our present concerns, however, seems to be the simple observation that, whenever else Prospero performs his magic, we never actually hear him speak.[10] Unlike Marlowe's Faustus, whose incantations are fully spelled out in the script, Prospero's magic words elude us. Throughout, this magus prefers to conjure silently, just as he demands silence from others: 'No tongue, all eyes. Be silent!' (4.1.59) On the metatheatrical level, the play-master is giving these injunctions to an audience whom he commands so as to make his own show work. As with all stage magicians, Prospero no less than Faustus, the main production of his art is theatre,[11] i.e. sheer spectacle and role play, and the main way of producing it is linguistic: by means of verbal fiat. Magic functions on the early modern stage as metatheatre because the art of players, too, works mainly by means of their words. On the bare stage, located in a wooden O as in a magic circle, without elaborate props or scenery, all scenes are verbally created by means of utterances – like Duncan's 'This castle hath a pleasant seat' (*Macbeth* 1.6.1) when all we may see are the seats of spectators – just as the stage magicians use their charms to conjure up whatever shape they please. This is the reason why language on the stage is principally 'conjunctive', in the term introduced by Thomas Greene (2005: 30–1), i.e. productive, or must aspire to be so: because it principally constitutes its referents, such as Macbeth's castle or Prospero's storm, with its own force, and brings about by verbal acts what is not otherwise existent.

Against this background, it seems all the more significant that Prospero's incantatory speech constitutes itself by means of *borrowed* language. The grand apostrophe 'Ye elves of hills, brooks, standing

lakes and groves' – in Culler's terms, 'a ritualistic, practically gratu-
itous action' (1981: 157) – opens a long and recognizable paraphrase of
Medea's incantation from Ovid's *Metamorphoses*,[12] a literary set-piece
often cited as an early modern textbook case of magic. At the point
where Shakespeare's magus finally comes into his own, where he
seems to summon all his powers to call on the various ghosts or media
of his magic art, a climax also in his powers of theatrical performance,
at just this point he draws on a given source and uses its perpetuated
language, citing the most famous witch of classical antiquity whose
verbal charms are iterated to the word. If Marlowe's Faustus, as we
saw, already entertained some doubt as to the 'virtue' of his words,
he still made it clear what kind of verbal power he aspires to. With
Prospero, this is far from clear, since his climactic verbal act is staged
by iteration. Throughout, his art is silent. Yet when even his farewell
speech proceeds through reminiscence and citation invoking literary
ghosts of the past, then he does not simply take his leave from magic
but also takes what he has left behind for an occasion of ventriloquy, as
if to remind us of what magic and poetic power may have – *must* have
– been, once upon a time, long gone, in a potent figure like Medea, with
a potent author like Ovid.

This, then, is the ultimate effect of this disturbing moment: to
mark the difference between classic precedent and modern actuality.
According to Keilen (2006: 93), Shakespeare generally dramatized
his attempts at English eloquence and potent verbal art as a constant
struggle with the precedent of Latin and with Ovid as his counterpart:
'in order to become eloquent, Shakespeare seems to have believed, he
had to be conquered by Latin'. But perhaps we may better view this
as a complex process of mutual conquest and reconquering, involving
emulation as well as appropriation, trying to transform the legacies of
old into a current idiom of writing and performance. To see literary
production as an act of genuine creation, with the author as a demiurge
of verbal fiat, is part of these classic legacies – a model of strong
authorship[13] partly revived and, at the same time, finally dismissed
in Prospero's farewell speech, a model for the modern artist no longer
readily available. Just before he says that he abjures his magic, the last
point Prospero mentions in his magic practices is waking the dead:
'graves at my command / Have waked their sleepers, ope'd and let
'em forth / By my so potent art' (5.1.48–50). Necromancy is just short
of actual creation, yet it stands here as a measure for the potency of art,
the greatest power it involves in calling the dead back to life – even as
such power is being abandoned. Prospero's farewell then performs a
double gesture: repeating and inserting difference. Grafted on the text
by Ovid and reenacting classic acts of sorcery, his speech does the same
to his magic that Miranda's opening speech did to the storm: it puts it

in inverted commas, so we may consider its effect. His next words, like Miranda's first, again use a deictic marker – '*this* rough magic' (5.1.50) – to frame the phenomenon and offer it for contemplation, as something that exists no more, or only at a remove from reality: the stuff that dreams are made on.

Modern authors, then, may dream of creativity and actual creation but what they actually do is different. This difference is inserted with the epilogue, staging the transition to a form of authorship where the author is no longer self-sustained and self-creating like a sovereign and magician, but contingent on the force of others, his spectators or readers, i.e. us:

> Let me not,
> Since I have my dukedom got
> And pardoned the deceiver, dwell
> In this bare island by your spell;
> But release me from my bands
> With the help of your good hands.
> Gentle breath of yours my sails
> Must fill, or else my project fails,
> ....
> And my ending is despair,
> Unless I be relieved by prayer.
> (Epilogue 5–16)

Thus the former master of the magic island pleads with his paying audience for help and for release. The spell now lies with us, the power to spell becomes ours. And thus his magic powers of authorial creation are translated, handed down from the single sovereign to the many who must now sustain him. With this 'decline of magic', to use Keith Thomas's term (1973), we see how authorship is being divested of divine sanctioning – just as kings eventually come to lose their divine right. What remains, for rulers and for writers in the modern age of crisis, is to hope for charisma, the elusive 'gift of grace' Max Weber analysed as the cultural compensation for traditional forms of transcendental power.[14] 'The charismatic bond is a bond of enchantment, formed by arousing hopes, expectations, adoration, faith and awe' (Horn 2011: 11), hence always involving the active support of a community. With the transfer of authority enacted in the epilogue, Shakespeare's *Tempest* seems to enlist spectators into such a support group, while trying to turn its central figure from a magic master into a charismatic leader, a representative of modern crisis who plays with us as much as we would play with him, in an ongoing process of mutual constitution: 'Taking its origin and legitimacy from a crisis, charismatic rule is itself in permanent crisis: the leader's power is ephemeral and fragile, in need of repeated success. The leader depends as much on the acclamation of his group as it depends on him for direction' (Horn 2011: 7). The play ends with a plea for applause, directing us to make him sail. Setting sail is the classic topos used by epic poets to refer to their work as a voyage (cf. Curtius 1993: 138), yet this classic mastery in literary navigation, the epilogue suggests, is no longer possible unless we make it happen ourselves: it is *our* 'gentle breath', no longer the *pneuma* of some divine spirit, that continues to inspire Prospero's 'project', i.e. enable literary creation, and may eventually bring it to completion and its destined happy ending, so he hopes, through prayer. Instead of magic potency, it now comes down to our prayer, our acts of verbal force. Prayer becomes what magic might have been: a way to change the world with words, now existing as a remnant of the former confidence in verbal efficacy.

'One of the greatest impediments that the seruants of God suffer in praier', wrote the English Jesuit and recusant patriot Thomas Wright in 1596, 'is a certain diffidence or doubting that they pray in vaine, that none heareth or attendeth what they say, whereupon followeth a tediousnesse and loathsomeness in praier' (1970: 32–3). Whether or not the messages we want delivered to the transcendental realm ever get there remains doubtful, ultimately a matter of faith. This is why a go-between is rather useful here, especially a medium such as Ellen Brand and a spirit such as Holger, some agent to intercede on our behalf. Such intermediaries, like the saints, however, are no longer available to believers in a protestant society, such as Shakespeare's England. All rituals and religious speech acts must principally be conducted without recourse to supporting figures whose integrity lies beyond doubt, just as all plays and all poetic speech acts should proceed here without drawing on inspired authorship and the magic potency of verbal art. The sources whence such power might have flowed can no more be tapped, the magic fountains are dried up or, if they exist somewhere, they remain hidden, 'occult' in the strict sense of the word.

Which brings us back to Krokowski's cabinet.

*

Here, in the catacombs of the mountain establishment, we are privileged to witness research into realms otherwise not easily accessible and into issues usually beyond experience, such as the principles of creativity. Here

> [t]he province of the subconscious, 'occult' in the proper sense
> of the word, very soon shows itself to be occult in the narrower

sense as well, and forms one of the sources whence flow the phenomena we have agreed thus to characterize. But that is not all. Whoever recognizes a symptom of organic disease as an effect of the conscious soul-life of forbidden and hystericized emotions, recognizes the creative force of the psychical within the material – a force which one is inclined to claim as a second source of magic phenomena.

(MM 654)[15]

As suggested earlier, this narrative is self-reflexive, like The Tempest, so that the phenomena and forces thus explored are the ones that actually make up the text we read. What is being questioned therefore is the magic fountain, in the sense just established: the source and potency of poetry.

Ellen Brand tells her enraptured audience that 'something whispered to her … whispered and told her what to do, softly, but quite clearly and distinctly' (MM 656), perhaps the sort of whispering that Marlowe's Faustus at times hears buzzing in his ears or like the humming voices that the shipwrecked party hears on Prospero's isle, but perhaps also the kind of whispering experienced by poets, artists and creators when they receive inspiration, the divine command that authorizes and enables their creation. Fräulein Brand we learn commands 'mysterious gifts' (MM 658),[16] that is to say, she is charismatic in the proper sense of the word, endowed with something that makes her different from us ordinary mortals, her wondrous powers of divination. It does not come as a surprise, then, that the spirit Holger, Elly's Ariel, as it were, who makes all this happen, introduces himself as a poet – or rather a Dichtr, to be precise: the condensation or, in Freudian terms, the Verdichtung of a real Dichter, a poet who is just a little imperfect, short of one letter, the letter e, which happens to be the most frequently used letter in the German language. Just as the alphabet of bone counters, which Hermine Kleefeld provides for the spelling séance with the wineglass, is one letter short and consists of 25 – a curious detail silently corrected in the English text where the number appears falsified as 26 (see MM 660, Der Zauberberg, hereafter referred to as Zb, 1001). By way of compensation, the English version gains a suggestive point in making the word poet short of t, so that Holger introduces himself in English as poe, like Edgar Allan Poe, whose haunting presence in this scene seems quite appropriate because of his key role in poetic occultism: several poems such as 'Farewell to the Earth' were dictated to a spiritual medium after Poe's death and declared by the naturalist and spiritist Alfred Russel Wallace to be 'finer and deeper and grander poems than any written by him in his earth-life' (Evans 2012: 55).

Be this as it may, with his purloined letter Holger figures as a Dichtr, an imperfectly spelled poet, and so reminds us that the quality of the imperfect may just be the stuff that poetry is made of, or has been made of since the Golden Age has waned and cannot be recovered any more. The following séance with the glass, at any rate, turns out to produce a 'surprising poem' (*MM* 663) which remains quite irrecoverable. In an alphabetic exercise the wine glass spells out every single word in letters, yet the poem as a whole is pure performance, like a bardic song or vatic vision, purely witnessed, without written evidence. So whatever we may gather of this 'lyric improvisation' (*MM* 664) remains tentative and ultimately silent. Like Prospero's magic words we never hear, Holger's work is rendered indirectly, like a stage direction, through the long passage of free indirect discourse in the narrative. But what we can make out sounds suspiciously like a scenario for Shakespeare's *Tempest*, complete with 'magic', 'sea-wrack', 'an islanded coast', the sea 'a long whispering in its dream', a 'hermit's hut', 'an open book, a skull, and in its slender frame the double-glass' (*MM* 663):[17] all the necessary keywords and paraphernalia appear. If Prospero traces a magic circle in which to catch his enemies 'spell-stopped' (5.1.61), as we saw before, we now see how Krokowski's séance retraces this circle, literally by all the spell stops of the wineglass, as if to catch us in the same condition. In this way, 'Highly Questionable' makes us consider or reconsider the model of strongly bardic, vatic, charismatic authorship which it performs and parodies, both revives and rejects.

As for the historical author figures involved in the cultural dynamics of this chapter, Maar (1995: 246) makes a persuasive case for Hans Christian Andersen, identified for instance through his birthplace Odense (which he shares with Elly) or his work *Holger Danske* (which points to the name of Holger). Yet in an intertextual network as densely over-determined as this novel there could still be more implied. Which is why I venture to propose the presence of another modern writer in this chapter, a close contemporary of Mann's, working and living partly in the same society and sometimes even in the same city, Munich, but a colleague to whose work and impact Mann used to keep a strictly guarded distance, even if he also sensed an elective affinity: Stefan George. On the one hand, Friedhelm Marx has shown (2006/7: 89), Mann felt insurmountable differences to the sacred antics of the George circle, on the other, he was sufficiently impressed by the ideas of this 'sphere' that he tried to inscribe them into *Der Zauberberg*. Such inscriptions may, I think, be traced especially in the present chapter and for various reasons. Not only is George a strong reference point for contemporary German dialogues with Shakespeare – through his own work as a translator just as through his inspiration for influential books like Friedrich Gundolf's *Shakespeare und der deutsche Geist* (1911), the defining study of his generation – he is also relevant as high priest of the kind of charismatic authorship culti-vated by a congregation of the chosen few, as parodied with Holger's pronunciations. Weber, in fact, named George and his *Kreis* as a prime example of contemporary charisma (Horn 2011: 11), confirmed in a recent study identifying George and the 'discovery of charisma' (Karlauf 2007). Significantly, in the early 1920s, just as he was completing the novel, Mann seems to have been rather fascinated by this author role himself and registered with some approval the occasion when he was associated with George's sphere (Marx 2006/7: 90); the only actual encounter between the two, described by Mann as 'unheimlich', i.e. uncanny, took place in 1924 (ibid.: 80). Against this background, I suggest seeing the séance as a specific engagement with the George cult and its otherwise outmoded model of strong authorship. The text, at any rate, may hold specific clues that prompt us to draw such a connection.

For instance, the obsession with letters and with spelling, prominent throughout the chapter, is remarkable in this respect, as is its engagement with numbers and addition. When Castorp asks Holger how long he is to stay in the mountain sanatorium, he receives the cryptic answer to go 'slanting through his room' (*MM* 665), in German 'quer durch sein Zimmer' (*Zb* 1008). As it turns out, Holger is instructing him to draw the *Quersumme* of his room number, i.e. the sum of digits; Castorp's room number being 34, the answer is that he will stay for seven years. Along these lines, engaging in the alchemy of letters and the cabbalistic play of numbers, we might search this secret circle for occult literary identifications. We might note, therefore, that Holger's name and George's both contain the same number of letters, namely six, just like George's fist name *Stefan* – and like the enigmatically misspelled *Dichtr*: perhaps this is why one letter is missing. We further note that the name *Holger* contains all the letters needed for the name *George*, with two extra letters in addition, *H* perhaps for Hans and *L* for Ludovico (i.e. Settembrini). When we now turn to numbers and, following standard occult practice, assign number values to the letters according to their position in the alphabet (A is 1, B is 2, and so on), we can add the numbers in these names and realize that both *Holger* and *Stefan* come to the same sum, namely 65. Should these be hints for us to take, silent signposts to identify the lyric spirit Holger with the poet Stefan George, Weber's real-life model for his concept of charisma? Are we on to something serious in magic, poetry and modern authorship? Or are we simply playing a spurious and highly questionable game? It may need some *ingenium*, i.e. the special gift shared by a *genius* like the romantic author notion and by an *engineer* like Castorp, to decide this question.

*

Time to sum up. What is at stake, I argue, in both Shakespeare's *Tempest* and Mann's *Zauberberg* is the potency of poets, i.e. the force of literature to cast a spell, to enchant others and make a difference in the world by means of words. In both texts, this quest or question of verbal creation is cast in corresponding roles, which are staged – as in the history of authorship – in terms of conjuring and magic. In just this sense, Prospero has long been read as Shakespeare's self-portrait, and Thomas Mann is routinely referred to as 'der Zauberer', i.e. the wizard or the magus, by his family and many others beside. Mann had no need to invent this role, he found it – 'Er fand lieber, als daß er erfand' – because he always found his material rather than making it up, as cited at the outset. What Mann could find in Shakespeare's Prospero, then, is a model for art to perform effects, a magic fountain of inspired writing. What we can find in Shakespeare after reading Mann, however, is the insight that such a model of authorship is always already obsolete. Once it is formed and formulated in literary production, it can no longer be a real production. To view *The Tempest* from the critical viewpoint of *Der Zauberberg* makes us see that the one-time magus is no more, if it ever was, but continues to exist only as a figure of the past, in inverted commas, as it were, for us to consider.

Let us therefore finally consider the famous formula in which the foreword to *Der Zauberberg* describes the authorial narrator: 'rounding wizard of times gone by' (*MM* 1). In Lowe-Porter's English version, the phrase loses the grammatical register used in German: 'der raunende Beschwörer des Imperfekt' (*Zb* 9), literally the murmuring or muttering or mumbling conjuror of the Past Tense. The term for Past Tense is the Latin *Imperfekt*, cognate also perhaps with the imperfections that writing of the modern kind described here necessarily involves – as suggested earlier with the imperfect spelling of Holger's role as *Dichtr*. More to the point, grammatically 'der raunende Beschwörer des Imperfekt' is a genitive construction that allows several readings. In its most immediate, straightforward sense, it functions as a *genitivus objectivus*: the Past Tense, or the past, is being conjured up. But there are two other possibilities at least implied, namely a *genitivus instrumentalis* so as to say the Past Tense is the means of magic or the instrument of conjuring; and a *genitivus qualitatis* suggesting that the conjuror himself is of the past, characterized by the Past Tense – a distanced, legendary figure from wondrous isles or remote mountain regions surviving perhaps still in occult catacombs and secret circles, but otherwise extinct.

So if the poet-demiurge is gone – 'The kings of the old time are dead', according to Yeats's diagnosis in one of his earliest poems (1997: 5), so 'Words alone are certain good' – should we be calling him to life again? Should we even make the effort to try and revive his ghost, as in the George circle and their cult of the vatic poet-leader, a dangerous and doubtful model which might lead, as Mann saw with great clarity, towards a modern cult of charismatic *Führer* figures: in May 1939 he noted in his diary 'die Hitlerei des Georgewesens' (Marx 2006/07: 97-8) – highly questionable indeed. So if we better let the figure of this master-poet stay in his grave, may we still mourn his legendary powers? 'But the calling back of the dead, or the desirability of calling them back, was a ticklish matter, after all … What we call mourning for our dead is perhaps not so much grief at not being able to call them back as it is grief at not being able to want to do so' (*MM* 675).[18] This is what the narrator tells us at the point where the medium offers necromantic service. And this is what my double session set out to explore: a double reading of *The Tempest* and *Der Zauberberg* for their shared work of mourning, in precisely such a sense: not being able to want to revive dead author magic even while grieving for its former potency.

'O Rocky Voice / Shall we in that great night rejoice?' With this apostrophe Yeats concludes his anxious dialogue with 'Echo' (1997: 354), cited at the outset, a poetic gesture as if to summon, one last time, the power of his former words, an address to the absent like Prospero's final conjuring, an invocation, in Culler's terms, that becomes 'a figure of vocation' (1981: 157), or in Auden's terms a 'way of happening, a mouth' (1976: 197). 'Poetry makes nothing happen', Auden declares in his elegy on Yeats. In a modern age of crisis, what is left to us may just be to redefine this 'nothing' as the something which poetry does make happen, after all, by words, the 'airy nothing' to which poets, according to Shakespeare's Theseus, give a local habitation and a name. After Prospero breaks his staff, we see how he turns to us: we now have the word and hold the key to spell in our hands. After Castorp breaks the spell by turning on the light, he goes to Krokowski and demands the key to leave the room – quite possibly the key also to poetic potency. Castorp does not tell us, for he leaves the room without a word.

Notes

1 See the contributions presented, for instance, in Caughie (1990), Kleinschmidt (1998), Jannidis et al. (1999), Detering (2002), Berensmeyer et al. (2012).

2 Kurzke opens his relevant chapter on a telling note: 'Es folgt ein peinliches Kapitel. Wir verstehen das nicht, wir billigen es nicht. Es ist nur schwer vorstellbar, aber der soignierte Bürger Thomas Mann hat sich verstohlen zu okkultistischen Séancen geschlichen' (2001: 336).

3 At this point I would like to thank Christian Begemann for generously sharing his powerful research into ghosts with me, as part of our joint seminar in 2012/13, and for helpful discussions on the ideas of this chapter.

4 *Es war einer mehr im Zimmer, als vordem* (*Zb* 1032).

5 *Man versteht schon, daß wir von unserer Gatten- und Vaterschaft sprechen, vom Akt der Geburt, dem Ellys Ringen tatsächlich so unzweideutig und unverwechselbar glich, daß auch derjenige ihn wiedererkennen mußte, der ihn noch gar nicht kannte, wie der junge Hans Castorp, welcher also, da auch er dem Leben nicht ausgewichen war, diesen Akt voll organischer Mystik in solcher Gestalt kennenlernte, – in was für einer Gestalt! Und zu welchem Behufe! Und unter welchen Umständen!* (Zb 1026).

6 See the contribution by Alexander Honold in this volume.

7 Wellbery shows that terms like 'begetting' and 'conception', 'pregnancy' and 'birth', 'genealogy', 'fatherhood' and 'motherhood' have long marked a discursive field to plot theories of artistic or intellectual production and thus to negotiate the relationship between nature and culture (Wellbery 2002: 10).

8 See Taussig (1993:193–211) for an inspiring discussion of the phonograph and its mimetic/magic power.

9 For this argument, see my articles on Marlowe's tragedy, Döring (2006) and (2008).

10 I have pursued this question more fully elsewhere, see Döring (2013).

11 See Healy (2004).

12 See Bate (1993: 251–5) for a full analysis of this celebrated passage.

13 For the notion of 'strong' as opposed to 'weak' authorship, see Berensmeyer et al. (2012: 14).

14 See: 'Charisma is self-determined and sets its own limits. Its bearer seizes the task for which he is destined and demands that others obey and follow him by virtue of his mission. If those to whom he feels sent do not recognize him, his claim collapses' (Weber 1978: 1112–13).

15 *Der Bereich des Unterbewußtseins, 'okkult' dem eigentlichen Wortsinne nach, erweist sich sehr bald auch als okkult im engeren Sinn dieses Wortes und bildet eine der Quellen, woraus die Erscheinungen fließen, die man aushilfsweise so benennt. Das ist nicht alles. Wer im organischen Krankheitssymptom ein Werk aus dem bewußten Seelenleben verbannter und hysterisierter Affekte erblickt, der anerkennt die Schöpfermacht des Psychischen im Materiellen, – eine Macht, die man als zweite Quelle der magischen Phänomene anzusprechen gezwungen ist* (Zb 992).

16 *Es flüsterte ihr zu ... Es werde ihr zugeflüstert, was sie zu tun habe, leise aber ganz scharf und deutlich.* (Zb 995); *Fräulein Brand geheimen Gaben* (Zb 998).

17 *ein durch und durch überraschendes Gedicht* (Zb 1005); *'lyrischen' Improvisation* (Zb1006); *eine magische Dingheit; Seemist; Bucht des Insellandes; Ein aufgeschlagen Buch, ein Totenschädel und im Gestell, im leichtgefügten Rahmen das dünne Doppelhohlgebläse* (Zb 1005-6).

18 *[D]och bleibt die Rückkunft Verstorbener, das heißt: die Wünschbarkeit solcher Wiederkehr immer ein verwickeltes und heikles Ding ... und was wir Trauer nennen, ist vielleicht nicht sowohl der Schmerz über die Unmöglichkeit, unsere Toten ins Leben kehren zu sehen, als darüber, dies gar nicht wünschen zu können* (Zb 1024).

Works Cited

Auden, W. H., 1976. *Collected Poems*, ed. Edward Mendelson. London: Faber.

Baßler, Moritz, Bettina Gruber, Martina Wagner-Egelhaaf (eds), 2005. *Gespenster. Erscheinung – Medien – Theorien*. Würzburg: Könighausen & Neumann.

Bate, Jonathan, 1993. *Shakespeare and Ovid*. Oxford: Clarendon Press.

Begemann, Christian and David E. Wellbery (eds), 2002. *Kunst – Zeugung – Geburt. Theorien und Metaphern ästhetischer Produktion in der Neuzeit*. Freiburg: Rombach.

Berensmeyer, Ingo, Gert Buelens and Marysa Demoor, 2012. 'Autorship as Cultural Performance: New Perspectives in Authorship Studies', in *Zeitschrift für Anglistik und Amerikanistik* 60:1, pp. 5–29.

Caughie, John (ed.), 1990. *Theories of Authorship: A Reader*. London, New York: Routledge.

Culler, Jonathan, 1981. 'Apostrophe', in *The Pursuit of Signs*. London, New York: Routledge, pp. 149–71.

Curtius, Ernst Robert, 1993 [1948]. *Europäische Literatur und Lateinisches Mittelalter*. Tübingen, Basel: Francke.

Detering, Heinrich (ed.), 2002. *Autorschaft: Positionen und Revisionen*. Stuttgart: Metzler.

Döring, Tobias, 2006. 'Magic, Necromancy and Performance: Uses of Renaissance Knowledge in Marlowe's *Doctor Faustus*', in *Magic, Science, Technology, and Literature*, eds Jamila Mildorf, Hans Ulrich Seeber and Martin Windisch. Münster: LIT, pp. 39–55.

Döring, Tobias, 2008. '*Doctor Faustus* bricht auf', in *Theater im Aufbruch: Das europäische Drama der Frühen Neuzeit*, eds Roger Lüdeke and Virginia Richter. Tübingen: Niemeyer, pp. 41–55.

Döring, Tobias, 2013. 'Learning to charm: on the virtue of words and the forgetting of language in *The Tempest*', in *Critical and Cultural Transformations: Shakespeare's The Tempest – 1611 to the Present*, eds Tobias Döring and Virginia Mason Vaughan. REAL, vol. 29. Tübingen: Narr, pp. 99–114.

Eliot, George, 2001. *Adam Bede*, ed. Carol A. Martin. Oxford: Clarendon.

Evans, Anthony, 2012. 'The Undead Author: Spiritualism, Technology and Authorship', in *The Ashgate Research Companion to Nineteenth-Century Spiritualism and the Occult*, eds Tatiana Koutou and Sarah Willburn. Aldershot: Ashgate, pp. 55–78.

Goethe, Johann Wolfgang, 1986. *Faust. Der Tragödie erster und zweiter Teil. Urfaust*, ed. Erich Trunz. München: Beck.

Greene, Thomas M., 2005. *Poetry, Signs, and Magic*. Newark: University of Delaware Press.

Gundolf, Friedrich, 1914. *Shakespeare und der deutsche Geist*. Berlin: Georg Bondi.

Healy, Thomas, 2004. '*Doctor Faustus*', in *The Cambridge Companion to Christopher Marlowe*, ed. Patrick Cheney. Cambridge: Cambridge University Press, pp. 174–92.

Horn, Eva, 2011. 'Introduction', in *New German Critique* 114, 38: 3 [special issue: Narrating Charisma], pp. 1–16.

James I, 1969 [1597]. *Daemonologie*. Facsimile Reprint. Amsterdam, New York: Theatrum Orbis Terrarum. Da Capo Press.

Jannidis, Fotis, Gerhard Lauer, Matias Martinez and Simone Winko (eds), 1999. *Rückkehr des Autors: Zur Erneuerung eines umstrittenen Begriffs*. Tübingen: Niemeyer.

Karlauf, Thomas, 2007. *Stefan George. Die Entdeckung des Charisma*. München: Blessing.

Keilen, Sean, 2006. *Vulgar Eloquence: On the Renaissance Invention of English Literature*. New Haven: Yale University Press.

Kleinschmidt, Erich, 1998. *Autorschaft: Konzepte einer Theorie*. Tübingen, Basel: Francke.

Kurzke, Hermann, 2001. *Thomas Mann. Das Leben als Kunstwerk*. Frankfurt am Main: Fischer Taschenbuchverlag.

Maar, Michael, 1995. *Geister und Kunst: Neuigkeiten aus dem Zauberberg*. München: Hanser.

Mann, Thomas, 2002a [1924]. *Der Zauberberg*, ed. Michael Neumann. Große Kommentierte Frankfurter Ausgabe, vol. 5.1. Frankfurt am Main: S. Fischer. [*Zb*]

Mann, Thomas, 2002b. 'Bilse und ich', in *Essays I, 1893–1914*, ed. Heinrich Detering. Große Kommentierte Frankfurter Ausgabe, vol. 14.1. Frankfurt am Main: S. Fischer, pp. 93–111.

Mann, Thomas, 2002c. 'Okkulte Erlebnisse', in *Essays II, 1914–1926*, ed. Hermann Kurzke. Große Kommentierte Frankfurter Ausgabe, vol. 15.1. Frankfurt am Main: S. Fischer, pp. 611–52.

Mann, Thomas, 2011 [1924]. *The Magic Mountain*, trans. H. T. Lowe-Porter. London: Vintage. [*MM*]

Marlowe, Christopher, 2005. *Doctor Faustus*, ed. David Scott Kastan. New York: Norton.

Marx, Friedhelm, 2006/07. 'Der Heilige Stefan? Thomas Mann und Stefan George', in *George-Jahrbuch*, vol. 6, eds Wolfgang Braungart and Ute Oelmann. Tübingen: Niemeyer, pp. 80–99.

Shakespeare, William, 1999. *The Tempest*, eds Virginia Mason Vaughan and Alden T. Vaughan. The Arden Shakespeare, Third Series. London: Thomson Publishing.

Sidney, Philip, 1989. *A Critical Edition of the Major Works*, ed. Katherine Duncan-Jones. Oxford: Oxford University Press.

Taussig, Michael, 1993. *Mimesis and Alterity: A Particular History of the Senses*. London, New York: Routledge.

Thomas, Keith, 1973 [1971]. *Religion and the Decline of Magic*. Harmondsworth: Penguin.

Weber, Max, 1978. *Economy and Society. An Outline of Interpretive Sociology*, eds Guenther Roth and Claus Wittich, trans. Ephraim Fischoff, Talcott Parsons et al. Berkeley: University of California Press.

Wellbery, David E., 2002. 'Kunst – Zeugung – Geburt. Überlegungen zu einer anthropologischen Grundfrage', in *Kunst – Zeugung – Geburt. Theorien und Metaphern ästhetischer Produktion in der Neuzeit*, eds Christian Begemann and David E. Wellbery. Freiburg: Rombach, pp. 9–36.

Wright, Thomas, 1970 [1596]. *A Treatise, Shewing the Possibilitie and Convenience of the Reall Presence of Our Saviour in the Blessed Sacrament*. Antwerp: Facsimile Reprint: Menston: Scolar Press.

Yeats, W. B., 1997. The Poems, ed. Richard J. Finneran. *The Collected Works of W. B. Yeats*, vol. 1. New York: Scribner.

Five

'A dark exception among the
rule-abiding': Thomas Mann
and Othello
Friedhelm Marx

This chapter tracks the traces that Shakespeare's *Othello* left in Thomas
Mann's oeuvre. Before looking at some pertinent passages, I would
first like to reconstruct which actors Mann could have seen, or actually
saw, playing the title role in Munich or elsewhere. All we know of
Mann's visits to the theatre in his younger years derives exclusively
from letters on the subject, as he destroyed his diaries from this period.
Within these letters, only one single passage speaks of a performance
of *Othello* at Munich's Schauspielhaus:

> Concerning the theatre, there was not much going on. Matkowsky,
> who I saw as Othello at the Schauspielhaus shortly before I left,
> has certainly made a strong impression on me. He is 'old-school'
> – without speaking more beautifully than others for that matter –
> and often chooses to impress with gimmicks. But he has powerful
> means, showed a lot of psychological insight and definitely is a
> personality.
> (Thomas Mann to Paul Ehrenberg, 18 July 1901; Mann 2002a: 172)[1]

Later on, other Othello actors are added to the list: Ernst von Possart,
possibly Paul Wegener; finally, in the years of his American exile where
Mann develops a growing interest in Shakespeare while working on
his *Doktor Faustus*, there is Paul Robeson.[2] The documents would not
suggest that Mann took more particular interest in *Othello* than in any
other Shakespeare play, were it not for a striking hint from the year
1907. In his essay 'Das Theater als Tempel' ('The Theatre as Temple'),
itself an earlier version of the more comprehensive and poetologically

Fig. 1: Adalbert Matkowsky as Othello

important essay 'Versuch über das Theater' ('Essay on the Theatre'), Shakespeare's Othello makes an unhoped-for appearance as a character. The figure is not actually named here, but in the case of Mann – who likes to omit particularly the important and obvious names (such as Lübeck in *Buddenbrooks* or Nietzsche in *Doktor Faustus*) – this rather signifies a special distinction. The passage in question reads:

> Every true, large-scale character of stage and theatre is a symbol. Let's imagine the following poetic personage: A man, noble and passionate, but branded in some way and in his soul a dark exception among the rule-abiding, among 'the wealthy curled darlings of our nation'; noble as an exception, but base in his sufferance, lonely, excluded from happiness, from the dalliance of happiness, fully building on achievement. Good preconditions, everything to surpass the 'darlings' who have no need for achievement; good preconditions for greatness. And it is through a tough, strict, hard life that he becomes great, publicly performs glorious deeds, is decorated with honours for his merits, – and yet, in his soul he remains a dark exception, very proud as a man of accomplishment, but full of distrust in his own human side, and with no faith that anyone could ever love him. Then – a young woman steps into his life, a bright, sweet, noble creature. She loves him for everything he accomplished and suffered; she disdains all curled darlings and chooses him. His incredulous delight teaches him faith. She becomes his wife, and he is far from jealousy in their marriage. 'Since she had eyes and chose me!' She is his reconciliation with the world, his justification, his perfection; she embodies his human nobility. And now, by diabolical, whispered insinuations, this man is being slowly poisoned with the suspicion that his wife betrays him with some sleek, common fellow. Slowly, tormenting doubt devours his pride, his emerging faith in felicity. Doubt overpowers him; uncertainty grows on him; the bitter insight comes to him that no-one of his ilk can ever be certain, that he should never have built his life upon happiness and love and that, along with his faith in such happy love, his life now is destroyed. 'Why did I marry?' He breaks down; and the rest is chaos, murder and suicide. – Imagine this man and husband as the hero of a narrative composition. The novelist will not necessarily feel obligated to paint on his face the insignia of his nature with picturesque brushstrokes. On the contrary, he might rather find it especially appealing to create an emphatic and ironical contrast between the man's external appearance and his affective constitution, – it will probably seem more lifelike to him this way. But on stage, as a theatrical

personage, this psychological type is – a Moor; he is black, his special nature can be seen from the highest balcony as blackness, he is not a type anymore, he is a figure, a symbol, – the elevated representative of all those who are 'black' in some sense and who would do wise not to marry.

(Mann 2002b: 119-20)[3]

In this passage, a strong interest for Othello's psychology as a character is combined with the question what shape such an outsider, such an 'exception among the rule-abiding', among 'the wealthy curlèd darlings of our nation' (*Othello* 1.2.69), should adopt on stage. For Mann, it is necessarily *black*. The question *how* black Shakespeare's tragic hero should appear on stage, and whether he is black *at all*, has at the time long been an issue of debate. At least since the late seventeenth century, the varied history of *Othello* productions has been constantly accompanied by critical controversies around the credibility, and indeed the meaning, of Othello's designation as a 'Moor'.[4] As early as 1693, Thomas Rymer doubted whether a Moor, in the sense of black African, could possibly be a Venetian commander and husband to an aristocratic woman. In 1814, Edmund Kean first staged a performance of Othello as a Mauretanian, i.e. from the early modern Arab-Muslim world of Northern Africa and Spain, an interpretation which sparked a vigorous tradition of readings and stagings well beyond England and America. Georg Brandes, for instance, in his classic 1898 Shakespeare study, follows this interpretation:

With his customary adherence to his original, Shakespeare, like Cinthio, calls his protagonist a Moor; but it is quite unreasonable to suppose from this that he thought of him as a negro. It was, of course, inconceivable that a negro should attain the rank of general and admiral in the Service of the Venetian Republic; and Iago's mention of Mauritania as the country to which Othello intends to retire, shows plainly enough that the 'Moor' ought to be represented as an Arab. It is no argument against this that men who hate and envy him apply to him epithets that would befit a negro.

(Brandes 1898: 439)[5]

In his essay 'Versuch über das Theater', Mann incidentally joins this debate – topical also in Germany – on how to understand this character. For him, Othello must necessarily be *black* on the stage, not because Shakespeare's text may suggest or require it, but because theatre demands it. According to Mann, all truly theatrical acting and doing is symbolic. And he uses his 'Versuch über das Theater' not only to identify such symbolism as specific to the theatre but, at the same time, also to distance himself from it. The symbolism of the theatre, Mann suggests, inevitably entails solemnity, ceremony, finally ritual and consecration – as may well be observed in Richard Wagner. On stage, even the leitmotif becomes a monstrance: thus, theatre and church come close, the artist turns into a priest, the theatre into a temple.

As narrator and novelist, Mann distances himself from such theatrical art of the temple that, in passing, he also identifies with Wagner. To this art form, which clearly needs immediate, overpowering sensory impressions, he opposes the renouncement of the picturesque in narrative. Within the medium of narration, the inner and outer aspects of the type embodied in Othello can be brought into ironical contrast. Here, the figure of a dark exception among the rule-abiding need not adopt a black shape, for it can do without external demonstration.

This argument quite overrides the entire philological debate in modern Shakespeare and *Othello* studies, which Mann is likely to have known through Brandes and others. Mann playfully imagines Othello as a part in narrative, because as type and character Othello evidently interests him: he functions both in the familiar narrative constellation of the artist figure in conflict with bourgeois society and as a mirror figure for Mann's biographical predicament.

Heinrich Detering (2005) has strongly made this point. Doubtless, Mann's own wedding to Katia Pringsheim in 1905 informs the subtext of his *Othello* reading. This attempt to 'give oneself a constitution', as he said in a letter to his brother Heinrich (17 January 1906, Mann 2002a: 340), resonates with the Shakespeare play, although Mann's union does not end as bloodily as Othello's brief happiness. In marrying Katia Pringsheim, Thomas Mann married something like a princess, a 'sweet, distinguished creature',[6] and his letters of the time convey a sense that he might actually have distrusted this unexpected marriage bliss. By the act of marrying, he exchanges his own artistic life of dark exceptionality for love and happiness – and he might have asked himself soon after whether this happiness was conducive to his artistic vocation. But that is not of interest here. Personal camouflage apart, Othello's blackness, according to Detering, acquires in this essay the status of a 'parable-like, universal formula for the outsider's existence per se' (2005: 12).[7] And indeed, Mann's early works contain quite a few dark outsiders among the rule-abiding: Othello's brothers, as it were – more of whom anon.

Let us first look at the way Mann's understanding of Othello develops and is received by his contemporaries. Direct reactions after 1907, when the essay was first published, are not known. Only when 'Versuch über das Theater' was reprinted in a 1921 collection entitled *Rede und Antwort (Statement and Response)*[8] did it provoke protest. In his article 'Thomas Manns Othello' published in the *Berliner Tageblatt und Handels-Zeitung* on 8 December 1921, writer and theatre critic Friedrich Michael addresses Mann's Othello reading – and dismisses it on grounds of philological arguments. Michael refers, among other things, to Shakespeare's own source, Giraldi Cinthio's novella, where the protagonist is already 'a Moor who plays the part later called Othello by Shakespeare' (*Berliner Tageblatt und Handels-Zeitung*, 8 December 1921).[9] According to Michael, then, it is not the theatre that made Othello a Moor (in the sense of black African), but the subject matter. The fact that Mann in turn rejects Michael's objections in a letter shows how much his own Othello reading means to him. On 20 December 1921, he replies:

> Dear Dr Michael,
> What you say is quite beyond contradiction, but still I cannot concede that the passage in question from the 'Versuch' is actually flawed. Its concern is not Shakespeare himself, and what he might possibly have thought or desired, but, in an impersonal sense, 'the Theatre', which precisely exposes this type, as I described it, as a Moor [*Mohr*]. This is also why it is utterly pedantic rationalism on Mr Harden's part when he assures us this chivalric Othello must not be a Moor [*Mohr*], but a Mauretanian [*Maure*]. Ridiculous. As if Shakespeare intended to present a race study. His Othello simply is a royal fairy-tale Moor [*Märchen-Mohr*], quite a fantastic breed.
>
> (Mann 2004a: 416)[10]

The letter indicates that in the meantime, Mann has apparently studied Maximilian Harden's Othello interpretation, i.e. two longer essays which Harden published (on the occasion of Jeßner's new staging of the play at the Berlin Schauspielhaus on 11 November 1921, starring Kortner as Othello, Hortmann 2001: 73–81) on 26 November and 3 December 1921 in his journal *Die Zukunft*.[11] There, Harden formulated a vehement polemic against Othello's black theatrical presence, using completely different arguments – without, however, critically referring to Mann's Othello reading. Like Brandes before him, Harden states Othello is not 'black (never would it [i.e. the city of Venice] yield the power of command to a Negro), but a Mauretanian African from the Mediterranean' (Harden 1921b: 238).[12] At the same time, he criticizes the increasingly drastic practices of theatre productions in recent years and decades:

> Fire and brimstone upon our Globe Theatre, when my mime ruins the commander ethnologically, body and spirit of a guileless

nature, grand in simplicity, and when he presents the groundlings with the howls, growls, sweat of a Negro. Whose acting, children, is ridiculously bad.

(Harden 1921b: 239–40)[13]

Harden carries on in his polemic against the practice that:

our Nigger Othellos grunt, roar, growl, hammer their ragged grimy breast with their fists, sweating for applause with ape-like leaps and exalted tragedicism, or grope the woman like a lecherous Congo fellow grasps his harlot in the brothel, who's greedily gasping for his damp.

(ibid.: 240–1)[14]

More specifically, he criticizes the 'grossly falsifying performance of the Senegalese Negro Ira Aldridge' (Harden 1921a: 264) and Max Reinhardt's *Othello* production, in which Albert Bassermann endowed the character 'with all kinds of Nigger attributes and submitted the audience to the torture of overdone screaming, a fearfully cracking voice, and creaking sound-crunching' (ibid.).[15]

For Thomas Mann, as we have seen, Harden's philological arguments in this debate are 'rationalist' in a negative sense, i.e. pedantic, ultimately ridiculous: 'as if Shakespeare intended to present a race study' (Mann 2004a: 416).[16] His irritation, when faced with Harden's preference for the *Mauretanian* Othello [*Maure*], however, makes him overlook the fact that this critic's *Othello* reading is actually quite close to his own. They converge in their understanding of what causes the catastrophe. Harden writes:

what seals Othello's fate is that he descended into this bourgeoisie with no intention of integrating. Race is just a costume here that helps identify him as a child of wild and free Nature, as a soul of vaster spaces and more sudden tempests; it is only an instrument to strengthen the external power of the image and the internal effectiveness of this special process.

(Harden 1921b: 239)[17]

Just like Mann, Harden reads Shakespeare's Othello as the type of an outsider who attempts in vain to enter bourgeois society whose rules, however, he does not want to accept. It is exactly this interpretative formula that Mann develops as early as 1907 and that raises his interest for Othello. For him, Shakespeare's protagonist is a 'dark exception among the rule-abiding' (Mann 2002b: 119): passionate and suffering, distinguished and branded, suspicious towards happiness, love and

Fig. 2: Ira Aldridge as Othello

all kinds of bourgeois order, that is to say, just such an artist figure as Thomas Mann has variously drawn and shown it in his works up to this time.[18] Friedrich Michael already pointed out this aspect in his 1921 article on 'Thomas Manns Othello'; his main intention was less to launch a philological critique than to argue that the central theme of Mann's own fiction can be identified in Mann's Othello reading. Here is the final paragraph of Michael's article:

Fig. 3: Albert Bassermann as Othello. Photographer: Hans Böhm, Berlin. Image held by The Kunst Historisches Museum

But these lines are not written pedantically to point out a mistake. The quoted passage rather contains one sentence that makes this whole flaw – if I may call it that – particularly dear to me. After Thomas Mann has analysed Othello's character, and before he speaks of his appearance on stage, he says: 'Imagine this man and husband as hero of a narrative composition. The novelist will not necessarily feel obligated to paint on his face the insignia of his nature with picturesque brushstrokes. On the contrary, he might rather find it especially appealing to create an emphatic and ironical contrast between the man's external appearance and his affective constitution, – it will probably seem more lifelike to him this way.'

What is this? Well, it is not only the rhyme scheme of the yet unwritten, and certainly not to be expected composition: 'Othello' by Thomas Mann, but the often varied and ever newly captivating main theme of this poet and his art in general. Ironical contrast – does that bring 'Luischen' to mind, to name just one character? Does it bring to mind the anecdote about the hero of this early novella, the violent encounter with a 'rude' serviceman, who ran over his foot with a hand cart – and the person harmed does not slap him, does not tackle him, oh no! This hero rather took off his hat and stammered: 'Forgive me, Sir!' And what did he look like, Jacoby, the advocate? A tiny, skinny, intimidated manikin, right? But it was 'a real colossus of a man!' This is Thomas Mann's 'Othello', the 'Othello' of the novelist. And his 'Versuch über das Theater' is, like everything he wrote and that is now rising in front of us in his 'Complete Works', a commitment to his art. Even if he is mistaken in this matter, he is right for himself, and it is precisely the consequence and certainty of his stance that continuously command our respect anew, or even more: our love.

(1921: 2)[19]

This insight into Mann's early oeuvre is as sharp as it is surprising. According to Michael, the 1907 Othello passage in 'Versuch über das Theater' highlights 'the main theme of this artist and his art in general' (*Berliner Tageblatt und Handels-Zeitung*, 8 December 1921).[20] Evidently, it is just this tension between the outsider's existence and bourgeois society that Mann is interested in and that underlies Harden's Othello reading fifteen years later – different though that is in focus – just as well. Mann sees Shakespeare's Othello as an artist figure and, as such, eminently suitable for the narrator and novelist. And indeed, just as Michael points it out, there are already many 'brothers' to Othello in his work – even if the name is nowhere actually mentioned.

Detering has unfolded the poetological implications of Mann's Othello reading with great precision. In his 2005 study *'Juden, Frauen und Litteraten'. Zu einer Denkfigur beim jungen Thomas Mann*, Mann's autobiographically transparent Othello reading is the starting point for describing and discussing Mann's poetics of the stigma. What 'Versuch über das Theater' illustrates by taking Othello as an example pervades, according to Detering, all of Mann's early oeuvre, where he incessantly tests and varies different ways to determine the relationship between outsiderdom and literature. On the one hand, there are the 'sleek and common fellows', 'the rich, curly darlings of our nation', the favourites of life. On the other, there are those that are somehow different, the strangers, the stamped, but also with a stamp of excellence, who seem stigmatized by a mark 'which brands the one that wears it as an outsider' (Detering 2005: 16).[21]

Based upon this observation, we can analyse the medial or generic difference between theatre and narrative prose in more detail, a difference that Mann brings into play in his essay. Whatever staging he had in mind in 1907 when he distanced himself as a novelist from Othello's obtrusive blackness as the immediate symbolism of outsiderdom, subsequent productions in following years, steeped in the aesthetics of expressionism, rather intensified such contrasts. Siegfried Jacobsohn comments on Max Reinhardt's 1917 *Othello* at the Schaubühne Berlin, with Paul Wegener in the title role:

Matkowski was a Mauretanian [*Maure*], Rossi a Moor [*Mohr*], Bassermann a Negro [*Neger*]. Wegener is a nigger [*Nigger*], stuck in animality by the legs, his head, not his mind, towering high above humankind, who will bring him down. He has crisp hair and pouty lips, but uses the solemn gestures, the ceremonial bows of his native country, and, in the commotion of pain, its native noises: shouting 'Doreolero' or something of the sort.

(Jacobsohn 2005: 145)[22]

Mann's Othello – his Othello as the character of a novel, a narrative – would not appear this obviously black, as black as stage Othellos, in his view, must be. His 'Versuch über das Theater' ascribes to the theatre symbolic, emblematic, visually apparent qualities which, in the worst case, lead to a catholicization, so to speak, of the theatre, where consecration, ceremony or monstrance come into play. This point is critically targeted at Richard Wagner's temple theatre and the institution of the Bayreuth festival. Mann's critique of the stage attacks its immediateness, its overload of theatrical sensuality. Twenty years later, Mann will extend this judgement to the new medium of film which, because of its sensory immediacy, seems almost artless to him.

When compared with competing media, be it theatre or later film, narrative composition appears by far more reserved, distanced, 'more lifelike'. At least, this holds for Thomas Mann's own narrative works where the stigma of the outsider is never as immediately recognizable as on stage. From time to time we may find corporeal signs of outsiderdom, like little Herr Friedemann's hump (in the novella named after its protagonist), but they still allow for a bourgeois existence. The actual

Fig. 4: Paul Wegener as Othello. Image held by the Frankfurt University Library (Universitätsbibliothek Johann Christian Senckenberg); Source: S36_F07193.

stigma is reflected and realized in the characters' interior. Whoever constitutes an exception from the rule-abiding and the favourites of life in Mann's early oeuvre can be recognized, above all, by his peers, by the ones equally branded on the inside. I would like to illustrate this with a glance at the 1903 novella *Tonio Kröger*. True, Tonio Kröger considers himself, just like every artist, the opposite of a 'proper, healthy, decent human being' (Mann 1998: 159),[23] but that is why he rejects eccentric clothing:

> Would you like me to be running around in a torn velvet jacket or a red silk waistcoat? [Tonio Kröger asks his girlfriend Lisaveta Ivanovna.] As an artist I'm already enough of an adventurer in my inner life. So far as outward appearances are concerned one should dress decently, damn it, and behave like a respectable citizen ...
>
> (Mann 1998: 157)[24]

He estimates that the inner adventurousness of the artist leads to the others's sensitivity for the brand, the 'sign on [his] brow'. In the course of the conversation he elaborates this point:

> Literature isn't a profession at all, I'll have you know – it's a curse. And when do we first discover that this curse has come upon us? At a terribly early age. An age when by rights one should still be living at peace and harmony with God and the world. You begin to feel that you are a marked man, mysteriously different from other people, from ordinary normal folk; a gulf of irony, of scepticism, of antagonism, of awareness, of sensibility, is fixed between you and your fellow men – it gets deeper and deeper, it isolates you from them, and in the end all communication with them becomes impossible. What a fate! Always supposing, of course, that you still have enough feeling, enough *love* left in your heart to know how appalling it is ... You develop an exacerbated self-consciousness, because you are well aware of being marked out among thousands by a sign on your brow which no one fails to notice ... A real artist is not one who has taken up art as his profession, but a man predestined and foredoomed to it; and such an artist can be picked out from a crowd by anyone with the slightest perspicacity. You can read in his face that he is a man apart, a man who does not belong, who feels that he is recognized and is being watched; there is somehow an air of royalty about him and at the same time an air of embarrassment. A prince walking incognito among the people wears a rather similar expression. But the incognito doesn't work, Lisaveta! Disguise

yourself, put on civilian costume, dress up like an attaché or a guards lieutenant on leave – you will hardly have raised your eyes and uttered a word before everyone will know that you are not a human being but something strange, something alien, something different …

(ibid.: 159–60)[25]

This self-assessment reveals Tonio Kröger as Othello's brother, if we read Othello – with Mann – as an artist figure. They are both outsiders; they are marked, marked as excellent, and they are dependent on their own achievement. In the medium of narrative, however, outsiderdom is not externally visible. As protagonist, Tonio Kröger bears a mark of strangeness: his first name. But it is balanced by his surname, his father's legacy. Only parts of him are strange and non-bourgeois, and his bourgeois dress code contributes to his being nowhere immediately recognized as an artist and a stranger. Clearly, Tonio Kröger's claim that no one can possibly miss the sign on his brow is refuted in the novella. Not only Lisaveta's answer shows it: 'And in any case you know very well that it is not necessary to take such a view of things as you are taking' (ibid.: 162).[26] But also the further course of the plot is indicative, the episode, for instance, in which Tonio Kröger is temporarily treated as a suspect in his hometown during his northbound travel, and is being interrogated. Obviously, he has been confused with a fraudster on the run who has also decided to get away from Munich to Denmark.

'Hm!' said the policeman. 'And you allege that you are not identical with an individial of the name of –' He said 'individial', and proceeded to spell out from the complicated document a highly intricate and romantic name which seemed to have been bizarrely compounded from the languages of various races; Tonio Kröger had no sooner heard it than he had forgotten it. 'An individial', the policeman continued, 'of unknown parentage and dubious domicile, who is wanted by the Munich police in connection with various frauds and other offences and is probably trying to escape to Denmark?'

(ibid.: 176)[27]

Tonio Kröger does not invoke his last name, or his well-known family, in this embarrassing situation, because he internally believes this institutional suspicion against him to be in some way justified.[28] The custodians of law and order, however, have not identified him by means of some sign on his forehead. Within the novella only those are able to recognize this sign who are themselves likewise branded in this imaginary sense, who are likewise dissociated from the favourites of life.

Tonio Kröger is not an isolated case. Mann's rather idiosyncratic 1907 interpretation of Othello sheds a light on his own literary triangulation of the relationship between outsider existence, art and bourgeois order. In his 'Versuch über das Theater' Shakespeare's Othello holds up the mirror to his own artistic way of life and is placed in elective affinity to the numerous artists of his own oeuvre, who all feel separated from the 'rule-abiding' by a 'sign on [the] forehead'. Unlike Othello, however, they almost always bear the sign of their exceptionality on the inside, so that only their especially perceptive peers, equally marked, can see the brand. As the protagonist of a novel or narrative, Thomas Mann's Othello would not be black or otherwise exotically different. This can be perceived as a conscious poetological choice in favour of a narrative likeness to life and against all too obtrusive theatrical sensuality – even where the eccentric expressionist *Othello* stagings are still to come. In his 'Versuch über das Theater', at any rate, the ironical novelist attempts to take a stand against the dramatist's fixation on stage symbolism, trying to justify his choice to renounce radical emblems of strangeness.

Thomas Mann's Othello is white.

Translated from German by Elisa Leroy and Johannes Ungelenk

Notes

1 *Was das Schauspiel angeht, so war nicht viel los. Matkowsky, den ich kurz vor meiner Abreise im Schauspielhaus als Othello sah, hat mir freilich starken Eindruck gemacht. Er ist ja 'alte Schule' – ohne daß er deshalb besonders schön spräche – und wirkt oft mit Mätzchen. Aber er hat gewaltige Mittel, zeigte viel psychologische Einsicht und ist entschieden eine Persönlichkeit* (Thomas Mann to Paul Ehrenberg, 18 July 1901; Mann 2002a: 172). All translations from German articles and letters cited here are by Elisa Leroy and Johannes Ungelenk, unless otherwise indicated.

2 Cf. Thomas Mann's own 1949 essay *Die Entstehung des Doktor Faustus* (*The Genesis of Doctor Faustus*).

3 *Jede rechte Bühnen- und Schaugestalt großen Stils ist ein Sinnbild. Man denke sich den folgenden dichterischen Charakter. Ein Mann, edel und leiden-schaftlich, aber auf irgend eine Weise gezeichnet und in seinem Gemüt eine dunkle Ausnahme unter den Regelrechten, unter 'des Volkes reichen, lockigen Lieblingen'; vornehm als Ausnahme, aber unvornehm als Leidender, einsam, ausgeschlossen vom Glücke, von der Bummelei des Glücks und ganz und gar auf die Leistung gestellt. Gute Bedingungen, das alles, um die 'Lieblinge' zu überflügeln, welche die Leistung nicht nötig haben; gute Bedingungen zur Größe. Und in einem harten, strengen und schweren Leben wird er groß, verrichtet öffentlich ruhmvolle Dinge, wird mit Ehren geschmückt für seine Verdienste,*

– bleibt aber in seinem Gemüt eine dunkle Ausnahme, sehr stolz als ein Mann der Leistung, aber voller Mißtrauen in sein menschliches Teil und ohne Glauben daran, daß man ihn lieben könne. Da tritt ein junges Weib in sein Leben, ein lichtes, süßes, vornehmes Geschöpf. Sie liebt ihn um deswillen, was er tat und litt, sie verschmäht alle lockigen Lieblinge und erwählt ihn. Sein ungläubiges Entzücken lernt den Glauben. Sie wird seine Frau, und er ist in der Ehe fern von Eifersucht. 'Sie hatte Augen ja und wählte mich!' Sie ist seine Versöhnung mit der Welt, seine Rechtfertigung, seine Vollendung, sie ist sein menschlicher Adel in Person. Und nun wird durch eine teuflische Ohrenbläserei dieser Mann langsam mit dem Verdacht vergiftet, daß sein Weib ihn mit irgend einem glatten und gewöhnlichen Burschen hintergehe. Langsam, unter Qualen zerfrißt der Zweifel seinen Stolz, seinen jungen Glauben an das Glück. Er ist dem Zweifel nicht gewachsen, er ist nicht sicher, die bittere Erkenntnis stellt sich ein, daß seinesgleichen nie sicher sein kann, daß er sein Leben niemals auf Glück und Liebe hätte gründen dürfen und daß mit dem Glauben an dieses Liebesglück nun auch sein Leben vernichtet ist. 'Warum vermählt' ich mich?!' Er bricht zusammen; und der Rest ist das Chaos, ist Mord und Selbstmord. – Man denke sich diesen Mann und Gatten als Helden einer erzählenden Dichtung. Der Romandichter wird sich nicht unbedingt genötigt fühlen, der Figur die Abzeichen ihrer Wesensart mit pittoresken Strichen ins Gesicht zu malen. Im Gegenteil wird er vielleicht einen besonderen Reiz darin finden, das Äußere des Mannes in einen betonten ironischen Gegensatz zu seiner seelischen Verfassung zu bringen, – so wird es ihn vielleicht lebenswahrscheinlicher dünken. Auf der Bühne aber, als Schaugestalt, ist dieser psychologische Typus – ein Mohr; er ist schwarz, seine besondere Art ist auf der höchsten Galerie als Schwärze sichtbar, er ist kein Typus mehr, er ist ein Sinnbild, ein Symbol, – der erhöhte Statthalter all derer, welche in irgend einem Sinne 'schwarz' sind und darum nicht klug tun, sich zu vermählen … (Mann 2002b: 119–20). The text of 'Das Theater als Tempel' supposedly originated independently and first appeared in the Berlin newspaper *Der Morgen*, 26 June 1907 (Mann 1907); it was immediately afterwards included in the essay 'Versuch über das Theater' (Mann 2002d).

4   For the historical and cultural implications of this contested term, see Vaughan (1997) and Neil (2006).

5   *Mit gewöhnlicher Folgsamkeit nennt Shakespeare gerade wie Cinthio die Hauptperson einen Mohren. Aber es ist ganz ungereimt deshalb anzunehmen, er habe sich ihn als Neger vorgestellt. Selbstverständlich ist es undenkbar, dass ein Neger einen Posten als Feldherr oder Admiral im Dienste der Republik Venedig hätte erlangen können. Auch zeigt Jago's Äußerung, Othello wolle sich nach Mauretanien zurückziehen, deutlich genug, dass er als Maure, d.h. als Araber gespielt werden muss. Es streitet keinesfalls gegen diese Auffassung, dass Männer, die ihn hassen und beneiden, ihn in ihrer Erbitterung mit Bezeichnungen stempeln, die auf einen Neger passen könnten* (Brandes 1904: 618).

6   *eine Verfassung zu geben* (Mann 2002a: 340); *süßes, vornehmes Geschöpf* ('Versuch über das Theater', 2002d: 119).

7   *zur gleichnishaft-universellen Formel des Außenseiterdaseins schlechthin* (Detering 2005: 12).

8   Concerning the revision of 'Versuch über das Theater' for the collection *Rede und Antwort* cf. Mann 2002c: 173–4; in July 1921 the chapter 'Das

Theater als Tempel' was republished separately in the *Rede und Antwort* version in the journal *Weimarer Blätter*.

9   *ein Mohr den von Shakespeare so genannten Othello spielt* (*Berliner Tageblatt und Handels-Zeitung*, 8 December 1921). Cf. Mann 2004a: 859–60: the Berlin writer, theatre critic and co-editor of the journal *Das Deutsche Buch* (1921–31) Friedrich Michael wrote numerous books and essays on the history of theatre. Thomas Mann supposedly knew him since 1920. On 10 April he thanked him the first time for works sent to him. In the years following (until 1932) Friedrich Michael wrote to Thomas Mann on a regular basis about the latter's works and sent him his books and essays, mainly treating theatre (cf. the letters of 10 January 1921, 31 May 1922, 11 August 1928 and 7 August 1932; Reg. 21/104, 22/49, 28/116 and 32/117).

10   *Sehr geehrter Herr Dr. Michael, Was Sie sagen, ist ja auch durchaus unwidersprechlich, und doch kann ich die betreffende Passage des 'Versuchs' als eigentlichen Schnitzer nicht anerkennen. Es handelt sich ja nicht um Shakespeare und um das, was er etwa gedacht und gewollt hat, sondern, unpersönlich, um das 'Theater', das eben diesen Typus, wie ich ihn nachzeichnete, als Mohren herausstellt. Darum ist es auch eine heillose rationalistische Pedanterie des Herrn Harden, wenn er versichert, der ritterliche Othello dürfe kein Mohr sein, er sei ein Maure. Lächerlich. Als ob Shakespeare eine Rassenstudie hätte liefern wollen. Sein Othello ist einfach ein königlicher Märchen-Mohr, durchaus phantastisch als Menschenschlag* (Mann 2004a: 416).

11   Cf. Maximilian Harden, 'Theater. Othello' (1921b) and 'Othello auf der Bühne' ('Othello on the stage') (1921a).

12   *nicht schwarz (nie liehe sie [die Stadt Venedig] einem Neger Befehlsgewalt), sondern maurischer Mittelmeerafrikaner* (Harden 1921b: 238).

13   *Pech und Schwefel aber auf unser Globus-Theater, wenn mein Mime den Feldherrn, den Körper und heldischen Geist argloser, in Schlichtheit großer Natur, mir ethnologisch verhunzt und den Parterregründlingen das Geheul, Gefauch, Geschwitz eines Negers vors Auge stellt. Der, Kinder, spielt ihn spottschlecht* (ibid.: 239–40).

14   *unsere Nigger-Othellos grunzten, brüllten, pfauchten, die zottige Russbrust mit Fausthämmern schlugen, mit Affensprung und Excentric-Tragirerei um Beifall schwitzten oder die Frau betätschelten wie ein angegeilter Kongokerl die gierig seinen Dunst schlürfende Bordelldirne* (ibid.: 240–1).

15   *robust fälschende Leistung des Senegalnegers Ira Aldridge* (Harden 1921a: 264); *allerlei Niggermerkmal anhing und die Qual gellen Überschreiens, ängstenden Tonkippens, knarriger Klangzerquetschung aufzwang* (ibid.).

16   *Als ob Shakespeare eine Rassenstudie hätte liefern wollen* (Mann 2004a: 416). The fact that Thomas Mann withdrew his contribution to the Festschrift on the occasion of Harden's birthday on 10 October 1921 at short notice belongs to the background of this irritation. He finally sent Harden the sketch of his 'little critical congratulation' – supposedly after the intervention of his mother-in-law – which led to the ultimate breaking-off of the relation (cf. Martin 1998: 151).

17   *ihm [Othello] wird zum Verhängniß, daß er, ohne den Willen, sich einzuordnen, in diese Bürgerlichkeit niederstieg. Rasse ist hier nur das Kleid, das ihn als das Kind wild-freier Natur, als die Seele weiterer Räume und jäherer Stürme*

erkennbar macht; ist nur ein Mittel, die äußere Bildkraft und innere Wirksamkeit des besonderen Vorgangs zu stärken (Harden 1921b: 239). Cf. also 'The man who has roamed the world with a shiny sword, of Mauretania or Venice, becomes sedentary; lowers himself from an untroubled free status into the limitations and bands of the bourgeoisie, whose law he nevertheless does not accept': *Der mit blankem Schwert, Mauretaniens oder Venedigs, durch die Welt getürmt ist, wird seßhaft; läßt sich aus sorglos freiem Stand in Schranken und Bande der Bürgerlichkeit herab, deren Gesetz er doch nicht anerkennt* (ibid.: 244). 'The unhoused without rest and repose lowers himself from an untroubled free status into bourgeoisie: and, nevertheless does not submit to the civil order Bürgerordnung]': *Der Unbehauste ohne Rast und Ruh ließ sich aus sorglos freiem Stand in Bürgerlichkeit herab: und fügt sich, dennoch, nicht in Bürgerordnung* (Harden 1921a: 261).

18 *dunkle Ausnahme unter den Regelrechten* (Mann 2004a: 119).

19 *Aber nicht, um kleinlich einen Irrtum festzustellen, werden diese Zeilen geschrieben. Es ist da vielmehr in der zitierten Stelle noch ein Satz, um des willen mir der ganze Irrtum – wenn ich es so nennen darf – lieb ist. Nachdem nämlich Thomas Mann den Charakter Othellos analysiert hat, und ehe er von seiner Bühnenerscheinung spricht, sagt er: 'Man denke sich diesen Mann und Gatten als Helden einer erzählenden Dichtung. Der Romandichter wird sich nicht unbedingt genötigt fühlen, der Figur die Abzeichen ihrer Wesensart mit pittoresken Strichen ins Gesicht zu malen. Im Gegenteil wird er vielleicht einen besonderen Reiz darin finden, das Äußere des Mannes in einen betonten, ironischen Gegensatz zu seiner seelischen Verfassung zu bringen, – so wird es ihn vielleicht lebenswahrscheinlicher dünken.'*

Was ist das? Nun, es ist nicht bloß der Reim einer ungeschriebenen, und gewiss nie zu erwartenden Dichtung: 'Othello' von Thomas Mann, sondern das oft variierte, uns stets neu fesselnde Grundthema dieses Dichters und seiner Kunst überhaupt. Der ironische Gegensatz – erinnert man sich da vielleicht an 'Luischen', um nur eine Figur zu nennen? Erinnert man sich jener Anekdote vom Helden dieser frühen Novelle, jenes Zusammenstoßes mit einem 'rüden' Dienstmann, der ihm mit einem Handwagen über den Fuß fuhr und dafür von dem Beschädigten – nicht geohrfeigt, nicht angelassen wurden, o nein! Dieser Held zog vielmehr den Hut und stammelte: 'Verzeihen Sie mir!' Und wie sah er aus, dieser Rechtsanwalt Jacoby? Ein kleines, dürres, verschüchtertes Männchen, wie? Aber er war 'ein wahrer Koloss von einem Mann'!

Das ist der 'Othello' Thomas Manns, der 'Othello' des Romanciers. Und sein 'Versuch über das Theater' ist wie alles, was er schrieb und was nun in den 'Gesammelten Werken' vor uns sich aufzubauen beginnt, Bekenntnis zu seiner Kunst. Auch wo er in der Sache irrt – für sich hat er recht, und eben die Geschlossenheit und Sicherheit seiner Haltung, sie ist's, die immer von neuem unsere Achtung mehr: unsere Liebe erobert (Michael 1921: 2).

20 *Grundthema dieses Dichters und seiner Kunst überhaupt* (Berliner Tageblatt und Handels-Zeitung, 8 December 1921).

21 *glatten und gewöhnlichen Burschen* (Detering 2005: 16); *des Volkes reiche ..., lockige ... Lieblinge ...* (ibid.); *die ihren Träger als Außenseiter brandmarkt* (ibid.).

22 *Matkowsky war ein Maure, Rossi ein Mohr, Bassermann ein Neger. Wegener ist ein Nigger, der mit den Beinen in der Tierheit steckengeblieben ist und mit*

*dem Haupt, nicht mit dem Kopf hoch über die Menschheit ragt, die ihn zur
Strecke bringt. Er hat krauses Haar und wulstige Lippen, aber die feierlichen
Armbewegungen, die zeremoniellen Verbeugungen seiner Heimat und im
Aufruhr des Schmerzes ihre Laute: 'Doreolero' oder ähnlich schreit er* (Jacobsohn
2005: 145).

23 *ein rechtschaffener, gesunder und anständiger Mensch* (Mann 2004b: 271).

24 *Wünschten Sie, daß ich in einer zerrissenen Sammetjacke oder einer rotseidenen
Weste umherliefe? Man ist als Künstler innerlich immer Abenteurer genug.
Äußerlich soll man sich gut anziehen, zum Teufel, und sich benehmen wie ein
anständiger Mensch...* (ibid.: 269).

25 *Die Litteratur ist überhaupt kein Beruf, sondern ein Fluch, – damit Sie's
wissen. Wann beginnt er fühlbar zu werden, dieser Fluch? Früh, schrecklich
früh. Zu einer Zeit, da man billig noch in Frieden und Eintracht mit Gott und
der Welt leben sollte. Sie fangen an, sich gezeichnet, sich in einem rätselhaften
Gegensatz zu den anderen, den Gewöhnlichen, den Ordentlichen zu fühlen, der
Abgrund von Ironie, Unglaube, Opposition, Erkenntnis, Gefühl, der Sie von
den Menschen trennt, klafft tiefer und tiefer, Sie sind einsam, und fortan giebt
es keine Verständigung mehr. Was für ein Schicksal! Gesetzt, daß das Herz
lebendig genug, liebevoll genug geblieben ist, es als furchtbar zu empfinden! ...
Ihr Selbstbewußtsein entzündet sich, weil Sie unter Tausenden das Zeichen an
Ihrer Stirne spüren und fühlen, daß es Niemandem entgeht. ... Einen Künstler,
einen wirklichen, nicht einen, dessen bürgerlicher Beruf die Kunst ist, sondern
einen vorbestimmten und verdammten, ersehen Sie mit geringem Scharfblick
aus einer Menschenmasse. Das Gefühl der Separation und Unzugehörigkeit,
des Erkannt- und Beobachtetseins, etwas zugleich Königliches und Verlegenes
ist in seinem Gesicht. In den Zügen eines Fürsten, der in Civil durch eine
Volksmenge schreitet, kann man etwas Ähnliches beobachten. Aber da hilft
kein Civil, Lisaweta! Verkleiden Sie sich, vermummen Sie sich, ziehen Sie sich
an wie ein Attaché oder ein Gardeleutnant in Urlaub: Sie werden kaum die
Augen aufzuschlagen und ein Wort zu sprechen brauchen, und jedermann wird
wissen, daß Sie kein Mensch sind, sondern irgend etwas Fremdes, Befremdendes,
Anderes...* (ibid.: 272–3).

26 *Übrigens wissen Sie sehr wohl, daß Sie die Dinge ansehen, wie sie nicht
notwendig angesehen zu werden brauchen...* (ibid.: 275).

27 *'Hm!' sagte der Polizist. 'Und Sie geben an, nicht identisch zu sein mit einem
Individium namens –' Er sagte 'Individium' und buchstabierte dann aus dem
bunt beschriebenen Papier einen ganz verzwickten und romantischen Namen
zusammen, der aus den Lauten verschiedener Rassen abenteuerlich gemischt
erschien, und den Tonio Kröger im nächsten Augenblick wieder vergessen
hatte. '– Welcher', fuhr er fort, 'von unbekannten Eltern und unbestimmter
Zuständigkeit wegen verschiedener Betrügereien und anderer Vergehen von der
Münchener Polizei verfolgt wird und sich wahrscheinlich auf der Flucht nach
Dänemark befindet?'* (ibid.: 293–4).

28 Cf. 'Should he make an end of the matter by disclosing who he was, by
informing Herr Seehase that he was not an adventurer of dubious domicile,
not born a gypsy in a green caravan, but the son of Consul Kröger, a member
of the Kröger family? No, he had no wish to say anything of the sort. And
were they not right, in a way, these representatives of bourgeois society? In

a certain sense he entirely agreed with them...' (Mann 1998: 176–7): *Sollte er der Sache ein Ende machen, indem er sich zu erkennen gab, indem er Herrn Seehaase eröffnete, daß er kein Hochstapler von unbestimmter Zuständigkeit sei, von Geburt kein Zigeuner im grünen Wagen, sondern der Sohn Konsul Krögers, aus der Familie der Kröger? Nein, er hatte keine Lust dazu. Und waren diese Männer der bürgerlichen Ordnung nicht im Grunde ein wenig im Recht? Gewissermaßen war er ganz einverstanden mit ihnen...* (Mann 2004b: 294).

Works Cited

Brandes, Georg, 1898. *William Shakespeare: A Critical Study*, 2 vols, trans. W. Archer. London: Heinemann.

Brandes, Georg, 1904. *Englische Persönlichkeiten. Teil 1–3: William Shakespeare*, in *Gesammelte Schriften*, vols 6–8. München: Langen.

Detering, Heinrich, 2005. *'Juden, Frauen und Litteraten' zu einer Denkfigur beim jungen Thomas Mann*. Frankfurt am Main: S. Fischer.

Harden, Maximilian, 1921a. 'Othello auf der Bühne', in *Die Zukunft* 30: 10, pp. 261–80.

Harden, Maximilian, 1921b. 'Theater. Othello', in *Die Zukunft* 30: 9, pp. 233–48.

Hortmann, Wilhelm, 1998. *Shakespeare on the German Stage. The Twentieth Century*. Cambridge: Cambridge University Press.

Hortmann, Wilhelm, 2001. *Shakespeare und das deutsche Theater im XX. Jahrhundert*. Berlin: Henschel.

Jacobsohn, Siegfried, 2005. *Theater – und Revolution? Gesammelte Schriften* vol. 3 (1915–26), eds Gunther Nickel and Alexander Weigel. Göttingen: Wallstein.

Mann, Thomas, 1907. 'Das Theater als Tempel', in *Der Morgen* 1: 7, pp. 214–7.

Mann, Thomas, 1921. 'Das Theater als Tempel', in *Weimarer Blätter* 3: 7, pp. 348–53.

Mann, Thomas, 1949. *Die Entstehung des Doktor Faustus*. Amsterdam: Bermann-Fischer.

Mann, Thomas, 1998 [1903]. 'Tonio Kröger', in *Death in Venice and other Stories*, trans. David Luke. London: Vintage, pp. 137–94.

Mann, Thomas, 2002a. *Briefe 1: 1889 –1913*, eds Thomas Sprecher, Hans R. Vaget, Cornelia Bernini. Große Kommentierte Frankfurter Ausgabe, vol. 21. Frankfurt am Main: S. Fischer.

Mann, Thomas, 2002b. 'Das Theater als Tempel', in *Essays 1: 1893–1914*, ed. Heinrich Detering. Große Kommentierte Frankfurter Ausgabe, vol. 14.1. Frankfurt am Main: S. Fischer, pp. 117–22.

Mann, Thomas, 2002c. *Essays 1: 1893–1914. Kommentar*, ed. Heinrich Detering. Große Kommentierte Frankfurter Ausgabe, vol. 14.2. Frankfurt am Main: S. Fischer.

Mann, Thomas, 2002d. 'Versuch über das Theater', in *Essays 1: 1893–1914*, ed. Heinrich Detering. Große Kommentierte Frankfurter Ausgabe, vol. 14.1. Frankfurt am Main: S. Fischer, pp. 123–68.

Mann, Thomas, 2004a. *Briefe 2: 1914–1923*, eds Thomas Sprecher, Hans R. Vaget, Cornelia Bernini. Große Kommentierte Frankfurter Ausgabe, vol. 22. Frankfurt am Main: S. Fischer.

Mann, Thomas, 2004b [1903]. 'Tonio Kröger', in *Frühe Erzählungen: 1893–1912*, ed. Terence J. Reed. Große Kommentierte Frankfurter Ausgabe, vol. 2.1. Frankfurt am Main: S. Fischer, pp. 243–318.

Martin, Ariane, 1998. 'Schwiegersohn und Schriftsteller: Thomas Mann in den Briefen Hedwig Pringsheims an Maximilian Harden', in *Thomas Mann Jahrbuch* 11, pp. 128–52.

Michael, Friedrich, 1921. 'Thomas Manns Othello.' *Berliner Tageblatt und Handels-Zeitung*, 8 December 1921.

Neil, Michael, 2006. 'Introduction', in *Othello. The Oxford Shakespeare*. Oxford: Oxford University Press, pp. 1–179.

Shakespeare, William, 2008. *The Tragedy of Othello the Moor of Venice*, in *The Norton Shakespeare*, eds Stephen Greenblatt et al. New York: Norton, pp. 2109–262.

Vaughan, Virginia Mason, 1997. *Othello: A Contextual History*. Cambridge: Cambridge University Press.

Six 'Who chooseth me must give and hazard all he hath': Shakespearean Overtones in Mann's *Der Tod in Venedig*
John T. Hamilton

The Merchant of Venice and *Death in Venice*, *Der Tod in Venedig* and *Der Kaufmann von Venedig* – the two titles alone, thus juxtaposed, are already provocative, suggesting some interrelation: some shared ground, some structural, thematic or motivic similarities. A comparison would appear to be justified, despite the historical, cultural and formal differences between the two works: between the end of the sixteenth century and the beginning of the twentieth, between English and German, between a theatrical comedy in verse and a tragic novella in prose, between a staged type (the *Merchant*) and a narrated allegory (*Death*), between being *of* Venice and being *in* Venice – all of which may ultimately shed light on the idea of being *between* in or of itself. Even when granting the nominal and prepositional differences – The *Merchant of* and The *Death in* Venice – the titles alone seem to entitle the reader to venture or hazard this comparison or thought experiment or, more precisely, this *hypothesis*, namely, that the two works bear some relation.

Allowance for this kind of comparatist approach invariably relies on a metaphor of *credit*. The meagre evidence of a relation between William Shakespeare's play and Thomas Mann's story is adduced as a deposit, which contracts the reading to pay off the loan and even to generate interest. For any hermeneutic speculation to yield profit, it is necessary to have faith in the enterprise, trusting that the interpretation will ultimately honour the fiduciary obligation. Hermes or Mercury, the god of crossing borders, the god of between-ness, the psychogogue who conducts souls from this world to the next, is also the god of commerce and interpretation, the patron of merchants and hermeneuts. Acting beneath this divine sponsorship, every hermeneut trades in mortgages; and by these mortgages, pledges compensation and profitability, even with his own life, his own flesh and blood – every mortgage is to some extent *un gage-mort*. Every hypothesis implies a potentially fatal *hypotheca*.

How credible, then, is the link between *Der Tod in Venedig* and *The Merchant of Venice*? What precisely would this hypothetical interrelation signify, what profit does it promise and what would be its value, if indeed it should be valid? To be sure, the proposed reading may after all be an interpretation of an interpretation. Insofar as the concepts of death and mercantilism share a hermetic source, it may be that Mann's novella already engages Shakespeare's play in some hermeneutic venture. We may ask, then, to what extent is Mann indebted to Shakespeare? What might be the terms of this debt? How was it secured and how might it be honoured?

*

A single sheet preserved in the Thomas Mann Archive in Zürich, dated circa 1905, bears the author's sketch for the layout of his library at home.[1] According to the plan, the top long shelf would hold German, English and Scandinavian works:

Deutsch, modern (Fontane, Hauptmann) | Shakespeare, Dickens, Englisch Eng | lisch Skandinavisch

What is immediately striking is that the name of Shakespeare, in addition to being placed in central position, is the only one underscored – a distinction shared with no other author listed on the plan, with the exception of Ibsen, who is found on the shelf directly below. It is understandable that, around 1905, Mann would have been particularly interested in dramatic texts, because it was in this year that he published his first and – as it would turn out – his last theatrical drama, *Fiorenza*. From the moment when he sent in the manuscript, just days before his wedding, Mann was deeply troubled by the play, which clearly tested his creative limits. Within weeks, after thanking his brother Heinrich for the wedding gifts, Mann confessed his anxiety:

> The play [*Fiorenza*] again caused an entirely unheard-of torment, and despite all precedents, this time I was mortally convinced [*zum Sterben überzeugt*] that the doubts with which I sent off the thick (much too thick) manuscript to Berlin were justified. Then, freed of the daily plague [*der täglichen Plage ledig*], I resigned myself. ... Since as early as *Tonio Kröger* I have allowed the

concepts 'Intellect' [*Geist*] and 'Art' [*Kunst*] to blur too much into each other. I had confused them and, in the play, set them hostilely against each other. That had led to this Solness-crash, this fiasco of endeavouring to fill an intellectual construction with life. About-face! Back to the naïveté of *Buddenbrooks*![2]

(2002a: 315)[3]

Fiorenza tormented its author because it rests on the intellectually sound and therefore artistically shaky ground of metaphysical positions, which may well support an ideal construct in the lofty regions of the mind but only by disdaining the life that swarms below. As Mann is willing to admit, his first major stab at the theatre all too rigorously – 'all too thickly' – proceeds by way of mercilessly inflexible positions, pitting the detached, moral critique of Girolamo Savonarola against the sensuous aestheticism of Lorenzo de' Medici's court. In brief, the play schematically sets the ascetic protocol of the 'Intellect' (*Geist*) against the dazzling allure of 'Art' (*Kunst*). In *Fiorenza*, Savonarola's Intellect is victorious over Lorenzo's Art; and it is precisely this victory that spells the death of Art.[4] Indeed, Mann's stark convictions in favour of Intellect, architectonically designed, now convinced him that he was poised, like Halvard Solness, Ibsen's master-builder, for a fatal fall. Although now 'freed [*ledig*] of the daily plague of writing', he already braces himself for performances and the harsh judgement they will presumably receive. The newlywed feels like he is 'single' (*ledig*), but his troubles are far from over.

Among the notes that made for a planned but never completed essay, to be entitled *Geist und Kunst*, Mann states the matter straightforwardly: 'Savonarola in "Fiorenza": Geist gegen Kunst' (Scherrer/Wysling 1967: 168).[5] As a representative of Spirit or Intellect, the austere monk of fifteenth-century Florence is associated with knowledge, criticism and Christian Neo-Platonism. This commitment to intellectual dualism, this capacity to make moral decisions and uphold them, links Savonarola emphatically to the pursuit of *literature*, which must resist the abysmal attractions of *art* and thereby abstain from the aestheticism, formalism and heathenism that are ascribed to Lorenzo's court. That Mann favours throughout Savonarola's ascetic ideals is fully attested in the play's composition. At the heart of Mann's position is his concern for the risk that he detected among artists of his own day, namely the risk of charlatanism, which is evinced most blatantly in the *Tristan* novella of 1903 with the depiction of the decadent aesthete, Detlev Spinell. The thorn in Mann's side is clearly the figure of Wagner, whose demagogic manipulation of the masses, grounded in theatrical flashiness and a general disdain for the critical distance afforded by literature, comes under direct attack in the notes for *Geist und Kunst.*[6] In *Fiorenza*, Savonarola vilifies Lorenzo's poets as working 'against the Intellect' (*wider den Geist*), their work being denounced as mere 'Augen- und Schaukunst' (1974, vol. 8: 1059–60). The critique is closely modelled on Nietzsche's objections voiced in *Der Fall Wagner*, yet the implications of Mann's reformulation are far from Nietzsche's general views on morality. In brief, whereas Nietzsche inveighs against Christian morality as an unhealthy system that renounces life and nourishes nihilism, Mann promotes Savonarola's literary austerity as a necessary moral corrective to aesthetic decadence.[7]

Having opted exclusively for cold intellectual reflection over the charming warmth of Art, for *Geist* over *Kunst*, the rookie playwright feared the worst. He realized that *Fiorenza*'s anti-Humanist, anti-Renaissance rhetoric would offend the art-loving bourgeoisie just as much as its strict dichotomization would exasperate the theatre critics. And his fears were in fact soon confirmed. In March 1906 Richard Schaukal, who early on ordained Mann as one of the most gifted and promising young writers in Germany, despairingly denounced *Fiorenza* as thin, poor, lifeless, 'simply literary' (*literarisch bis aufs Mark*, Schaukal 1969: 42); he singled out the tediously long monologues as 'soulless chatter' (*seelenloses Geredsel*, ibid.: 43) and recommended that the author restrict his work to novels and the novella, in which he clearly excelled, and thus avoid the theatre, where he just as clearly did not.

Again, Mann would have to agree. In the letter to Heinrich, he looks back on *Tonio Kröger*, written in 1901, which confused warm-blooded appeal of sensuous form (*Kunst*) and cold critical analysis (*Geist*). Midway through this novella, when the fatal attractions of beauty and form become particularly troubling, Tonio Kröger vehemently rejects his friend's suggestion that he should recuperate in Italy:

> I am indifferent to Italy to the point of despising it! It's a long time since I felt that I belonged there. Art, yes? Velvet-blue sky, hot wine and sweet sensuality ... In brief, I don't like it. I renounce. All that *bellezza* makes me nervous. I also can't stand all those frightfully vivacious people down there with their black bestial gaze. Those Romans [*Diese Romanen*] have no conscience in their eyes ... No, I'll make a short trip to Denmark.
>
> ...
>
> I want to stand on the battlements of Kronberg, where the 'Spirit' [*Geist*] came to Hamlet and brought anguish and death upon the poor, noble young men ...
>
> (2004: 281–2)[8]

The *Geist* or ghost of Shakespeare thus appears precisely at the moment when a moral stand must be asserted, when the alluring charm of the South must be resisted. The dangerous fascination of 'these Romans' (*diese Romanen*) – and also perhaps of certain kinds of 'novels' (*Romane*) – lie in a lack of moral conscience that belongs properly to the dramatic North. Ultimately, however, having fled in search of Shakespearean resolve, Tonio realizes that, although embodying two worlds, he belongs to neither. Tonio's failure to blend Northern intellect and Southern art – this resulting aporia, which closes the novella – apparently drove Mann to clarify the issues, to force Intellect free from Art in the dramatic form that Shakespeare had mastered. Accordingly, *Fiorenza* emphatically stages the triumph of *Geist* over *Kunst*. Yet, as we have seen, this violent gesture led, in turn, to an embarrassing 'fiasco' – to a deadly 'plague', like cholera, which threatened to precipitate the author's death. Well before the critics publicly announced Mann's fatal theatrical endeavour, the playwright himself was mourning a stillbirth.

All the same, despite the pestilential *Fiorenza*-fiasco, Mann was not a man who would allow self-pity to paralyse him for long. Having taken a position, he was determined to maintain it. An implicit argument fuels his 'Versuch über das Theater' ('Essay on the Theatre'), which he began drafting as the frightful reviews of his first play rolled in. His theatre essay is in fact an elaborate exercise in self-justification: it is not that his *Fiorenza* failed to meet the criteria of good theatre but rather that modern stagecraft was not capable of rising to the high literary, intellectual and moral standards of his work. As a popular spectacle, reeking of greasepaint and flaunting conventional décor, today's theatrical performances appeal to the uneducated, unsophisticated, non-literary masses. Although theatre 'makes concessions to literature' (2002b: 123), it is perfectly content to proceed without its moral insights. Consequently, contemporary drama is hardly dramatic at all, because it is committed to presenting characters that are simplified and flat, ready to stoop to the audience's intellectual torpor. In contrast, the development of true drama is to be found in the novel, a genre that boldly combines the subjective impulse of lyric and the objective drive of epic, producing figures that are 'more precise, more complete, more knowledgeable, more conscientious, more profound' (ibid.: 130).[9] If one still believes in drama, one should shy away from the playhouse and turn instead to literature, which better realizes drama's original vocation.

Mann reinforces his critique of modern theatre by summoning the authority of Shakespeare. To begin, he rehearses the argument formulated in Richard Wagner's *Oper und Drama*, which celebrates Shakespeare's genial capacity for transforming the folk material of

Romance into high art (ibid.: 134).[10] However, whereas Wagner typically sees his own musical drama as the epitome of what Shakespeare initiated, Mann – also typically – locates drama's true artistic consummation in novelistic narrative. Among his notes, Mann vilifies Wagner's contempt for 'mere literature' – that is, for literary texts not orchestrated with Wagner's own music. In Mann's view, Wagner's turn to the theatre, his insistent claim to have united Shakespeare and Beethoven, perilously enlists literature into the service of enticingly beautiful art (*Kunst*) and thereby jeopardizes literature's moral value. Mann's 'Versuch über das Theater' suggests that Wagnerism contributes to the decadence of the age, insofar as it purchases uncritical, artistic beauty at the expense of literature's penetrating insights and capacity for critical analysis. Wagner's art may be radiant, but not all that glisters is gold. On the contrary, today's theatre, including Bayreuth, has fallen far from its original Shakespearean ideal by choosing seductive beauty and superficial effects over literature's psychologically incisive approach.

With Shakespeare on his side, Mann sent his theatre essay in for publication on 7 May 1907, just days before the Frankfurt Schauspielhaus was to stage the premiere of *Fiorenza*. It is thus possible to read the theatre essay as a pre-emptive strike. Days before audiences in Frankfurt would complain about Mann's theatrical failure, the author could demonstrate how theatre itself has failed. Rather than drag himself to the Hessian capital for the performance, Mann decided instead to accompany his wife Katia for several weeks' vacation in Venice.

*

Throughout the decade that followed the massive and unexpected commercial success of *Buddenbrooks*, the now famous son of Lübeck's merchant-senator regarded his adopted positions as the very coin with which he must trade for continued creative viability. The central and emphatic position of Shakespeare in Mann's library, noted above, is emblematic of the English playwright's donation to the German writer's moral purse. Be that as it may, despite great effort and indefatigable resolve, Mann's investment in strong positions bore little profit of note. Many projects were proposed but eventually abandoned: *Maja*, a novel of manners set in contemporary Munich; a historical novel on Frederick the Great; and, as mentioned, the essay on *Geist und Kunst*, in which the author would settle all the pertinent aesthetic accounts. Then, with a pile of aborted projects on his desk, in the spring of 1911, unlike Tonio Kröger who had chosen the spirit of Hamlet's merciless Denmark over the fatal beauty of the art-saturated, sun-drenched

South, Mann once again ventured forth with his wife to the welcoming shores of Venice and returned with an idea for a novella that would venture much more.

Der Tod in Venedig boldly broaches the rather scandalous theme of an older man who risks everything for an infatuated bond with a beautiful boy. Although the name of Shakespeare nowhere appears in the work that Mann would come to describe as treating this 'daring if not impossible object' (2002a: 483),[11] the novella readily betrays close affinities to the Bard's most sustained reflections on risk-taking, bonds and exchange. Often considered in relation to the sonnets, *The Merchant of Venice* has long been read as evidence of Shakespeare's homoerotic tendencies, which is made to account for the inexplicable sadness that afflicts the merchant Antonio at the very head of the play:

> In sooth I know not why I am so sad.
> It wearies me, you say it wearies you;
> But how I caught it, found it, or came by it,
> What stuff 'tis made of, whereof it is born,
> I am to learn;
> And such a want-wit sadness makes of me
> That I have much ado to know myself.
> (1.1.1–7)[12]

Despite his explicit denials, it soon becomes clear that the root cause of Antonio's despondency is his emotional bond with the penniless Bassanio, who is planning to court Portia, the wealthy princess of Belmont. These vectors of triangulated desire consequently bind the bonds of friendship and marriage to the fiduciary bonds that make such unions possible.[13] Bassanio approaches Antonio for a loan to finance his courtship at Belmont. After conceding that he already owes his friend a great sum, Bassanio argues that risking further investment will bring greater return. To demonstrate, he recalls a story from his youth: how he was able to retrieve a lost arrow by shooting a second shaft in 'the selfsame way':

> In my school-days, when I had lost one shaft
> I shot his fellow of the selfsame flight
> The selfsame way, with more advisèd watch,
> To find the other forth; and by adventuring both
> I oft found both. I urge this childhood proof
> Because what follows is pure innocence.
> I owe you much, and like a wilful youth
> That which I owe is lost; but if you please
> To shoot another arrow that self way

Which you did shoot the first, I do not doubt,
As I will watch the aim, or to find both
Or bring your latter hazard back again
And thankfully rest debtor for the first.
(1.1.140–52)

Bassanio's conclusion, with which he hopes to persuade his friend: 'hazard' a second loan and you will redeem both. Antonio of course has already learned this core lesson; all his funds have been invested in merchant ventures across the globe. He therefore implores his friend to '[t]ry what [his] credit can in Venice do' (1.1.180), to use his good name to secure a loan from the Jewish usurer, Shylock, who himself must borrow the capital from the powerful Tubal. With Shakespeare, one good risk deserves another and another.

Thomas Mann's riskiest novella may have been further motivated by the contemporary biographical criticism of Shakespeare. Crucial in this regard is the work of Georg Brandes, the Danish and Jewish scholar, whose monumental study of Shakespeare, translated into German in 1895, was a decisive source for Mann, not least because of the work's decidedly Nietzschean flare. Indeed, Tonio Kröger's attraction to Denmark, inspired by the critical force of *Hamlet*, corresponds very specifically with Brandes' insightful reading of the tragedy.[14] For his reading of *The Merchant of Venice*, Brandes adduces the biographical context: Shakespeare turned to this comedy about property, exchange and false appearances precisely at the point in his life when he began to acquire land and applied for a coat-of-arms (1898, 1: 178–85). Tellingly, *Der Tod in Venedig* famously opens with an analogous depiction of Aschenbach, who is said to have recently acquired the coveted *particule de noblesse*. 'Gustav Aschenbach oder von Aschenbach' is a well-respected author of significant accomplishment, a cultural institution unto himself, and an obvious projection of who the thirty-five-year-old Thomas Mann might become when he reached the inverted age of fifty-three.

Accordingly, Aschenbach is credited for having completed all the works that Mann himself recently abandoned in frustration: the Maja novel and the novel on Frederick the Great, as well as the essay on *Geist und Kunst*. This success is due to Aschenbach's aptitude for discipline and self-control. Whereas Mann desperately struggled to find his position, oscillating between the blinding radiance of art and the reflective brilliance of critique, between becoming a poet (*Dichter*) or remaining a man of letters (*Literat*), Aschenbach discovered a way somehow to reconcile both demands by becoming a mature master (*Meister*)[15] who has learned to exchange his youthful scepticism, irony, and cynicism for difficult, honest work. Like Bassanio, he now brings '[g]ifts of rich value' (2.9.90) to his nation, but the splendid life that courts his nation's culture is, also like Bassanio's splendour, a life purchased on credit, still in debt to life's ultimate, final Creditor. A poet's immortality has always been but a euphemism for death.

Perhaps the most important intertextual link between Shakespeare's comedy and Mann's novella may be found in the former's famous episode of the three caskets, which could be read as an allegory of Aschenbach's achievements and consequently Mann's aspirations. Before Bassanio may have Portia's person and her purse, he must, like every suitor, participate in a contest set up by the princess's deceased father. Three caskets are on display in Belmont: one of gold, one of silver, and one of lead. Only one contains Portia's portrait and thus the prize. The first contestant, the Prince of Morocco, wrongly selects the casket of gold, whose inscription reads: 'Who chooseth me shall gain what many men desire' (2.7.5). Morocco fails to recall that he asked Portia not to judge his substance by his outward, sun-burnished appearance; and so, when the casket is opened, it reveals nothing but skeletal remains to which a note is appended: 'All that glisters is not gold' (2.7.65). The second suitor, the Prince of Aragon, opts for the silver casket, which states: 'Who chooseth me shall get as much as he deserves' (2.9.35). He makes his judgement on the basis of pride, that he is not one to 'be honorable / Without the stamp of merit' (2.9.37–8); but when the lid is removed, only a fool's portrait is discovered. Whereas Morocco acted negligently, ignoring the distinction between internal content and external form, Aragon pursued his moral convictions. Both therefore overlook the casket of lead, whose inscribed message is perhaps far too enigmatic: 'Who chooseth me must give and hazard all he hath.' Bassanio, who is already well schooled in the profitable lessons of venture, correctly chooses the base metal and finds his 'fortune' and his 'bliss' (3.2.136). Desire and pride lose what risk gains.

Eduard Stucken, the Berlin scholar and playwright, and one of Thomas Mann's literary acquaintances, linked the fable of the three caskets to archaic cults in his voluminous study of *Astral Myths*, published between 1896 and 1907. According to Stucken, the gold represents the Sun, the silver represents the Moon, and the lead represents the 'Bright Star of Youth' (*Sternenknabe*) (Stucken 1896–1907, 5: 655–6). The three caskets thereby rehearse a pattern prevalent across ancient mythology and Germanic folktales, including Cinderella or 'Aschenputtel', the poor but starred young maiden who catches the prince's eye. In *Der Tod in Venedig*, Mann subtly engages this constellation of motifs. In the first chapter, Aschenbach, like Aschenputtel herself, overtaxed by hard work, takes an afternoon stroll and wanders into a cemetery, where, like Shakespeare's Morocco, he is drawn to the 'symmetrically ordered inscriptions in gold letters' (2004b: 502).[16] He is torn from his reverie by the sudden appearance of a strange man who is standing 'in the portico' (*im Portikus*), a detail that may remind us of Belmont's princess. At any rate, the attraction of gold, reinforced by the classically beautiful form, inspires a *desire* to abandon his study and travel abroad. Across Mann's early work, the desire to go south, toward the sun, is linked to the appeal of art and a concomitant renunciation of literary detachment. However, before Aschenbach pursues his desire, we learn of the discipline of his strict writing habits, which, at least up to this point, have awarded him the honours that he somewhat arrogantly feels he has rightly deserved.

> He began his day early by splashing cold water on his chest and back; and then, a pair of tall wax candles in silver holders at the head of his manuscript, he spent two or three fervently consci- entious morning-hours offering up to art the powers he had gathered in sleep as a sacrifice.
>
> (ibid.: 510)[17]

Aligned with silver, the indoor candlelight, further linked to the shock of cold water, stands in contrast to the sun's golden warmth. Whereas the dazzling gold inscription sparked a *desire*, here the silvery light of reflection belongs to a system based on *merit*.

In Stucken's interpretation of the three caskets – a reading that Freud would explicitly adopt in his discussion of the narrative[18] – Mann could have found confirmation of the symbolic schemes that organized much of his early work. In these first stories, the glistening gold of *Kunst* is consistently linked to sunlit charm and opposed to the cold silver of *Geist*, which is linked to the moon. In *Gladius Dei* (1902), which clearly anticipates the tensions elaborated in *Fiorenza*, the gleaming surfaces blind the citizens of Munich to the seriousness of literature: literary journals are stuffed into coat pockets and remain unread; the bookshop window displays nothing but art books; and the young men, who lasciviously gawk at a revealing painting of the Madonna, blissfully make plans to go to the theatre. Mann frequently vilified his Bavarian neighbours for mistrusting literature as the antithesis of art, as a practice that presumably had little contact with real life. Only in Berlin, Mann notes, can one detect some literary sensibility, thanks to the influence of the Jewish population, the 'people of the Book' (Scherrer/ Wysling 1967: 157).[19]

The tension between the gleaming gold of art and the silvery incisiveness of critique motivates one of Mann's first publications, *Enttäuschung* (1896), written in the wake of his first escapade to Venice. Tellingly, the 'disappointment' or 'disillusionment' that disrupts enjoyment plays out on the Piazza San Marco beneath a full, silvery moon. Together, the solar, golden allure of *Kunst* and the lunar, silvery distance of *Geist*, comprise the two sides of the Apollonian coin, denoted by the god's harmonious lyre and penetrating bow, which Mann tellingly adopted as his own monogram. Yet, Apollo, the god of the lyre and the bow, the god of harmonious art and incisive critique, proves insufficient. As an avid reader of Nietzsche, Mann would realize that dealing exclusively with the cult of Apollo must ultimately pay homage to Dionysus, lest the author suffer the fate of Pentheus. If gold and silver – desire and merit, beauty and critique, *Kunst und Geist* – represent the tension that organizes the first phase of Mann's writing career, it is the hazardous lead that signals the breakthrough to the next phase, a phase linked to the floating city of Venice, to La Serenissima, which conceals underground the dark, lead-lined recesses of the *Piombi*.

In his reading of *The Merchant of Venice*, Brandes states that the fable of the three caskets may be derived from the Buddhist legends of India. And it is, of course, along the maddening path of the alien, Asiatic god, Dionysus, that Aschenbach will forget his indebtedness both to the shining gold of art and the reflective silver of critique, and instead plumbs the depths of his wild dreams, giving and hazarding all he has. Aschenbach's love for the Polish boy Tadzio has led him to disdain his position as master:

> The magisterial poise of our style is a lie and a farce, our fame and social position are an absurdity, the crowd's trust in us is altogether ridiculous, the use of art to educate the people and the youth, a daring undertaking that should be forbidden.
>
> (2004b: 589)[20]

The Apollonian coin with which Aschenbach had traded for his entire career is now exposed as devalued currency. The sunlit allure of art, tempered by laborious, pre-dawn discipline, blinds us to the fact that art is 'daring' (*gewagt*) – that it 'risks everything' (*alles wagt*) – and therefore should be 'forbidden'. Tadzio announces the promise and the threat that Shakespeare consigned to lead. In Schlegel's translation, 'Wer mich erwählt, der gibt und wagt sein alles dran' (Shakespeare 2010: 410).

For Aschenbach, Venice becomes the site of a plumbiferous adventure. When the distinguished writer first approaches the maritime capital, he observes how the 'sky and sea remained dull and leaden [*bleiern*]' (2004b: 520). This lead or *Blei* quickly goes on to distinguish Tadzio as the 'bright star of youth' – the *Sternenknabe* – expressed by the cognate adjective 'bleich' (*pale or sallow*), like the skin of someone 'anemic' (*bleichsüchtig*). It is the *Blei* – itself an anagram of both the living, fleshly body (*Leib*) and a designation of what is held dear (*lieb*) – that seems to draw the venerable writer fatally to the beautiful boy. Indeed, Aschenbach is first attracted to Tadzio's 'pale countenance' and his 'jagged and colorless' teeth, which lack 'the enamel of health', displaying 'a strangely brittle transparency, like one finds sometimes among the anemic' (*bei Bleichsüchtigen*, ibid.: 541). Although Tadzio's hair is 'golden', his leaden complexion distances him from the Apollonian sphere and aligns him with the Dionysian. Moreover, he is accompanied by three sisters, whose uniform dress is explicitly the colour of 'slate' (*schieferfarb*, ibid.: 530), a hue that visually rhymes with melancholic lead, the lustreless, malleable matter of alchemy, governed by Saturn. The presence of these 'three maidens', may further allude to Lear's daughters, who, according to Stucken and, following him, Freud, are understood as relating to the three caskets, where the apparently worthless is worth everything. As Achenbach pursues the family in a gondola, which is in fact described as a 'casket' (*Kästchen*), the sky once again is 'slate-like' (*schieferig*, ibid.: 567). Finally, as the writer languishes on the sands of the Lido, debilitated by cholera, he believes he sees Tadzio pointing to the setting sun, beckoning him, waving him on, 'into the immensity full of promise' – *ins Verheißungsvoll-Ungeheure* – 'as if the pale and lovely soul-summoner [*der bleiche und liebliche Psychagog*] was smiling at him' (ibid.: 592). In these final lines, in addition to deploying the anagrammatic resonance of *bleich* and *lieblich*, Mann transforms Tadzio into Hermes, into the leaden god of merchants and interpreters – a Mercury of Venice who accompanies the soul beyond the life of art and intellect, sealing a 'monstrous' (*ungeheuer*) 'promise' (*Verheißung*) that gives credit where credit is ultimately due.

Thus, the intertextual links to Shakespeare's drama that Mann engages are less grounded in elements of plot or character, and more in allusive, quasi-symbolic details, most notably in the figuration of the three caskets. For Mann, the shared motif of risk, of hazarding all one has, points the way out of an otherwise aporetic oscillation between the demands of golden *Kunst* and silvery *Geist*. In this way, *Der Tod in Venedig* not only profits from its Shakespearean loans, but also arguably discloses elements hitherto neglected in the earlier play. Bassanio furnishes the text for the *Liebestod* that gently conveys Aschenbach to some promised land – *ein Land der Verheißung* – the joyful but also monstrous consequence of longing:

But thou, thou meager lead
Which rather threaten'st than dost promise aught,
Thy paleness moves me more than eloquence,
And here choose I. Joy be the consequence!
(3.2.104–7)

Notes

1 The image is reproduced as the cover illustration and frontispiece to Reed (1996).

2 Unless noted otherwise, all translations are mine.

3 *Es war wieder eine ganz unerhörte Qual damit, und trotz aller Präcedenzfälle war ich diesmal zum Sterben von der Berechtigung der Verzweiflung überzeugt, mit der ich das dicke (viel zu dicke) Manuskript nach Berlin absandte. Dann, der täglichen Plage ledig, resignierte ich mich. ... Schon seit dem Tonio Kröger waren mir die Begriffe 'Geist' und 'Kunst' zu sehr in einandergelaufen. Ich hatte sie verwechselt und sie, in diesem Stück, doch feindlich gegen einander gestellt. Das hatte zu diesem Solness-Absturz geführt, diesem Fiasko in dem Bemühen eine geistige Construction mit Leben zu erfüllen. Umkehr! Zurück zur Buddenbrook-Naivetät!* (Mann 2002a: 315).

4 See Robertson (2005).

5 For an excellent overview of Mann's project, see Reed (1966).

6 See, e.g. the passage marked 'Wagnerkritik' in Scherrer and Wysling (1967: 178).

7 For a sustained comparison of Mann and Nietzsche in relation to *Fiorenza* and the *Geist und Kunst* notes, see Burgard (1983).

8 *Italien ist mir bis zur Verachtung gleichgültig! Das ist lange her, daß ich mir einbildete, dorthin zu gehören. Kunst, nicht wahr? Sammetblauer Himmel, heißer Wein und süße Sinnlichkeit ... Kurzum, ich mag das nicht. Ich verzichte. Die ganze bellezza macht mich nervös. Ich mag auch alle diese fürchterlich lebhaften Menschen dort unten mit dem schwarzen Tierblick nicht leiden. Diese Romanen haben kein Gewissen in den Augen ... Nein, ich gehe nur ein bißchen nach Dänemark.*

...

Ich will mich auf der Terrasse von Kronberg stehen, wo der 'Geist' zu Hamlet kam und Not und Tod über den armen, edlen jungen Menschen brachte ... (Mann 2004a: 281–2).

9 *Zugeständnisse an die Literatur* (Mann 2002b: 123); *genauer, vollständiger, wissender, gewissenhafter, tiefer* (ibid.: 130).

10 Cf. Wagner (1984: II.1).

11 *gewagten, wenn nicht unmöglichen Gegenstandes* (Mann 2002a: 483).

12 William Shakespeare, *The Merchant of Venice*, Orgel and Braunmuller (eds) *The Complete Pelican Shakespeare*. All subsequent citations are from this edition.

13 For a sustained reading along these lines, see Shell (1982: 47–83).

14 For a comprehensive account of Mann's complex indebtedness to Brandes, see Sandberg (1972).

15 See Mann, *Tonio Kröger* (2004a: 318).

16 *symmetrisch angeordnete Inschriften in Goldlettern* (Mann 2004b: 502).

17 *[Er] begann seinen Tag beizeiten mit Stürzen kalten Wassers über Brust und Rücken und brachte dann, ein Paar hoher Wachskerzen in silbernen Leuchten zu Häupten des Manuskripts, die Kräfte, die er im Schlaf gesammelt, in zwei oder drei inbrünstig gewissenhaften Morgenstunden der Kunst zum Opfer dar* (ibid.: 510).

18   See Freud's 1913 essay 'Das Motiv der Kästchenwahl'.
19   On this point, see Reed (1996: 124–5).
20   *Die Meisterhaltung unseres Stiles ist Lüge und Narrentum, unser Ruhm und Ehrenstand eine Posse, das Vertrauen der Menge zu uns höchst lächerlich, Volks- und Jugenderziehung durch die Kunst, ein gewagtes, zu verbietendes Unternehmen* (Mann 2004b: 589).

Works Cited

Brandes, Georg, 1898. *William Shakespeare: A Critical Study*, 2 vols, trans. W. Archer. London: Heinemann.

Burgard, Peter, 1983. '*Fiorenza*: Mann contra Nietzsche', in *Modern Language Quarterly* 44, pp. 359–72.

Freud, Sigmund, 1968–78 [1913]. 'Das Motiv der Kästchenwahl', in *Gesammelte Werke*, vol. 10, eds Marie Bonaparte, Anna Freud. Frankfurt am Main: S. Fischer, pp. 23–37.

Mann, Thomas, 1974. *Gesammelte Werke*, 13 vols. Frankfurt am Main: S. Fischer.

Mann, Thomas, 2002a. *Briefe 1: 1889–1913*, eds Thomas Sprecher, Hans R. Vaget, Cornelia Bernini. Große Kommentierte Frankfurter Ausgabe, vol. 21.1. Frankfurt am Main: S. Fischer.

Mann, Thomas, 2002b. *Essays 1: 1893–1914*, ed. Heinrich Detering. Große Kommentierte Frankfurter Ausgabe, vol. 14.1. Frankfurt am Main: S. Fischer.

Mann, Thomas, 2004a [1903]. 'Tonio Kröger', in *Frühe Erzählungen*, ed. Terence J. Reed. Große Kommentierte Frankfurter Ausgabe, vol. 2.1. Frankfurt am Main: S. Fischer, pp. 243–318.

Mann, Thomas, 2004b [1912]. 'Der Tod in Venedig', in *Frühe Erzählungen*, ed. Terence J. Reed. Große Kommentierte Frankfurter Ausgabe, vol. 2.1. Frankfurt am Main: S. Fischer, pp. 501–92.

Reed, Terence J., 1966. 'Geist und Kunst: Thomas Mann's abandoned Essay on Literature', in *Oxford German Studies* 1, pp. 53–101.

Reed, Terence J., 1996. *Thomas Mann: The Uses of Tradition*, second edition. Oxford: Clarendon Press.

Robertson, Ritchie, 2005. 'Savonarola in Munich: A Reappraisal of Thomas Mann's *Fiorenza*', in *Publications of the English Goethe Society* 74, pp. 51–66.

Sandberg, Hans-Joachim, 1972. 'Suggestibilität und Widerspruch: Thomas Manns Auseinandersetzung mit Georg Brandes', in *Nerthus: Nordisch-deutsche Beiträge* 3, pp. 119–63.

Schaukal, Richard, 1969. 'Thomas Mann und die Renaissance', *Berliner Tageblatt*, 5 March 1906, in *Thomas Mann im Urteil seiner Zeit*, ed. Klaus Schröter. Hamburg: Wegner, pp. 41–6.

Scherrer, Paul and Hans Wysling (eds), 1967. *Quellenkritische Studien zum Werk Thomas Manns*. Bern: Francke.

Shakespeare, William, 2002. *The Merchant of Venice*, in *The Complete Pelican Shakespeare*, eds Stephen Orgel and A. R. Braunmuller. New York: Penguin, pp. 285–323.

Shakespeare, William, 2010. *Der Kaufmann von Venedig*, trans. August Wilhelm Schlegel, in *Sämtliche Werke*, ed. Günter Klotz. Berlin: Aufbau Verlag, pp. 379–461.

Shell, Marc, 1982. *Money, Language, and Thought*. Berkeley: University of California Press.

Stucken, Eduard, 1896–1907. *Astralmythen der Hebraeer, Babylonier und Aegypter: Religionsgeschichtliche Untersuchungen*, 5 vols. Leipzig: Pfeiffer.

Wagner, Richard, 1984. *Oper und Drama*, ed. K. Klopfringer. Stuttgart: Reclam.

Seven

Shakespeare to Mann, via Wagner
Dave Paxton

In 1911 Thomas Mann introduced into his short story 'Wie Jappe und Do Escobar sich prügelten' ('The Fight between Jappe and Do Escobar') the ballet-teacher and bathing-master François Knaak, an old man with 'plump' hips and 'extraordinary and fastidious mannerisms', who is 'reported to wear a corset' and who gnaws 'his soft brown moustache with his under lip'. Herr Knaak arouses the 'suspicions' of the youth of Travemünde, to whom he sometimes gives 'private lessons', but he is prevented by his age and social position 'from being convicted and unmasked' (Mann 2001: 409–10).[1]

In the novella which Mann began writing this same year, *Der Tod in Venedig* (*Death in Venice*), the sinister bathing-master seems to transform into the disturbing companion of the 'young men' on board the boat to Venice: an 'old' man with 'wrinkles around his eyes' and 'rouge' on his cheeks, who lifts 'a wrinkled, ringed finger' and licks 'the corners of his mouth with the tip of his tongue in a revoltingly suggestive manner' (*Death in Venice*, hereafter referred to as *DV*, 28–9, 33).[2] Aschenbach the austere German artist is horrified by this figure, but he ends the novella in a similar state, staggering through the back alleys of Venice, his own lips 'slack, cosmetically embellished', his own wrinkles smothered 'beneath face cream and the glow of youth' (ibid.: 136, 132).[3] *Der Tod in Venedig* imagines the descent of an exemplary man-of-letters, 'whose style schoolboys were exhorted to emulate', into an urban underworld of 'degeneracy', 'debauchery' and 'prostitution' (ibid.: 135, 122–3).[4]

Aschenbach is dragged from the 'disciplined, decently austere' path set out by his noble German 'forebears' (ibid.: 12)[5] by his experience of desire for the fourteen-year-old boy Tadzio. Mann builds this desire, however, out of the noblest models from German high-culture in general, and from Richard Wagner's operas in particular. Mann was passionately attached to these operas from his youth, when his experiences of *Tannhäuser*, *Lohengrin* and *Tristan und Isolde* filled him 'with a longing, envious and infatuated, to produce something similar' (Mann 1985a: 46),[6] and in 1931 he felt in 'no doubt that the traces of my early and continuing experience of Wagner's work are manifest in everything I have written' (Mann 1985e: 88).[7] Mann's Wagner-engagement was from the start fundamentally erotic: if, as Mann wrote to his brother Heinrich Mann in 1901, '[i]t is all metaphysics, music, and adolescent sexuality – adolescence hangs on with me' (Mann 1975c, 22),[8] then it was from Wagner more than anyone else that Mann found the metaphysics and music into which he could tangle his desire. As Ronald Hayman writes: 'The sensuality of Wagner's music seems to have had a catalytic effect on Thomas's youthful sexuality, at once intensifying the flow of desire and helping him to sublimate it dreamily into the kind of fantasy he could distill into fiction' (1995: 109).

Der Tod in Venedig was its author's work of erotic self-revelation, into which Mann confessed a 'personal' experience of '"forbidden" love' (Mann 1975a: 95),[9] so it is inevitable that, as William H. McClain has written, it seems 'the most Wagnerian' of all Mann's books (1964: 482). It resonates especially with Act 3 of *Tristan und Isolde*: the agonized hero who lies on the rocky cliffs of Kareol, looking over the 'wide sea horizon' to see 'Moving o'er the paths / Of ocean' a woman smiling at him and bringing him 'last release' (Wagner 1981: 79, 85–6)[10] seems to turn into the old German artist who lies on Venice beach looking at the boy on the horizon 'smiling at him, beckoning to him, as if ... he were pointing outward' into the 'promising immensity' of death (*DV* 141–2).[11] Mann did not have to twist Wagner too much to fit him into the new cross-generational context: Wagner would himself talk 'about the past' and muse, contra Goethe, 'that the eternal feminine drags one downward' (C. Wagner 1980: 565),[12] and even Tristan's resolutely straight desire takes him, via Isolde, into a distant past which has as its end-point

> the sacred
> Realm of night
> From which my mother
> Sent me forth.
> (Wagner 1981: 77)[13]

Wagner conceived *Tristan und Isolde* in 1854 as a drama based on *Romeo and Juliet*,[14] and *Der Tod in Venedig* is oddly appropriate to an experience which Wagner had with Shakespeare's play the following year. Staying in London to conduct a series of concerts with the Philharmonic Society, he attended a performance of the play at the Haymarket Theatre: 'the part of Romeo', he later explained, 'had been given to ... an old man, who appeared to be at least sixty, and who seemed to try to retrieve his lost youth by laboriously adopting a rather sickeningly sweet, feminine air' (Wagner 1983: 525).[15] Tristan, before the opera to which he gave his name had been written, was already in 1855 threatening to collapse into a dirty old man.

If *Der Tod in Venedig* seems to enact that collapse, then this is also more broadly a collapsing of Wagnerian mythology into the psychiatric-sexual landscape which unfolded in Europe through the late nineteenth and early twentieth centuries when, as Michel Foucault put it in 1975, 'a large domain of intervention, the domain of ... the abnormal, opened up before psychiatry' (Foucault 2003: 167). In 1857, two years after Wagner's experience at the Haymarket, the French doctor Ambroise Tardieu opened up the category of deviancy into which Mann would deposit Wagner:

> Hair curled, face made up, neck bared, waist cinched to accentuate his curves, the fingers, ears, and chest covered with jewels, the most penetrating perfume wafting from the whole person, and in his hand a handkerchief, flowers or some needlework: such is the strange, repulsive, and by all rights suspect physiognomy that betrays pederasts.
>
> (Tardieu 2013: 309)

Mann wrote to Wolfgang Born in 1921 of the subject-matter of *Der Tod in Venedig*: 'the pathological element exerts a powerful intellectual attraction upon me, and always has' (Mann 1975d: 100)[16] – but what was Mann's intention in dissolving Wagner's high-Romanticism into the new psychiatric landscape of abnormality and perversion? Was he trying to destroy Wagner? Not quite: it was more that he was trying to bring to light the perversity *which already lay in Wagner* – to show that the space which opened up to psychiatric intervention was already the space of Wagner's creative practice. Nietzsche noticed this crossover in 1888: 'transposed into hugeness,' he snarled, 'Wagner does not seem to have been interested in any problems except those which now preoccupy the little decadents of Paris. Always five steps from the hospital. All of them entirely modern, entirely metropolitan problems' (1967: 176).[17]

Mann could draw on Wagner to articulate Aschenbach's desire for Tadzio, as well as collapse Wagner into Tardieu's category of 'the pederast', because a conception of dissident, cross-generational desire was already embedded in Wagner's oeuvre. In this essay I make the perhaps surprising claim that this conception had generated quite specifically out of Wagner's creative engagement with William Shakespeare. I explore the three stages of Wagner's Shakespeare-engagement in order to show how in 1840 they became enmeshed and generated a motif of *sexual desire for the lost past*, which Wagner immediately blew up into the grandest realms of mythology and which Mann in turn locked onto and made his own: a study of the Wagner-Shakespeare link thus opens a genealogy leading into *Der Tod in Venedig*. John Hamilton makes *The Merchant of Venice* central to his analysis of Mann's novella, but I focus primarily on *Measure for Measure*, and my attempt to trace a line of influence between that play and the novella adds another layer of Shakespearean complexity to this work of 'dense ... intentions and relationships' (Mann 1975b: 73),[18] while it also opens out a context for Jonathan Dollimore's consideration of Aschenbach in relation to Shakespeare's own erotic (anti)hero Angelo.[19]

*

The first of the three stages of Wagner's Shakespeare-engagement came when, as a young adolescent, Wagner rebelled against his family, school and 'plain middle class' (C. Wagner 1978: 495)[20] world and fell in love with Shakespeare, which name he pronounced '*Shick*sper', associating it 'with Fate and battle' (*Schicksal* = fate, *Speer* = spear): he read the plays as 'daemonic and fantastic' and he sought 'a mystical meaning in Falstaff' (ibid.: 766).[21] The youth was preoccupied with 'the idea of emancipation from school and family' (Wagner 1983: 20),[22] and when at the age of fourteen he moved from Dresden to Leipzig he secretly stopped attending classes in a 'complete turnabout from the path of formal academic training' (ibid.: 22)[23] in order to dedicate himself to a private study of his 'exemplar' (Wagner 1892b: 4).[24]

Out of Wagner's study of Shakespeare there arose a 'vast tragic drama' which the youth had conceived in Dresden: *Leubald*, though Wagner would always misremember the title as *Leubald und Adelaïde*. 'I had put together', he later explained, 'a drama to which Shakespeare, principally through *Hamlet*, *Macbeth*, and *Lear* ... had contributed. The plot was essentially a variation of *Hamlet*' (Wagner 1983: 25).[25] In this gory tragedy, Leubald ('a mixture of Hamlet and Hotspur'), having been sworn to vengeance by the ghost of his father, undertakes a 'wild vendetta' to murder the race of Roderich, only to then fall in love with Roderich's daughter Adelaïde (ibid.: 26).[26] At its mid-point the play transforms from *Hamlet* into *Romeo and Juliet* as its hero, now 'driven less by thirst for blood than by longing for death', dedicates himself to the 'fiery love affair', but this dedication is thwarted by the arrival on-stage of 'the ghosts of all the ... members of the clan slaughtered' – 'according to the method adopted by Shakespeare in

Richard III' (ibid).[27] Wagner later recalled, inaccurately but memorably: 'two-and-forty human beings died in the course of this piece, and I saw myself compelled, in its working-out, to call the greater number back as ghosts, since otherwise I should have been short of characters for my last Acts' (1892b: 4).[28] At the drama's conclusion Leubald, caught between the ghostly torment and his desire for his beloved, stabs Adelaïde to death, 'finds himself suddenly at peace, sinks his head in her lap, and enjoys her last caresses while her life-blood streams over their dying bodies' (1983: 27).[29]

The 'voluminous masterpiece' was completed in 1828. It seemed to Wagner's family the product of 'perverted talent', an 'aberration' and a 'crime', but the fifteen-year-old decided to continue down this dangerous path: he felt that his drama would work better with a soundtrack so he set out to take music lessons, intending to 'start composing immediately' (ibid.: 25–7).[30] 'I ... wanted', he later remembered, 'to write incidental music for *Leubald und Adelaïde*, like Beethoven's for *Egmont*; the various categories of ghosts belonging to my spirit world would first receive their distinctive coloring from the corresponding musical accompaniment' (ibid.: 31).[31] He became obsessed with Beethoven: 'There ... arose in me', he later remembered, 'an image [of Beethoven] of the highest supernal originality, beyond comparison with anything. This image melded with that of Shakespeare: in ecstatic dreams I met both, saw and talked to them; upon awakening I was bathed in tears' (ibid.: 30).[32]

*

The second stage of Wagner's Shakespeare-engagement came when in 1834 Wagner cast off the 'brooding seriousness' (1983: 81)[33] of his youth and threw himself 'upon the immediate surroundings of life' (Wagner 1892a: 294).[34] At this time he 'closely studied' (1983: 83)[35] *Measure for Measure*, finding three things in Shakespeare's play: first, in the evocation of Vienna, a picture of a sensual and disease-ridden society in which the observer sees 'corruption boil and bubble / Till it o'errun the stew' (5.1.314–15);[36] second, in the nun Isabella, a 'chaste' (2.4.185) woman who, retreating from the corruption into a cloister, seems to Lucio 'a thing enskied and sainted, / By [her] renouncement an immortal spirit' (1.4.34–5); third, in the governor Angelo, a man whose own retreat from sensuality, striving for 'austereness' (2.4.156) and attempt at moral-political reform arouses in him an intense sexual desire for Isabella herself, which Angelo interrogates in a soliloquy:

Can it be

That modesty may more betray our sense

Than woman's lightness? Having waste ground enough
Shall we desire to raze the sanctuary
And pitch our evils there? ...
                              ... Most dangerous
Is that temptation that doth goad us on
To sin in loving virtue.

(2.2.172–6, 185–7)

Wagner responded intensely to all of this: 'I could see', he later
recalled, 'only the somber, strait-laced governor ... aflame with a
frightful passion for the beautiful novice' (1983: 83),[37] and he was
'inspired' by Isabella herself, this 'superb woman' with her 'chaste
soul' (1892a: 295).[38]

In 1836 Wagner completed *Das Liebesverbot* (*The Ban on Love*), a
full-scale opera of Shakespeare's play in which Isabella turns into a
freedom-fighter and prophet of the sexual revolution, and Angelo
into the sinister German lawgiver Friedrich – the 'antithesis of love'
(2008: 29)[39] – whose regime is toppled at the drama's conclusion;
Wagner later explained that he had adapted Shakespeare's 'solemn'
play 'very freely', caring only 'to uncover the sinfulness of hypocrisy
and the artificiality of the judicial attitude toward morality' (1983:
83).[40] The themes and motifs which Wagner had found in *Measure for
Measure* continued, however, to preoccupy him even after his opera
was completed, and by the 1840s he was using Shakespeare's motifs of
desire and renunciation to evoke the plight of the nineteenth-century
German artist – a man bound by an 'oath of renunciation', seeking
'protection and salvation behind peaceful monastery walls' (Wagner
1973d: 23–5),[41] living in one of Europe's 'private sanctuaries' (Wagner
1973c: 103),[42] but also a man whose approach to art is born of 'desire'
(1892a: 340)[43] and whose striving for 'utter chastity' causes him to 'be
consumed by an almost lascivious delight' (1973c: 104).[44] The artist
here is at once Isabella and Angelo.

*

The third stage of Wagner's Shakespeare-engagement came when,
as a lost adult, Wagner returned to the spirit of his Shakespearean
adolescence. He was working in a series of provincial theatres and
feeling 'in a constant state of distraction' in 'the vortex of theatrical
activity' when he 'attended with huge interest not only the performances themselves but also the rehearsals' of a production of *King
Lear*, and these contributed to a 'favorable change' in the direction of
his 'taste, heretofore badly warped by the theatrical customs of the
time' (Wagner 1983: 124, 145, 149).[45] 'It was', Wagner later recalled,

'most gratifying to feel my old and serious predilection for the spoken drama reawakened', and he experienced a 'reversion' of his 'innermost inclinations to the passionately serious side of [his] being that had been dominant in … earliest youth' (ibid.: 149–51).[46]

Wagner decided to move to Paris to make his fortune as an opera composer, and his journey by boat took him past 'the beautiful castle of Elsinore, the sight of which brought back [his] youthful impressions of *Hamlet*' (1983: 161).[47] Stopping in London, he visited Westminster Abbey to see Shakespeare's monument in Poet's Corner, and standing before it he was 'led to a train of thought' in which his friend Ferdinand Praeger was later convinced he 'could discern the germ of [Wagner's] daring revolution in musical form' (Praeger 1892: 76). In Paris, he saw a rehearsal of Beethoven's Ninth Symphony, and once again he was taken back into the past: 'the conception of this marvelous work', he later explained, 'which I had dimly formed in the enthusiastic days of my youth … suddenly stood before me bright as day and as palpable to my touch' (Wagner 1983: 175).[48] Wagner had strayed from Beethoven at the age of seventeen but now he returned:

> That whole period of deterioration in my musical taste, which dated precisely from the time I went astray about Beethoven's last compositions and had grown so much worse during all my superficial theatrical activities, now sank away before me as if into an abyss of shame and remorse.
>
> (Wagner 1983: 175)[49]

Wagner's experiences with *Lear*, *Hamlet* and the Ninth Symphony 'revived [his] former spirit and gave it new life and strength' (ibid.: 175).[50] Having broken into Shakespeare and Beethoven as an adolescent, Wagner now returned to the spirit of this adolescence, finding there a springboard to his future: 'I recalled the image of the impressions of my youth', he later explained, 'In order to assure myself of what it was, in particular, that I held dear in the German Home for which I was yearning' (1892a: 313).[51] 'We Germans are luckier [than others]', Wagner would later muse: 'our origins lie in ourselves, and we can delude ourselves that we are able to bring our past back to life' (C. Wagner 1980: 176).[52]

*

In 1840 Wagner's use of the motifs which he had found in *Measure for Measure* became entangled with his fantasy-return to adolescence. He wrote a short-story, *Eine Pilgerfahrt zu Beethoven* (*A Pilgrimage to Beethoven*), which like Shakespeare's play is set in a Vienna of 'superficial sensuality' and 'frivolous, indiscriminate pleasure-seeking', and which tells the story of two people, one of whom disgustedly retreats from the sensuality into 'the sanctuary' and another who, driven by 'burning desire', tries to enter that sanctuary and find fulfilment there. Angelo turns into R—, a German artist intent on visiting his musical hero, and Isabella turns into Beethoven himself (Wagner 1973a: 746, 68).[53] Wagner uses these Shakespearean contours to put into print his own return to the past: 'It was as though', R— explains about his erotic pilgrimage, 'I were a lover journeying back after long separation to the beloved of his youth!' and when the young man makes it into the sanctuary and asks Beethoven for advice about opera composition, the old man replies 'with something like violence' that R— should do 'As Shakespeare did when he wrote his plays!' (ibid.: 66, 80).[54]

In this unofficial sequel to *Measure for Measure*, the desiring hero finds in the Viennese sanctuary not a nun but instead a great composer who stands in symbolically for the adolescence to which Wagner was at that time returning: a demonic revenant which responds 'with something like violence' to the desiring adult standing before it, offering him the gift of his own future. This is a *positive* recuperation of *Measure for Measure* to tell a story about the German artist's quest for his own culture. However, R—'s return to the past catapults him into a terrible fate in the sequel which Wagner wrote to his short-story: *Ein Ende in Paris* (*Death in Paris*[55]), 1841. R— now finds himself cast back into the French capital – 'it was into a *swamp*, into a *morass*, that I sank' – where, 'haunted by the wailful ghostly tone of an oboe', he is elbowed into the gutter by 'street-urchins' and 'seized by an irresistible desire to pay a visit to the devil' (1973b: 84, 94–7).[56] As he descends into madness, his body decays: 'How I welcomed the dissolution', he explains, 'which I could feel creeping through every part of my emaciated body! Impervious to the outside world, I unconsciously went wherever my tottering legs carried me … I … was dying for a faith' (ibid.: 99–100).[57] Wagner's hero dies, crying that on earth he has been 'a dissonant chord', pledging himself to the German cultural tradition, and threatening the Day of Judgement on those 'who dared to exploit this chaste and noble Art … for the sake of sensual pleasure' (ibid.: 101).[58] In this strange tale, which emerged at the intersection of Wagner's return to his Shakespearean youth and his study of *Measure for Measure*, the German artist's return to the past leads him onto a terrible path of disease, devilry and death in a foreign land.

*

Wagner, claimed Nietzsche, took 'problems … which … preoccupy the little decadents of Paris' and 'transposed [them] into hugeness': thus

R—, the man who dies in Paris, was immediately transposed into the ageing eponymous hero of the opera which Wagner wrote next, *Der Fliegende Holländer* (*The Flying Dutchman*, 1841), who also finds death through a return to the past. Looking at a 'child' standing before him, Wagner's hero breathes:

> This maiden's image speaks to me
> as from the distance of time long past:
> as I had dreamt of it through eternities of dread,
> now I see it before my eyes.
>
> (Wagner 2012: 133)[59]

If in 1840 Isabella had transformed into Beethoven, now Beethoven in turn transformed into the girl Senta – a passionate youth who stands before a lost old man and, speaking to him from 'time long past', offers him fulfilment. In *Ein Ende in Paris* Wagner had tried to hang onto his motif of return by displacing death onto the French capital (R— dies because he ends up in a sensuous foreign land) but in *Der Fliegende Holländer* death is reincorporated into desire as its telos and idealized as 'redemption': at the opera's conclusion Senta and the Dutchman, having sunk to their deaths, 'rise from the water, both transfigured' (ibid.: 163).[60] If the narrative-arc of Wagner's Paris stories was here blown up into the grandeur of mythology, then the anxiety of *Ein Ende in Paris* was also replaced by a new statement of optimism.

Wagner did not achieve the redemption that he gave to his character: when he returned to Germany from France in 1842 it was intended to be *his* 'hour of redemption', but when he arrived in Dresden, the place where he had first read Shakespeare and conceived *Leubald*, he found that this 'city in which I had spent such meaningful years of childhood and boyhood made a chilling and deadening impression on me... everything that might remind me of my youth seemed to have passed away' (1983: 216–19).[61] Wagner tried to revivify the past by digging out the *Leubald* manuscript for his friends, but the reading was interrupted and 'the ghosts remained in their weird realm' (Schmole 1950: 122).[62] At this time Wagner conceived and wrote his fifth opera *Tannhäuser* (1845), the eponymous hero of which, having sojourned in the sensuous Venusberg and been called back to Christian society by the name of his first girlfriend, returns looking for fulfilment but instead desecrates Elisabeth with his erotic fantasies. In all of this we can see Wagner's positive recuperation of *Measure for Measure* gradually twisting back around to return to Shakespeare's original metaphysic of sin: if Wagner had first displaced death onto the foreign other, then reincorporated it into the self by idealizing it, now he reincorporated it in a negative form. Tannhäuser's cry of horror, as Elisabeth kneels before him in prayer, finally returns Wagner to Angelo and Isabella proper:

> To save a sinner from damnation
> an angel came to guard my days,
> but I, I saw her, and desired her,
> soiled her with sly and lustful gaze.
>
> (Wagner 2011b: 82)[63]

*

Wagner's attempt to integrate his motif of returning to youth into the erotic contours of *Measure for Measure* succeeded in *Tannhäuser* at the cost of turning the German hero into a sex-criminal: Angelo the 'outward-sainted deputy' who 'is yet a devil' (3.1.88–91) now stood on-stage anew as Tannhäuser himself, the 'son of sin' who enters society with 'a mask of smooth hypocrisy' (Wagner 2011b: 82)[64] and pollutes it. Wagner returned to this terrain in his last opera *Parsifal* (1882), but he tried to salvage his two Shakespearean structures by splitting them apart: the youth's job is now not to respond to the hero's erotic advance but instead to redeem him from sex.

Angelo transforms, via Tannhäuser, into Amfortas, a ruler who, having left his kingdom in order to enact a moral reform and eradicate 'sinful joys and hell's damnation', returns home to find himself aroused by the Holy Grail itself: 'thrilled by the agony of ecstasy', he feels his 'sinful blood / ... gush in wild terror / into the world of sinful passion', and the Grail cries to Parsifal from its 'profaned sanctuary': 'Redeem me, rescue me / from hands defiled by sin!' (Wagner 2011a: 125, 147, 195).[65] Here is Angelo's 'desire to raze the sanctuary / And pitch [his] evils there' over forty years after Wagner had first encountered it and now with no hint of a utopian recuperation. As if to emphasize his Shakespearean debt, Wagner gives to the Grail the exact music – the Dresden Amen – which he had given to Isabella's sanctuary in *Das Liebesverbot* in 1836. The redemption for which both Amfortas and the Grail yearn is provided by a youth, in this case the opera's eponymous hero, a young adolescent experiencing 'the awakening of sensual feelings', but this youth can provide redemption only because he is 'deprived ... of sensual urges' (C. Wagner 1980: 92, 99)[66] and turned into 'the innocent fool' (2011a: 115).[67] Senta had offered erotic fulfilment, but Parsifal offers a portal out of a world sunk in desire. Wagner's creative career had begun in a Shakespearean world of massacres and love-deaths; now it ended with a radical erotic purification.

*

Thomas Mann saw *Parsifal* at the Bayreuth Festspielhaus in 1909, and afterwards he wrote to his friend Walter Opitz:

> The music is the ultimate in modernism. Nobody has ever gone beyond it ... What a terrifyingly *expressive* art! The accents of contrition and torment that [Wagner] practised all his life achieve their ultimate intensity only here. Tristan's longing pales beside this Miserere. Piercing details, gripping moments, the most refined and ardent cruelties.
>
> (1985g: 45)[68]

Wagner's last opera registered with Mann's own experience of desire, and a quarter-century later, he was still thinking about this work with its 'love-sick high priest, who awaits redemption at the hands of a chaste boy', this boy himself 'another case of remote peculiarity' (Mann 1985d: 129).[69] He mused that the 'extremism' of Wagner's characters 'would have been more obvious ... had they been presented in the guise of a novella': it is the work's music, he claims, which *masks* its extremism, so 'the whole thing emerges not as gruesome-facetious nonsense ... but as a deeply religious sacred drama' (ibid.).[70] If, as Nietzsche had mocked, Wagner 'transposed into hugeness' problems afflicting those who are 'five steps from the hospital', then here the novella-form functions to undo that transposition and follow Nietzsche's demand that one 'translate Wagner into reality, into the modern' (1967: 175),[71] thereby bringing the perversion of his art to the light of day.

Two years after he saw *Parsifal* Mann started work on his perverted novella *Der Tod in Venedig*, which tells the familiar Wagnerian story of a man who encounters an adolescent who returns him to 'ancient thoughts passed on to him in his youth' and whom he follows into 'the golden dusk of the sanctuary' (*DV* 82, 101),[72] a story now set in the city in which Wagner had died in 1883. The spear-struck Amfortas turns into Aschenbach with his 'conception of manliness' which 'stands by calmly ... while swords and spears pierce its flesh' (ibid.: 16), and Parsifal turns into Tadzio, the boy of 'mute divinity' (ibid.: 56) who promises redemption to the erotic sufferer lying before him.[73] Mann, however, synthesizes the Amfortas–Parsifal relationship with its Wagnerian predecessors, thereby injecting it anew with desire from the past and undoing *Parsifal*'s erotic purification. Amfortas is collapsed not only into the desiring hero Tristan, but also further back into the agonized Dutchman: as a lost old man who sails the sea and meets a 'pale' (*DV* 141)[74] child who beckons him to death, Aschenbach draws on that Wagner-character whom Mann found 'extraordinarily moving'

(Mann 1985c: 41)[75] and in whom he saw himself reflected, ending a letter in 1902 quoting Senta's redemption-theme and wondering 'if *this* Flying Dutchman will ever be granted a "redemption"' (1985f: 23).[76] Mann pushes his Wagnerian models not only backward but also *downward*: in 1841 Wagner had 'transposed' his own R— 'into hugeness' to become the Dutchman, and now Mann seems to undo that transposition and collapse the Dutchman back into R—, a middle-class German artist who makes a pilgrimage to the past, driven by 'a fervent youthful craving … long outgrown and forgotten' (*DV* 5)[77] only to be spun into the dystopia of disease, devilry and death in a foreign land.

Der Tod in Venedig collapses Tristan into the Haymarket's 'sickeningly sweet' Romeo, and Wagnerian mythology into a psychiatric category, but this is also a collapsing of Wagner back into himself – and Mann reaches so far back into Wagner that he locks onto the Shakespeare play which Wagner had 'closely studied' in 1834. *Der Tod in Venedig*, in its evocation of a sensual and diseased city, and its story of a man whose attempt to repudiate sensuality in favour of 'austerity' (*DV* 60)[78] leads him to an agonizing experience of desire, resonates incredibly intensely with *Measure for Measure*: if Angelo was the governor whose refusal of sex in favour of chastity caused him a yearning 'to raze the sanctuary / And pitch [his] evils there', then Aschenbach is the brilliant German master who rejects 'bohemian excess and the murky depths' in favour of 'exemplary purity' only to find that 'form and innocence … lead to intoxication and desire … they too lead to the abyss' (*DV* 135–7).[79] *Der Tod in Venedig* may have grown out of its author's experience of *Parsifal* in 1909, but the novella is most importantly a *correction* of Wagner's last opera: Amfortas, yearning for redemption in a pure boy, had forgotten the important lesson which Wagner had learned from *Measure for Measure*, and which now sends Aschenbach spiralling into the Venetian underworld – that untouchable purity can be the most dangerously arousing thing of all.

Mann was conflicted about his own sexuality, but he was even more conflicted about Wagner. In 1908, in his 'Versuch über das Theater' ('Essay on the Theatre'), he had told the story of someone who, '[d]riven on by an exotic urge', had entered a 'tropical landscape' filled with 'dancing savages' and 'drank of it, drank deep, intoxicating draughts, and found oblivion', also 'nausea and remorse' but perhaps *also* a 'first experience of beauty' (1985b: 28).[80] Mann was here telling the story of his own introduction to the theatre, where he had his 'first encounter with the art of Richard Wagner' – to whose 'ideal world' one 'gazes up, swiftly intoxicated by the music, with shame and questioning in one's heart' (ibid.: 29–30)[81] – and the essay provides a blueprint for *Der Tod in Venedig*, the (anti)hero of which falls in love with a boy whom he sees as 'a distant work of art' (*DV* 61).[82] Mann even gives to

Aschenbach authorship of his own 1911 essay 'Auseinandersetzung mit Wagner' ('Coming to Terms with Richard Wagner'), in which he describes the 'homesickness ... nostalgia for my youth' (1985a: 48)[83] which comes upon him when he listens to his favourite composer. Sitting on Venice beach Aschenbach writes this very essay, modelling his prose on Tadzio's body, sinking afterwards into exhaustion 'as if his conscience were reproaching him after a debauch' (*DV* 86).[84] *Der Tod in Venedig* encodes into Aschenbach's desire for Tadzio the story of Mann's own Wagner-engagement – and if Tadzio stands in for Wagner, then he is Wagner as a fourteen-year-old, presumably writing a gory Shakespearean tragedy in his hotel room when he can escape from the 'women guarding' him (ibid.: 111).[85]

*

When in 1855 Richard Wagner saw the 'sickeningly sweet' old Romeo in the Haymarket Theatre, it was as though his own Shakespearean motif of erotic-return was played back to him, *in the context of Shakespeare*, but in a perverted form. When, however, he and his friend Carl Lüders consulted the theatre programme they were amazed to find that the dirty old man was actually the actress Charlotte Cushman: '"By thunder!"' Lüders cried, '"It's a woman!"' (Wagner 1983: 525).[86] This detail is oddly appropriate to the conclusion which Aschenbach draws from his desire for Tadzio: though men may try to be 'chaste warriors', he claims, 'they nevertheless are as women' (*DV* 136).[87] In this tradition both freedom and perversion are located in trans-historical and cross-generational male interactions, and set against the suffocation of female domesticity, yet the telos of male deviancy is here claimed as an *un-manning* and opening into women's eroticism, and not as a final escape from the perverse, but as an ultimate, ecstatic entry into it.

In *Der Tod in Venedig* the women surrounding Tadzio anxiously call him back when he approaches Aschenbach, and the old man has 'to be concerned about standing out or arousing suspicion' (*DV* 111)[88] when he gazes at his beloved boy, but by codifying Aschenbach's desire as female the novella opens up a new, dangerous possibility: that it is the women who are the original perverts. In that case, Aschenbach has to die not because his desire sullies the economy of female love but instead because, having become filtered through that economy, it inadvertently brings to light the perversion which already lies there, but which is disavowed. *Der Tod in Venedig* threatens to tell a startlingly modern story about sexual dissidence, scapegoating and punitive violence: Angelo may have wanted 'To sin in loving virtue', and that logic of desire may have transferred through Wagner into Aschenbach's yearning for Tadzio, but Mann's novella also reminds its reader that it is in the name of 'virtue' that those like Aschenbach who 'are incapable of taking to the heavens' (*DV* 137)[89] have to be killed – and *this too*, the book silently urges on its reader, is a sin.

Notes

1 *fett namentlich in der Hüftgegend* ('Wie Jappe und Do Escobar sich prügelten', hereafter referred to as GKFA 2b: 491); *unerhörten, demonstrativen Gewähltheit seiner Manieren* (ibid.); *über den das unwiderlegte Gerücht im Umlauf war, daß er ein Korsett trage* (ibid.: 492); *erfaßte seinen weichen braunen Schnurrbart mit der Unterlippe* (ibid.: 493); *Verdacht* (ibid.: 492); *Privatkursus* (ibid.); *überführt und entlarvt zu werden* (ibid.:).

2 *junger Leute* ('Der Tod in Venedig', hereafter referred to as GKFA 2a: 518–19); *Er war alt* (ibid.); *Runzeln umgaben ihm Augen und Mund* (ibid.); *Das matte Karmesin der Wangen war Schminke* (ibid.); hob seinen beringten, runzeligen Zeigefinger (ibid.: 522); *und leckte auf abscheulich zweideutige Art mit der Zungenspitze die Mundwinkel* (ibid.).

3 *schlaffen Lippen, kosmetisch aufgehöht* (ibid.: 588); *unter Crème und Jugendhauch* (ibid.: 586).

4 *an dessen Stil die Knaben sich zu bilden angehalten wurden* (ibid.: 588); *Entsittlichung; Unmäßigkeit; Schamlosigkeit* (ibid.: 580).

5 *Vorfahren* (ibid.: 508); *ihr straffes, anständig karges Leben* (ibid.).

6 This is a free translation, based on 'Auseinandersetzung mit Wagner' (hereafter referred to as GKFA 14a: 301–2).

7 *und zweifle nicht, daß die Spuren meines frühen und fortlaufenden Wagner-Werk-Erlebnisses überall deutlich sind in dem, was ich herstellte* (Vaget 2005: 79), from 'Wie stehen wir heute zu Richard Wagner', Mann's response to a new production of *Lohengrin* in Würzburg in September 1927.

8 *Das Ganze ist Metaphysik, Musik und Pubertätserotik: – ich komme nie aus der Pubertät heraus* ('Brief an Heinrich Mann, 7. März 1901', hereafter referred to as GKFA 21c: 160).

9 *ein persönlich-lyrisches Reiseerlebnis, das mich umstimmte, die Dinge durch Einführung des Motivs der,Verbotenen' Liebe auf die Spitze zu stellen ...* ('Brief an Carl Maria Weber, 4. Juli 1920', hereafter referred to as GKFA 22a: 349–50).

10 *einen weiten Meereshorizont* (Wagner 1912–14h: *Tristan und Isolde*, 57); '*Siehst du sie noch nicht? / Wie sie selig, / hehr und milde / wandelt durch / des Meer's Gefilde?'* (ibid.: 69); *letzte Labung* (ibid.).

11 *ihm lächle, ihm winke; als ob er ... hinausdeutete, ... ins Verheißungsvoll-Ungeheure* ('Der Tod in Venedig', hereafter referred to as GKFA 2a: 592).

12 *Bei Tisch spricht er von Vergangenheit, das Ewig-Weibliche zieht herunter, sagt er, an früher denkend* (C. Wagner 1967: 628).

13 '*es ist das dunkel / nächt'ge Land, / daraus die Mutter / einst mich sandt'* (Wagner 1912–14h: *Tristan und Isolde*, 55).

14 Cf. C. Wagner (1980: 55). Cosima records her husband's comment about *Tristan und Isolde*: 'my model was *Romeo and Juliet.*' Richard Wagner was

thinking specifically of Bellini's *I Capuleti e i Montecchi*, but his interest in this opera was from the start driven by his love for Shakespeare's play.

15 *daß man den Romeo von einem so alten, wenigstens als sechzigjährigen gewürdigten Manne, spielen ließ, welcher seine weitabliegende Jugend durch ein süßliches, weibisches Wesen mühsam ersetzen zu wollen schien* (Wagner 1912–14n: 103).

16 *Ich leugne nicht, daß das Pathologische mich geistig mächtig anzieht und daß es dies immer gethan hat* (Mann 1962: 184).

17 *Ja, in's Grosse gerechnet, scheint Wagner sich für keine andern Probleme interessirt zu haben, als die, welche heute die kleinen Pariser décadents interessiren. Immer fünf Schritte weit vom Hospital! Lauter ganz moderne, lauter ganz grossstädtische Probleme!* (Nietzsche 1989: 34).

18 *ein dichtes Gewebe von Absichten und Beziehungen* ('Brief an Elisabeth Zimmer, 6. September 1915', hereafter referred to as GKFA 22b: 93).

19 Cf. John Hamilton and Jonathan Dollimore in this volume.

20 *schlichte Bürgerschaft* (C. Wagner 1966: 530).

21 *mit Schicksal und Kampf; dämonisch phantastisch; bei Falstaff einen mysteriösen Sinn suchend* (ibid.: 828).

22 *Begriff der Emanzipation von Schul- und Familienzwang* (Wagner 1912–14I: 27).

23 *völliges Abweichen von den Pfaden einer regelmäßigen Schulausbildung* (Wagner ibid.: 29).

24 *mein Vorbild* (Wagner 1912–14a: 'Autobiographische Skizze', 5).

25 *großen Trauerspiel* (Wagner 1912–14I: 34); *In dieser Schrift hatte ich nun ein Drama aufgezeichnet, zu welchem Shakespeare hauptsächlich durch 'Hamlet', 'Macbeth' und 'Lear' … beigetragen hatte … Die Handlung begründete sich eigentlich auf eine Variation des 'Hamlet'* (ibid.).

26 *ein Gemisch von 'Hamlet' und 'Percy Heißsporn'* (ibid.: 34); *ungestümer Fehde* (ibid.).

27 *weniger von Blutdurst als von Todessehnsucht angetrieben* (ibid.: 35); *glühendes Liebesverhältnis* (ibid.); *nach der von Shakespeare in Richard III. befolgten Methode schließen sich ihm die Geister der übrigen durch Leubald hingerichteten Glieder der Familie seiner Geliebten an* (ibid.).

28 *zweiundvierzig Menschen starben im Verlaufe des Stückes, und ich sah mich bei der Ausführung genötigt, die meisten als Geister wiederkommen zu lassen, weil mir sonst in den letzten Akten die Personen ausgegangen wären* (Wagner 1912–14a: 5).

29 *findet sich dann plötzlich beruhigt, senkt sein Haupt auf ihren Schoß und läßt sich ihre letzte Liebkosung gefallen, während ihr eigenes Blut über den Sterbenden dahinströmt* (Wagner 1912–14I: 36).

30 *voluminöse Manuskript* (ibid.: 33); *verschrobene Richtung* (ibid.: 36); *Verirrung* (ibid.: 34); *Gegenstand des Verbrechens* (ibid.); *welche ich nächstens auszuführen demnach beabsichtigte* (ibid.: 36).

31 *Zu 'Leubald und Adelaide' wollte ich nun eine Musik schreiben, wie die Beethovensche zu Goethes 'Egmont'; namentlich sollten die so unterschiedlichen Gattungen der Gespensterwelt angehörenden Geistererscheinungen durch die entsprechende musikalische Begleitung ihr rechtes Kolorit erst erhalten* (ibid.: 42).

32 *In mir entstand bald ein Bild erhabenster überirdischer Originalität, mit welcher sich durchaus nichts vergleichen ließ. Dieses Bild floß mit dem Shakespeares in mir zusammen: in ekstatischen Träumen begegnete ich beiden, sah und sprach sie; beim Erwachen schwamm ich in Tränen* (ibid.: 41).

33 *grübelnden Ernste* (ibid.: 110).

34 *unmittelbarer auf die nächste Lebensumgebung* (Wagner 1912–14g: 253).

35 *des Süjets von Shakespeares 'Maß für Maß' bemächtigt* (Wagner 1912–14l: 113)

36 William Shakespeare, 1991. *Measure for Measure*, ed. Brian Gibbons. Cambridge University Press. All references are to this edition.

37 *ich sah nur den finstern, sittenstrengen Statthalter, selbst von furchtbar leidenschaftlicher Liebe zu der schönen Novize entbrennend* (Wagner 1912–14l: 114).

38 *Isabella war es, die mich begeisterte* (Wagner 1912–14g: 254); *herrlichen Weibe* (ibid.); *keusche Seele* (ibid.).

39 *Liebesantipode* (Wagner 1912–14j: *Das Liebesverbot* (libretto), 97).

40 *ernste* (Wagner 1912–14l: 114*); in sehr freier Weise* (ibid.: 113); *das Sündhafte der Heuchelei und das Unnatürliche der grausamen Sittenrichterei aufzudecken* (ibid.: 114).

41 *Gelübde der Entsagung* (Wagner 1912–14k: 51); *heilsamen Schutze friedvoller Klostermauern* (ibid.: 54).

42 *ihr Heiligtum* (Wagner 1912–14d: 181).

43 *Verlangens* (Wagner 1912–14g: 294).

44 *reinsten Keuschheit* (Wagner 1912–14d: 182); *ein etwa unzüchtiger Selbstgenuß entzücken können* (ibid.).

45 *Zerstreuung* (Wagner 1912–14l: 167); *Theatergewirr* (ibid.: 196); *eine Aufführung des 'König Lear' ..., welcher ich nicht nur in den Aufführungen, sondern auch in den Proben mit höchstem Interesse beiwohnte* (ibid.: 201); *günstige Wendung meiner bis daher durch die Theaterpraxis auffallend verdorbenen Geschmacksrichtung* (ibid.).

46 *Sehr erfreulich war es mir, daß ich durch recht gute Aufführungen des rezitierenden Schauspiels meine alte ernste Neigung wieder angeregt fühlen durfte.* (Wagner 1912–14l: 201); *Umkehr meiner innern Neigungen nach der in frühester Jugend mir eignen, inbrünstig ernsten Seite meines Wesens hin* (ibid.: 204).

47 *schönen Schlosse von Helsingör ... dessen Anblick mich in unmittelbare Berührung mit meinen Jugendeindrücken von Hamlet setzte* (ibid.: 218).

48 *so daß, wie mit einem Schlage, das in meiner Jugendschwärmerei von mir geahnte Bild von diesem wunderbaren Werke ... nun sonnenhell, wie mit den Händen greifbar, vor mir stand* (ibid.: 237).

49 *Die ganze Periode der Verwilderung meines Geschmackes, welche, genau genommen, mit dem Irrewerden an dem Ausdrucke der Beethovenschen Kompositionen aus dessen letzter Zeit begonnen, und durch meinen verflachenden Verkehr mit dem schrecklichen Theater sich so bedenklich gesteigert hatte, versank jetzt vor mir wie in einem tiefen Abgrund der Scham und Reue.* (ibid.: 237)

50 *gewann doch nun ... der neugewonnene alte Geist erst wirkliche Lebenskraft* (ibid.: 237).

51 *Um mich zu vergewissern über das, was ich an der deutschen Heimat, nach der ich mich doch sehnte, denn eigentlich liebte, führte ich mir das Bild der Eindrücke meiner Jugend zurück ....* (Wagner 1912–14g: 270).

52 *wir Germanen hätten es besser, wir stammten von uns ab, und wir können*
uns einbilden, daß wir unsere Vergangenheit lebendig wieder machen können
(C. Wagner 1967: 204).

53 *oberflächliche Sinnlichkeit* (Wagner 1912–14b: 104); *leichtsinnige und nicht*
sehr unterscheidende Genußsucht (ibid.: 104); *höchsten Heiligtums* (ibid.: 102);
heißeste Sehnsucht (ibid.: 95) .

54 *Kein Liebender konnte seliger sein, der nach langer Trennung zur Geliebten*
seiner Jugend zurückkehrt (ibid.: 93); *fast heftige* (ibid.: 109); *'Wie es*
Shakespeare machte, wenn er seine Stücke schrieb' (ibid.).

55 Robert L. Jacobs and Geoffrey Skelton choose this title for dramatic effect,
to translate *Ein Ende in Paris*, whereas William Ashton Ellis simply uses *An*
End in Paris.

56 *daß es Sumpf und Morast war, in dem ich versank* (Wagner 1912–14c: 128); *den*
klagenden, geisterhaften Ton einer Hoboe (ibid.: 129); *Gamins* (ibid.: 114); *daß*
mich eines Tages die unwiderstehliche Lust anwandelte, den Teufel aufzusuchen
(ibid.: 130).

57 *Wie begeisterte mich das Vorgefühl einer nahen Auflösung, das ich plötzlich in*
allen Teilen dieses verwüsteten Körpers wahrnahm! – Für alle äußern Umstände
unempfänglich, … unbewußt, wohin mich mein schwankender Schritt trug, …
ich starb … für die Einfalt meines Glaubens … (ibid.: 133).

58 *ein dissonierender Akkord* (ibid.: 135); *die es wagten, in dieser Welt Wucher mit*
der hohen keuschen Kunst zu treiben, die sie schändeten und entehrten aus …
schnöder Gier nach Sinnenlust (ibid.).

59 *'Wie aus der Ferne längst vergang'ner Zeiten / spricht dieses Mädchens Bild*
zu mir: / wie ich's geträumt seit bangen Ewigkeiten, / vor meinen Augen seh'
ich's hier. –' (Wagner 1912–14e: 279). Translation of libretto © Lionel Salter
Library, www.lionelsalter.co.uk. Reprinted by kind permission of Graham
Salter.

60 *In weiter Ferne entsteigen dem Wasser der Holländer und Senta, beide in*
verklärter Gestalt (ibid.: 291).

61 *Stunde der Erlösung* (Wagner 1912–14l: 292); *Die Stadt, in welcher ich so*
bedeutungsvolle Kinder- und Knabenjahre verlebt, machte unter dem Eindruck
trüber, rauher Witterung einen kalten, toten Eindruck auf mich; wirklich schien
mir alles, was an meine Jugend mich erinnern konnte, dort erstorben (Wagner
1912–14m: 4).

62 *die Geister verblieben in ihrem unheimlichen Reiche* (Schmole 1953: 171).

63 *Zum Heil den Sündigen zu führen, / die Gott-Gesandte nahte mir: / doch, ach! sie*
frevelnd zu berühren / hob ich den Lästerblick zu ihr! (Wagner 1912–14f: 28).

64 *der Sünde fluchbelad'ner Sohn* (ibid.); *mit heuchlerischer Larve* (ibid.).

65 *zu böser Lust und Höllengrauen* (Wagner 1912–14i: 333); *durchzückt von*
seligsten Genusses Schmerz (ibid.: 342); *sündigen Blutes Gewell / in wahnsin-*
niger Flucht / muß mir zurück dann fließen, / in die Welt der Sündensucht / mit
wilder Scheu sich ergießen (ibid.); *verrat'ne Heiligtum* (ibid.: 359); *erlöse, rette*
mich / aus schuldbefleckten Händen! (ibid.). Translation of libretto © Lionel
Salter Library, www.lionelsalter.co.uk. Reprinted by kind permission of
Graham Salter.

66 Cf. C. Wagner (1980: 152): 'Yesterday evening he [i.e. Richard Wagner] was
pleased with Parsifal as a character, said he had correctly indicated the

things which a noble impression in adolescent years produces, overturning the natural instincts.' – *Gestern Abend freute er sich des Parsifal's als Gestalt, er habe darin das richtig angegeben, was in der Entwicklungszeit ein erhabener Eindruck hervorbringt, so daß der Naturtrieb umschlägt* (C. Wagner 1977: 178).

67   *der reine Tor* (Wagner 1912–14i: 328).

68   *Die Musik das Modernste und Letzte. Niemand ist darüber hinaus. ... Welch furchtbare Ausdruckskunst! Die Accente der Zerknirschung und der Qual, an denen er [Wagner] sein ganzes Leben lang geübt hat, finden erst hier ihre endgültige Intensität. Tristans Sehnsucht weit überboten durch dies Miserere. Durchdringende Einzelheiten, Klemmungen, feinste, inbrünstigste Grausamkeiten* ('Brief an Walter Opitz, 26. August 1909', hereafter referred to as GKFA 21b: 427–8).

69   *ein liebesiecher Oberpriester, der auf die Erlösung durch einen keuschen Knaben harrt; ebenfalls ein Fall entlegener Sonderbarkeit* (Mann 1982: 757).

70   *eines romantischen Extremismus ... ihre novellistische Einkleidung würde das leichter erkennbar machen* (ibid.: 757-8); *aus dem das Ganze sich nicht wie bei dem Literaturromantiker als schaurig-scherzhafter Unfug, sondern als hochreligiöses Weihespiel gebiert* (ibid.: 758).

71   *'Aber der Gehalt der Wagnerischen Texte! ihr mythischer Gehalt, ihr ewiger Gehalt!' – Frage: wie prüft man diesen Gehalt, diesen ewigen Gehalt?— Der Chemiker antwortet: man übersetzt Wagnern in's Reale, in's Moderne* (Nietzsche 1989: 34).

72   *uralte, seiner Jugend überlieferte ... Gedanken* (GKFA 2a: 553); *die goldene Dämmerung des Heiligtums* (ibid.: 565).

73   *Konzeption 'einer ... Männlichkeit' ..., 'die ... ruhig dasteht, während ihr die Schwerter und Speere durch den Leib gehen'* (ibid.: 511); *das Göttlich-Nichtssagende* (ibid.: 537).

74   *bleich* (ibid.: 591).

75   *eine überaus rührende dichterische Gestalt* (Mann 1999: 33).

76   *Ob auch wohl mir Fliegendem Holländer einmal eine,Erlösung' gleich der Ihren zutheil werden wird?* ('Brief an Walter Opitz, 26. August 1909', hereafter referred to as GKFA 21a: 205).

77   *ein jugendlich durstiges Verlangen ... längst entwöhnt und verlernt* (GKFA 2a: 505).

78   *vormännlich hold und herb* (ibid.: 539).

79   *der in so vorbildlicher Form dem Zigeunertum und der trüben Tiefe abgesagt* (ibid.: 588); *Aber Form und Unbefangenheit führen zum Rausch und zur Begierde, ... führen zum Abgrund, zum Abgrund auch sie* (ibid.: 589).

80   *aus exotischem Trieb ersehnt* ('Versuch über das Theater', hereafter referred to as GKFA 14b: 138); *tropischer Landschaft* (ibid.); *umtanzt von Wilden* (ibid.); *man trank, man betrank sich und vergaß sich darin* (ibid.); *Katzenjammer und Reue* (ibid.); *Ein erstes Schönheitserlebnis!* (ibid.).

81   *daß mir zuerst die Kunst Richard Wagners entgegentrat* (ibid.: 139); *das Ideal* (ibid.: 140); *zu dem man, rasch trunken von Musik, emporstarrt* (ibid.).

82   *in bildmäßigem Abstand* (GKFA 2a: 541).

83   *Heim- und Jugendweh* (GKFA 14a: 304).

84   *als ob sein Gewissen wie nach einer Ausschweifung Klage führe* (GKFA 2a: 556); cf. Mann (1985g: 45), footnote.

85   *die Frauen, die Tadzio behüteten* (GKFA 2a: 572).
86   *'Donnerwetter! Es ist ja ein Frauenzimmer.'* (Wagner 1912–14n: 103)
87   *züchtige Kriegsleute* (GKFA 2a: 589); *so sind wir wie Weiber* (ibid.).
88   *es war dahin gekommen, daß der Verliebte fürchten mußte, auffällig geworden und beargwöhnt zu sein* (ibid.: 572).
89   *wir vermögen nicht, uns aufzuschwingen* (ibid.: 589).

Works Cited

Foucault, Michel, 2003. *Abnormal: Lectures at the Collège de France 1974–1975*, trans. Graham Burchell. New York: Verso.

Hayman, Ronald, 1995. *Thomas Mann: A Biography*. New York: Scribner.

Mann, Thomas, 1962. 'Brief an Wolfgang Born, 18. März 1921', in *Briefe 1889–1936*, ed. Erika Mann, vol. 1. Frankfurt am Main: S. Fischer, pp. 184–6.

Mann, Thomas, 1975a. 'Letter to Carl Maria Weber, 4 July 1920', in *Letters of Thomas Mann*, trans. Richard and Clara Winston. London: Penguin, pp. 93–7.

Mann, Thomas, 1975b. 'Letter to Elisabeth Zimmer, 6 September 1915', in *Letters of Thomas Mann*, trans. Richard and Clara Winston. London: Penguin, pp. 72–3.

Mann, Thomas, 1975c. 'Letter to Heinrich Mann, 7 March 1901', in *Letters of Thomas Mann*, trans. Richard and Clara Winston. London: Penguin, pp. 22–3.

Mann, Thomas, 1975d. 'Letter to Wolfgang Born, 18 March 1921', in *Letters of Thomas Mann*, trans. Richard and Clara Winston. London: Penguin, pp. 100–2.

Mann, Thomas, 1982. 'Leiden und Größe Richard Wagners', in *Leiden und Größe der Meister. Gesammelte Werke*, ed. Peter de Mendelssohn. Frankfurt am Main: S. Fischer, pp. 716–79.

Mann, Thomas, 1985a. 'Coming to Terms with Richard Wagner', in *Pro and Contra Wagner*, trans. Alan Blunden. London: Faber, pp. 45–8.

Mann, Thomas, 1985b. 'From "An Essay on the Theatre"', in *Pro and Contra Wagner*, trans. Alan Blunden. London: Faber, pp. 25–37.

Mann, Thomas, 1985c. 'From "Mind and Art"', in *Pro and Contra Wagner*, trans. Alan Blunden. London: Faber, pp. 37–44.

Mann, Thomas, 1985d. 'The Sorrows and Grandeur of Richard Wagner', in *Pro and Contra Wagner*, trans. Alan Blunden. London: Faber, pp. 91–149.

Mann, Thomas, 1985e. 'Wagner and the Present Age', in *Pro and Contra Wagner*, trans. Alan Blunden. London: Faber, pp. 88–9.

Mann, Thomas, 1985f. 'Letter to Kurt Martens, 12 July 1902', in *Pro and Contra Wagner*, trans. Alan Blunden. London: Faber, p. 23.

Mann, Thomas, 1985g. 'Letter to Walter Opitz, 26 August 1909', in *Pro and Contra Wagner*, trans. Alan Blunden. London: Faber, pp. 44–5.

Mann, Thomas, 1999. *Im Schatten Wagners: Thomas Mann über Richard Wagner: Texte und Zeugnisse 1895–1955*, ed. Hans Rudolf Vaget. Frankfurt am Main: Fischer Taschenbuchverlag.

Mann, Thomas, 2001 [1911]. 'The Fight between Jappe and Do Escobar', in *Collected Stories*, trans. H.T. Lowe Porter. London: Everyman's Library, pp. 409–10.

Mann, Thomas, 2002. 'Brief an Kurt Martens, 12. Juli 1902', in *Briefe 1. 1889–1913*, eds Thomas Sprecher, Hans R. Vaget and Cornelia Bernini. Große Kommentierte Frankfurter Ausgabe, vol. 21. Frankfurt am Main: S. Fischer, p. 205. [GKFA 21a]

Mann, Thomas, 2002. 'Brief an Walter Opitz, 26. August 1909', in *Briefe 1. 1889–1913*, eds Thomas Sprecher, Hans R. Vaget, Cornelia Bernini. Große Kommentierte Frankfurter Ausgabe, vol. 21. Frankfurt am Main: S. Fischer, pp. 427–8. [GKFA 21b]

Mann, Thomas, 2002a. 'Auseinandersetzung mit Wagner', in *Essays 1. 1893–1914*, ed. Heinrich Detering,. Große Kommentierte Frankfurter Ausgabe, vol. 14.1. Frankfurt am Main: S. Fischer, pp. 301–4. [GKFA 14a]

Mann, Thomas, 2002a. 'Versuch über das Theater', in *Essays 1. 1893–1914*, ed. Heinrich Detering. Große Kommentierte Frankfurter Ausgabe, vol. 14.1. Frankfurt am Main: S. Fischer, pp. 123–68. [GKFA 14b]

Mann, Thomas, 2002b. 'Brief an Heinrich Mann, 7. März 1901', in *Briefe 1. 1889–1913*, eds Thomas Sprecher, Hans R. Vaget, Cornelia Bernini. *Große Kommentierte Frankfurter Ausgabe, vol. 21. Frankfurt am Main: S. Fischer, pp. 160–1.* [GKFA 21c]

Mann, Thomas, 2004. 'Brief an Carl Maria Weber, 4. Juli 1920', in *Briefe 2. 1914–1923*, eds Thomas Sprecher, Hans R. Vaget and Cornelia Bernini. Große Kommentierte Frankfurter Ausgabe, vol. 22. Frankfurt am Main: S. Fischer, pp. 347–53. [GKFA 22a]

Mann, Thomas, 2004. 'Brief an Elisabeth Zimmer, 6. September 1915', in *Briefe 2. 1914–1923*, eds Thomas Sprecher, Hans R. Vaget and Cornelia Bernini. Große Kommentierte Frankfurter Ausgabe, vol. 22. Frankfurt am Main: S. Fischer, pp. 92–3. [GKFA 22b]

Mann, Thomas, 2004a [1912]. 'Der Tod in Venedig', in *Frühe Erzählungen*, ed. Terence J. Reed. Große Kommentierte Frankfurter Ausgabe, vol. 2.1. Frankfurt am Main: S. Fischer, pp. 501–92. [GKFA 2a]

Mann, Thomas, 2004b [1911]. 'Wie Jappe und Do Escobar sich prügelten', in *Frühe Erzählungen*, ed. Terence J. Reed. Große Kommentierte Frankfurter Ausgabe, vol. 2.1. Frankfurt am Main: S. Fischer, pp. 482–500. [GKFA 2b]

Mann, Thomas, 2005 [1912]. *Death in Venice*, trans. Michael Henry Heim. New York: Ecco. [*DV*]

McClain, William H., 1964. 'Wagnerian Overtones in *Der Tod in Venedig*', in *Modern Language Notes* 79:5, pp. 481–95.

Nietzsche, Friedrich, 1967. *The Case of Wagner*, in *The Birth of Tragedy and The Case of Wagner*, trans. Walter Kaufmann. New York: Random House, pp. 153–98.

Nietzsche, Friedrich, 1989 [1888]. 'Der Fall Wagner', in *Der Fall Wagner. Götzen-Dämmerung. Der Antichrist. Ecce Homo. Dionysos-Dithyramben. Nietzsche contra Wagner*, Kritische Studienausgabe, eds Giorgio Colli, Mazzino Montinari, vol. 6. München: dtv, pp. 9–54.

Praeger, Ferdinand, 1892. *Wagner As I Knew Him*. London: Longmans, Green, and Co.

Schmole, Marie, 1950. 'The Dresden years', in *Letters of Richard Wagner: The Burrell Collection*, ed. John N. Burk. New York: The Macmillan Company, pp. 118–35.

Schmole, Marie, 1953. 'Die Dresdner Jahre', in *Richard Wagner Briefe. Die Sammlung Burrell*, ed. John N. Burk. Frankfurt am Main: S. Fischer, pp. 165–87.

Shakespeare, William, 1991. *Measure for Measure*, ed. Brian Gibbons. Cambridge: Cambridge University Press.

Tardieu, Auguste Ambroise, 2013 [1878]. *Etude médico-légale sur les attentats aux moeurs*, quoted in Julie Peakman, *The Pleasure's All Mine: A History of Perverse Sex*. Clerkenwell, London: Reaktion.

Vaget, Hans Rudolf (ed.), 2005. *Im Schatten Wagners. Thomas Mann über Richard Wagner. Texte und Zeugnisse 1895–1955*, revised edition. Frankfurt am Main: Fischer Taschenbuchverlag.

Wagner, Cosima, 1976. *Die Tagebücher. Band 1. 1869 –1877.* München: Piper.

Wagner, Cosima, 1977. *Die Tagebücher. Band 2. 1877–1883.* München: Piper.

Wagner, Cosima, 1978. *Diaries,* vol. 1, trans. Geoffrey Skelton. London: Collins.

Wagner, Cosima, 1980. *Diaries,* vol. 2, trans. Geoffrey Skelton. London: Collins.

Wagner, Richard, 1892a. 'A Communication to my Friends', in *Richard Wagner's Prose Works,* vol. 1, trans. William Ashton Ellis. London: Kegan Paul, Trench, Trübner & Co, pp. 267–392.

Wagner, Richard, 1892b. 'Autobiographic Sketch', in *Richard Wagner's Prose Works* vol. 1, trans. William Ashton Ellis. London: Kegan Paul, Trench, Trübner & Co, pp. 1–19.

Wagner, Richard, 1912–14a. 'Autobiographische Skizze', in *Sämtliche Schriften und Dichtungen,* vol. 1, 6th edn. Leipzig: Breitkopf & Härtel, pp. 4–19.

Wagner, Richard, 1912–14b. 'Eine Pilgerfahrt zu Beethoven', in *Sämtliche Schriften und Dichtungen,* vol. 1, 6th edn. Leipzig: Breitkopf & Härtel, pp. 90–113.

Wagner, Richard, 1912–14c. 'Eine Ende in Paris', in *Sämtliche Schriften und Dichtungen,* vol. 1, 6th edn. Leipzig: Breitkopf & Härtel, pp. 114–35.

Wagner, Richard, 1912–14d. 'Der Künstler und die Öffentlichkeit', in *Sämtliche Schriften und Dichtungen,* vol. 1, 6th edn. Leipzig: Breitkopf & Härtel, pp. 180–5.

Wagner, Richard, 1912–14e. *Der fliegende Holländer* (libretto), in *Sämtliche Schriften und Dichtungen,* vol. 1, 6th edn. Leipzig: Breitkopf & Härtel, pp. 258–91.

Wagner, Richard, 1912–14f. *Tannhäuser* (libretto), in *Sämtliche Schriften und Dichtungen,* vol. 2, 6th edn. Leipzig: Breitkopf & Härtel, pp. 3–40.

Wagner, Richard, 1912–14g. 'Eine Mitteilung an meine Freunde', in *Sämtliche Schriften und Dichtungen,* vol. 4, 6th edn. Leipzig: Breitkopf & Härtel, pp. 230–344.

Wagner, Richard, 1912–14h. *Tristan und Isolde* (libretto), in *Sämtliche Schriften und Dichtungen,* vol. 7, 6th edn. Leipzig: Breitkopf & Härtel, pp. 1–81.

Wagner, Richard, 1912–14i. *Parsifal* (libretto), in *Sämtliche Schriften und Dichtungen,* vol. 10, 6th edn. Leipzig: Breitkopf & Härtel, pp. 324–75.

Wagner, Richard, 1912–14j. *Das Liebesverbot* (libretto), in *Sämtliche Schriften und Dichtungen,* vol. 11, 6th edn. Leipzig: Breitkopf & Härtel, pp. 59–124.

Wagner, Richard, 1912–14k. 'Pariser Fatalitäten für Deutsche', in *Sämtliche Schriften und Dichtungen,* vol. 12, 6th edn. Leipzig: Breitkopf & Härtel, pp. 46–64.

Wagner, Richard, 1912–14l. *Mein Leben. Erster Teil: 1813–1842,* in *Sämtliche Schriften und Dichtungen,* vol. 13, Leipzig: Breitkopf & Härtel.

Wagner, Richard, 1912–14m. *Mein Leben. Zweiter Teil: 1842–1850,* in *Sämtliche Schriften und Dichtungen,* vol. 14, Leipzig: Breitkopf & Härtel.

Wagner, Richard, 1912–14n. *Mein Leben. Dritter Teil: 1850–1861,* in *Sämtliche Schriften und Dichtungen,* vol. 15, Leipzig: Breitkopf & Härtel.

Wagner, Richard, 1973a. 'A Pilgrimage to Beethoven', in *Wagner Writes from Paris…,* trans. Robert L. Jacobs and Geoffrey Skelton. London: George Allen & Unwin, pp. 64–83.

Wagner, Richard, 1973b. 'Death in Paris', in *Wagner Writes from Paris…,* trans. Robert L. Jacobs and Geoffrey Skelton. London: George Allen & Unwin, pp. 84–102.

Wagner, Richard, 1973c. 'The Artist and the Public', in *Wagner Writes from Paris…,* trans. Robert L. Jacobs and Geoffrey Skelton. London: George Allen & Unwin, pp. 103–8.

Wagner, Richard, 1973d. 'Traps for Unwary Germans in Paris', in *Wagner Writes from Paris…,* trans. Robert L. Jacobs and Geoffrey Skelton. London: George Allen & Unwin, pp. 18–35.

Wagner, Richard, 1981. *Tristan and Isolde*, English National Opera Guide. Richmond: John Calder.

Wagner, Richard, 1983. *My Life*, trans. Andrew Gray. Cambridge: Cambridge University Press.

Wagner, Richard, 2008. *Das Liebesverbot* (libretto), trans. Richard Arsenty. New York: The Wagner Society of New York, Inc.

Wagner, Richard, 2011a. *Parsifal* (libretto), trans. Lionel Salter. Overture Opera Guide. Richmond: Overture Publishing.

Wagner, Richard, 2011b. *Tannhäuser* (libretto), trans. Rodney Blumer. Overture Opera Guide. Richmond: Overture Publishing.

Wagner, Richard, 2012. *Der fliegende Holländer* (libretto), trans. Lionel Salter. Overture Opera Guide. Richmond: Overture Publishing.

Eight 'Yes—yes, no': Mann, Shakespeare and the Struggle for Affirmation
Ewan Fernie

When Thomas Mann, in *Doktor Faustus*, looked hardest at Shakespeare, he found various things there. He found erotic turbulence, bisexuality, the problems and confusions of working through a sexual go-between, the love of a fair youth, the faint hope for redemption of a lost innocence. All strong stuff! And yet, beyond this and most shockingly, Mann found in Shakespeare an early, implicit theology of modernity. It's shocking, first of all, because we don't think of Shakespeare as a theological writer. Of course I know some recent scholarship has found Shakespeare theologically interesting; I've even contributed to that case myself, firstly in *Shame in Shakespeare*, then in *Spiritual Shakespeares*, and (most recently) in *The Demonic*, where I argued, for instance, that *Macbeth* is the bravest of all artistic responses to Luther's injunction to 'sin bravely'.[1] But we don't and shouldn't think of Shakespeare as *above all* a theological writer like, say, Dante – indeed, that might be exactly why he's become theologically interesting in our more secular age. Nor do or should we think of modernism as fundamentally theological. Of course I know about Joyce's agon with Catholicism, his deep reading in and contemplation of theological writers like Aquinas and Bruno; I know about the way he breathes a sort of immanent theology – eschatology even – into the comic triumph of Bloomsday. And there's the reactionary theological modernism of *Four Quartets*; and the most religious English-language poet of modernism, David Jones, expressly writes against a situation where the word 'wood' has ceased automatically to evoke the Cross of Christ.[2] But all the theology in modernism, including Joyce, is reactionary inasmuch as it attempts to re-enchant the wasteland. Whereas what Mann finds in Shakespeare is that modern art, culture and indeed experience is already essentially theological. Only not in a good way.

Because Mann's partly Shakespeare-derived theology of modern life is unchurched, seductive, devastating: in short, it is a theology of the damned. And what's worse is, once you've seen it, this is hard to get around. You get sucked in; Mann certainly did. This essay tells the story of his struggle to see life otherwise. It suggests, also, that *Shakespeare* tried to see life otherwise. And it suggests this might help *us* to get to grips with a fundamental need in modernity and ourselves.

But first we need to remind ourselves of what this theology of the damned, this most improbable thing – a *Shakespearean* theology of modern life – consists in. According to Mann in *Doktor Faustus*, it boils down to 'gravity's revolt to wantonness' (*Love's Labour's Lost*, 5.2.74).[3] On the one hand, gravity's revolt involves creative liberation from the ordinary restrictions of life. But, equally, it is unhealthily cut off from life, as witnessed in the maddest, most nonsensical passages of Shakespeare's early comedy.[4] Such wild abstraction is a first kind of 'wantonness', but gravity's revolt also engenders a compounding and opposite kind, a violent hunger for the ordinary life left behind. This pattern whereby the rejection of life is followed by perverse hunger to repossess it Mann sees as Shakespeare's spiritual signature, and the secret truth of our own times and lives.

But why is this theological? The pattern of revolt from then wrecking re-engagement with life is of course Faustian. But why's *that* theological? It is theological because it outrages, and not once but twice, the ultimate givenness of Being. Its sins against life are sins against God. That's why Adrian Leverkühn becomes such easy prey for the Devil while working on his operatic version of *Love's Labour's Lost*. I've written before about Mann and Shakespeare in *Doktor Faustus*; about how their unexpected conjunction reveals the formative negativity of modern culture in its most agonized form.[5] Here I want to take up the alternative story of Mann's and Shakespeare's struggle to affirm modern life in spite of this.

I believe the creative collision between Mann and Shakespeare raises some important questions for all of us:

Given the seemingly intractable alienation of the human mind in modernity, is there any alternative to the theology of the damned? And if so, what is it?

*

Tracking Mann and Shakespeare takes us right into a major problem of contemporary culture in the West: the problem of religion. Mainstream culture today stands at one remove at least from what we might call spontaneous or natural religion. And Mann expresses what many feel: *can't live with it, can't live without it*. 'I cannot say that I believe in God,' he writes, 'and even if I did believe, it would be a long time before I said so' (trans. and quoted in Heller 1979: 148);[6] but we should not take this as mere secularism, as Erich Heller intimates: 'He doubts, and even believes in doubt, for doubt is better than a false belief'. 'Thus, from the depth of his unbelief,' Heller goes on, 'Thomas Mann religiously denounces the heretical believer' (ibid.).

Doubt is more authentic, unbelief more religious, than religion is: doubt and unbelief have a better fix on the ultimately ambivalent and uncertain nature of things insofar as we can know them.

And yet, at the same time as he rejects belief, Mann abhors the thought of any inchoate, self-indulgent 'spirituality'. At the graveside of an unnamed poet (in fact, Frank Wedekind)[7] who had, in his extremity, 'longed for salvation', he is horrified to hear sophisticated talk of 'our duty towards the spirit which we call religion'. With that, he says simply, 'I put on my hat and went home' (ibid.: 142).[8]

The English philosopher Gillian Rose challenges Mann on religious grounds in her book *The Broken Middle*. Rose inveighs against the German author as a prize modern example of what she calls a Gnostic, by which she means a spiritually ambitious person who stands aloof from any ecclesiastical, or rabbinic, tradition.[9] 'Ultimately, in criticising Mann,' Andrew Shanks explains, 'Rose is aiming at all that great multitude of modern intellectuals who, in their disenchantment with institutionalized religion, have more or less decided to replace it, as an education for the moral imagination, with the reading of serious novels, the watching of serious plays or films' (2008: 104). Now this seems well aimed as a critique of disengaged intellectuals; but I'm not sure we should stop reading Mann and head out for Evensong or the synagogue – although, to tell the truth, many people, at least in contemporary Britain, have stopped doing both in droves. *I put on my hat and went home*: as we've seen, Mann does *not* favour a conveniently privatized spirituality. In fact, he takes the objective claims of religion very seriously: that's why he can't glibly credit them. He also, and in *Joseph und seine Brüder* – the very novel that Rose criticizes – takes seriously the power of religion to recreate an indifferent multitude as a mobilized and militant church of God; he absolutely sees the political energy and potential for beauty in this. Where he does differ from Rose is a matter of emphasis; but then emphasis in important matters makes for important differences.

Rose recognizes the difficulty and ambivalence of modern life. She seeks to resolve it, not in the sense of bringing it to an end but instead by reconceiving the role of traditional religious institutions in terms of *doing justice* to the complexity of modern culture. The very mission of the church in the world, according to her, is to mediate tirelessly between the different truths, creeds, institutions and parties that make up modern life. Mann, as we have seen, is far from denying the power of official religion. But religious revival tends to strike him as perverse or nostalgic or both: consider the disturbing, atavistic theology of *Der Zauberberg* (*The Magic Mountain*) or *Doktor Faustus*. For Rose, Gnosticism is – *again* it is – the great religious temptation. For Mann, official religion is a noble historical phenomenon, but one which always remains historical. Gnosticism isn't a temptation Mann even takes very seriously. According to him, our contemporary spiritual conditions have forced us out of a natural and virtuous at-homeness in the church. That means that nowadays, as we see from the religion of Naphta or Schleppfuß, religion itself is the real temptation.

But how, then, is the soul to come home?

*

Well, we can start to answer that question by observing that when Mann broods on questions of spirit, he is often thinking about Shakespeare as well.

In *The Ironic German*, Heller suggests that Mann's contemporary Hugo von Hofmannsthal 'defined most succinctly the disquieting quality of the literary situation' (1979: 21) which Mann faced, and defined it in expressly Shakespearean terms.

Hofmannsthal's 'Ein Brief' is the confession of early modern culture as such in the guise of an imaginary letter written by one Lord Chandos, an invented Elizabethan intellectual, to Francis Bacon.[10] It expresses the devastation of tradition and meaning by knowledge, in a way which resonates with the fates of, as Heller observes, 'Doktor Faustus, who goes to Hell because he wants to know, and of Hamlet, who lives in Hell because he knows' (ibid.: 21). As we saw in the Introduction, Heller also points to *Tonio Kröger*, where Mann explicitly conjures a Shakespearean ghost (ibid.: 13–14). 'There is something I call being sick of knowledge...,' says Tonio, 'when it is enough for a man to see through a thing in order to be sick to death of it – the case of Hamlet' (Mann 1936: 106–7). This sickness of knowledge, which Nietzsche also recognized in Shakespeare's Prince, renders life obscene, and it cannot be accommodated or defused in positive religion. The upshot is an agony of spiritual guilt: 'To see things clearly, even if through tears, to recognize, observe, even at the very moment when hands are clinging and lips meeting, and the eye is blinded with feeling – it is infamous, indecent, outrageous ....'[11] (ibid.).[12] In Mann's first master-piece, *Buddenbrooks*, Heller tells us Thomas Buddenbrook is Thomas Mann's 'merchant-Hamlet. ... And with his son Hanno the play *is* the thing, and music becomes the only reality: music and death, the great romantic liberators of the soul, the powers that move in with noble excess where the balance between question and answer is upset – the balance called tradition' (1979: 14). In that liberation, Hanno already foretells Adrian Leverkühn's Shakespearean musical adventure into a demonic passion for the negative in *Doktor Faustus*.

Heller further points out that Mann followed Friedrich Schlegel in seeing Shakespeare as one of the first self-conscious writers, and as such a main source of the contradiction and complexity which burst forth in Romanticism. This literature, according to Schlegel, offered an 'indirect mythology' (quoted in Heller 1979: 201).[13] And what else but *indirect* mythology could stand a chance in our modern spiritual conditions of self-conscious knowledge and dislocation from natural, unmediated experience?

Mann saw that there are two ways of dealing with the burden of self-conscious knowledge our cultural belatedness bequeaths. There is the way of ironic engagement with life, and the way of destructive negation of it. The discovery of both in *Love's Labour's Lost* leads Leverkühn and modern music to Hell, and is crucially if obscurely implicated in the horrors of the Third Reich. But elsewhere in his oeuvre, Mann tried to deal with the negativity and alienation of modern life in a more productive fashion.

*

I argued in the Introduction that Mann offers Peeperkorn in *Der Zauberberg* as a Shakespearean, Falstaff-inspired solution to what he had already begun to see as a partly Shakespearean problem of demonic abstraction. But Peeperkorn is a sketch only, and it is the corrupted Jesuit, Naphta, who wins the battle of ideas in the novel. In *Betrachtungen eines Unpolitischen* (*Reflections of a Nonpolitical Man*), Mann admitted straightforwardly, 'I have Schopenhauer's morality – a popular word for the same thing is "pessimism" – as my basic psychological mood, that mood of "cross, death and grave" that appeared as early as in my first efforts'[14] (1983: 54). In an earlier age, that might have led to a positive religious vocation; but now, as *Der Zauberberg* and *Doktor Faustus* recognize, it lays Thomas Mann open to the fiend. The gigantic effort represented by his most 'gigantic novel' is what it takes to protect himself and, as Hermann Kurzke suggests, 'legitimize his own rejection of [this] sympathy with death' (2002: 394).

In *Joseph und seine Brüder*, Mann apparently has to leave Shakespeare behind in order to improve on Peeperkorn and his case for affirmation; but *Joseph* I suggest can 'bounce' us into a new view of one of Shakespeare's major comedies – *As You Like It* – as an analogous effort to imagine a life which defuses negativity and can so be comprehensively affirmed.

Today *Joseph* is perhaps the least read and discussed of Mann's masterpieces, but it is the work which offers the most convincing alternative to the demonic spirituality which in *Doktor Faustus* Mann associates with Shakespeare and finds at the heart of modern culture. *Joseph* also rescues modern spirituality from the embarrassment of being kitsch, floundering unmoored from the concreteness and communitarian politics of religion. Mann's epic novel works hard over 1,500 pages of closely printed type to give unchurched spirituality form and dignity, as well as a very worldly and engaged aspect that, to my mind, arms it in advance against Rose's critique of Mann as a modern 'Gnostic'.

For a start, Mann doesn't underestimate official religion in *Joseph*; and nor, for that matter, does his hero. Certainly, Mann's Pharaoh, Akhenaton, withdraws from political responsibility into blissful and edifying metaphysical dreams – which, it should be admitted, entail a real advance, moving from pantheistic tribalism towards a peaceful, universal monotheism. Still, as Pharaoh dreams, Joseph on his behalf is building granaries, forestalling famine, feeding the Egyptian people. Moreover, Mann gives significant attention and indeed honour, in this novel, to Jewish religiosity. He perceives that the germ and genius of Jewish religion is its particular but self-transcending vocation for the universal. Akhenaton's mystical raptures represent the universal as a refuge from political urgency, but Mann portrays Jewish universalism much more politically positively. This is a religious morality that is not of the world, but it is far from Gnosticism. If it stands apart from life-as-it-is, it does so in the hope of bringing a newer and more absolute world into being.

Mann's celebration of Jewish morality, just at the point of the worst persecution of the Jews in history, is noble and impressive. As Heller observes, Jaakob's 'divine anxiety' is 'so much at the centre of Thomas Mann's work that he sometimes thought he would have to call it *Jacob and his Sons*' (1979: 244). In this most positively religious of his works, Mann goes hungrily back to the origin of the Judeo-Christian tradition in search of that clarity of vision and purpose which inevitably was lost as it became established and involved in the world it opposes. Jaakob's story glints with the vision of a fresh possibility *for us moderns* of a religious community rebuilt on the basis of the solidarity of those not at home in the world.

But it's true that, even in *Joseph und seine Brüder*, Mann turns decidedly away from institutionalized religion, and what he recognizes in Jaakob's story as its radical, collective negation of accustomed life. And here he does so without falling into the Devil's arms.

In *Joseph*, Mann tries to carve out an accommodating position which stands between a principled, religious negation of life such as Jaakob's and joyous participation in it. We first meet Joseph offering 'his youthful nakedness to the moon' (2005: 59),[15] which straightaway makes the point that a more harmonious spirituality will be coextensive with an accepting, even comprehensive sexuality. To his sterner, more wracked father, Joseph's lunar escapade smacks concerningly of 'folly', 'lewd frenzy' and 'unclean regions of the soul' (ibid.: 337).[16] But we are told by Mann that Joseph 'had a better understanding of God's living reality and would prove more supple in dealing with it than Jacob' (ibid.: 923).[17] Moreover, the very, all-but-universal extensiveness of Joseph's sexual interests depends on a kind of chastity. He is not actually drawn into 'lewd frenzy' even though Potiphar's smitten wife, Mut-em-enet, subjects him to 'one of the strongest temptations that has ever laid siege to a lad in the history of the world' (ibid.: 976).[18] That said, such is his openness that he does not altogether refuse Mut-em-enet's blandishments either. 'One may call it curiosity and frivolity,' writes Mann, 'call it an aversion to finally giving up the possible choice of evil, the wish to keep the choice between good and evil still open, though with no intention whatever of siding with evil' (ibid.: 977).[19] Unlike Jaakob's church of self-castigating sinners, Joseph does not engage in the crude definiteness of sheer moral judgement or refusal. He is a *'virtuoso* of virtue'[20] (ibid.: 931; my emphasis). We may imagine him exercising his morality as though playing a violin, bowing light into and out from the darkness without capitulating to the demonic. Joseph reveals and effects a much deeper and more extensive relation between the sacred and the ordinary world. In him, affirmation begins to look possible.

Crucial to this aptitude for affirmation is the supple flexibility of Joseph's wit. As Mann puts it:

> wit is by nature a messenger who goes back and forth, a nimble ambassador between two opposing spheres and influences – for example, between the forces of the sun and moon, the father's legacy and the mother's legacy, between the blessing of the day and the blessing of the night – indeed, to put it in direct and all-inclusive terms, between life and death.
>
> (ibid.: 1438)[21]

Wit absorbs the negative pole into affirmation; it absorbs negation itself into affirmation. It doesn't actually entail the neglect of customary morality as Rose claims Mann does in his Joseph books but, instead, seeks to reconcile tradition with self-expressive non-conformity. As Joseph himself says:

For the pattern of tradition comes from the deeps that lie below, and is what binds us. But the I is from God and is a child of the spirit, which is free. This, however, is civilised life – that the binding pattern from the depths is fulfilled in the divine freedom of the I, and there is no human civilisation without either one or the other.

(ibid.: 1158)[22]

Thus Mann's Joseph reconciles in his own life the oppositions between church and world, spirit and flesh, talent and tradition.

The most explicit and worked out formulation of Joseph's happy spirituality is Mann's disquisition on his traditionally distinguishing feature of *tâm*: 'a strangely equivocal word for which "upright" is a very poor translation, for its meaning includes both the positive and the negative, the yes and the no, light and dark, life and death'. Ultimately Mann translates it: 'Yes—yes, no': 'that is, with a yes and no prefixed by the coefficient of another yes'. 'In purely mathematical terms', he explains, 'since a yes and a no cancel one another out, only the additional yes is left over; but such pure reckoning has no colour and this sort of mathematics disregards the dark coloring of the yes that evidently remains as an aftereffect of the canceled no'. 'It is', he concludes, as if with a disarming smile, 'all very complicated' (ibid.: 1230–1).[23]

Here in truth is what Heller calls a 'theology of irony': a theology of nuance, complexity and shadedness.[24] And Mann's charming shrug of the shoulders is in fact belied by the X-ray lucidity of his formulation, 'Yes—yes, no', his fine defiance of mathematical convention in insisting that 'the dark coloring of the yes...evidently remains as an aftereffect of the canceled no'. Mann's discussion of Joseph's *tâm* affords a whole alternative perspective on the religious negativity of Jaakob and the tribe of Israel, which in this light seems less like righteous refusal of corruption than a falsifying evasion of truth in its essentially mixed nature. The negative, it appears, still has an ineradicable share in the development of spirit. But the negative hypostasized is a false positive. This is not what *tâm* affirms as 'Yes—yes, no'. Instead, *tâm* positively affirms *movement*. It affirms movement between alternatives, between negation and affirmation, just such movement as is expressed in Joseph's opulent multi-coloured life.

Joseph, I suggest, is Thomas Mann's incarnation and icon of a comprehensively affirmed life.

And yet –

'All that we saw was owing to your metaphysics' (2008: 141), says Blake in *The Marriage of Heaven and Hell*, and Mann is spiritually honest enough to see the limits to Joseph's happy spirituality. Jaakob pronounces upon his favoured son 'a rare blessing ... the spirit of charming mediation ... a lovely blessing', while at the same time admitting that it is 'not the highest or most stern'. 'Behold,' he says gravely to Joseph, 'your precious life lies in all its truth before the eyes of a dying man'. And the truth of Joseph's life is 'play', 'allusion', 'a confiding, cordial state of favour, hinting at salvation and yet not fully summoned and admitted to true seriousness' (2005: 1476).[25]

There is beauty in this but at the same time, as is painfully clear to a father's heart, also the sadness of significant restriction. And yet, so dialectically duplicitous is Mann as an artist that so soon as we admit this Joseph's spirituality seems again to assert itself, in its most gracefully expansive aspect. Certainly no one in the novel says anything better than this:

> [T]he feast is to be observed with every high delight and amusement. For high delight, my friend, and the subtle jest are the best that God gave us, and the profoundest knowledge we have of this complicated, equivocal life.
>
> (ibid.: 1304)[26]

Could there be wiser advice as to how to live? And this spirit of festive affirmation is no kind of wishful thinking; it is rather a heroic 'Hermes humour' which can see off even evil and pain. For Joseph insists:

> One cannot answer them with a long face. The human spirit can rise above them only in serene delight, so that in its own profound amusement over what is unanswerable, it may move God himself, the great unanswering God, to laughter.
>
> (ibid.: 1304)[27]

Joseph's smile may well in the end be the best – the *strongest* – answer to the furious negativity of a Naphta, or the creative torment of a Leverkühn. To take up the terms of Mann's allegorical prelude, he unites in his own person the otherworldly energy of 'the spirit' and the this-worldly energy of 'the soul' (ibid.: 3–40).[28] Rose scorns this. In the words of her most lucid commentator:

> Implicitly, the message is: let the antagonism of the two principles be softened into a gentle dialectic of amused, and amusing, irony! Wherever Soul and Spirit appear to be at war, let irony go to work on both sides, to mollify their mutual resistance. And, supremely – let ironic novels be written, like this one.
>
> (Shanks 2008: 103)

But Mann tentatively suggests that the union of these two principles accomplishes 'the mystery', and even perhaps the fruition of 'God's quiet hope', 'actualizing in the present a humanity that would be blessed with blessings of heaven above and blessings of the deep that lies below' (Mann 2005: 35).[29] It seems wrong to scoff at this. Or, indeed, at such softening and gentleness as manage to take the edge off a purely negative spirituality whose influence, we should recall, Mann discerns in the catastrophe of Nazism and World War Two. Joseph's worldly, accommodating, indeed partly pagan (Egyptian) spirituality involves a massive expansion of religious experience, and truly shares in the grand openness and heteroglossia of the enormous novel which expresses it. It also turns Jaakob's religious agonies into permissive, accommodating joy. It is Thomas Mann's most satisfying answer to modern negativity, and there is nothing better than his own phrase for it: 'the holy game'.[30]

*

But what of Shakespeare? Well, if 'the holy game' is Mann's answer to the serious problem of self-conscious abstraction in modern life which he thought of in partly Shakespearean terms, it is also a perfect description of the spirituality of affirmation which Shakespeare drama-tizes in *As You Like It*.

Opening with jealous sibling rivalry which leads to the repudiation and exotic exile of a talented and attractive brother who nevertheless wins out after being tested sexually, *As You Like It* clearly strikes lights with the biblical story which so inspired Mann. But Orlando is just a place-holder for Joseph, whose memory is more completely fulfilled, in Shakespeare's transvestite comedy, in Rosalind. It is Rosalind who most flourishes in exile; it is she who, like Joseph, is witty, 'heavenly' (1.2.241), and able to do 'strange things' (5.2.47).[31] And if Mann found in the biblical Joseph potential for a shimmering, multivalent sexual charisma, Shakespeare had already endowed his heroine with exactly that quality. Reading *As You Like It* in conjunction with *Joseph und seine Brüder* enables the recognition that in Rosalind Shakespeare had already fashioned just such an avatar and champion of the spirituality of affirmation as Mann's Joseph was destined to become.[32]

In *Doktor Faustus*, Mann was right, I think, to see Shakespeare's imagination as essentially unchurched. This doesn't mean that questions of religion – or even *the* question of religion – aren't 'live' in Shakespeare's work. The church is, historically speaking, always just off stage in Shakespeare: the great, vexed totem of moral authority. As such Shakespeare doesn't need to evoke it. His drama is already 'by the church', and operating in relation to it.[33] Of course there are religious figures in Shakespeare but they are not – surely, nobody would say they are? – his greatest characters, and, where they figure at all, they tend to figure the relation between church and state. It would seem Shakespeare has relatively little interest in the church as an autonomous religious community, lit by its own light of dissenting values etc. Censorship, for sure, would have proscribed much of this, and much of it would have been too politically 'hot'. But, had Shakespeare been particularly interested in the life of the church, it is difficult not to think he would have found ways of writing about and dramatizing it.

That said, like *Joseph und seine Brüder*, *As You Like It* keeps in play the possibility that religious renunciation might be the best solution to the problem of living. Jacques yearns prophet-like to cleanse the foul body of this infected world (2.7.58–61); and yet, he himself, as Duke Senior exclaims, is covered in 'th'embossèd sores and headed evils' (2.7.67) he bewails. In reply, Jacques evokes a mental picture of sin flowing 'as hugely as the sea / Till that the weary very means do ebb' (2.7.72–3).

There is sin, and sin, and nothing but sin – except, if we're lucky, its exhaustion.

And that calls for radical conversion: 'to forswear the full stream of the world and live in a nook, merely monastic' (3.3.345–6). The play provides some vivid instances of conversion, including the transformation of Oliver, who says of his previous, unregenerate self:

'Twas I, but 'tis not I. I do not shame
To tell you what I was, since my conversion
So sweetly tastes, being the thing I am.

(4.3.130–2)

And what works for Oliver turns out to work for the unregenerate Duke Frederick as well. An amazing trend has begun whereby all the nobles are leaving Frederick's illegitimate court to join the rightful Duke in the forest. Desperate Frederick leads a great army there, meaning to put his exiled brother to the sword; but in 'the skirts' of the 'wild wood' he bumps into 'an old religious man', and is promptly 'converted / Both from his enterprise and from the world' (5.4.143–6). This world-denying strain of the play compares with Jaakob's more severe spirituality in Mann's novel. Hearing of the Duke's radical conversion, Jacques runs off to meet him, for 'out of these convertites' much is 'to be heard and learned' (5.4.168–9).

Maybe there is, but we don't, in *As You Like It*, hear the homilies of the reformed Duke Frederick. Just like Mann in *Joseph und seine Brüder*, Shakespeare establishes religious renunciation as a viable way of being in the world but nonetheless keeps it on the fringes, expressly confined to 'the skirts' of the forest, interest and action. In Mann, the highest and sternest blessing may be deflected from Joseph to Ezra, the man of sin; but the novel nonetheless disposes its own double blessing, from above and below, on its own hero, the beautiful and worldly Joseph. Similarly, *As You Like It* tenders an otherworldly crown to its sinners – Oliver, Frederick, Jacques – while shamelessly lavishing the lion's share of attention on its sexy this-worldly heroine, Rosalind.

As You Like It works hard to endue the Forest of Arden with a spiritual aura. There, we hear, the exiled Duke and his entourage 'fleet the time carelessly as they did in the golden world' (1.1.95). This perhaps conjures a pagan Eden, but it resonates more with biblical spirituality that 'three or four loving lords have put themselves into voluntary exile with him', that this exile is associated with wandering, and that old Adam later limps there in pure love (1.1.81–3, 131). 'True it is that we have seen better days', says the Duke, 'And have with holy bell been knolled to church' (2.7.121). That he '[f]inds tongues in trees, books in the running brooks, / Sermons in stones, and good in everything' might raise suspicions of pastoral mendacity but 'good in *everything*' intimates a passionate mysticism, and this is hard-won inasmuch as it includes 'adversity' (2.1.16–17, 12). Certainly, the Duke himself behaves in accord with the good he finds in nature when he responds to Orlando's arrival with a drawn sword with this movingly simple invitation: 'Sit down and feed, and welcome to our table' (2.7.105).

But *As You Like It* is an *erotic* comedy, the spirituality of Arden of an expressly sexy stripe. Jacques says at the end of the play, 'There is sure another flood toward, and these couples are coming to the ark' (5.4.35–6); but Shakespeare's comedy suggest salvation in sex and sensuality as much as it evokes the heavenly thunderer. Or perhaps it reveals a sort of blessed sexuality of coupling – *two by two* – that primordially escaped wrathful judgement.[34]

'Heavenly Rosalind' (1.2.241) is the bearer of the play's erotic promise. And thanks to the observances of her lover Orlando, what the 'tongues in trees' speak is her name, so, as Orlando says, 'That every eye which in this forest looks / Shall see [her] virtue witnessed everywhere' (3.2.7–8). This makes Rosalind the embodiment of the life-force in general. Her beauty is such as to reveal that 'Heaven Nature charged / That one body should be filled / With all graces wide-enlarged' (3.3.116–18). And though this is in part amorous and poetical hyperbole, it is also truer than Orlando knows, inasmuch as the diverse and undulating creature he hymns is currently living as a man in the very forest he is decorating with his testimonies to her. Like Mann's Joseph, Rosalind is an expressly sexy version of the incarnation. And since Shakespeare's play is a comedy, in her eros and salvation come together as the teleology of the work as such.

Given that life in general is hallowed in Rosalind as it is in Joseph, bisexuality is fundamental to both works. Rosalind like Joseph expresses human sexiness in general, mediating in her own person between male and female.[35] '[T]he wiser, the waywarder' is *As You Like It*'s dictum since the customary singleness of self and world is misconceived (4.1.129–30). The truest poetry is the most feigning (3.3.16). That's why in leaving her defined and, therefore, limited social identity behind Rosalind goes '[t]o liberty, and not to banishment' (1.3.128). In losing their established selves, Joseph and Rosalind both attain a transcendent freedom which expresses the *more* that they more truly are.

There are consequences for others as well. Joseph is an avatar of subjective possibility; confronted with him Potiphar's wife wants to *live*. Rosalind is *As You Like It*'s vitally unfixing element, truly as much Ganymede as she is Rosalind, and therefore the agent not just of a homosexual flirtation (between Ganymede and Orlando) but equally – and brilliantly – of a heterosexual marriage that is simultaneously achieved and queered *by means of a homosexual flirtation.*

As much as they share a surpassing sexiness, Rosalind and Joseph share a creative wit. In her paean to 'a woman's wit', Rosalind crows:

Make the doors upon a woman's wit, and it will out at the casement; shut that, and 'twill out at the keyhole; stop that, 'twill fly with smoke out at the chimney.

(4.1.130–2)

Such explosive creativity cannot be pinned down, the paradox here being that it exceeds even the truth of gender it purportedly expresses: remember it is spoken by a female character in male drag (who, on the original Shakespearean stage, was played by a boy ...). Rosalind's alter-ego Ganymede is himself a work of her wit, and such flamboyantly transgressive self-creation brings us in the orbit of the Dostoevskian dictum: 'everything is permitted!' (2004: 649). But *As You Like It* and *Joseph und seine Brüder* do not go to the Devil. Instead, these works *positively* embrace difference within a more open and conditional mode of being which defuses the threat of the negative. 'Your "if" is the only peacemaker: much virtue in "if"' (5.4.87–8). Axiomatic here is the way in which Rosalind draws into the richness of a more encompassing love everything that threatens it: the battle of the sexes, sexual cynicism, cuckold's horns.

So I want to pair off Rosalind with Thomas Mann's Joseph! After all, Orlando was never good enough for her!

We have seen that these two characters – from different epochs, from different national literatures – stand for the energy of affirmation. What they affirm is the whole range of human possibility. Joseph in Egypt,

Rosalind in Arden: they affirm the *exoticism* of human possibility. Joseph is associated with 'the wisdom of the East': a heterodox, venturesome spirituality. And Rosalind associates herself with something similar when she says, 'I have, since I was three year old, conversed with a magician, most profound in his art and yet not damnable' (5.2.47–9).

And yet not damnable: Joseph and Rosalind admit more of wonder and religion, as well as more of the world, into religion. Perhaps they even stand for the possibility of a new religion?

Now there's a thought!

And yet, for all of his venturesomeness, Joseph remains pious; for all of hers, Rosalind remains a good girl. It's instructive she speaks of the 'strange things' she can do in relation to reverting to conventional gender and marriage. It is as if in broaching the galaxy of possibilities, she has made convention strange, and therefore not so much a falsely naturalized imperative as it is truthful and choosable in its very strangeness.

Joseph and Rosalind manage to affirm customary morality *and* subversive creativity. Their comprehensive affirmation includes cultural convention, but it is not at all limited to it. '*Yes—yes, no*': both yes and no are affirmed in an encompassing affirmation. But something of the energy of the negative, as Mann insists, 'remains as an aftereffect of the canceled no'. This will be too accommodationist for some readers, who will lean instead to the complete renunciation of the world that is also canvassed in *Joseph* and *As You Like It*, but it is a real and impressive answer to the question of how to live. Much of this book shows how the juxtaposition of Shakespeare and Mann reveals the challenge and importunacy of the negative in modern culture. Reading *As You Like It* and *Joseph und seine Brüder* together presents 'the holy game' as a possible solution to that challenge.[36]

Notes

1   More than twenty-five years ago now, Debora Shuger made the case that religion was 'the master-code of pre-capitalist society' and 'the cultural matrix for explorations of virtually every topic' (1990). Ken Jackson and Arthur F. Marotti subsequently detailed 'the turn to religion in early modern English studies' (2004). One dominant strand of this turn described Shakespeare and his contemporaries in either Catholic or Protestant terms: see, for instance, Richard Wilson (2004) and Adrian Streete (2009). For a recent, even-handed approach, see David Scott Kastan (2014). 'The current focus on political theology in Shakespeare studies', according to Jennifer R. Rust, 'is largely devoted to tracing how Shakespeare's dramas illuminate the structural link between religious and political forms in both early modernity and modern liberal

democracy' (2009: 175). This confirms the worldly slant of recent accounts of Shakespearean religiosity in general. 'Perhaps we do better to think of Shakespeare as creating resonances between the situations in his plays and the religious archetypes at the foundations of his culture; as invoking what Rosalie Colie, writing of *King Lear*, calls "Biblical echo"', as Louis Adrian Montrose wrote in the first blush of the new historicism (1981: 46). For my own contributions to these debates, see Fernie (2002, 2005, 2012).

2   Joyce's theology has been a serious topic of scholarly enquiry since Robert Boyle (1978). See David Jones, Preface to *The Anathemata* (2010).

3   All references are to the Arden *Love's Labour's Lost*, ed. H. R. Woudhuysen.

4   For more on this, see Fernie (2012: 115–41).

5   Ibid.

6   *Ich darf nicht sagen, daß ich an Gott glaube, – es würde lange dauern, glaube ich, bis ich es sagen würde, auch wenn ich es täte* (Mann 2009: 581).

7   Hermann Kurzke identifies Wedekind (2002: 244).

8   *nach ihrem Heil langende Seele* (Mann 2009: 582); '*Die Verpflichtung zum Geiste, … die wir Religion nennen*' (ibid.); *da setzte ich meinen Zylinder auf und ging nach Hause* (ibid.).

9   Thus, says Rose (1992: 147), 'the feast is spoiled'.

10   See Hugo von Hofmannsthal 'Ein Brief', in *Gesammelte Werke, Prosa II*, pp. 12ff.

11   *Es gibt etwas, was ich Erkenntnisekel nenne, Lisaweta: Der Zustand, in dem es dem Menschen genügt, eine Sache zu durchschauen, um sich bereits zum Sterben angewidert … zu fühlen, – der Fall Hamlets* (Mann 2004: 276); *Hellsehen noch durch den Thränenschleier des Gefühls hindurch, erkennen, merken, beobachten und das Beobachtete lächelnd bei Seite legen müssen noch in Augenblicken, wo Hände sich umschlingen, Lippen sich finden, wo Menschen Blick, erblindet von Empfindung, sich bricht, es ist infam, Lisaweta, es ist niederträchtig, empörend … (ibid.).*

12   Nietzsche on Hamlet is comprehensively and reliably discussed in Roger Paulin (2003). Mann himself confessed to an identification with Hamlet around February/March 1902: 'Hamlet – : his enthusiastic weakness, the hyperaesthesia of his conscience, his penchant for pondering, his heated fantasy and denial of reality, his pessimism, his aversion to realization (as far as Ophelia, women, courtiers, all of existence is concerned) (It suffices for him to see through in order to be repulsed) — — — ecce ego!' (Mann quoted in Kurzke 2002: 130): *Hamlet–: seine enthusiastische Schwäche, die Hyperästhesie seines Gewissens, seine Reflektionskrankheit, seine hitzige Phantasie und sein Versagen der Wirklichkeit gegenüber, sein Pessimismus, sein Erkenntnis-Ekel (was Ophelia, die Frauen, die Höflinge, das ganze Dasein betrifft) (Es genügt ihm, zu durchschauen, um angewidert zu sein) — — — ecce ego!* (zitiert nach Kurzke 1999: 146).

13   *indirekte Mythologie* (Schlegel 1967: 319).

14   *Wenn ich von Schopenhauer den Moralismus – ein populäreres Wort für dieselbe Sache lautet 'Pessimismus' – meiner seelischen Grundstimmung habe, jene Stimmung von 'Kreuz, Tod und Gruft', die schon in meinen ersten Versuchen hervortrat* (Mann 2009: 87).

15   *dem Monde … seine junge Nacktheit darzustellen* (Mann 1983a: 77).

16   *eine Narrheit* (Mann 1983b: 31); *geiler Taumel* (ibid.); *mit dieser unreinen Seelengegend* (ibid.: 32).

17   *daß Joseph ... sich auf diese Lebendigkeit Gottes sogar besser verstehen und ihr geschmeidiger werde Rechnung zu tragen wissen als Jaakob* (Mann 1983c: 471).

18   *eine der stärksten Versuchungen ..., die wohl je in der Welt einen Jüngling bestürmt haben* (ibid.: 537).

19   *Nenne man es Neugier und Leichtsinn, nenne man es Abneigung, den Wahlfall des Bösen entgültig aufzugeben, den Wunsch, die Wahl zwischen Gut und Böse, wenn auch keineswegs in der Absicht, auf die Seite des Bösen zu fallen ...* (ibid.: 538).

20   *ein Virtuosenstück der Tugend* (ibid.: 482).

21   *daß der Witz die Natur hat des Sendboten hin und her und des gewandten Geschäftsträgers zwischen entgegengesetzten Sphären und Einflüssen: zum Beispiel zwischen Sonnengewalt und Mondesgewalt, Vatererbe und Muttererbe, zwischen Tagessegen und dem Segen der Nacht, ja, um es direkt und umfassend zu sagen: zwischen Leben und Tod* (Mann 1983d: 487).

22   *Denn das musterhaft Überlieferte kommt aus der Tiefe, die unten liegt, und ist, was uns bindet. Aber das Ich ist von Gott und ist des Geistes, der ist frei. Dies aber ist gesittetes Leben, daß sich das Bindend-Musterhafte des Grundes mit der Gottesfreiheit des Ich erfülle, und ist keine Menschengesittung ohne das eine und ohne das andere* (ibid.: 151).

23   *Aber 'tâm' ist ein seltsam oszillierendes Wort, das mit 'redlich' sehr schwach übersetzt ist, denn sein Sinn umfasst beides, das Positive und das Negative, das Ja und das Nein, Licht und Finsternis, Leben und Tod. ... 'Ja – ja, nein', also mit einem Ja-Nein, das noch mit dem Vorzeichen eines zweiten Ja versehen ist. Rein rechnerisch gesehen, bleibt da freilich, da ein Ja und ein Nein einander aufheben, nur das zusätzliche Ja übrig; aber das Rein-Rechnerische hat keine Farbe, und zum mindesten läßt solche Mathematik die dunkle Färbung des resultierenden Ja außer acht, die offenbar eine Nachwirkung des rechnerisch doch aufgehobenen Nein ist. – Das alles ist, wie gesagt, verwickelt* (ibid.: 237–8).

24   Heller's sixth chapter, and his treatment of *Joseph and his Brothers*, is titled 'The Theology of Irony', pp. 215–58.

25   *ein seltener Segen ... der Geist anmutigen Mittlertums* (Mann 1983d: 533); *Denn es ist ein lieblicher Segen, aber der höchste und strengste nicht. Siehe, dein teures Leben liegt vor des Sterbenden Blick in seiner Wahrheit. Spiel und Anspiel war es, vertraulich, freundliche Lieblingsschaft, anklingenden ans Heil, doch nicht ganz im Ernste berufen und zugelassen* (ibid.).

26   *Und mit festlichem Spaß soll es ausgeführt sein aufs allerheiterste. Denn die Heiterkeit, Freund, und der verschlagene Scherz sind das Beste, was Gott uns gab, und sind die innigste Auskunft vor dem verwickelten, fragwürdigen Leben* (ibid.: 326).

27   *Man kann sie im Ernst nicht beantworten. Nur in Heiterkeit kann sich der Menschengeist aufheben über sie, daß er vielleicht mit innigem Spaß über das Antwortlose Gott selbst, den gewaltigen Antwortlosen, zum Lächeln bringe* (ibid.: 326).

28   Cf. Mann (1983a: 7–53): 'Vorspiel' *Höllenfahrt*, in 'Die Geschichten Jaakobs'.

29   *Das Geheimnis aber und die stille Hoffnung Gottesliegt vielleicht in ihrer Vereinigung, nämlich in dem echten Eingehen des Geistes in die Welt der Seele,*

in der wechselseitigen Durchdringung der beiden Prinzipien und der Heiligung des einen durch das andere zur Gegenwart eines Menschentums, das gesegnet wäre mit Segen oben vom Himmel herab und mit Segen von der Tiefe, die unten liegt (Mann 1983a: 47).

30 This is the culminating section of his epic novel, Part Six of *Joseph the Provider*. *'Das heilige Spiel'*.

31 *As You Like It*, ed. Michael Hattaway (2000).

32 Shakespearean criticism has not, so far as I know, previously made the connection between *As You Like It* and the story of Joseph, though it has come close. Hannibal Hamlin works with Shakespeare's allusions to Jacob in (2013: 74, 102, 232); but in turning to *As You Like It*, Hamlin invokes neither Jacob nor Joseph, but only the Prodigal Son (pp. 9–10). In his earlier book on the same topic, Steven Marx also failed to pick up resonances between *As You Like It* and the Joseph story, perceiving instead: 'Resemblances between Genesis's Joseph and Shakespeare's Prospero are detailed and striking' (2000: 31). Shakespeare explicitly refers to the Joseph story in *1 Henry IV* when Falstaff says, 'If to be fat be to be hated, then Pharaoh's lean kine are to be loved' (2.5.429–30). And Russell Fraser's 'Shakespeare's Book of Genesis' detects a general affinity with the first book of the Bible and *As You Like It* but without mentioning Joseph (1991).

33 I take the expression 'by the church' from Feste's witty descant on it in *Twelfth Night* (3.1.4ff.). See note 1 for the suggestion that recent investigations of Shakespeare and religion tend to have a worldly accent.

34 In an interesting recent reading, Paul A. Kottman has argued that the best that *As You Like It* can do in the direction of rebuilding society in general is achieved in its rediscovery and refashioning of romantic love between Rosalind and Orlando (2009: 23ff.). Hugh Grady, however, persuasively argues that, though 'the creation and celebration of a still-current category of the personal and private' is indeed a major Shakespearean achievement here, in fact 'far from resting at this step, the play moves forward in a fascinating process of cultural house-building in the cleared space of Arden' (1996: 190).

35 For the classic treatment of the deconstruction of gender in *As You Like It*, see Catherine Belsey (1985).

36 Interested readers can trace this reading of *As You Like It* as a profoundly affirmative play in a range of earlier responses to Shakespeare. Kiernan Ryan, for instance, calls *As You Like It* 'Shakespeare's most amenable comedy' (2009: 204). In William Hazlitt's response to the play, what might otherwise be censured as decadent – growing soft and delicate, 'riot', 'idleness', being 'spoiled', 'heedless', 'wanton', 'giddy' – is liberated and allowed (Hazlitt 2008: 33–4). In his classic study of Shakespearean comedy, C. L. Barber's remarks on *As You Like It* also present the play in terms of a more comprehensive and inclusive vision, though here the vision combines mindful self-awareness with sensuous immediacy (1967: 239). And Helen Gardner writes, 'Although life in Arden is not wholly idyllic, and this place set apart from the world is yet touched by the world's sorrows and can be mocked at by the worldly wise, the image of life which the forest presents is irradiated by the conviction that the gay and

the gentle can endure the rubs of fortune and that this earth is a place where men can find happiness in themselves and in others' (2008: 160). Phebe Jensen sees a Catholic-aligned challenge to 'the Protestant rejection of festivity associated with "mirth"' in the spiritualized affirmation of life I am presenting as key to Shakespeare's play (2008: 131).

Works Cited

Barber, C. L., 1967. *Shakespeare's Festive Comedy: A Study of Dramatic Form and Its Relation to Social Custom*. London: Meridian Books.

Belsey, Catherine, 1985. 'Disrupting sexual difference: meaning and gender in the comedies', in *Alternative Shakespeares*, ed. John Drakakis. London: Methuen, pp. 166–99.

Blake, William, 2008 [1790–93]. 'The Marriage of Heaven and Hell', in *William Blake: Selected Poetry and Prose*, ed. David Fuller, rev. edn. London: Pearson.

Boyle, Robert, 1978. *James Joyce's Pauline Vision*. Carbondale: Southern Illinois University Press.

Brown, John Russell (ed.), 2002 [1979]. *Shakespeare*: Much Ado About Nothing *and* As You Like It, Casebook Series. Basingstoke: Palgrave.

Dostoevsky, Fyodor, 2004. *The Brothers Karamazov: A Novel in Four Parts with Epilogue*, trans. Richard Pevear and Larissa Volokhonsky. London: Vintage.

Fernie, Ewan, 2002. *Shame in Shakespeare*. London: Routledge.

Fernie, Ewan, 2005. *Spiritual Shakespeares*. London: Routledge.

Fernie, Ewan, 2012. *The Demonic: Literature and Experience*. London: Routledge.

Fraser, Russell, 1991. 'Shakespeare's Book of Genesis', *Comparative Drama* 25: 2, pp. 121–8.

Gardner, Helen, 2008 [1979]. 'Let the Forest Judge', in *Shakespeare*: Much Ado About Nothing *and* As You Like It, ed. John Russell Brown. Basingstoke: Palgrave, pp. 149–65.

Grady, Hugh, 1996. *Shakespeare's Universal Wolf: Studies in Early Modern Reification* Oxford: Clarendon Press.

Hamlin, Hannibal, 2013. *The Bible in Shakespeare*. Oxford: Oxford University Press.

Hazlitt, William, 2008 [1818]. 'Characters of Shakespeare's Plays', in *Shakespeare*: Much Ado About Nothing *and* As You Like It, Casebook Series, ed. John Russell Brown. Basingstoke: Palgrave, pp. 33–4.

Heller, Erich, 1979. *Thomas Mann: The Ironic German*. South Bend: Regenery/ Gateway.

Hofmannsthal, Hugo von, 1952 [1902]. 'Ein Brief', in *Gesammelte Werke, Prosa II*. Frankfurt am Main: S. Fischer, pp. 7–22.

Jackson, Ken and Arthur F. Marotti, 2004. 'The Turn to Religion in Early Modern English Studies', in *Criticism* 46, pp. 167–90.

Jensen, Phebe, 2008. *Religion and Revelry in Shakespeare's Festive World*. Cambridge: Cambridge University Press.

Jones, David, 2010. *The Anathemata*. London: Faber.

Kastan, David Scott, 2014. *A Will to Believe: Shakespeare and Religion*. Oxford: Oxford University Press.

Kottman, Paul A., 2009. *Tragic Conditions in Shakespeare: Disinheriting the Globe*. Baltimore: The Johns Hopkins University Press.

Kurzke, Hermann, 1999. *Thomas Mann: Das Leben als Kunstwerk*. München: Beck.
Kurzke, Hermann, 2002. *Thomas Mann: Life As a Work of Art*, trans. Leslie Wilson. Princeton: Princeton University Press.
Mann, Thomas, 1936. *Stories of Three Decades*, trans. H. T. Lowe-Porter. London: M. Secker and Warburg.
Mann, Thomas, 1983 [1918]. *Reflections of a Nonpolitical Man*, trans. and intro. Walter D. Morris. New York: Frederick Ungar.
Mann, Thomas, 1983a [1933]. 'Die Geschichten Jaakobs', in *Joseph und seine Brüder*, ed. Peter de Mendelssohn. Gesammelte Werke in Einzelbänden, Frankfurter Ausgabe, vol. I. Frankfurt am Main: S. Fischer.
Mann, Thomas, 1983b [1934]. 'Der junge Joseph', in *Joseph und seine Brüder*, ed. Peter de Mendelssohn. Gesammelte Werke in Einzelbänden, Frankfurter Ausgabe, vol. II. Frankfurt am Main: S. Fischer.
Mann, Thomas, 1983c [1936]. 'Joseph in Ägypten', in *Joseph und seine Brüder*, ed. Peter de Mendelssohn. Gesammelte Werke in Einzelbänden, Frankfurter Ausgabe, vol. III. Frankfurt am Main: S. Fischer.
Mann, Thomas, 1983d [1943]. 'Joseph, der Ernährer', in *Joseph und seine Brüder*, ed. Peter de Mendelssohn. Gesammelte Werke in Einzelbänden, Frankfurter Ausgabe, vol. IV. Frankfurt am Main: S. Fischer.
Mann, Thomas, 2004 [1903]. 'Tonio Kröger', in *Frühe Erzählungen*, ed. Terence J. Reed. Große Kommentierte Frankfurter Ausgabe, vol. 2.1. Frankfurt am Main: S. Fischer, pp. 243–318.
Mann, Thomas, 2005 [1933–43]. *Joseph and his Brothers: The Stories of Jacob, Young Joseph, Joseph in Egypt, Joseph the Provider*, trans. John E. Woods. London: Alfred A. Knopf.
Mann, Thomas, 2009 [1918]. *Betrachtungen eines Unpolitischen*, ed. Hermann Kurzke. Große Kommentierte Frankfurter Ausgabe, vol. 13.1. Frankfurt am Main: S. Fischer.
Marx, Steven, 2000. *Shakespeare and the Bible*. Oxford: Oxford University Press.
Montrose, Louis Adrian, 1981. 'The Place of a Brother in *As You Like It*: Social Process and Comic Form', in *Shakespeare Quarterly* 32: 1, pp. 28–54.
Paulin, Roger, 2003. *The Critical Reception of Shakespeare in Germany 1682–1914: Native Literature and Foreign Genius*. New York: Georg Olms.
Rose, Gillian, 1992. *The Broken Middle: Out of Our Ancient Society*. Oxford: Blackwell.
Rust, Jennifer R., 2009. 'Political Theology and Shakespeare Studies', in *Literature Compass* 6: 1, pp. 175–90.
Ryan, Kiernan, 2009. *Shakespeare's Comedies*. London: Palgrave.
Schlegel, Friedrich, 1967. 'Rede über die Mythologie', in *Kritische Friedrich Schlegel-Ausgabe*, ed. Hans Eichner, vol 2. Paderborn: Ferdinand Schöningh, pp. 311–28.
Shakespeare, William, 1998. *Love's Labour's Lost*, ed. H. R. Woudhuysen. The Arden Shakespeare, Third Series. London: Methuen.
Shakespeare, William, 2000. *As You Like It*, ed. Michael Hattaway. Cambridge: Cambridge University Press.
Shakespeare, William, 2008. *The Norton Shakespeare*, eds Stephen Greenblatt et al. New York: Norton.
Shanks, Andrew, 2008. *Against Innocence: Gillian Rose's Reception and the Gift of Faith*. London: SCM Press.
Shuger, Debora, 1990. *Habits of Thought in the English Renaissance: Religion, Politics, and the Dominant Culture*. Berkley: University of California Press.

Streete, Adrian, 2009. *Protestantism and Drama in Early Modern England*. Cambridge: Cambridge University Press.

Wilson, Richard, 2004. *Secret Shakespeare: Studies in Theatre, Religion and Resistance*. Manchester: Manchester University Press.

Nine   Teenage Fanclub: Mann and Shakespeare in the Queer Pantheon

Heather Love

This essay addresses the connections between Thomas Mann and William Shakespeare via an account of their reception by two ambitious, conflicted queer American women: Willa Cather and Susan Sontag. Both women were passionately invested in high culture and sought models that would help them to achieve their outsize dreams of literary fame. Provincial childhoods – Cather grew up in rural Virginia and small town Nebraska, and Sontag grew up in Long Island, New York, Tucson, Arizona, and, finally, Los Angeles – led to intense artistic ambition and geographical restlessness. Particularly in their early writing – in diaries, school essays, and newspaper articles written when they were still in their teens – Cather and Sontag read their futures in the lives of great men. Borrowing from the energies of bona fide geniuses, these young women attempted to rocket themselves out of geographical isolation, out of biographical time, even out of human particularity altogether. The aim of their wild enthusiasm is, paradoxically, death, since the endgame is immortality: they long to be, as Cather wrote about Shakespeare when she was twenty years old, 'a truth, a law, not to be influenced by external circumstances or discoveries' (1970: 89). The fact that, for both Cather and Sontag, the desire to be untouched by external circumstances was related to their experience of sexual and gender difference does not diminish the significance of their artistic ambition; instead it shows the extent to which artistic achievement and social alienation were bound up for them.

Through their identifications with Mann and Shakespeare, Cather and Sontag reflected on themselves as artists, as intellectuals, and as social exiles. Shakespeare represented an unimpeachable standard of greatness for both women, his aesthetic production so manifestly perfect that it had the capacity to defeat time. As a living example of European sophistication, stylistic virtuosity, and philosophical seriousness, Mann troubled Cather and Sontag in ways Shakespeare did not. Mann represented continuity with the past – the survival of 'great art' into the modern period. Like any survival, though, his life was shadowed by decadence. By contrast with Shakespeare, Mann's name was not sanctified by death and the passage of time; he still might write lesser books, and his reputation might be subject to reversals down the line. Furthermore, as a contemporary (rather than a biographical cipher), Mann's life was subject to scrutiny. While the homoeroticism of Shakespeare's work was mellowed by time and ignorance, Mann's example was too close at hand. Through the careful management of secrecy and knowledge, Mann successfully avoided the stigma associated with the medical-legal category of homosexuality, and was therefore a model for the two women; however, the presence of queerness in several of his greatest works offered the disturbing suggestion that literary merit might be deeply tied to same-sex desire. In an essay published after the death of Paul Verlaine, Cather offered an ambivalent commentary on the poet's 'unmentionable and almost unheard of crimes' (1896: 9): 'This is all disease you say; certainly it is, but we all gather the pearls fast enough in this world and nobody troubles himself much about the disease of the oyster which produced it. Oysters do not grow pearls under normal conditions nor do men write great poems' (1970: 283). The women found themselves in a double bind: how could they reap the aesthetic rewards of queerness without being subject to public censure or deflation on the market?

Shakespeare and Mann both suggest possibilities, having defeated biography through monumental achievement. Shakespeare offers a more appealing – if inimitable – example. His unassailable greatness as an artist disqualified criticism, while his distance from the present shrouded his life in mystery. In 'Notes on Camp', Sontag muses about Shakespeare's exceptional status, wondering: 'Why is the atmosphere of Shakespeare's comedies (*As You Like It*, etc.) not epicene, while that of *Der Rosenkavalier* is?' (1982a: 109). She answers her own question in 'On Style': 'A work of art, so far as it is a work of art, cannot – whatever the artist's personal intentions – advocate anything at all. The greatest artists attain a sublime neutrality. Think of Homer and Shakespeare, from whom generations of scholars and critics have vainly labored to extract particular 'views' about human nature, morality, and society' (1982b: 146).

In contrast to Shakespeare's sublime neutrality, Mann's renown and his freedom from stigma are an achievement rather than a given. Mann's real-time struggles with the relationship between the artist and the bourgeois meant that his example was much closer to home for Cather and Sontag. Both women found the possibility of a European departure from American social and sexual norms immensely alluring, but they also worried over possible consequences of such a departure. Mann was deeply identified with European aestheticism and decadence, his fiction awash in male homoeroticism, illness, and longing for death. However, like Shakespeare, he had the knack of converting queerness into canonicity. Mann was unusual in combining the role of the queer bohemian and bourgeois family man. Was it possible to be a great artist without becoming a social outcast? How had Mann, unlike the martyr Wilde or the outlaw Verlaine, managed to have it both ways?

Because of their age difference – Cather was born in 1873, Sontag in 1933 – Mann occupied a different position in the imaginary of the two women. But they wrote about him at roughly the same time: Cather in the 1930s and Sontag in the 1940s. Cather was in her sixties when she wrote her essay 'Joseph and his Brothers', however the piece is a reflection on precocious youth: it recalls the brilliant, eccentric figure Cather had cut as a gender-deviant teenager in Red Cloud, Nebraska, dressing in boys' clothes and signing her name William Cather, M.D. Sontag began writing about Mann as just such a precocious youth: when she was fourteen years old, Sue Sontag wrote a school essay on *Der Zauberberg* (*The Magic Mountain*) that concludes with the breathless and confident claim that it is the finest prose work she has ever read. Both Cather and Sontag reflected on their artistic and geographical ambitions through the example of Mann. Their understanding of his career was inflected by their grandiose fantasies about the future but also by anxiety about their queerness and the fate it might condemn them to. Although their geographical and temporal longings promised to propel them into a larger world, they were alert to the possibility that they might be headed for an even more constricted future. Mann, like Shakespeare, seems to promise the integration of artistic genius (with its suggestions of deviance and marginality) and worldly success, maturity, and social recognition. But Mann's status as a living author (and, for the high school student Sue Sontag, one living across town in Los Angeles) made him vulnerable to devaluation in a way that Shakespeare – securely dead – was not.

*

Cather's essay on Mann, 'Joseph and his Brothers', was originally published in the *Saturday Review* on 6 June 1936; it appeared again later that year in a collection of Cather's essays called *Not Under Forty*. *Not Under Forty* is often read as a sign of Cather's increasing literary and social conservatism, a departure from the restlessness and rebellion of her early years. A prefatory statement to the collection warns away readers under forty years of age, for whom, she writes, the book 'will have little interest'. The note reads:

> The title of this book is meant to be 'arresting' only in the literal sense, like the signs put up for motorists: 'ROAD UNDER REPAIR', etc. It means that the book will have little interest for people under forty years of age. The world split in two in 1922 or thereabouts, and the persons and prejudices recalled in these sketches slid back into yesterday's seven thousand years. Thomas Mann, to be sure, belongs immensely to the forward-goers, and they are concerned only with his forwardness. But he also goes back a long way, and his backwardness is more gratifying to the backward. It is for the backward, and by one of their number, that these sketches were written.
>
> (1992d: 812)

For Cather, writing as an anti-modernist, disdains new directions in literature and culture after the breaking point of 1922 – the *annus mirabilis* of Anglo-American modernism, which saw the publication of James Joyce's *Ulysses* and T. S. Eliot's *The Waste Land*. Linking aesthetic innovation with immaturity, Cather distances herself from the present and its 'forward' youth, taking up the mantle of seven thousand years of history. Mann is a crucial example for her, since he is an iconic modernist and therefore a representative of the twentieth century that Cather – just two years his elder – disdains. But Cather also claims Mann through his biblical fiction, which she saw as his most mature work. Although she cannot abide the modernist Mann, Cather identifies him as a stealth traditionalist, an author with roots deep in the past.

Themes of temporality and aging are central to Cather's appreciation of Mann's tetralogy in progress, *Joseph und seine Brüder*, which she praises for its long historical view and the calm dignity of its narrative.[1] Cather writes, 'There is nothing in *Joseph and his Brothers* more admirable than the tempo, the deliberate, sustained pace. (In this age of blinding speed and shattering sound!)' (1992a: 860). According to Cather, Mann's subject matter allows him not to rush: 'He can listen to the herdsmen telling their stories over and over, go backward and forward with their "dreamily indefinite" habits of thought. He has all the time there is; Mediterranean time, 1700 B.C.' (ibid.). The essay turns on a contrast between Joseph and Jaakob (as Jacob's name appears in Mann's novel): Joseph is the precocious, charismatic, gifted youth and his father Jaakob, whom Cather calls 'the rod of measure' (1992a:

871), has been tested by time and takes the long view. He is a figure of mature artistic achievement. Suggesting a contrast between the young, aestheticist Mann and his later, wiser self, Cather sides with Jaakob: 'The world is always full of brilliant youth which fades into grey and embittered middle age: the first flowering takes everything. The great men are those who have developed slowly, or who have been able to survive the glamour of their early florescence and to go on learning from life' (ibid.: 868). The critic Bernice Slote comments on the 'presence of the young Willa Cather' (1966: 31-112, 90) in this essay; the ambivalent portrait of Joseph recalls Cather as a glittering, brilliant youth rampant in small-town Nebraska. At stake for Cather in these reflections is not only the 'glamour of early florescence' but also the suggestion of deviance that glamour and earliness carry.

The question of Cather's queerness became the subject of heated debate in 2002 when Joan Acocella published her book, *Willa Cather and the Politics of Criticism*. While the dust may have settled now – particularly after the publication of Cather's letters in 2014 – Acocella's take on Cather is nonetheless instructive. Acocella refuses a lesbian reading of Cather because, she argues, such a focus misses the primacy of aesthetic concerns for Cather; she blames contemporary critics for imposing narrow political concerns on a body of work that is universal in its reach. Acocella's reading focuses on a passage in Cather's essay 'The Novel Démeublé' which was crucial to Sharon O'Brien's 1984 article, '"The Thing Not Named": Willa Cather as a Lesbian Writer'.

> Whatever is felt upon the page without being specifically named there – that, one might say, is created. It is the inexplicable presence of the thing not named, of the overtone divined by the ear but not heard by it, the verbal mood, the emotional aura of the fact or the thing or the deed, that gives high quality to the novel or drama, as well as to poetry itself.
>
> (1992b: 873)

O'Brien interprets 'the thing not named' as a specific evocation – i.e. same-sex desire. By contrast, Acocella claims that Cather's subject is 'not … homosexuality but … literature' (2002: 50). For Acocella, the fact that Cather is talking about art constitutes proof that she is not talking about homosexuality. However, a reading of Cather's work – particularly her overheated journalism of the 1890s – makes clear that whenever she is talking about art she is also always talking about homosexuality: passion, according to Cather, is *every* artist's secret.

Before Cather became one of the great novelists of the twentieth century, she spent many years scrambling as a journalist, churning out articles on everything from women's fashion to Wagner. Unlike the late Mann – or the ancient herdsmen that were his subject – Cather did not have all the time in the world: she was trying to make it big while still a young woman, in a publication sphere that moved very fast. From her years writing freelance in Nebraska to her job editing Pittsburgh's *Home Monthly*, Cather wrote reviews and essays about her favorite authors, among them a number of *poètes maudits* whose example she hoped to follow, but not too closely. Writing in the shadow of the Wilde trial, Cather anxiously responds to a range of aesthetic objects, attempting to stake out a position that will ensure literary success while keeping social abjection at bay. The temptations of Europe and of aestheticism for Cather are palpable: in these deeply ambivalent reflections one sees Cather struggling – often in vain – to drive a wedge between good art and bad living.

In 1897, soon after arriving in Pittsburgh, Cather observed: '[A]ll Pittsburgh is divided into two parts. Presbyteria and Bohemia, and the former is much the larger and more influential kingdom of the two' (1970: 505). For Cather, Bohemia names both the promise of youth and the terrible spectre of failure. To become an artist is to risk a life outside of normative aims, habits, and temporal and spatial trajectories. The figure of the exile-artist is both a model of resistance to the deadening realm of social convention and a sign of the dangers of corruption, arrested development, and failure.

Cather had always thrown in her lot with the Bohemian, the outsider, and the artist, but in her twenties she made a gradual and self-conscious decision to migrate to the more powerful kingdom. In a review of the play *Bohemia*, based on Henri Murger's *Scènes de la vie de Bohème*, Cather writes,

> When all is said and done, Bohemia is pre-eminently the kingdom of failure, at least it is the province of non-success. For a young man it may be a temporary abiding place whose skies are not altogether hopeless, ... a land of youth where he tarries but a moment and from which the serious business of life will call him away. But an old man who is still hanging about the outskirts of Bohemia is a symbol of the most pitiful failure on earth.
>
> (1970: 294)

For the young dreamers in Cather's work, there are only two options: phenomenal artistic success or social death. Though Bohemia was the kingdom of the artist, Cather feared that lingering there would mean failure. To be an artist but not to take on the social identity of the artist or bohemian was the trick.

While the target of Cather's aggression in her review of *Bohemia* is the aging artist, in 'Joseph and his Brothers' she turns that aggression on the brilliant youth: Joseph, a stand-in for the young Cather. At seventeen, Joseph is entertained by his own ideas, pleased by his ability to please. The background against which Cather paints Joseph is one familiar to her; she presents his dilemma as that of a talented youth in a provincial backwater.

> Nothing very interesting ever happens now in Jacob's great family; so Joseph decorates the trivial events: he exaggerates, gossips, talks too much, and is extravagantly given to dreams. These are not the dreams of lassitude, nor are they sensual. They are violent, dizzy – nightmares of grandeur. The qualities which are to make his great future are in him, potential realities, just as they were in Napoleon at seventeen; and they have nothing to grapple with.
>
> (1992a: 867)

Cather's ambivalent attraction to this figure is apparent; unlike the hero of her story 'Paul's Case' – another queer-ish boy narratively punished by Cather – Joseph is beautiful and talented. Though she is drawn to the magnitude of Joseph's ambition, she is suspicious of his allure; one hears a disciplinary note in her response to his extravagance, the effeminate quality of his brilliance. But Joseph is saved from his life of easy frivolity, according to Cather, by the hardship he suffers when his brothers beat 'the conceit and joy out of him' (ibid.: 869), and send him into Egypt as a slave. In Cather's fiction, brutality is necessary to compel dreamy boys to abandon the charmed world of youth.

Cather reveals her investment in this story at the end of the essay; she argues that Joseph must be sacrificed in order to place Jacob his father in his rightful place at the centre of the history. Cather writes:

> Jacob is the rod of measure. He saw the beginning, the new-born creature, and believed even then that this was the child of destiny. He knew Joseph before Joseph knew himself. When the 'true son' disappeared into darkness at the dawn of his promise, it was Jacob, not Joseph, who bore the full weight of the catastrophe, and tasted the bitterness of death. And he lived to see the beautiful conclusion; not the worldly triumph only, but the greatness of heart which could forgive wrongs so shameful and cruel. Had not Jacob been there to recognize and to foresee, to be destroyed by grief and raised up again, the story of Joseph would lose its highest value. Joseph is the brilliant actor in the scene, but Jacob is the mind which created the piece itself. His brooding spirit wraps the legend in a loftiness and grandeur which actual events can never, in themselves, possess. Take Jacob out of the history

of Joseph, and it becomes simply the story of a young genius; its cruel discipline, its ultimate triumph and worldly success. A story ever new and always gratifying, but one which never wakens the deep vibrations of the soul.

(ibid.: 871)

Jacob leaves behind a brilliant youth, choosing the path of the complete artist: not a character actor strutting around Bohemia, but a brooding observer, Jaakob is a withdrawn, sorrowful god – not god incarnate but god the creator. Jaakob's apotheosis depends on Joseph's suffering: Jaakob must taste 'the bitterness of death' (ibid.), and be able to forgive 'shameful and cruel' (ibid.) wrongs. Cather suggests that the making of a true artist requires violence against the figure of the bright and talented youth. To become Jaakob, one must first kill one's inner Joseph.

*

There are few authors who can equal Cather in her passion for self-creation – but Susan Sontag is a viable candidate. The sheer energy of Sontag's adolescent intellectual ambition has become clear since the posthumous publication of the first volume of her diaries, *Reborn* (2008). A typically dramatic entry, written in the spring of 1948, begins, 'what is it to be young in years and suddenly wakened to the anguish, the urgency of life?' (2008: 4). Sontag was fifteen. Throughout her adolescence, Sontag idolized Mann, seeing in him an author whose sensitivity to the anguish and the urgency of life matched her own. On 1 September 1948, Sontag wrote in her diary: '*The Magic Mountain* is a book for all of one's life. I know that! *The Magic Mountain* is the finest novel I've ever read. The sweetness of renewed and undiminishing acquaintance with this work, the peaceful and meditative pleasure I feel are unparalleled' (ibid.: 6). Many of Sontag's pronouncements draw on the rhetoric of age and eternity, as if she sought to borrow a sense of temporal stability from Mann's greatness.

As it turned out, *Der Zauberberg* was less a book for all of Sontag's life than it was for her life from fourteen to seventeen years of age; at least judging from the diary entries, reading Mann did not seem to give her much in the way of 'peaceful and meditative pleasure'. Sontag's passionate identification with Mann is subject to sudden reversals. An entry from 1949 suggests Sontag's ongoing efforts to fix her estimation of Mann's work: 'Somewhere, in an earlier notebook, I confessed a disappointment with the Mann Faustus ... This was uniquely undisguised evidence of the quality of my critical sensibility! The work is a great and satisfying one, which I'll have to read many times before I can possess it' (ibid.: 19). Throughout her journals, Sontag records events related to her discovery of Mann: learning of *Der Zauberberg* from Clifton Fadiman's middlebrow guide to literature *Reading I've Liked*, or getting caught shoplifting *Doktor Faustus* in her local bookstore. Most dramatically, she records visiting Mann in his Los Angeles bungalow in 1949 with two school friends: 'E, F, and I interrogated God this evening at six' (ibid.: 56). Back home after this encounter, Sontag meticulously recalled Mann's table talk, recording verbatim his opinions about Joyce and Proust as well as his reflections about translations of his novels. A marginal note, presumably added later, strikes a contrast with these enthralled transcriptions of the words of the master: 'The author's comments betray his book with their banality' (ibid.: 58).

Sontag treated her obsession with wry retrospect in an essay, 'Pilgrimage', published in *The New Yorker* almost forty years later. Sontag narrates the visit to Mann as an encounter between 'an embarrassed, fervid, literature-intoxicated child and a god in exile who lived in a house in Pacific Palisades':

> But when I was borne aloft by 'The Magic Mountain', I wasn't thinking that he was also, literally, 'here'. To say that at this time I lived in Southern California and Thomas Mann lived in Southern California – that was a different sense of 'lived', of 'in'. Wherever he was, it was where-I-was-not. Europe. Or the world beyond childhood, the world of seriousness. No, not even that. For me, he was a book.
>
> (1987: 44)

Sontag, writing in her fifties, attempts to do justice to the mixture of idealization and disappointment that Mann inspired in her when she was a teenager. Since he was for her an unreal, superhuman figure, it was almost impossible to imagine that he had consented to live in Southern California – or to be incarnated at all. But as she realizes that the author is in fact a person and *not* a book or a set of ideas, Sontag lashes out. She notes that she expected Mann to speak like a book but instead he spoke like a book review, and not even a good one. Cather had published her essay on Mann in *The Saturday Review* just over a decade earlier. In 'Pilgrimage', Sontag notes that Mann spoke the accessible prose of *Saturday Review* (which she felt she had 'outgrown') rather than the 'fancy prose' of *Partisan Review* (ibid.: 48).

The intermittent aggression toward Mann both in the diaries and the *New Yorker* essay is genuine, yet it is clear that the real target here is Sontag, the young woman so hungry for transcendence that she mistook a man for a god. What is striking about Mann is his complacency, his suburbanity, the middlebrow transparency of his speech: these are just the qualities that Sontag had sought to escape by over-identifying with his writing, and by herself taking up residence – at least in her mind – high in the Swiss Alps. As a result, the primary note that Sontag strikes in retrospect is shame. 'Pilgrimage' begins: 'Everything that surrounds my meeting with him has the color of shame. December, 1947. I was fourteen, steeped in vehement admirations and impatience for the reality to which I would travel once released from that long prison sentence, my childhood' (ibid.: 38). In meeting a living symbol of Europe and high art, Sontag was ashamed of her youth, her lack of experience, her Americanness, and her ignorance. The fact that Sontag represents herself as fourteen here – when in fact the entry about the Mann visit is dated 12/28/49, when she was sixteen – suggests ongoing shame about the episode: as if at sixteen Sontag should have known better, whereas such extravagance is excusable two years earlier. Sontag's treatment of her younger self in 'Pilgrimage' is more knowing and more ironic than Cather's in 'Joseph and his Brothers'; nonetheless, she seems to agree that reaching maturity as an artist requires killing off the precocious teenager inside.

For Sontag, reaching maturity also required full expression of her sexuality, which meant having sex with women and men, achieving orgasm, and finding a way to live in her body. The contrast with Cather is sharp, and generational difference as well as personality played a role: from a young age, Sontag had access to queer subculture, and she visited lesbian bars in her teens. It's an interesting thought experiment to imagine what Cather's reflections on maturity and the artist's life would have looked like if she had lived in Sontag's time – and in California. In an entry from 1949, after having sex with a woman for the first time, Sontag makes clear how crucial queer sexuality is to her self-understanding as an artist and an intellectual:

> And what am I now, as I write this? Nothing less than an entirely different person ... My concept of sexuality is so altered – Thank god! – bisexuality as the expression of fullness of an individual – and an honest rejection of the – yes – perversion which limits sexual experience, attempts to de-physicalize it ... I know now a little of my capacity ... I know what I want to do with my life, all of this being so simple, but so difficult for me in the past to know. I want to sleep with many people – I want to live and hate to die – I will *not* teach, or get a master's after I get my B.A. ... I don't intend to let my intellect dominate me, and the last thing I want to do is worship knowledge or people who have knowledge! ... I intend to do everything ... to have one way of evaluating experience – does it cause me pleasure or pain, and I shall be very cautious about rejecting the painful – I shall anticipate

pleasure everywhere and find it, too, for it *is* everywhere! I shall involve myself wholly ... *everything matters!* ... I am alive ... I am beautiful ... what else is there?

(2008: 27–8)

Sontag's desire to live the life of the body and leave the intellect behind was by most measures a failure: in marrying Philip Rieff less than two years later, taking her MA in philosophy and doing doctoral research at Harvard, and becoming one of the most famous intellectuals and critics of the twentieth century, Sontag hardly ceased to worship knowledge or the people who have it. Furthermore, her sense of release from shame was short-lived: writing in the late 1950s, Sontag observes, 'I am just becoming aware of how guilty I feel being queer' (ibid.: 223). This link between transcendent experience and shame can help to explain why even Sontag's attempts at pleasure are touched by the desire for greatness (a desire to 'do everything'), a transcendent ambition that aims for but invariably misses access to ordinariness and the life of the body.

In her journal entries from the early 1960s, Sontag reflects on bad romance, even developing a shorthand for the psychic structure that seems to make satisfaction in love impossible for her. She calls it 'X'. What is X? Its meaning in Sontag's journal is remarkably unstable. Calling it 'the scourge' (ibid.: 245), Sontag accounts for X by listing the characteristic behaviours that constitute it: being 'an object, not a subject' (ibid.: 246); 'X is the one-night stand, the inability to say no' (ibid.: 230); X is 'connected with the sense of shame. X = the compulsion to be what the other person wants' (ibid.); 'People who have pride don't awaken the X in us. They don't beg. We can't worry about hurting them. They rule themselves out of our little game from the beginning. Pride, the secret weapon against X. Pride, the X-cide' (ibid.: 247); 'America is a very X-y country' (ibid.: 246). It is not really possible to sum up X, but its primary meanings seem to include: erotic ambivalence, self-hatred and hatred of the other, over-investment, projective identification, head-games, and unrequited love as the model of all love.

A figure of misrecognition and crossed love, X might also describe the love the young Sontag bore for Mann, expecting him to rescue her not only from the prison of her youth but also from the potentially much more constraining prison of her future. Given the fantastic hopes that she invested in him, Sontag couldn't help turning Mann into a scourge. But even when she turned against him, the object of Sontag's contempt was never Mann himself; Sontag reserved her fiercest contempt for his passionate teenage fan, who could never be old – or young – enough.

*

If Mann was deeply implicated in Cather and Sontag's little games, Shakespeare appeared to stay out of the fray, beyond the reach of their anxious self-invention and self-management. But the gravitational field of their ambition was remarkably powerful. In a 1957 diary entry, Sontag writes:

> What *do* I believe?
>
> In the private life
> In holding up culture
> In music, Shakespeare, old buildings.

(2008: 99)

Situating Shakespeare between the pair of music and old buildings, Sontag identifies the greatest author with culture itself, attempting to anchor her own wild and shifting enthusiasms. But the fact that this list begins with a belief in 'the private life' suggests just how shaky the foundations of high culture were for Sontag. Having invested in 'safe as houses' high culture as a means of redemption and as a path to privacy (privacy as transcendence), we see that the whole building threatens to collapse around her – culture is not a fact, it is rather an achievement, something that Sontag will have to hold up if it will continue at all.

For Sontag, Shakespeare was so wholly identified with great art that he transcended it. Writing in her diary in 1964, she opines: 'Great art has a beautiful monotony – Stendhal, Bach. (But not Shakespeare.) A sense of the inevitability of a style – the sense that the artist had no alternatives, so wholly centered is he *in* his style ... The greatest art seems secreted, not constructed' (2012: 21). Sontag describes the production of art as an emanation of the individual; aesthetic value is not worked up by stylists but rather is produced as a regular, even secretion from the cells of great authors. But Shakespeare, as always, is *hors de combat*, his greatness incomparable to even the greatest of artists. While he does not work up false variety like a lesser artist, Shakespeare also escapes the monotony of a being that inevitably produces its own essence again and again. Instead, she implies, Shakespeare creates art that is both inevitable and infinitely varied. In settling on the term 'secreted' to describe this process, Sontag suggests that Shakespeare is a crypt turned inside out, an engine for turning secrets into works of art – public, indelible, and more lifelike than life itself.

Cather also saw Shakespeare as an exception to all rules and as a means to transcendence. In an 1893 review for the *Nebraska State*

Journal, Cather describes the Shakespeare portrait that hangs in a local theater as if it were a crucifix:

> Over the drop curtain in the Funke there is a very fair copy of one of the best pictures of Shakespeare that any artist ever painted. It is rather doubtful whether any theatre in the world is quite worthy to hold the picture of the man who consummated literature, but that picture has been loved by many of us. It has been a comfort, sometimes, to look away for a while from the things on the stage, which were better left unseen, and to look up at that great face and know that once upon this planet such a man had lived and worked. The picture has been there for years and years, looking down on tragedy, comedy, and melodrama alike with that mournful, tender, 'father-forgive-them' smile.
>
> (1970: 29)

In contrast to Mann, whose divine status is never assured, Shakespeare's image remains on the wall, looking down on life's little tragedies (and comedies) while remaining safely beyond them. Shakespeare's image provides a refuge for the young Cather when she wants to turn away from things 'better left unseen': she refers to the poorly staged dramas he should not see; however, given the dynamics of sin and forgiveness she evokes, Cather suggests that he should look away from other unspeakable or secret aspects of human existence.

The implication is that Shakespeare cannot be touched by such dramas, that the great man is in the theater but not of it. But it is a fair copy of his image that hangs in the Funke Opera House in Lincoln, Nebraska, and the dramas that take place there are enacted in his name. More to the point, the very strength of Cather's idealization of Shakespeare in these early writings threatens to bring him down to earth. In another review in the *Nebraska State Journal* written a year later, Cather approvingly describes the 'high seriousness and earnestness' of Shakespeare's plays, her admiration reaching a fever pitch:

> The fact that for three hundred years these plays have wrought the great minds of every nation up to the highest pitch of intensity and emotion, is proof positive that they were written at the white heat of intensity by the greatest mind of all. They are the most serious product of the most serious of races, the high-water mark of the literature of the world. Whatever they may conceal they reveal more of the highest triumph of human art, more of the deepest reading of human life than any other of the works of man. As to Shakespeare himself it doesn't matter much ... It is immaterial. But the plays will stand till the judgment after the

name of the builder is forgotten, enduing throughout time, the admiration of all generations past, the wonder of all generations to be.

(1970: 89)

As it turns out, even Shakespeare is not safe from the profound longings and ambivalence of a young dreamer. While he stands as a monument to human achievement, the intensity of Cather's desire for self-making through his example infects even 'the greatest mind of all'. Working to throw fuel on the flames of feverish young minds every-where, Shakespeare in Cather's hands is a very X-y writer.

*

Burning with ambition, in love with culture, and desperate to escape the provinces, both Cather and Sontag saw a way out through identi-fication with Great Men. That pursuing this escape route from all that was familiar and ordinary demanded great sacrifices was something that both women came to understand only later. Cather already under-stood this sacrifice at the time of her writing on Mann: that knowledge explains the melancholy of the preface to *Not Under Forty* (written 'for the backward, and by one of their number') and the iron law of necessity that demands the sacrifice of the young and charming Joseph. It also informs her well-known statement about human relations as the 'tragic necessity of human life', in the essay on Katherine Mansfield featured in this collection. She writes:

> One realizes that even in harmonious families there is this double life: the group life, which is the one we can observe in our neigh-bor's household, and, underneath, another – secret and passionate and intense – which is the real life that stamps the faces and gives character to the voices of our friends. Always in his mind each member of these social units is escaping, running away, trying to break the net which circumstances and his own affections have woven about him. One realizes that human relationships are the tragic necessity of human life; that they can never be wholly satis-factory, that every ego is half the time greedily seeking them, and half the time pulling away from them.

(1992c: 878)

Sontag came to a similar sense of the violence of greatness as she aged. Throughout the journals from the late 1960s, she describes her anguish at not having access to ordinary pleasures and reflects on her formation as a creature of the mind rather than the body. She writes:

Cocteau says: Primitives make beautiful things because they've never seen any others. Analogous to what I did as a child. I started thinking using my mind, because I'd never seen anyone do it. I didn't think anyone had a mind except in the Pantheon (mostly dead, foreign) – Mme. Curie, Shakespeare, Mann, etc. Everyone else was like my mother, Rosie, Judith. If I'd known about the middle ground – all the intelligent, thoughtful, sensitive people, who knows? I might never have gone on + on + on with my mind. For partly I did that because I thought no one was taking care of that at all. The mind needed my help to survive.

(2008: 204)

For Cather and Sontag, the identification with high culture was a matter of survival. Through their passionate identifications with Mann and Shakespeare, they constructed a Pantheon in which they sought to live alongside the figures they adored, and to escape the world that they knew – and which knew them – all too intimately. By identifying with figures of unquestionable greatness, they sought to access the glamour and dynamism of the aesthetic while escaping its associations with deviance and stigma. But in that rarefied world of their own making, there was little in the way of human sustenance. Having vaulted themselves beyond the 'middle ground' of ordinary pleasures, the life of the body, and mortal affection, they found greatness but still longed for the good.

Note

1   Mann had published *Die Geschichten Jaakobs* (*The Tales of Jacob*, 1933), *Der junge Joseph* (*The Young Joseph*, 1934), and *Joseph in Ägypten* (*Joseph in Egypt*, 1936) at the time Cather wrote her essay; *Joseph, der Ernährer* (*Joseph the Provider*) did not come out until 1943.

Works Cited

Acocella, Joan, 2002. *Willa Cather and the Politics of Criticism*. New York: Vintage.

Cather, Willa, 1896. 'The Death of Verlaine', in *Nebraska State Journal*, February 2, p. 9.

Cather, Willa, 1970. *The World and the Parish, vol. I: Willa Cather's Articles and Reviews 1893–1902*. Lincoln, Nebraska: University of Nebraska Press.

Cather, Willa, 1992a. 'Joseph and his Brothers', in *Stories, Poems, and Other Writings*, ed. Sharon O'Brien. New York: The Library of America, pp. 859–71.

Cather, Willa, 1992b. 'The Novel Démeublé', in *Stories, Poems, and Other Writings*, ed. Sharon O'Brien. New York: The Library of America, pp. 834–7.

Cather, Willa, 1992c. 'Katherine Mansfield', in *Not Under Forty*, collected in *Stories, Poems, and Other Writings*, ed. Sharon O'Brien. New York: The Library of America, pp. 872–83.

Cather, Willa, 1992d. 'Prefatory Note', in *Not Under Forty*, collected in *Stories, Poems, and Other Writings*, ed. Sharon O'Brien. New York: The Library of America, p. 812.

O'Brien, Sharon, 1984. '"The Thing Not Named": Willa Cather as a Lesbian Writer', in *Signs* 9.4, pp. 576–99.

Slote, Bernice, 1966. 'The Kingdom of Art,' in *The Kingdom of Art: Willa Cather's First Principles and Critical Statements, 1893–1896*, ed. Bernice Slote. Lincoln, Nebraska: University of Nebraska Press.

Sontag, Susan, 1982a. 'Notes on Camp', in *A Susan Sontag Reader*. New York: Farrar, Straus and Giroux, pp. 105–19.

Sontag, Susan, 1982b. 'On Style', in *A Susan Sontag Reader*. New York: Farrar, Straus and Giroux, pp. 137–55.

Sontag, Susan, 1987. 'Pilgrimage', in *The New Yorker*, December 21.

Sontag, Susan, 2008. *Reborn: Journals and Notebooks 1947–1963*, ed. David Rieff. New York: Picador.

Sontag, Susan, 2012. *As Consciousness is Harnessed to Flesh: Journals and Notebooks 1964–1980*, ed. David Rieff. New York: Farrar, Straus and Giroux.

Ten A Kind of Loving: Hans Castorp as Model Critic
David Fuller

Professional criticism tends to degenerate into the merely professional, and needs constantly to be refreshed by a feeling for art that is in the full sense *amateur* – loving. Hans Castorp's thoughts and feelings about the music to which he listens on gramophone recordings towards the end of *Der Zauberberg* (§7, 'Fülle des Wohllauts') are a model for this kind of literary-critical thinking – professionally *amateur*. Discussing this with examples from Shakespeare, similarly through recorded performances, is an experiment with two backgrounds. One: a love of recorded performances, especially performances by singers who worked in periods before recording became usual – their style valuing creative spontaneity over the more calculated (or electronically corrected) 'perfection' supposedly required by frequent iteration; and especially performances by actors who worked in periods before television set norms – their style preferring a histrionic theatricality not moderated by naturalism. The other: experiments I have attempted with modes of criticism based on the idea of art as emotional knowledge, giving prominence to interaction between the work and the reader, part of the meaning of which derives from the fact of interaction – who the reader is, what the reader brings, and what he or she becomes. 'Fülle des Wohllauts' draws together this love and these experiments.[1]

As Hans comments on it, the music to which he listens is integrated with who he is, what he feels, and how he thinks and acts. His modes of thinking, though not trained or systematic in relation to music, are real in their knowledge of the works concerned, and that knowledge is sophisticated by the ways in which it is brought into relation with Hans's other thinking – thinking about love and personal relationships, about religion, and about the 'advanced' social currents of his age. It offers new models of criticism precisely because it combines the sophisticated with the untrained and unsystematic – that is, it is not confined to learned routines, which are always in danger of becoming damagingly separated from the life that gives them meaning. Some elements of critical 'formulae' can be adduced – not in themselves very learnable: passionate identification, both complete and problematized; visceral pleasure in form – really visceral: the mind engaged through the body. But the fundamental issue is not critical practices but modes of being.

In this Hans is a model for all critical thinking about art: perceptions based in real experience can always lead to new and surprising places. Hans's thinking, based in music, has special applications to Shakespeare because Shakespeare, like all great poets, is a musician; and the meanings of Shakespeare's music involve mysteries that, being valuably resistant to conceptual thinking, have a natural affinity with Hans's modes of thought. Underlying assumptions are indicated by a fundamental paragraph about Hans Castorp's mode of thinking in the novel, which has parallels in German aesthetics.

> He had a special term for this responsible preoccupation with his thoughts …: he called it 'playing king' – a childish term taken from the games of his boyhood, and by it he meant that this was a kind of entertainment that he loved, although with it came fear, dizziness, and all sorts of heart palpitations that made his face flush even hotter.[2]

Mann's crucial term, 'Regieren' – to rule, govern – is used here in a paradoxically extended sense associated with childhood, play, and Hans's illness. It involves childlike, even visionary wonder, but allied to a sophisticated adult range and depth of thought. Used throughout the second half of the novel, the word suggests an investigative, imaginative dwelling on experiences, and on conflicting ideas about their interpretation; extracting insights from complex feelings and ideas that apparently point in opposite directions.[3] Mann prepares for Hans's 'sonderbares Wort' by invoking his liberal and reactionary mentors, Settembrini and Naphta, and the whole dialectic of their opposition. Hans's thinking as 'Regierung' is also characterized by its antithetical symbolic locations: the blue-blossoming meadow of ego-dissolving wisely passive contemplation; the snow-storm of ego-affirming active seeking. Truths to different experiences, giving rise to opposite ethics, understood through complementary modes of thinking. In this sense 'governing': bringing to order complexes of thought and feeling that are all but ungovernable. The activity combines subtlety and comprehensiveness of thought with freedom of imagination and intensity of feeling that breaks through normal social constraints. The connection with illness also associates it with the heightened states of being and depth of vision that Hans extracts from his 'magic mountain' experience. All this is 'Regierung' – and a model for critical thinking: intellect, imagination, feeling, discovery.

Mann's emphasis on 'play' of imagination, and on the interaction of work and reader, perception and interpretation, has a history in German aesthetics going back to Lessing, Schiller and Goethe. For Lessing:

> That alone is significant and fruitful which gives free play to the imagination. The more we see, the more must we be able to add by thinking. The more we add thereto by thinking, so much the more can we believe ourselves to see.
>
> (1988: 34)[4]

Free play of imagination, 'freies Spiel': by this the reader engages more of him- or herself, and so comes to a more investigative-creative understanding. This must be understood by its exemplification in Lessing's critical practice: not random perceptions loosely attached to unregulated fancifulness, but contemplation of 'the object as in itself it really is' (Matthew Arnold's phrase) and imaginative thought given to all the implications of its articulation. 'Spiel' is similarly a central term in Schiller's aesthetics, again play that is paradoxically disciplined, and that harmonizes traditionally opposed faculties of being, spiritual and sensuous.[5] Even more emphatically than Lessing, Goethe brings out the issue of response and interpretation engaging the reader's creativity.

> A work of art, especially a poem, that leaves nothing to conjecture is not a true work of art, fully worthy of the name. Its highest function must always be to stimulate reflection, and it can only really commend itself to ... the reader by compelling him to interpret it in his own way, and to complete it, so to speak, by creative re-enactment.
>
> (1909–11: 4.477)[6]

These fundamental ideas about imaginative play and the creative reader can be paralleled from any number of writers, of different kinds and from different cultures. They indicate fundamental orientations for Hans's activity of 'Regierung' as applied to thinking about art.

But before Hans's thinking, his listening: it has apparently not been noticed that Mann has Hans play recordings that actually existed when he is assumed to be listening, just before the outbreak of World War I.[7] Mann describes some of the performances in detail, so that – as often with the historical grounding of his fiction – the imaginative aspects of the account are integrated with a quasi-documentary basis. With all, Mann's thematically-based choices were historical possibilities in the era of early acoustic recording. Mann is never tied to history. All his choices for Hans's most concentrated listening are significant in relation to the novel as a whole; but all of them actually existed, some (the Caruso performances of Puccini and Verdi) as recordings to which Mann refers. While much of what the reader needs to know about the music and its performance is written into the novel, it should help recreate the experience of thinking like Hans Castorp to imagine the now historic performance qualities that Mann's first readers would assume. (For details of the music and the recordings see the appendix).

Mann signals plainly the intensity of the gramophone's effect on Hans:

> Somewhere inside him a voice said: 'Wait! Look out! An epoch begins! For me!' He was filled with the very definite premonition of a new passion and enchantment, a new burden of love. What he felt was no different from what a lad in the flatlands feels when he casts the first glance at a girl and Cupid's barbed arrow unexpectedly pierces his heart.
>
> (*MM* 761)[8]

It is crucial to see how much words connected with love and wonder are used about Hans's feelings in relation to the machine, the performances, and the music. Familiarity intensifies love: Hans can relish more fully every inflection. Hans's characteristic modes of engagement and understanding are most evident with his favourite items – fragments of Verdi, Debussy, Bizet, Gounod and Schubert. It is indicative that only one of these is German.[9] In articulating a non-Germanic Romance or Latin ethos, the music helps Hans become who he wishes to be. Hans's engagements need to be understood in the context of the novel as a whole: there are meanings he recognizes, and meanings that remain unconscious for him but can be heard by the reader. And while aspects of Hans's response are personal and idiosyncratic, it is Mann's argument that only a limited amount of anybody's experience is specific to the individual. Hans's responses are also representative.

> A human being lives out not only his own personal life as an individual, but also, consciously or subconsciously, the lives of his epoch and contemporaries; and although he may regard the general and impersonal foundations of his existence as unequivocal givens and take them for granted, having as little intention of ever subjecting them to critique as our good Hans Castorp himself had, it is nevertheless quite possible that he

senses his own moral well-being to be somehow impaired by the lack of critique.

(MM 36–7)[10]

Seclusion in the conditions of the mountain prompts Hans to develop the critique lacking in his culture for those who live only the semi-conscious life of the ordinary world ('Flachland'). By 'Fülle des Wohllauts' he is a developed and subtle interpreter, both idiosyncratic and supra-personal.

Hans's favourite listening is never purely disinterested. It is always engaged with his non-aesthetic experience. The music is made real to him by being drawn into relation with that experience. Some of this involves recreation in terms that are sometimes conscious, sometimes unconscious. Three fragments among Hans's favourites involve military figures whom he sees as parallel to his cousin, Joachim, though finally two of these – Radamès and Don José – act in ways opposite to Joachim, preferring love to duty. They are congruent not with Joachim but with Hans himself. His crucial Mardi Gras conversation with Clawdia Chauchat – on not seeking morality in discipline but in abandoning oneself to what can destroy – implies precisely the positive perspective on the 'derelictions' of Radamès and Don José that engages Hans with their music, which presents a new ethic albeit from within the framework of an old. Parallels with Joachim are a blind to conceal from Hans the congruence with his own experience – part actual, part desired – that gives these characters their compelling attraction.

Dramatic situations are important: so too is expressivity of vocal sound. Singers are characters, but also musical instruments: Amneris, but also the 'königlichen Alt mit dem Stimmbruch' ('mezzo with the break in her register'); Radamès, but also the 'tragisch verblendeten … Tenor' ('tragically infatuated tenor'); 'rein akustisch genommen' ('from a purely acoustic point of view') the justifiably rejected Amneris fully deserves Radamès (*Zb* 976/*MM* 765). The performer is a creative intermediary, complicating emotional effects (*Zb* 975/*MM* 765); and it is not only that vocal inflection conveys meaning and performance is a mode of criticism; pure vocal sound also signifies.[11] Both music and the performing voice may convey meanings quite different from the content of the text and dramatic situation. With the Aida–Radamès duet, though the situation is preparatory to death by starvation, for Hans the music obliterates any point of view not derived from its beauty (*Zb* 978/*MM* 768–9). Mann, drawing a parallel with the transfiguration in death of Wagner's Isolde, described it as an 'italienischer Liebestod' (1979: 375). There are inter-actions of drama with music and performance in which form entirely dominates content.

In Verdi Hans responds to experiences shaped from what he finds in himself – ideals realized through conflict. Debussy shows another way. The *Prélude à l'après-midi d'un faune* is a direct contrast to the surrounding fragments – not only a new ethic, but a new ethic because a new form. The faun, through whom Hans imagines a self he might become, is the opposite of Radamès and Don José: 'Es war die Liederlichkeit mit bestem Gewissen, die wunschbildhafte Apotheose all und jeder Verneinung des abendländischen Aktivitätskommandos' (*Zb* 980; 'it was depravity with the best of consciences, the idealized apotheosis of a total refusal to obey Western demands for an active life', *MM* 770). As Mann argues, every work implies a world-view (*Zb* 987–8/*MM* 775). Here that is pagan and sensual, a wisdom of passive receptivity. To characterize this Mann has to struggle against the implications of German vocabulary: 'Liederlichkeit mit bestem Gewissen' (Lowe-Porter, 'slackness' – placed in inverted commas). The new ethos is expressed by new musical methods: not dramatized conflicts of feeling but music 'angetan, die Seele in Traum zu spinnen' (*Zb* 979; 'calculated to set the soul spinning a web of dreams', *MM* 769), music of contrived indeterminacy, modernist – and French – in rhythm, harmony, structure, and orchestration. Hans's response – discernibly based in what the music really is, but also free-wheeling and rhapsodic – again opens him to imaginative engagement with what he wishes to become. It is a perfect example of 'Regierung' in the creative-recreative mode required by Goethe.

While the relation of dramatic content to musical form is different, the scenes from *Carmen* repeat the fundamental conflict of *Aida* between love and duty. Hans hears in the drama 'eine Urfeindschaft gegen das Prinzip, das durch diese … Clairons … rief' (*Zb* 982; 'an ancient hostility to the principle behind those … bugles', *MM* 771) – the bugles summoning the soldier back to life governed by regulation. There is a general meaning: the drama of the gypsy and the soldier epitomizes *Aida*'s opposition of freedom and duty – with the difference that Don José is more impressed than Radamès by the conflict. Hans connects Don José with Joachim, but the reader can again see that unconsciously, through the power of the music, he identifies with being drawn out of the safely familiar by love and desire.

Hans is comically unconscious of this, but Mann implies the unrecognized identification variously. José's Flower Song is invoked when Hans first speaks to Clawdia (*Zb* 308/*MM* 280): he associates José's suffering and passive fidelity with his own feelings. As the gramophone episode recalls (*Zb* 814/*MM* 770), Hans also alludes to *Carmen* in his climactic conversation with Clawdia's companion, Pieter Peeperkorn (*Zb* 769/*MM* 727). Having outlined the opera's plot, he prompts the reader: 'warum fällt sie mir ein?' (*Zb* 926; 'why did it occur to me', *MM* 728).

Why? Because in cutting himself off from the flatlands for the love of an exotic woman who is out of reach Hans is Don José. As he is in cherishing the flower she gave him – or in Hans's case, the X-ray plate. And could anything be more Carmenesque than the ethic of Clawdia's carnival proposition: abandon yourself to what will destroy you. Hans identifies with the pathos of José's hopeless love. 'Carmen, ich liebe dich!'; '"Ja, ja!" sagte Hans Castorp schwergemut und dankbar' (*Zb* 983; 'Carmen I love you'; '"Yes, yes" Hans Castorp said in sombre gratitude', *MM* 772–3).

The aria of Valentin from Gounod's *Faust* Hans more straightfor- wardly connects with Joachim, but here he consciously re-creates: Joachim is Valentin; Hans is Marguerite, the sister for whose protection Valentin-Joachim prays. As with the Flower Song, the music is integrated into the novel beyond 'Fülle des Wohllauts'. The transsexual implica- tions of Hans seeing himself as Marguerite connect with his bisexual view of love (for Clawdia and her avatar, the beautiful boy, Pribislav Hippe). Putting himself in the role of sister connects too with Joachim's protective farewell and its violation of convention in the affectionate use of personal pronouns and personal names (*Zb* 537/*MM* 503). It is this recording that prompts the final appearance to Hans of the dead Joachim (*Zb* 856/*MM* 811). As with all Hans's favourites, there is a comprehensive integration of real-life and aesthetic experience. The experiences Hans has, how he understands himself, and finally who he is, are all involved with art. This means what Lessing et al. argue real aesthetic experience must mean – imaginative activity on the part of the reader-listener, based on things in the work, drawing on the reader- listener's experience, actual or desired.

This complexity of interpretative interactions reaches its most intense form with the last of Hans's favourites, Schubert's song, 'Der Lindenbaum'. The discussion of this is more extended and even more elaborately integrated into the novel as a whole. With 'Der Lindenbaum' Mann introduces the idea that a work of art epitomizes issues larger than its explicit subject.

An object created by the human spirit and intellect, which means a significant object, is 'significant' in that it points beyond itself, is an expression and exponent of a more universal spirit and intellect, of a whole world of feelings and ideas that have found a more or less perfect image of themselves in that object – by which the degree of its significance is then measured. Moreover, love for an object is itself equally 'significant'. It says something about the person who feels it, it defines his relationship to the universe, to the world presented by the created object and, whether consciously or not, loved along with it.

(*MM* 775)[12]

Hans's love of 'Der Lindenbaum' is the index of his feeling for the world it implies. But, unlike with the Flower Song, Hans is fully conscious of this: in his 'Regierung' about 'Der Lindenbaum' (Mann invokes the idea repeatedly: *Zb* 988/*MM* 776) he is able to criticize the work, the world it implies, and his love for both – to see all three for what they are; all of which indicates what Mann calls 'zweifelnde Liebe' (*Zb* 988; 'scrupulous love', *MM* 776) – integrated feeling and thought.[13]

Another new issue here concerns how understanding elicits implications contrary to evident meanings. What does 'Der Lindenbaum' imply? Death (*Zb* 988/*MM* 777). Is that surprising? What does a flatland perspective say about the song? 'Ei ja, ja, ja, das war recht schön' (*Zb* 988; 'Oh my, oh my – that was all very pretty', *MM* 776). And parts are simply beautiful: the rippling piano prelude representing the iridescent fountain; the major key in which the song begins and ends: Nature offers comfort to human misery. But there is an opposite current: the minor key of the central verse, in which the rippling piano, now turbulent, becomes the assault of cold winds epitomizing the lover's rejection; and though the music returns to the piano-fountain, it offers comfort that might have been, but is not, and never will be; the rest the lover did not accept from the Lindenbaum he will find only in death.

There are reasons in the poem and the setting, then, for understanding 'death' as the meaning of the song. But there are also reasons in the listener. 'Eine Lebensfrucht, vom Tode gezeugt und todesträchtig' (*Zb* 989; 'a fruit of life, sired by death and pregnant with death', *MM* 777), 'Der Lindenbaum' also draws together Hans's experiences of, dialogues about, and mediations on death. Experiences of death: above all the death of Joachim. Dialogues about death: Settembrini with Hans (§5, 'Ewigkeitssuppe und plötzliche Klarheit'); Settembrini and Naphta in conflicts that epitomize the opposition of their world-views (§6, 'Operationes spirituales'); Clawdia with Hans: love as associated with the mysteries of the body, corruptible matter, and death (*Zb* 437/*MM* 406) – a view utterly opposite to that of the optimist Settembrini, but endorsed by the novel, if Hans's feeling for Clawdia is the creative, revelatory force he understands it to be. Meditations on death: Hans's near-death experience when, semi-volitionally lost in a snowstorm, he hallucinates opposite visions of human life (as peaceful and loving; as violent and predatory) and reflects on these, resolving the contradictions of Settembrini and Naphta. The resolution of these experiences, dialogues, and meditations does not admit of simple formulation – but Hans's conclusions indicate one fundamental direction of thought:

Man is the master of contradictions, they occur through him, and he is more noble than they. More noble than death, too noble for it – that is the freedom of his mind. More noble than life, too noble for it – that is the devotion of his heart. There, I have rhymed it altogether, dreamed a poem of humankind. ... *For the sake of goodness and love, man should grant death no dominion over his thoughts.*

(*MM* 588)[14]

In being poised between opposite implications about death, 'Der Lindenbaum' epitomizes a central issue of *Der Zauberberg*.

Some of Hans's most significant experiences, then, underlie the discussion of the lied. He hears the thing as in itself it really is; but he is also a creatively engaged listener, bringing to the work feelings and ideas that allow him to respond with special intensity to its full implications. It is the way in which the song is shown to be so deeply integrated with Hans's thoughts and feelings that gives his 'Regierung' about it its authority. As with Valentin's aria, Mann marks this with a final climactic recall: Hans is singing 'Der Lindenbaum' the last time we see him, in World War I, disappearing into battle (*Zb* 1084/*MM* 852–3).

What, then, are the special qualities of Hans's listening? Passionate identification, conscious and unconscious; such pleasure in form that form is content; becoming through the music a new self; but underlying all this, and more generally, as Hans comments on it, the music is thoroughly integrated with his thinking, feeling, and being. This integration comes from repeated listening – dwelling in the work, inhabiting its details with full attention and with love; love recognized as reaching beyond the work to its implied world-view. But 'love' here does not mean simple endorsement: this is 'scrupulous love'. Difficult to formulate, this is exemplified in Mann's deeply engaged but also finally equivocal 'Leiden und Größe Richard Wagners' (1933), a lecture delivered shortly after the election of Hitler, for which Mann was denounced and (in effect) driven into exile (1985: 91–153). It exemplifies Mann's practice of aesthetic criticism with 'world-view' implications extrapolated – aesthetic criticism which thus becomes a form of cultural and political criticism; here about the world-view implied by Wagner's music, and specifically its political import, submission to power and to the irrational that Mann connects with Nazism. But the basis of the critique is love. Ideologically approved 'scruple' not made problematic by engagements of love, commentary from those who have not felt their fundamental being – as Mann felt his – in part created by the art they discuss, comes too easily to be valuable.

Not all of this is transferable, perhaps, to anything we can think of as criticism. But then the issue here is only partly about critical practices. It is first about coming into relation with works of art in a different way: *Regierung*, a kind of loving, the blue-blossoming meadow and the snow-storm. What is at stake is not primarily a change of techniques but a re-direction of being. Hans's re-direction comes from engaging with the debates of Settembrini and Naphta; from his anti-social bisexual love; and his gradual exchange of flatland mode for the mode of the mountain, with its altered consciousness of time and purposiveness. Some of this I know from experience: Settembrini was the idol of my youth, as Naphta is the temptation of my age. Some Pribislav Hippe I find all too readily. But norms of critical discourse, which are not those of the meadow and the snow-storm, insidiously insinuate a sense of time and purpose seen from a flatland perspective.

What can all this do with Shakespeare?

I have chosen two recordings of Shakespeare, one film, one audio: *Richard III* (1955) with Laurence Olivier as Richard; and *The Winter's Tale* (1963) with John Gielgud as Leontes and Peggy Ashcroft as Paulina. These are performances I first loved when I was more impressionable, more volatile and suggestible – more childlike, in the ways Mann desiderates. If I have worked out the implications of those passions, while my teenage commitments were more intense than discriminating, they should have become 'scrupulous loves'.

'Der Mensch lebt nicht nur sein persönliches Leben als Einzelwesen'; but also, 'Epoche! Das kam zu mir' – and the gramophone comes to Hans as it does not come to others. In his idiosyncratic way, Hans is living the life of his age; but, having exchanged the flatlands for mountain, meadow and snowstorm, he is also living outside it. It is by this alienation that he has become a sophisticated interpreter. Alienation, immunogenic in relation to the dulling comforts of joining the herd, has been his creative teacher.

I saw Olivier, Gielgud and Ashcroft on stage, at the same time seeing Nureyev and Fonteyn in their non-realist form of theatre, and becoming obsessed with the myth and romance dramas of Wagner, of which I had the good fortune to see the stylized productions of Wieland Wagner at Bayreuth. My enthusiasm for these forms of theatre, as distant as could be from realism in mode and naturalism in performance, was, like Hans's pleasure in the gramophone, immunogenic – in relation to the Shakespeare criticism I then encountered which, if it was derived from theatre at all, was not derived from theatre of this kind. Poetic drama as I knew it in Olivier and Gielgud performances was congruent with this general sense of theatre: extremes of feeling presented through stylization. It was from this that I drew my sense of what Shakespeare criticism should engage with and understand. It is on this that Hans's listening reflects.

Olivier's *Richard III* as I found it can be connected with Hans straightforwardly. There were unconscious meanings (Hans and the Flower

Song) – meanings of which I am conscious now, but was not conscious of when I first loved this film – and meanings about becoming who you wish to be (Hans and the Faun). The performance is full of the kinds of thing I shall be admiring with Gielgud and Ashcroft as central to the aesthetics of poetic drama. The verse-speaking combines feeling for structure so practised as to seem intuitive, with flexible inflection ranging from conversational to semi-sung; and that range is especially striking here, because the verse is so obviously formal. The film is also a striking example of re-contextualization that changes meaning (Hans as Marguerite). Isolating Richard's murders from the action of *Henry VI*, and cutting Queen Margaret and her curse (of which Richard is the executor), transforms Richard from the agent of a providential pattern to an independent initiator of action. That his energies are still attractive is therefore all the more striking, and it was those energies that when I first saw the film I found so thrilling – as I find them still. I connected Olivier's Richard with the thrillingly evil characters in Wagner, Alberich and Hagen, and concluded, with pleasure, that art was generally of the devil's party. A good deal in me was yearning for William Blake before I discovered him. In this way the film is also like Hans's Flower Song: isolated from its context it signifies differently – here the villain more villainous without being less attractive.

This is because Olivier presents Richard as both highly sinister and very funny: his charisma does not moderate either extreme. For on-stage dynamism and intensity he seemed to me a sort of Callas-plus-Nureyev of poetic drama – utterly uninhibited about Romantic extravagance, whether of stylized speech, gesture and movement, or tableau. His style of declamation and physical theatre relates poetic drama to opera, and to ballet – to ballet because movement is so often stylized, and because, important as words are, the meanings of the film as a whole lie also in the structured sequence of embodied actions and images, and all the ways in which they interact with and comment on the poetry. Though the intensity of Shakespeare's poetry can make us forget this, Olivier emphasizes drama as in part embodied sequence: action, image, tableau – broad tones, built up from minute inflections. He shows the meaning of Nietzsche's at first sight bizarre reflection on *Hamlet*: 'The structure of the scenes and the vivid images reveal a deeper wisdom than the poet himself can put into words and concepts' (1999: 81).[15]

Later I came to think Olivier's Richard even more like Don José for Hans, in that part of its attraction for me was unconscious. I was growing up thinking of myself as 'queer' – that was the word then used – in a context in which this was entirely disallowed. This could be at times melancholy and terrifying, but I was also able to generate for myself the defiant idea that my feelings were not, as everything around me implied, wickedness and error. I dealt with this by evolving a persona that simultaneously showed and concealed – a sort of behavioural A. E. Housman (whose gazing at Shropshire lads could seem entirely acceptable in the pastoral conventions within which it was presented). The showing–concealing persona was dangerous, but it was also exciting. In retrospect I see that Olivier's Richard thrilled me as a character who had the energy to be self-determining with an illicit purpose, exuberant in the performance of masks, provoked by seeing how near one could go to violating them. 'I thank my God for my humility' in a context of unbridled ego-assertion (2.1.73); 'See where his grace stands 'tween two clergymen' in the context of the deposition and murder of his brother's sons (3.7.95); and many other examples of wonderfully exuberant camp role-playing. For those enjoying the performance of an anti-self – the Devil as pious Christian – the effect is to watch dupes who are taken in (the stage audience), postulate another group (moralists in the theatre audience) who are scandalized by ruthlessness enjoying its own brilliance, while focussed on the performance of the mask – amoral pleasure in the flamboyant energies of boldly self-determining egotism. On this reading the implied world-view is Nietzschean: delight in energy regarded by conventional perspectives as wicked.[16] It was a training in reading 'against the grain', or, as I now think of it, reading for one's preferences – that is, as with Hans and 'Der Lindenbaum', highlighting elements genuinely present in the work, but with emphases coloured by the predispositions brought to it. Not meaning that ignores history and otherness – art as catalyst igniting only what is brought to it: solipsistic. Not meaning that confines itself to history and otherness – criticism as scholarship igniting no real connection: sterile. But real meaning negotiated between the work and the self. The negotiation should be, as far as possible, conscious: we should understand what we are doing insofar as we can – but that is never more than partially. The reality of a reading to experience is more important than the degree of its self-consciousness. I understood as a teenager that there was a pious reading of *Richard III* in which Good defeated Evil, and order was restored after chaos; but, while I doubt that I could have articulated a Nietzschean pleasure-in-energy reading, I would have been clear that I did not believe its opposite. This was inarticulate understanding in a mixture of Hans Castorp modes: a powerful albeit largely unconscious meaning; art helping to release who one wishes to be.[17]

There is not only one way of engaging with art. Unconscious identification can be quite as profound and satisfying as sophisticated detached multiple perspectives. The self-consciousness of modern criticism can be all very well: but to think of this as the only mode of sophisticated consciousness of art is pitiful and corrupt. For the reader-listener who can never unselfconsciously give him- or herself, as to a lover, there is a kind of knowledge many works of art expect and require that can never be experienced. Hans's blindness to his identification with Don José is concomitant with his full understanding of the feelings embodied in José's music. Sophisticated intelligence is not always able to understand why works of art affect us as they do. Criticism needs sometimes to be humble in its pretentions and recognize the limitations of conscious understanding – perhaps precisely with works that affect us most strongly, where their power may be related to feelings impossible to bring to consciousness. Intuition is not necessarily an uncultivated faculty: it can be the spontaneous consequence of much anterior conscious thought. There must be an interaction between spontaneous feeling and conscious thinking in which feeling can correct thought as much as thought feeling. Without this, in the delicate balance of thinking and feeling, thinking has a corrupt dominance.

The Winter's Tale: first Gielgud speaking verse, insofar as sound can be conveyed silently. Layout may suggest how the shapes of syntax as spoken expressively reconfigure the shapes of form:

Ha' not you seen, Camillo?
but that's past doubt: you have, or your eye-glass is thicker than a cuckold's horn;
    or heard,
for to a vision so apparent rumour cannot be mute;
    or thought,
for cogitation resides not in that man that does not think:
my wife is slippery?

                                      (1.2.269–75)

And yet within this the shapes of form – the metrical pulsation, the line so cut across by the syntax – can still be heard. And to further heighten this disrupted structure, alternation between address to Camillo and recoil into self-communing is brought out by changes of volume and pitch from which each unit (*seen / heard / thought*) rises in intensity as it approaches the revelatory accusation. It is the music of impassioned paranoia. Of course the point is not that another actor should do precisely what Gielgud does, which relates to the idiosyncrasies of Gielgud's voice and the state of the spoken language in his time; but that the poetry's fundamental expressivity should be recreated, whether by an actor or in the mind's ear, in terms fully alive to all the aspects of articulation (rhythm, syntax, pitch, volume) that convey intensity of thought and feeling.

Only a limited amount of this can be described. Finally learning about sound can come only through the ears. And what Eliot calls 'the inexplicable mystery of sound' (1962: 233) in poetry is in part beyond articulation, something to which one can only point and say, 'listen: as I hear these things, there it is'. Even as I was learning about it, was inarticulately full of it, I was not learning to think it. On the contrary, I was distracted from understanding what I was really discovering through Gielgud's performance by criticism that directed attention to modes of thought less engaged with the experience of theatre – a problem that does not arise for Hans Castorp, whose passions are not deflected by any programme of education.

Listening to the Gielgud–Ashcroft *Winter's Tale* made me alive to the music of poetic drama. This might seem straightforward enough were it not common experience that critics regularly cannot hear it nor actors deliver it. Gielgud and Ashcroft made it audible. I heard a fundamental skill of complete technical competence: an understanding of form so practised as to be intuitive; not wary of freedom (structures well established could be boldly varied); with the whole attention on meaning and feeling. Voices produced by the whole vocal mechanism – all the organs of the mouth and throat, but also from deeper in the body: the whole physical being engaged, because it is the bodily experience of emotion that allows a voice to bring out the poetry's full range of colour. Voices that can participate without forcing in a wide range of feelings with variety of delivery, responsive to heightened drama and heightened formal structures, projected by more singing tones; the speaking voice, as Hans finds the singing voice, a quasi-musical instrument. With Gielgud and Ashcroft I heard the colloquial base of Shakespeare's poetry – voices speaking with all the individual tones that register an engaged particular identity; and I heard the singing line – voices transmuted towards song by responsiveness to the formal structures of art. Individuality of inflection, rooted in idiosyncratic living being; the singing line, art's transcendence of the purely personal: it is the Shakespearean drab-aureate gamut. Both Gielgud and Ashcroft were exponents of Valéry's principle of performing verse so as to bring out its fundamental nature: without deserting the expressivity of colloquial speech, verging on the complementary expressivity of song.[18] If there is for me one thing more important than any other with performing or hearing Shakespeare's poetry it is that fundamental ability to project its tonal range. From Gielgud and Ashcroft I heard the sounds of sensibility and intelligence able to engage completely with the subject matter in the forms in which the poetry articulates it. And not only emotional and imaginative intelligence in a general way: in myriad decisions about interpretation (sense, tone, music) which were intellectually convincing and emotionally compelling I heard a revelation of the basic nature of the medium.[19]

Implicit in the Gielgud–Ashcroft style of performance is a view of poetic drama in which music is fundamental to its expressivity

– music both local and structural. While the form in which ideas about the music of poetry have entered modern criticism may come from Mallarmé through Pound and Eliot, the ideas themselves are implicit in Shakespeare's practice. They are characteristically formulated in Eliot's 'The Music of Poetry': music is not only a matter of local effects; it is a question of the entire poem or play (1957a: 26-38). The reader should hear the music in the part (line, speech), but also in the whole, which can be understood as analogous to a musical structure – not the structure of a symphony, which, with whatever expansions and variations, is a set pattern, but the more organic structure of a tone poem or Wagnerian music-drama. As in the *Aida* 'Liebestod' as that is heard by Hans Castorp, it is form, not content, that is decisive about meaning. In Eliot's formulation:

> I have before my eyes a kind of mirage of the perfection of verse drama, which would be a design of human action and of words, such as to present at once the two aspects of dramatic and of musical order. It seems to me that Shakespeare achieved this at least in certain scenes ... and that this was what he was striving towards in his late plays.
>
> (1957b: 87)[20]

Just as there is a local music of words, so there is also a structural music of scenes.

It is more difficult to experience the effects of this with a play than with a score. Realizing the structural music implied by a verbal text, on the stage or in the imagination, is a less determinate process than realizing structure notated musically. Opera is a helpful analogy to poetic drama because, while pure music exists as sound only, opera, like poetic drama, is both aural and visual, with the fundamental structures and tones of narrative and dramatic sequence congruent or interacting with those of the words. Dramatic structure – a sequence of tones minutely varied moment by moment, broadly varied in larger units – is rarely experienced in ways fully congruent with the implications of a text as the libretto for a happening. Even when a play is read as a sequential experience, criticism finds it difficult to attend to the music of structure. In the theatre pacing and proportion are regularly changed by cutting; and rarely does performance consistently give dramatic realization to the implied tonal qualities of every area of a play. It is difficult, therefore, in reading or in the theatre, to have experiences of drama from which to think about the effects of musical design that Eliot adumbrates. The Gielgud–Ashcroft *Winter's Tale*, with its moment-by-moment aurality so vividly realized, and uncut, so that the play's total aural design is in place, offers just such an experience.

Much more could be adduced and applied from Hans Castorp's listening: reading for one's preferences, conscious and unconscious; the part played by large implied backgrounds in our feelings about a work; realizing through art passions disallowed by one's cultural circumstances; becoming through art who one wishes to be. But Hans Castorp does not offer a 'model' primarily in the sense of methods. He suggests a mode of thinking with feeling that is fundamentally a way of being; a characteristic manner of contemplation the irregular nature of which Mann marks by his unusual term, 'regieren', with its complex and paradoxical definition, its symbolic locations, and all the exemplifications that precede Hans's thinking about music. Hans's thinking about art is congruent with his thinking about everything else that seizes his feelings and imagination. It is thinking that involves a heightened sense of being, a kind of loving that Mann calls 'zweifelnde Liebe', scrupulous love. Hans recognizes that, thoroughly entered into, the music he loves, in the ways in which he loves it, offers knowledge of himself and his world. Both love and understanding arise from what Hans has learned from all his experience – a diffused or sometimes a precisely focussed presence in his thinking about everything. Does this mean it helps in thinking about literary criticism? At bottom the most important thing is one's fundamental orientation towards works of art. For me, Hans Castorp's thinking with feeling refreshes and clarifies that, and helps to understand it in new ways.

Appendix

'Fülle des Wohllauts' (*Zb* 963-90 /*MM* 759–78): the Music and Recordings. (The music is listed here in the order in which items are referred to in the novel.)

Many of the vocal items listed below have been reissued on CD by Naxos Historical, Nimbus Prima Voce, Pearl, Preiser Lebendige Vergangenheit, and other specialist recording publishers.

Offenbach, *Orpheus in der Unterwelt* (*Orphée aus Enfers*). 'Ach, ich habe sie verloren', aria of Orpheus, quoted in the overture; a popular piece, variously recorded before 1913 (for example, conducted by Eduard Künneke, Odéon, 1910).

Rossini, *Il Barbiere di Siviglia*, 'Largo al factotum', from Act 1, sung by a 'famous Italian baritone'. Possibly Titta Ruffo (1877–1953), the most famous baritone contemporary of Caruso, who first recorded the aria in 1912. Possibly Giuseppe de Luca (1876–1950), who also sang with Caruso, and who recorded the aria (but with piano accompaniment) in 1907 (second recording, with orchestra, 1917). A medley of popular items of various kinds, including an aria from Verdi, *La Traviata* (the description suggests 'Sempre libera' from Act 1, recorded by Luisa Tetrazzini, 11.07.1911); (Anton) Rubinstein, violin and piano 'romance' (the popular Romance in E flat, op. 44, no.1, recorded by Jóska [Joseph] Szigeti, 1. 11. 1908); and the barca-rolle from Offenbach's *Les Contes d'Hoffmann* (frequently recorded, in various forms, before 1913, as by the orchestra of 'The Palace Theatre London' [no conductor named], Odéon, 1908).

Wagner, *Tannhäuser*, 'Blick' ich umher in diesem edlen Kreise', from Act II: Wolfram at the song contest; recorded by Fritz Feinhals (1869–1940), 1909; Otto Goritz (1873–1929), 1911; and Walter Soomer (1878–1955), 1913.

Puccini, *La Bohème* ('a modern Italian opera': 1896), 'Da mi il braccio, mia piccina', from the duet of Rodolfo and Mimì in Act I, 'O soave fanciulla'. The 'world-famous tenor' and 'soprano with a voice sweet and clear as glass' are Enrico Caruso (1873–1921) and Nellie Melba (1861–1931); recorded, 24.03.1907. (Caruso also recorded the duet with Geraldine Farrar in 1912, but the recording was not issued until 1942.)

Hans Castorp's favourites:

Verdi, *Aida*, the duet of Radamès and Amneris from Act 4; Caruso as Radamès, Amneris sung by Louise Homer (1871–1947); recorded 29. 12. 1910 (matrices C-9748-1, C-9749-1).

Amneris, Ramfis, and chorus of priests from Act 4, 'Ohimè, morir mi sento … Radamès, tu rivelasti … Sacerdoti, compiste un delitto'; Bianca Lavin de Cases as Amneris, F. Rizzo as Ramfis, La Scala Orchestra, cond. Carlo Sabajno; recorded 6.11.1909 (issued as three sides, of which Hans Castorp, for whom the music apparently breaks off just before Amneris's denunciation 'Sacerdoti, compiste un delitto', has only the first two).

The duet of Radamès and Aida from Act 4; Caruso as Radamès, Aida sung by Johanna Gadski (1872–1932); recorded 6./7.11.1909 (matrices C-8353, C-8348-2).

Debussy, *Prélude à l'après-midi d'un faune*. The earliest recording is of an abridged version, conducted by Landon Ronald with the New Symphony Orchestra (from 1915 Royal Albert Hall Orchestra). HMV D130; matrices Ac 5827f and HO 1836ao; recorded 16.12.1911 (issued in Germany 1914) and 6.05.1916 (issued 1918). The 'complete' (abridged) recording was first issued on two single-sided records, 0722 in July, and 0723 in September 1918, with the double-sided D130 following later, along with a double-sided issue in France, W317, in December 1919. (The abridged version contains: side 1: bars 1–4, 8–30, 37–51; side 2: bars 55-78, 94–110. 27 bars were cut.)

Bizet, *Carmen*, Act 2 duets. The best-known recording of these from the period has Emma Calvé (1858–1942) as Carmen and Charles Dalmorès (1871–1939) as Don José; recorded 20.03.1908 (matrices C-6042-1, C-6043-2).

Flower Song of Don José, Act 2, recorded by Caruso, 7.11.1909 (matrix C-8350). Also recorded by Dalmorès, 25.10.1912 (matrix C-4249-3). (A complete recording of *Carmen* was made by Pathé Frères in 1911.)

Gounod, *Faust*, Act 2, air de Valentin, 'Avant de quitter ces lieux', recorded by Henri Weber, 1903; Maurice Décléry (1873–1957), 1903; Henri Albers (1866–1925), 1907; and at least two other French baritones before 1913 (Lucien Rigaux, 1908; Léonce Teissié, 1908). (A 'complete' recording of *Faust*, with Jean Noté (1859–1922) as Valentin (but omitting 'Avant de quitter'), was made by Pathé Frères, 1911–12.)

Schubert, 'Der Lindenbaum', song 5 from the cycle *Die Winterreise*. The song was well-known apart from the cycle, and frequently recorded, but there were only two recordings before 1913 by tenors: by Jan Sztern (1867–1949), G&T 22194, recorded 1901; and by Carl Brahm, Globophon 51324, recorded 1911. Neither singer was well-known. There were two further recordings by tenors made before *Der Zauberberg* was published. Leo Slezak (1873–1946) recorded the song in June 1923 (accompanied by Bruno Seidler-Winkler; Polydor 65774). Richard Tauber (1891–1947) recorded the song at least three times, the first time in March 1923; German Odéon, matrix xxB 6849; cat. Rxx 80846 (pianist not named). If Mann had in mind a particular performance of 'Der Lindenbaum' it was almost certainly one of these. In 1923 Slezak (recording from 1905) was famous in opera and song, but Tauber (in 1923 less well-known) became an iconic performer of Schubert lieder. Mann's account of the performance corresponds closely to Tauber's over the ending, the same phrase repeated with contrasting vocal colourings: chest voice, head voice (*Zb* 986/*MM* 775).

Notes

1   See Fuller 1988, in which the final chapter argues for and exemplifies a mode of criticism explicitly engaged with the experiences and values with which the literary arguments are in dialogue; and 2011 which approaches the same issue in a different way, relating Shakespeare's sonnets to

their fundamental ideas about love in philosophy (Plato), visual art (Michelangelo), fiction (Mann), music (Britten) and film (Jarman).

2 *The Magic Mountain*, trans. John E. Woods (2005), p. 463; hereafter referred to as *MM. Er hatte ein sonderbares Wort für diese seine verantwortliche Gedankenbeschäftigung …: er nannte sie 'Regieren', – gebrauchte dies Spiel- und Knabenwort, diesen Kinderausdruck dafür, als für eine Unterhaltung, die er liebte, obwohl sie mit Schrecken, Schwindel und allerlei Herztumulten verbunden war und seine Gesichtshitze übermäßig verstärkte* (Zb 589). Helen Lowe-Porter translates the 'sonderbares Wort' prosaically as 'stock-taking' and entirely omits the association with childhood and play (Mann 1960: 390).

3 For the word's various uses see the German text *Zb* 621, 631, 640, 712, 719, 929, 987–9 (four uses here), 1063 and 1085, and especially 748 (Hans Castorp's vision in the snow). On the word's association with Hans's attempts to resolve the disputes of Settembrini and Naphta see *Zb* 879, where they are 'Regierungsräte'. Wood misses the connection here, translating 'viziers' (*MM* 691). Lowe-Porter translates 'auditors', with reference added to her translation of *regieren* as 'stock-taking'. The place Hans especially associates with the activity, the 'blue-blossoming meadow', is his symbolic choice for the location of the Settembrini/Naphta duel (*Zb* 1063/*MM* 836).

4 *Dasjenige aber nur allein ist fruchtbar, was der Einbildungskraft freies Spiel lässt. Je mehr wir sehen, desto mehr müssen wir hinzu denken können. Je mehr wir dazu denken, desto mehr müssen wir zu sehen glauben* (Lessing 1965: 71).

5 See Friedrich Schiller's *Über die ästhetische Erziehung des Menschen, in einer Reihe von Briefen*, 1794, Letter 27, §8–9; *On the Aesthetic Education of Man in a series of Letters*, trans. Elizabeth M. Wilkinson and L. A. Willoughby (1967: 214–15), and the discussions of play of association, the play-drive/play-impulse, and serious play (*Spiel und Ernst*) in their extended introduction (pp. xi–cxcvi).

6 *Ein Kunstwerk, besonders ein Gedicht, das nichts zu erraten übrig liesse, sei kein wahres, vollwürdiges. Seine höchste Bestimmung bleibe immer, zum Nachdenken aufzuregen, und nur dadurch könne es dem … Leser recht lieb werden, wenn es ihn zwänge, nach eigener Sinnesweise es sich auszulegen und gleichsam ergänzend nachzuschaffen* (Goethe, conversation with Friedrich von Müller, 1827; 1909–11: 4.477). Translation by the author.

7 Neither Vaget 2006 nor Mertens 2006 discuss the recordings.

8 *In ihm hieß es: 'Halt! Achtung! Epoche! Das kam zu mir.' Die bestimmteste Ahnung neuer Passion, Bezauberung, Liebeslust erfüllte ihn. Dem Jüngling im Flachland, dem beim ersten Blick auf ein Mädchen Amors widerhakiger Pfeil unverhofft mitten im Herzen sitzt, ist nicht gar anders zumute* (Zb 969).

9 When Mann chose his own favourite recordings for an American magazine in 1948 he selected a completely different, almost exclusively German repertoire (Mann 1985: 204–5).

10 *Der Mensch lebt nicht nur sein persönliches Leben als Einzelwesen, sondern, bewußt oder unbewußt, auch das seiner Epoche und Zeitgenossenschaft, und sollte er die allgemeinen und unpersönlichen Grundlagen seiner Existenz auch als unbedingt gegeben und selbstverständlich betrachten und von dem Einfall, Kritik*

daran zu üben, so weit entfernt sein, wie der gute Hans Castorp es wirklich war,
so ist doch sehr wohl möglich, daß er sein sittliches Wohlbefinden durch ihre
Mängel vage beeinträchtigt fühlt (Zb 53).

11   On the revelatory force of a performing voice as pure sound, see Mann's
      extended image of the (visual) effect of gradually unfolding mountain
      landscape in 'Schnee' (*Zb* 738-9/*MM* 580–1).

12   *Ein geistiger, das heißt ein bedeutender Gegenstand, ist eben dadurch 'bedeutend',*
      daß er über sich hinausweist, daß er Ausdruck und Exponent eines Geistig-
      Allgemeineren ist, einer ganzen Gefühls- und Gesinnungswelt, welche in ihm
      ihr mehr oder weniger vollkommenes Sinnbild gefunden hat, – wonach sich
      denn der Grad seiner Bedeutung bemißt. Ferner ist die Liebe zu einem solchen
      Gegenstand ebenfalls und selbst 'bedeutend'. Sie sagt etwas aus über den, der sie
      hegt, sie kennzeichnet sein Verhältnis zu jenem Allgemeinen, jener Welt, die der
      Gegenstand vertritt, und die in ihm, bewußt oder unbewußt, mitgeliebt wird (Zb
      987).

13   On 'the thought that can wholly become emotion, the emotion that can
      wholly become thought' (*... der Gedanke, der ganz Gefühl, ... das Gefühl,*
      das ganz Gedanke zu werden vermag [Mann 2004: 555]) see *Death in Venice*
      (Mann 1971), p. 118.

14   *Der Mensch ist Herr der Gegensätze, sie sind durch ihn, und also ist er*
      vornehmer als sie. Vornehmer als der Tod, zu vornehm für diesen, – das ist die
      Freiheit seines Kopfes. Vornehmer als das Leben, zu vornehm für dieses, – das
      ist die Frömmigkeit in seinem Herzen. Da habe ich einen Reim gemacht, ein
      Traumgedicht vom Menschen ... Der Mensch soll um der Güte und Liebe
      willen dem Tode keine Herrschaft einräumen über seine Gedanken (Zb
      748).

15   *Das Gefüge der Scenen und die anschaulichen Bilder offenbaren eine tiefere*
      Weisheit, als der Dichter selbst in Worte und Begriffe fassen kann (Nietzsche
      1988: 109-10).

16   Cf. Nietzsche's view of *Macbeth*, *Morgenröte*, §140 (Nietzsche 1982): the
      play's image of ambition prompts joy; it shows Shakespeare 'enamoured
      of the passions as such'. Cf. Shaw on Richard's 'Conscience is but a word
      that cowards use / Devised at first to keep the strong in awe' (5.6.39–40),
      with much else in the play, as implying a fundamentally Nietzschean view
      (letter to Sir Johnston Forbes-Robertson, 1965–88, vol. 2: 383–4).

17   For readings of *Romeo and Juliet* and *Antony and Cleopatra* based in a
      similar objective-subjective interplay, see Fuller 2012.

18   See Valéry, 1957–75, vol. 7, pp. 159–66, 'On Speaking Verse'.

19   Much of this was written from also listening to another Shakespeare
      performance by Peggy Ashcroft, her recording of Lucrece in *The Rape*
      of Lucrece (directed by George Rylands, British Council/Argo, 1962) –
      different in being non-dramatic, an early work, more patterned in rhetoric
      and form (rhyme royal stanzas), but showing many of the same qualities
      as her Paulina in the projection of verse.

20   Cf. 'To work out a play in verse is to be working like a musician ...
      Underneath the action ... there should be a musical pattern which inten-
      sifies our excitement by reinforcing it with feeling from a deeper and less
      articulate level' (Eliot 1936: 994–5).

Works Cited

Eliot, T. S., 1936. 'The Need for Poetic Drama', in *The Listener* XVI: 411, 5 November, pp. 994–5.

Eliot, T. S., 1957a [1942]. 'The Music of Poetry', in *On Poetry and Poets*. London: Faber, pp. 26–38.

Eliot, T. S., 1957b [1951]. 'Poetry and Drama', in *On Poetry and Poets*. London: Faber, pp. 72–88.

Eliot, T. S., 1962. *Collected Poems, 1909–1962*. London: Faber.

Fuller, David, 1988. *Blake's Heroic Argument*. New York: Routledge.

Fuller, David, 2011. *The Life in the Sonnets*. Shakespeare Now! London: Continuum.

Fuller, David, 2012. 'Discovering Transgression: Reading from the Passions', in *Shakespeare and I*, eds Will McKenzie and Theodora Papadopolou. London: Continuum, pp. 61–77.

Goethe, Johann Wolfgang, 1909–11. *Goethes Gespräche*, ed. W. Freiherr von Biedermann, 5 vols. Leipzig: Biedermann.

Lessing, Gotthold Ephraim, 1965 [1766]. *Laokoon*, ed. Dorothy Reich. Oxford: Oxford University Press.

Lessing, Gotthold Ephraim, 1988 [1766]. *Laokoon*, trans. W. A. Steel (1930), revised H. B. Nesbit (1985), in *The Origins of Modern Critical Thought: German Aesthetic and Literary Criticism from Lessing to Hegel*, ed. David Simpson. Cambridge: Cambridge University Press.

Mann, Thomas, 1960 [1928]. *The Magic Mountain*, trans. Helen Lowe-Porter. Harmondsworth: Penguin.

Mann, Thomas, 1971 [1912]. *Der Tod in Venedig*, ed. T. J. Reed, Oxford: Oxford University Press.

Mann, Thomas, 1979. *Tagebücher, 1918–1921*, ed. Peter de Mendelssohn. Frankfurt am Main: S. Fischer.

Mann, Thomas, 1985. *Pro and Contra Wagner*, trans. Allan Blunden. London: Faber.

Mann, Thomas, 2002 [1924]. *Der Zauberberg*, ed. Michael Neumann. Große Kommentierte Frankfurter Ausgabe, vol. 5.1. Frankfurt am Main: S. Fischer. [*Zb*]

Mann, Thomas, 2004 [1912]. 'Der Tod in Venedig', in *Frühe Erzählungen*, ed. Terence J. Reed. Große Kommentierte Frankfurter Ausgabe, vol. 2.1. Frankfurt am Main: S. Fischer, pp. 501–92.

Mann, Thomas, 2005 [1924]. *The Magic Mountain*, trans. John E. Woods. New York: Everyman's Library. [*MM*]

Mertens, Volker, 2006. *Groß ist das Geheimnis: Thomas Mann und die Musik*. Leipzig: Militzke.

Nietzsche, Friedrich, 1982 [1881]. *Daybreak: Thoughts on the Prejudices of Morality*, trans. R. J. Hollingdale. Cambridge: Cambridge University Press.

Nietzsche, Friedrich, 1988. *Die Geburt der Tragödie*, in *Kritische Studienausgabe*, eds Giorgo Colli and Mazzino Montinari, vol. 1. München/Berlin: dtv/De Gruyter, pp. 9–156.

Nietzsche, Friedrich, 1999 [1872]. *'The Birth of Tragedy' and Other Writings*, eds Raymond Geuss, Ronald Speirs. Cambridge: Cambridge University Press.

Schiller, Friedrich, 1967 [1794]. *On the Aesthetic Education of Man in a Series of Letters*, trans. Elizabeth M. Wilkinson and L. A. Willoughby. Oxford: Clarendon.

Schiller, Friedrich, 2009 [1794]. *Über die ästhetische Erziehung des Menschen, in einer Reihe von Briefen*, ed. Stefan Matuschek. Frankfurt am Main: Suhrkamp.

Shakespeare, William, 2008. *The Norton Shakespeare*, eds Stephen Greenblatt et al. New York: Norton.

Richard III, directed by Laurence Olivier. London Films 1955, republished on DVD variously.

The Winter's Tale, directed by Howard Sackler. Caedmon 1963, republished on CD by HarperCollins.

Shaw, George Bernard, 1965–88. *Collected Letters*, ed. Dan H. Laurence, 4 vols. London: Reinhardt.

Vaget, Hans Rudolf, 2006. *Seelenzauber: Thomas Mann und die Musik*. Frankfurt am Main: S. Fischer.

Valéry, Paul, 1957–75. 'On Speaking Verse', in *On the Art of Poetry*, trans. Denise Folliot, introd. T. S. Eliot, *Collected Works* vol. 7, ed. Jackson Matthews. London: Routledge, pp. 159–66.

Eleven   Changing the Subject
Ulrike Draesner

Angles and angels

I started to read Thomas Mann before I read Shakespeare. I started to read Thomas Mann when I was about twelve or thirteen years old, and it happened by accident. The accident used my mother's body to enter the world, it crept into her head in the shape of a blurred memory and some diffuse cultural knowledge like 'Thomas Mann, valuable', and 'didn't I read his books myself without any negative effects?'

Easter 1974: imagine me, a girl on the verge of puberty, lying on my bed, reading Mann's last and unfinished novel *Die Bekenntnisse des Hochstaplers Felix Krull* (*Confessions of Felix Krull. Confidence Man*). Imagine posters of Karl May's Winnetou and Boney M. on my walls, imagine an edition of *Bravo* somewhere in the room, next to a schoolbag containing the textbooks *General Erdkunde* and *Learning English 3*. Being a hungry reader I found myself quickly absorbed by Krull's story and definitely fascinated when I reached the scene where Felix, serving as the liftboy Armand in a grand hotel, sneaks into a female guest's room. He met Madame Houpflé at the station, he stole some jewellery from her. And now?

Thomas Mann was aged seventy-nine when his last novel was published – a text he had started to work on in 1910. There had been many interruptions, many distractions, many in(ter)ventions triggered equally by inner and outer 'Ereignisse' (political distortions, rashly revolving constellations in family and society, exile and home) entering the 'Eigen'-Raum of Thomas Mann, figuring the writer Mann, figuring the person Mann, busily concealing shifts in the scope of phantasmatic identities.

Obviously, the vision of Krull, a young man, almost a boy, of beauty, eros and ever changing identity hadn't loosened its grip on Mann's writerly imagination. The narrative constellation chosen for *Krull* mirrors the narrative genesis of his tale: both, narrator and author, are men looking back into their respective histories. Mann simulates a middle-aged Felix, writing the biography of his youth, whereas the advanced and famous old writer Thomas Mann, going back to narrative ideas he worked on as a middle-aged writer, pushes on the novel which will turn out to be his last one. I was ravished. I found myself in the middle of a sex scene.

Clearly, vibrantly, and fairly outspoken. Obviously, my mother suffered from partial amnesia or had never really read *Krull*. 'How's the book?' she asked when I was half-way through; a muttered 'geht so' made her leave my room again. Krull and his Madame supplied me with the first bed scene I really found worthwhile. Being a child of the early seventies, I had been introduced to the 'whole stuff' quite directly in biology lessons at school – and ever since had marvelled why mankind hadn't died out long ago. But now, how amazing: what I read was much better even and more effective than the weekly photo-series in *Bravo*, showing what, allegedly, anybody of my age was craving to see. They started to bore, inevitably, whereas Thomas Mann's words sent shivers over my back and belly and enabled me to *imagine* a 'something' which I didn't know yet.

Mann's prose in *Krull* may sound somewhat outmoded and artificial; though almost brittle in some paragraphs, it might easily bring to full life a character in the subsequent passage in just two or three lines, surprising and amusing in its ironical overtones. I think I was slightly entranced by the slow movement of words and thoughts over the page, evolving time and bringing to the fore, to my eyes today, the acceleration of our lives ever since. The difference between 1974 and today is so striking that I am almost shocked about how *much* time seems to have passed – about my own accumulating years, passed and gone forever.

Aged twelve, lying on my bed, dangling my legs, all this was entirely irrelevant. I identified with Felix, the happy one. He was young, appealing, witty. My female and his male sex didn't impede my identification with him, the hero of the tale, in the least. If I didn't want to remain alone in reading, I had to identify with men in ninety-nine per cent of my books. I had got so used to that shift that I didn't notice it any more.

No surprise then that I easily and even comfortably used Krull's eyes in order to assess the old woman he was having sex with on that hotel bed. Ever so clearly I remember the twilight of the room, its heavy embroidered curtains, a chest of drawers. And la Madame, naked between the sheets, whereas Krull himself, naked, seen as the divine messenger Hermes or as Amor, walks the room looking for further prey – in flesh and jewellery. And how dangerous it was! The double risk of discovery comes back so vividly to my mind that I can almost taste it in my mouth: it heightened the act of the characters as well as my reading.

[I]nstead of answering I bent all the way down to her and pressed my lips against hers. She not only carried this kiss to even greater lengths than the one that afternoon – with no lack of co-operation from me – she also took my hand from its support and guided it inside her décolletage to her breasts, which were very nicely fitted to the hand, moving it about by the wrist in such a way that my manhood, as she could not fail to notice, was most urgently aroused.

(Mann 1965: 168–9)[1]

Finally: Felix, in the identity of Armand, the liftboy, is stretching and exercising his beautiful limbs on the bed of rich Madame Houpflé. To my absolutely reliable recollection, this Diane is an old hag, *steinalt* – wrinkles all over, breasts dangling to her navel. In rereading, she turns out to be about fifteen years younger than I am today. Wonderful! She entertains a young lover, who pleases her in various ways. For her, his Hermes-like beauty is as arousing as his low social rank. His avowal, that it was him who snapped her jewellery case from her at the station, is perceived as an exquisite form of degradation by her. So she decides to remunerate the second time Felix makes love to her by allowing him to steal from her again. It enhances her jouissance. A wonderful bargain: he pays for the first robbery by sleeping with her ('I had given her my best, had in my enjoyment made proper recompense', ibid.: 170),[2] she pays for his second love-making by tolerating yet another act of robbery, which she may attend to or *beiwohnen*, as Mann puts it, using a verb, nowadays old fashioned, denoting sexual intercourse. Doubly dear, this callboy of happiness. And subtle the art of the writer Thomas Mann, when he allows the scene to culminate yet again *after* everything seems to have happened twice already:

And so I obeyed her. Cautiously I left her and took what the room offered – too easy a theft … Despite the complete darkness I had no trouble finding the key to the bureau in the corner cupboard. I opened the top drawer almost noiselessly and had only to take out a few items of lingerie …

(Mann 1965: 176)[3]

Hermes, messenger, angel. A game of triangles, facilitated by a character with wings, naked, endowed with extra-terrestrial lustre. This is Felix in *Felix Krull*, bound to an old, ugly, cock-eyed female of thirty-five. This is, even more strongly, Thomas Angelus Mann, incubus, succubus, an angel-like bodily being, who, since he cannot take part in flesh, wants to take part at least by creating flesh and glancing at it. Who is glance, nothing but glance, covetous gaze from man to man. Deprecating the woman, whom he needs in order to allow himself to allow the angel to appear.

It pays the effort to have a closer look at the narrative installation to be found here. There is a supposedly mature Felix, telling us of his adventures as young Felix-Armand, coming alive in Armand's mask – his body. And there is the author, Thomas Mann, looking and moving through the conceptual 'mask' of his younger self in order to creep into Felix and, using Felix, into Armand. Four male personae, evolving one from the other and merging into the next, three of them virtually present in the scene, to endow one male with a 'real' (fictitious) body. Four males, bathing in the glance and desire of one female, Diane Houpflé, who praises Armand's beauty by slighting her own – and thereby delights all of them. Obvious and subtle in one: the high eroticism of the scene, which I felt even as a fairly innocuous reader, is created by the multi-presence of eyes and wishes, and by the generation and expression of male desire via a female body which is essentially used as *Sprachrohr* – a propped up character, present in the scene to reveal and describe the beauty and erotic flair of a male body. That's why Madame Houpflé has to be rather old: her attractiveness has to be minimized. The focus is clear – and the desirous gaze and feelings of Felix and Thomas Mann, in Felix's mask, through Madame Houpflé's eyes and in Armand's bodily movements, can be felt clearly in the scene.

As an author I have had numerous occasions to doubt or at least to think freshly about the distinction of author and narrator. I have become interested in areas where this difference gets blurred, grey areas of intersection or merging. You may argue that it will never be the author coming up in a text; so let's call the voice I am trying to talk about an authorial function, a spectre, creeping into fiction through identification, cunning and playfulness. It's hard to grasp, I myself am tentative about it – but Mann, considering his lifelong active interest in narrative authorization and undermining, seems to me to be a good case for experiments touching this point.

In contrast to the reader of twelve, I recognize now how the shining and glowing of the diamonds and of a certain, much desired area of moist female flesh, mirror each other. Mann's text uses them as mutual signifiers: lust emerges where they blend; it counts among his strategies to defeminize the eroticism of the female-male encounter. But something else happens to me as a reader: today I can visualize Armand's *and* Madame Houpflé's perspectives, beyond Mann's narrative engineering, and I feel that even in 1974 I didn't look exclusively through Armand's eyes. I also used my own vision concerning female pleasure, even though Thomas Mann acts carefully against it, at least on the surface of his text. The woman is as ugly as can be, she herself confirms it, so you have to believe it, don't you? [4]

There was something else. I rely on myself as a twelve-year-old who didn't know anything about Thomas Mann, and not much about misogyny or homosexuality, but who was captured by the vibrant eroticism of these pages in *Felix Krull* and their double meanings. On the one hand Madame Houpflé's speech about herself, given to her by the author. On the other hand the truth of the text: sexual arousal, set free from conventional roles, thereby floating. And augmented by the risk of being discovered, by the carnivalization of social roles, by the carnal and financial transgression of laws of property, propriety and possession. The excited nerves of my pubertal body perceived the ensuing tensions of ambivalence as clearly as the fact that the body of the woman acting in Mann-Krull's bed differed considerably from the body that was being described. Sexy, full of lust and life, intimate with techniques of sexual refinement of which, to my opinion, none of the real life females I knew would have been capable. Felix let himself be paid off well and had had as much fun as Diane, who managed to betray her husband doubly, and as myself, who learnt from this book, who felt something new and who – after reading it – had something to be kept secret, hidden away from the grown-ups around me.

Threefold constellations have ever since interested me most in Mann's writing – the movement of at least three bodies in a clearly circumscribed space, where the bodies, in Mann, tend to include only two characters of the book (male and female or both male), while the third 'person' palpably present is a mask or spectre of the author – present not only in his directing the text and in his language, but also in something one might be tempted to call his own desire. I would prefer to speak of an author's 'interest', his inter-esse in a scene. Mann taught me, in the long run, to use writing in order to look into spaces, tabooed in the society we live in and according to the rules we apply to ourselves. His slant biographical use of writing as a means of covered self-apparition in scenic mirrors of language, which he tries to fill with bodily material, is as innovative as it is fascinating. Mann doesn't use it too often; and I remember how disappointed I felt, when, still aged thirteen or fourteen and excited by *Krull*, I read his novel *Buddenbrooks*, waiting and waiting for a scene of this kind – in vain.

Fiction and poetry both are fed by a double source: 'reality' and literature. Thinking of literary triangles of the male-male-female kind will lead us to Shakespeare's sonnets – and their male praises of female-male beauty, their tri-angel-uation: undulating conventional praise of women's beauty so as to extend it to a young male body by playing with the variability of the positions 'you', 'I' and the omnipresence of the writer's eye – and mouth.

Let me add one last thought about the translating process of reading before looking more deeply into processes of writing with the help of

Shakespeare's poetry and its translations. Reflecting on my encounter with Mann's novel *Felix Krull*, I think that I owe my first lessons in how to write a novel to Mann. *Krull* opened up a multi-angular space of perspectives, it made me move and see by heterogeneity and the use of sensory perception in many modes. As a twelve-year-old, a child still, I seem to have found it much easier to skim differences of sex (and gender) than today. Not being grown up meant not to belong to the realm of either men or women. I still found myself on my way into these 'realities' and their framework of roles. Maybe some remnants of this agile identification are kept in our memories-as-readers? So that the identificatory gender positions, even when we read as grown-ups, move more effortlessly than in 'real life'? Mann's fiction is an invitation to reflect on this possibility. My short story *Zucken und Zwinkern* (published in *Hot Dogs*) takes up Mann's *Wälsungenblut*. It diligently avoids attributing sex and gender to its narrator. The reader will create his or her own images; of course my female authorial name will contribute its share, but it may be that in a second read the reader will change position and enjoy the freedom to do so, reacting to an echo stemming from happy reading hours during childhood.

Influence and infatuation

In Shakespeare's sonnets the writer stages himself as doubly privileged: he may overcome death via the fleshly creation of a new body as well as by his 'eternal' writing, thereby eternalizing the beauty of his beloved counterpart and of his own desire. I want to suggest that Mann's fascination with Shakespeare is grounded in the 'energeia'[5] of his texts: an art of writing enacted not as the translation of ideas into action or the mimetic rendering of character, but as the endeavour to incorporate bodily life as powerfully as possible into words.

I am interested in this process myself; and it is easily understood why scenes that deal with sex or, more precisely, with constellations of (possible) (bodily) reproduction offer themselves to epitomize the principle – content and wording strategies may mirror each other. Mann and Shakespeare, separated by time, space and language, widely diverge in writing attitudes and aesthetics. But they are connected by their lasting fascination with bodily reproduction that both continually use to mirror processes of writing. Legion are the constellations of intercourse violating social and cultural boundaries in Mann's stories and novels, ubiquitous the topic of matching, disguising and reversing gender in Shakespeare's tragedies and comedies. And vital to his sonnets, evolving around two male bodies and one female body in their interaction with writing and time.

Looking at Mann and Shakespeare simultaneously means to move in a literary space stretching over centuries, a space connected by a writer's creative picking from another writer's work, by his translating and subjective answer, following his own possibilities of being 'touched' or 'inflamed', excited into action. In accordance with this subjectivism we find ourselves reading airy traces, whose rendering, in addition, must be informed by my own writerly ideas about and experience with 'inspiration' stemming from others' literary art. Therefore I won't enlarge on parallels between the sonnets and Krull's bed encounter or some other scenes taken from Mann's *Wälsungenblut* and *Der Tod in Venedig*, where Mann, yet again, highlights his characters by using attributes of classical or celestial beauty. Instead, I want to try to grasp the subject from a third angle, looking more deeply into two highly different processes of translation, thereby triangulating the connection between Mann-Shakespeare by means of a Draesnerian process of reshaping Shakespeare into a lingo-productive version of German.

Radical sonnets
One afternoon in the late spring of 1999 I found myself sitting on the floor of my room, picking up the single pages of my student's edition of Shakespeare's sonnets. I had wanted to quote from sonnet 18, had taken the book out of the shelf – and was now reassembling its parts. My eyes settled on sonnet 5. I was transfixed: the poem talked about cloning.

Undeniably: it dealt with artificial reproduction – the topic that had been dominating the headlines for weeks. Dolly the lamb had been born, and everybody was excited about the human genome project. Fears and utopias, misunderstandings, discussions and excitement were flaring; the excitement persisted and in June 2000 the *Frankfurter Allgemeine Zeitung* published a feuilleton just consisting of the letters ACTG.

In the light of this context Shakespeare's verses took on new dimensions, gleaming almost as arcanely as Dolly's eyes. Shakespeare tackles procreation obsessively. A male ego addresses a male partner, turns to a female, turns to both of them. The constellation gets more ambivalent if one detaches the identity of the sonnets' ego from the male name of their author, who, acutely aware of life's and beauty's futility, uses his poems as instruments to dream of immortality. Shakespeare's sonnets envision marriages; their energy is set against all-devouring time – the real 'other' in their triangles of creation and memory.

Cloning seems to be our expression of the all too human dream of survival; the language being technical instead of poetic. Possibilities of – and ideas about – genetic manipulation have been altering the meanings of (natural) creation, mortality, individuality and reproduction over the last decades. My radical translations transform

Shakespeare's sonnets into intertwining sequences of speech by a person who is being cloned, by the clone created, by clones among each other in a world of hybrid identities.

These speeches are radical in various senses. They exhibit my frame of thinking and interpreting, bringing it almost offensively to the fore. And they follow a radical linguistic device by taking Shakespeare's words at their roots, turning their meanings upside down, wilfully misreading them. Of course the strategy is not truly wilful – it is putting up a show of wilfulness, digging up hidden meanings, etymological connections, false friends, implications of idioms (in German). It aims at reading the underlying structures of language and its ways of pasting and cloning, of copying and deciphering the world via resemblance.

My learning more about modern bio-technological means to interfere with the set-up of life shoved the poems into a new perspective and set off an artistic response. In order to translate Shakespeare's reproduction sonnets I needed transformations in content and form. :to change the subject the project was called in the end, subjecting the original poems to strategies of copying – and mistaking.

The first line of the first sonnet already offered gorgeous possibilities: 'From fairest creatures we desire increase'. All German translators of the sonnets whom I had read had chosen 'schön' (beautiful) for 'fair'. My decision to put 'hell' (light, fair) is not spectacular, seen from the English basis, but opened up the possibility to further move into our tongues' nets. It allowed me to introduce the German idiom 'helle sein', used to indicate that someone is intelligent (bearing a lot of light in his or her head). Immediately the very first line of my translation, 'von hellsten kreaturen begehren wir anstieg', may be read as talking about the criteria of selection among cloned embryos, evaluating the *Lebenswürdigkeit* of artificial sperm-egg-unities. The decision to replace any copying or storing device (writing, collecting, picturing), mentioned by Shakespeare, by a more modern, technical equivalent (fridges, computers, digitalization etc.) evolved hand in hand. Simultaneously, the form of the poems underwent a continued process of erosion via multilateral copying mistakes. My sonnets resemble ruins – retaining the number of 14 lines, the fall of verse, but dislocating rhymes and ignoring metre by the addition of syllables which either seem to run wild or finally tumble off the line – due to a lack of stamina.

1

Shakespeare

From fairest creatures we desire increase,
That thereby beauty's rose might never die,

But as the riper should by time decrease,
His tender heir might bear his memory:
But thou, contracted to thine own bright eyes,
Feed'st thy light's flame with self-substantial fuel,
Making a famine where abundance lies,
Thyself thy foe, to thy sweet self too cruel.
Thou that art now the world's fresh ornament,
And only herald to the gaudy spring,
Within thine own bud buriest thy content,
And, tender churl, mak'st waste in niggarding.
Pity the world, or else this glutton be,
To eat the world's due, by the grave and thee.

(2010 :113)

Shakespeare x Draesner

von hellsten kreaturen begehren wir anstieg,
daß das mandelbrot der gekrümmten schönheit nie sterbe,
doch wie die fertigen mit der zeit verschwinden, so mag ein
                                                    kopierer-
be lockend die erinnerung an sie tragen: in sich.
du aber, getackert an die schlauheit deiner augen
fütterst die flamme des anscheins mit dem selbst
referentiellen öl der sprache des einzelnen,
wo überfluß zu zellen gerinnt, bist dir mit dir
genug, das ornament dieser welt: naturident
blühn im kasten die karten deines kontinents
auf, durch deinen glasstabkörper, steigt sie längst
im spendesaal, die zarte locke dna.
bedaure die gezeugten, sonst ist es antropophagie,
das ihre zu essen, wie ihr grab, behandelst du sie.

(2000: 13)

5

Shakespeare

Those hours that with gentle work did frame
The lovely gaze where every eye doth dwell,
Will play the tyrants to the very same,
And that unfair which fairly doth excel;
For never-resting Time leads summer on
To hideous winter, and confounds him there;
Sap check'd with frost, and lusty leaves quite gone,

Beauty o'versnow'd, and bareness everywhere:
Then, were not summer's distillation left,
A liquid prisoner pent in walls of glass,
Beauty's effect with beauty were bereft,
Nor it, nor no remembrance what it was.
But flowers distill'd, though they with winter meet,
Leese but their show; their substance still lives sweet.

(2010: 121)

Shakespeare x Draesner

die stunden, die mit weichem mull den rahmen spannten
deines blicks, in dem so gern ein fremdes auge schwimmt,
werden die transplanteure geben, als sich, an dich,
und ausgeleuchtet wird, was das leuchtendste übertraf:
die in atomen tickende zeit überführt den sommer
in strahlenderen winter, und zergründet ihn dort:
saft, im kühlschrank erstarrt, fleischige membranen, welk,
schönheit überkrustet von frost, nacktheit, an jedem ort:
stünde dann nicht das destillat des sommers im fach,
flüssiger gefangener zwischen wänden und gas,
wäre die fruchtblase der schönheit durch schönheit zerstoben
weder sie, noch erinnerung bliebe, daran, was war.
aber blumenartiges, extrahiert, in den winter geschoben,
schwappt als zellcode, milchiger saft, die zukunft ans glas.

(2000: 14)

Translating (another's) masks

Shakespeare's plays make use of their audiences – they abound in devices set up to set the boundaries between fiction and reality swinging (e.g. asides, direct addresses, plays within the play). Mann seems to answer this in his late fiction by his usage of masks, which seem to become a vital part of his narrators and of many of his characters; sometimes, as in *Der Tod in Venedig*, a certain carnivalization of characters and roles can be observed.

A character is two at once; he seems to peel himself from himself, appears in a visible shape and in a second sub-shape – which need not be his 'true' form, but just another form of disguise or meaning. There is a certain 'blurring', which I wouldn't like to call just another effect of uncertainty or unreliability – because these terms divest us of the aesthetic effects of this means of writing. In Mann it is even used as a means contradictory to uncertainty: it reveals subcutaneous meanings – as when in the beginning of *Der Tod in Venedig* Gustav Aschenbach during his Munich promenade discovers a strange-looking man:

The man was moderately tall, thin, beardless and remarkably snub-nosed; he belonged to the red-haired type and had its characteristic milky, freckled complexion. ... His head was held high, so that the Adam's apple stood out stark and bare on his lean neck where it rose from the open shirt; and there were two pronounced vertical furrows, rather strangely ill-matched to his turned-up nose, between the colorless red-lashed eyes with which he peered sharply into the distance. There was thus – and perhaps the raised point of vantage on which he stood contributed to this impression – an air of imperious survey, something bold or even wild about his posture; for whether it was because he was dazzled into a grimace by the setting sun or by reasons of some permanent facial deformity, the fact was that his lips seemed to be too short and were completely retracted from his teeth, so that the latter showed white and long between them, bared to the gums.

(Mann 1988: 196–7)[6]

The man, baring his teeth, the man ready to bite, becomes even more imminent:

Aschenbach's half absentminded, half inquisitive scrutiny of the stranger had no doubt been a little less than polite, for he suddenly became aware that his gaze was being returned: the man was in fact staring at him so aggressively, so straight in the eye, with so evident an intention to make an issue of the matter and outstare him, that Aschenbach turned away in disagreeable embarrassment and began to stroll along the fence, casually resolving to take no further notice of the fellow. A minute later he had put him out of his mind.

(ibid.: 197)[7]

The glance of the uncanny man elicits a surprising reaction in Aschenbach, something unpredictable, irrational – a leap or crack. If I talked of triangeluation in *Krull*, we are now able to elucidate further the idea and function of subcutaneous threefold relationships, demanding the characters' *and* the author's full (and foolish) strength. The man who appeared out of nowhere has no name, but an identity. He, too, is an angel, though a fallen one: red-haired, limping, bearing a weapon, almost no nose (as a skeletal head would show no nose), transparent hue, frightful presence, 'gekreuzt' instead of 'gekreuzigt' – clad in a transvestite suit, a devil connected to death. The third position in the game is taken up by a cultural frame of reference, 'the third' being a figure ambivalent by nature, starting another game of jumps and falls with Aschenbach: triangeluation turns into hopscotch. Mann and his imagination are hopscotching Aschenbach, Mann's alter ego, between the rectangles or forces of his imagination, his desires, discipline and some brute and interesting mixture of free will and destiny, which in this novella are being presented by Mann as a reciprocal system of interactions – of willing and letting happen.

The devil-angel's effect turns out to be especially telling in this context:

> A minute later he had put him out of his mind. But whether his imagination had been stirred by the stranger's itinerant appearance, or whether some other physical or psychological influence was at work, he now became conscious, to his complete surprise, of an extraordinary expansion of his inner self, a kind of roving restlessness, a youthful craving for far-off places, a feeling so new or at least so long unaccustomed and forgotten that he stood as if rooted, with his hands clasped behind his back and his eyes to the ground, trying to ascertain the nature and purport of his emotion.
>
> It was simply a desire to travel; but it had presented itself as nothing less than a seizure, with intensely passionate and indeed hallucinatory force, turning his craving into vision.
>
> (ibid.: 197)[8]

Aschenbach witnesses a process of translation – it's him who is being translated. To us, as readers equally of Mann's story and Mann's aesthetics, it gives an example of influence. Influence, enacted. Mann's passage seems to deliver a precise description of the ways in which a writer at least sometimes can take from another writer. You notice something – you feel seen. You don't recognize the full impact. You are attracted. You are pushed. It makes you – move. Differently. Inserts you into a game that you don't play on your own.

Aschenbach is moved into visions, tears and infection. He is lifted out of his routines. He sees tigers, plants, phalli and vaginas. He feels the need to alter the plans for his summer – he starts a search. That's helpful, too, for any process of aesthetic translation, and very precise. Aschenbach seems to know a direction – he knows that he wants to travel and he turns south, but first ends up in the wrong place, in Pola. Only after having arrived there is he able to redirect his thoughts, and the proper end of his journey, still initiated by the Munich figure, becomes obvious to him. It may seem surprising to read this process of perception and reaction, of passive and active search, as an epitome of creative transference. But I can call on Mann to have my reading supported: Aschenbach is a writer and most of the reflections of the novella revolve around the conditions of production. Mann puts it very beautifully – he has the gift of becoming extremely precise in handling terms, using them in order to pinpoint:

> The morning's writing had overstimulated him: his work had now reached a difficult and dangerous point which demanded the utmost care and circumspection, the most insistent and precise effort of will, and the productive mechanism in his mind – that *motus animi continuus* which according to Cicero is the essence of eloquence – had so pursued its reverberating rhythm that he had been unable to halt it even after lunch, and had missed the refreshing daily siesta which was now so necessary to him as he became increasingly subject to fatigue.
>
> (ibid.: 195)[9]

Mann's narrator in *Der Erwählte* (*The Holy Sinner*) mirrors Shakespeare's playing around with the mirror-capacities of the stage. To speak of one narrator is wrong, of course. There are at least two, the first being extremely ridiculous and stagey: Mann calls him 'Geist der Erzählung'. A spirit, a sprite, a 'most unlikely thing', in *Hamlet*'s term, and a ghost, excavated from the depth of the tradition of narration and its verification. He rings the bell of any town where you might start reading the book, he rings all the bells of Rome, of the globe – of all times. He is nothing and everything, fiction and non-truth: the means to allow the author by ridiculing himself and his art, to enter the stage of narration a second time and tell the most unlikely story of the medieval man Gregorius, who had two children with his own sister, went off to do penance and lived on a rock in the middle of a lake for more than twenty years, where he shrunk to the size of a toad, dried out, didn't eat but lichen from its stones and didn't drink but licked drops of rain. After twenty years of fittest survival he was elected pope in Rome. Mann's narrative of Hartmann von Aue's narrative is offered to us by a monk, as narrative tradition would have it – but superseded by the sprite, a self-ridiculing mask of Thomas Mann's. Here it is used in an easy, off-hand game – the risk of telling about transgressing sexuality kept away from the author Thomas Mann by the distance to his main character in time, in profession (Gregorius doesn't have one) and by narrative framing. How risky the narration of *Der Tod in Venedig* in comparison – close in time, close even in place, similar in profession – Gustav Aschenbach obviously mirrors Thomas Mann's career and position as a writer – how outspoken where male to male desire is concerned. In *Der Tod in Venedig* the masks of narration have become airy 'things' themselves – appearing and disappearing on characters, similar to voices: the man in Munich, the old man, dressed up as a young one on the boat to Venice, the impresario of the comedians in

Venice in the hotel, who presents himself wearing a series of masks – and finally Aschenbach himself, after his visit to the hairdresser, made up to look much younger – a mimicry now of the old man mimicking a young one. Masks, shrinking and thereby coming closer, translated into Aschenbach's final dream of lust and desire, of copulation and cannibalism; masks, dissolved into the air – viral (inducing death, for some) and powerful.

Adventurous conjunctions?

The playwright Christian Dietrich Grabbe, a German writer of the early nineteenth century, whose plays were notorious for their mass scenes and quick changes, used to scribble abundant notes in the margins of his texts. Recently a colleague told me an anecdote about Grabbe's eccentricity which – if only for its beauty and narrative precision – is worth sharing. Once, while one of Grabbe's plays was rehearsed, the director of the theatre proudly announced that, indeed, they would be able to bring a real elephant onto the stage. Instead of being grateful, awful Grabbe got himself into a fit of fury: he needed 193 elephants!

The (fictitious) number illuminates what a novel or a story can achieve – in contrast to the theatre: fiction can do 600 elephants. And so can Thomas Mann, in the end. *Der Erwählte* does not content itself with less than everything. It turns the entire globe into sound. What a writerly dream:

> The ringing of bells, the surging and swelling of bells supra urbem, above the whole city, in its airs overfilled with sound. Bells, bells, they swing and sway, they wag and weave through their whole arc on their beams, in their seats, hundred-voiced, in Babylonish confusion. Slow and swift, blaring and booming – there is neither measure or harmony, they talk all at once and all together, they break in even on themselves … Who is ringing the bells? Not the bell-ringers. They have run into the street like all folk, to list the uncanny ringing. Convince yourself: the bell-chambers are empty. Lax hang the ropes, and yet the bells rock and the clappers clang. Shall one say that *nobody* rings them? – No, only an ungrammatical head, without logic, would be capable of the utterance. 'The bells are ringing': that means they are rung, and let the bell-chambers be never empty. – So who is ringing the bells of Rome? – It is *the spirit of story-telling*. – Then can he be everywhere, hic et ubique, for instance at once on the Tower of St. George in Velabro and up in Santa Sabina, which preserves columns from the abominable Temple of Diana? At a hundred consecrate seats at once? – Of a certainty, that he can. He is as air, bodiless, ubiquitous, not subject to distinction of here

and there. He it is that says: 'All the bells were ringing'; and, in consequence, it is he who rings them. So spiritual is this spirit and so abstract that grammatically he can be talked of only in the third person and simply referred to as 'It is he'.

(Mann 1992: 3–5)[10]

Irony: of course.
  Self-mockery? Of course.
  More than that? Of course.
  Clever camouflage. Introduction of a scandalous topic with the help of the masks of monk and fool.
  This.
  And: 600 elephants.

Notes

1 … *neigte ich mich statt aller Antwort vollends zu ihr hinab und senkte meine Lippen auf ihre. Nicht nur aber, dass sie den Kuss noch weitgehender ausgestaltete als den ersten vom Nachmittag, wobei es an meinem Entgegenkommen nicht fehlte, – so nahm sie auch meine Hand aus ihrer Stütze und führte sie in ihr Décolleté zu ihren Brüsten, die sehr handlich waren, führte sie da am Gelenk herum auf eine Weise, dass meine Männlichkeit, wie ihr nicht entgehen konnte, in den bedrängendsten Aufstand geriet* (Mann 2012: 203).

2 *[i]ch hatte ihr mein Bestes gegeben, hatte, genießend, wahrlich abgezahlt* (ibid.: 204).

3 *So war ich ihr denn zu Willen. Behutsam hob ich mich fort von ihr und nahm im Zimmer, was sich darbot – überbequem zum Teil … Trotz tiefer Dunkelheit fand ich auch gleich im Eckschränkchen den Schlüssel zur Kommode, öffnete deren oberste Schublade fast lautlos und brauchte nur ein paar Wäschestücke aufzuheben …* (ibid.: 211–12).

4 'We women are lucky that our curves please you. But the divine, the masterpiece of creation, the model of beauty, that's you, you young, very young men with Hermes legs' (Mann 1965: 171): *Wir Weiber mögen von Glück sagen, daß unsere runden sieben Sachen euch so gefallen. Aber das Göttliche, das Meisterwerk der Schöpfung, Standbild der Schönheit, das seid ihr, ihr jungen, ganz jungen Männer mit den Hermesbeinen* (Mann 2012: 206).

5 The old Greek word, signifying the appearance of gods among men, deals with cases of extraordinary presence. It is this sense that I would like to reactivate here, using 'energeia' as a term to talk about directness and extraordinary presence in art.

6 *Mäßig hochgewachsen, mager, bartlos und auffallend stumpfnäsig, gehörte der Mann zum rothaarigen Typ und besaß dessen milchige und sommersprossige Haut. … Erhobenen Hauptes, so dass an seinem hager dem losen Sporthemd entwachsenden Halse der Adamsapfel stark und nackt hervortrat, blickte er mit farblosen rotbewimperten Augen, zwischen denen, sonderbar genug zu*

seiner kurz aufgeworfenen Nase passend, zwei senkrechte, energische Furchen standen, scharf spähend ins Weite. So – und vielleicht trug sein erhöhter und erhöhender Standort zu diesem Eindruck bei – hatte seine Haltung etwas herrisch Überschauendes, Kühnes oder selbst Wildes; denn sei es, dass er, geblendet, gegen die untergehende Sonne grimassierte oder dass es sich um eine dauernde physiognomische Entstellung handelt: seine Lippen schienen zu kurz, sie waren völlig von den Zähnen zurückgezogen, dergestalt, dass diese, bis zum Zahnfleisch bloßgelegt, weiß und lang dazwischen hervorbleckten (Mann 2004a: 502-3).

7   *Wohl möglich, dass Aschenbach es bei seiner halb zerstreuten, halb inquisitiven Musterung des Fremden an Rücksicht hatte fehlen lassen, denn plötzlich ward er gewahr, dass jener seinen Blick erwiderte, und zwar so kriegerisch, so gerade ins Auge hinein, so offenkundig gesonnen, die Sache aufs Äußerste zu treiben und den Blick des andern zum Abzug zu zwingen, dass Aschenbach, peinlich berührt, sich abwandte und einen Gang die Zäune entlang begann, mit dem beiläufigen Entschluss, des Menschen nicht weiter achtzuhaben. Er hatte ihn in der nächsten Minute vergessen* (ibid.: 503).

8   *Er hatte ihn in der nächsten Minute vergessen. Mochte nun aber das Wanderhafte in der Erscheinung des Fremden auf seine Einbildungskraft gewirkt haben oder sonst irgendein physischer oder seelischer Einfluss im Spiele sein: eine seltsame Ausweitung seines Innern ward ihm ganz überraschend bewusst, eine Art schweifender Unruhe, ein jugendlich durstiges Verlagen in die Ferne, ein Gefühl, so lebhaft, so neu oder doch so längst entwöhnt und verlernt, dass er, die Hände auf dem Rücken und den Blick am Boden, gefesselt stehenblieb, um die Empfindung auf Wesen und Ziel zu prüfen.*

    Es war Reiselust, nichts weiter; aber wahrhaft als Anfall auftretend, und ins Leidenschaftliche, ja bis zur Sinnestäuschung gesteigert (ibid.: 503–4).

9   *Überreizt von der schwierigen und gefährlichen, eben jetzt seine höchste Behutsamkeit, Umsicht, Eindringlichkeit und Genauigkeit des Willens erfordernden Arbeit der Vormittagsstunden, hatte der Schriftsteller dem Fortschwingen des produzierenden Triebwerkes in seinem Inneren, jenem „motus animi continuus", worin nach Cicero das Wesen der Beredsamkeit besteht, auch nach der Mittagsmahlzeit nicht Einhalt zu tun vermocht ...* (ibid.: 501).

10   *Glockenschall Glockenschwall supra urbem, über der ganzen Stadt, in ihren von Klang überfüllten Lüften! Glocken, Glocken, sie schwingen und schaukeln, wogen und wiegen ausholend an ihren Balken, in ihren Stühlen, hundertstimmig, in babylonischem Durcheinander. Schwer und geschwind, brummend und bimmelnd – da ist nicht Zeitmaß noch Einklang, sie reden auf einmal und alle einander ins Wort, ins Wort auch sich selbst... Wer läutet die Glocken? Die Glöckner nicht. Die sind auf die Straße gelaufen wie alles Volk, da es so ungeheuerlich läutet. Überzeugt euch: die Glockenstuben sind leer. Schlaff hängen die Seile und dennoch wogen die Glocken, dröhnen die Klöppel. Wird man sagen, dass niemand sie läutet? – Nein, nur ein grammatischer Kopf ohne Logik wäre der Aussage fähig.,Es läuten die Glocken', das meint, sie werden geläutet, und seien die Stuben auch noch so leer. – Wer also läutet die Glocken Roms? – Der Geist der Erzählung. – Kann der denn überall sein, hic et ubique, zum Beispiel zugleich auf dem Turme von Sankt Georg in Velabro und droben in Santa Sabina, die Säulen hütet vom gräulichen Tempel der Diana? An hundert weihlichen Orten auf einmal? – Allerdings, das vermag er. Er ist luftig, körperlos, allgegenwärtig,*

nicht unterworfen dem Unterschiede von Hier und Dort. Er ist es, der
spricht:,Alle Glocken läuten', und folglich ist er's, der sie läutet. So geistig ist
dieser Geist und so abstrakt, dass grammatisch nur in der dritten Person von ihm
die Rede sein und es lediglich heißen kann,Er ist's.' (Mann 1980: 7).

Works Cited

Draesner, Ulrike, 2000. 'Twin Spin. Sonette von Shakespeare,
  Radikalübersetzungen', in *:to change the subject*. Göttingen: Wallstein, pp. 11–33.
Draesner, Ulrike, 2004. *Hot Dogs. Erzählungen*. München: Luchterhand.
Mann, Thomas, 1965 [1954]. *Confessions of Felix Krull. Confidence Man*, trans.
  Denver Lindley. New York: Alfred A. Knopf.
Mann, Thomas, 1980 [1951]. *Der Erwählte*, ed. Peter De Mendelssohn. Gesammelte
  Werke in Einzelbänden, Frankfurter Ausgabe. Frankfurt am Main: S. Fischer.
Mann, Thomas, 1988 [1912]. 'Death in Venice', in *Death in Venice and other Stories*,
  trans. David Luke. New York: Bantam, pp. 249–320.
Mann, Thomas, 1992 [1951]. *The Holy Sinner*, trans. Helen Lowe-Porter. New York:
  Alfred A. Knopf.
Mann, Thomas, 2004a [1912]. 'Der Tod in Venedig', in *Frühe Erzählungen*, ed.
  Terence J. Reed. Große Kommentierte Frankfurter Ausgabe, vol. 2.1. Frankfurt
  am Main: S. Fischer, pp. 501–92
Mann, Thomas, 2004b [1906/21]. 'Wälsungenblut', in *Frühe Erzählungen*, ed.
  Terence J. Reed. Große Kommentierte Frankfurter Ausgabe, vol. 2.1. Frankfurt
  am Main: S. Fischer, pp. 429–63.
Mann, Thomas, 2012 [1954]. *Bekenntnisse des Hochstaplers Felix Krull*, eds Thomas
  Sprecher, Monica Bussmann. Große Kommentierte Frankfurter Ausgabe, vol.
  12.1. Frankfurt am Main: S. Fischer.
Shakespeare, William, 2010. *Shakespeare's Sonnets*, ed. Katherine Duncan-Jones. The
  Arden Shakespeare. London: Methuen.

Afterword
Elisabeth Bronfen

The explicit reference to *Love's Labour's Lost* in Thomas Mann's *Doktor Faustus* is the declared point of departure for far wider but also more tenuous links between the two authors which the essays in this collection set out to explore. Begun during the last years of World War II, Mann's 'Germany novel' targeted cultural antecedents to the national catastrophe of Nazi totalitarianism and its violation of human life. In inhuman abstraction and separation from the ordinary, it recognized something of both the German catastrophe and the twentieth-century avant-garde. Looking back in hindsight, and particularly in light of the holocaust, the demonic inspiration on which Adrian Leverkühn's twelve-tone compositions are shown to have been predicated compels us to consider not only the murky interface between politics and aesthetics which we have inherited from modernism. We are more specifically called upon to ask in what way Shakespeare's early modern imagination anticipates the ethical consequences of gravity getting lost in the course of a radical liberation from all constraints of the ordinary. One key issue in the transhistorical relations these essays trace is certainly the question of the degree to which Mann is indebted to Shakespeare; equally important, however, is the counter-move: how far could we read or perform Shakespeare today in light of the ways in which Thomas Mann understood the modern condition in part through his reading and engagement with Shakespeare?

For such an investigation into literary correspondences and connections, transcending as they do issues of acknowledged influence and explicit citation, I propose the critical term *crossmapping* so as to underscore the double move at work in the conversation between Mann and Shakespeare which this volume enables. On the one hand, one can claim that Mann maps certain constellations he finds in Shakespeare onto contemporary cultural and philosophical concerns in his novellas and novels. On the other hand, one can also claim that, given certain, discernible analogies between both oeuvres (regarding character figurations, thematic concerns, word play and rhetorical strategies), it is equally fruitful and perhaps more revelatory to map onto a set of Shakespeare's plays the ways in which Mann's novels responded to their own contemporary cultural crises. Crossmapping thus entails using the historically later texts as the starting point for a speculation on their cultural origin and, in so doing, it looks at Shakespeare through the lens of his subsequent refiguration by authors who succeeded him, which here includes Mann but also intermediaries like Nietzsche and Wagner. Rather than simply proposing a relation of influence, cross-mapping Mann and Shakespeare sheds light on neuralgic points that connect both cultural moments. The lines of connection opened allow us to read Shakespeare's plays as anticipating something that will come to be significant again in modernism, albeit in a different guise. At the same time, the sort of hermeneutic strategy assayed in this book can also help us set about discussing what Shakespeare can teach us about modernity, and in particular the troubled enmeshment of the political and the aesthetic, which *Doktor Faustus* traces back to Shakespearean comedy and which is so characteristic for modernism in general.

And yet, to uncover suggestive relations between an earlier and a later text not only allows us to discover those passages for which our readings may offer fresh meaning. Equally productive is the way in which, having found certain correspondences, the one text shines through the other precisely because the mapping in fact produces no perfect fit. Asking about the manner in which Shakespeare anticipates thematic and rhetorical constellations that will bear fruit *again* in modernism also means noticing seminal differences in the dramaturgic resolutions the renaissance poet offers. At issue is not just that a given oeuvre has had a resilient afterlife but also what shifts have occurred in the course of such cultural survival. If one of the most resilient lines of connection between these two oeuvres thrives on the tension between an escape into the aesthetic from the quotidian responsibilities of the world, and an ethical call to return to the gravity of the ordinary, then the closures Shakespeare's plays present also draw attention to the way difference nevertheless comes into play within the very survival of cultural energies his texts have engendered over the ages.

To take an example: Given that King Ferdinand's academy of men, separate from everyday society and predicated as it is on the excessive desire to exclude women, is the point of connection to *Doktor Faustus*, it is useful to remember that this experiment fails because he, along with his fellow scholars, falls prey to precisely the knowledge of women he has sought to ban. In Shakespeare it is the women who ultimately dictate the time and terms of the enforced return to the ordinary, with which this comedy of wanton verbal excess finds closure. Rosaline, the

Princess's witty attendant, is the one who speaks the lines so seminal to Mann's Germany novel: 'The blood of youth burns not with such excess / As gravity's revolt to wantonness' (5.2.73–4).[1] A revolt in the name of gravity, in other words, proves to be as excessive as what it revolts against: the promiscuous, the profusely luxuriant, the playfully lively. Important for the reinstatement of gravity on which this comedy ends, in turn, is that if King Ferdinand and his lords were initially guilty of a wantonness of wit, their ultimate debunking follows upon a second display of wantonness, now involving the manner in which they choose to court the women they had first sought to repudiate.

It is as a follow-up of her mockery of their ridiculous disguise as Muscovites that the Princess of France, having been informed of the death of her father, dictates an excessive collective return to gravity. She demands that King Ferdinand go to some 'forlorn and naked hermitage, / Remote from all the pleasures of the world' (5.2.777–8), while she will shut herself up in a 'mourning house, / Raining the tears of lamentation / For the remembrance of my father's death' (5.2.790–2). Berowne, in turn, is sent by his lady Rosaline to spend the year visiting those who are diametrically opposed to his verbal prowess, the speechless sick. With all the fierce endeavour of his wit he is 'to enforce the pained impotent to smile' (5.2.831). Shakespeare's answer to the sophisticated allusiveness of his courtiers brings what seems a contradictory compassion into play. Berowne may initially claim that 'to move wild laughter in the throat of death? / It cannot be, it is impossible: Mirth cannot move a soul in agony' (5.2.882–4), and yet he ultimately consents to the jesting in the context of real pain upon which his lady insists.

By looking back at the Shakespearean text through the lens of Mann's appropriation, my interest is drawn to the fact that it is the women who successfully fuse an ethical acknowledgement of the inescapable law of mortality with a subversive creativity, and in a manner particularly compelling – once again – for art performed in the aftermath of the global catastrophe of political totalitarianism. In Mann's Germany novel, wantonness, of course, plays itself out in yet a further sense of the word, namely as deliberate and unprovoked cruelty. With this in mind, we may glean from Shakespeare's closure not just a lament regarding the impossibility of finding a poetic and critical language that might adequately represent Auschwitz. Of continued pertinence, also, is the recognition that in the face of death a recourse to the wantonness of poetic words, the very excess that makes this mode of expression both wildly contingent and uncontainable, might just be the only adequate manner in which to record and counter global suffering. In that it not only gives final authority to the voices of women but also invokes the possibility that a comic restitution may still – after the long proposed twelvemonth of separation – be an option, Shakespeare's call to self-restraint and a re-anchoring of wit in the ordinary world seems different from Mann's conviction that after Auschwitz there is no redemption in sight. My intuition is that in turning back to Shakespeare's sense of the limit which the facticity of death imposes on all poetic imaginations – even while his comic resolution proposes that aesthetic refiguration of the world finds its most compelling challenge when faced with real suffering – we might find the beginnings of fresh answers to Mann's disillusionment in regard to the destruction which World War II wrought.

But as much as we may wish to keep totalitarian politics and art neatly distinct, what the conjunction of Mann and Shakespeare suggests is that we must instead address the disturbing links between them. On the one hand, we would like to hold on to the discrepancy that while Nazi ideology valorized authenticity, resoluteness, health, strength, and a redemptive final solution (the so-called *Endlösung*) based on exterminating all cultural qua racial difference, the modernist aesthetic response entailed a celebration of the inauthenticity of masquerade and surface appearances, sickness, the impure and infected, along with anti-cathartic closures and open ends. But Leverkühn's musical adventure is not just a trope for the masculine artist's desire to avert the ordinary, and separate artistic prowess from sensual happiness. The political analogy intended by Mann sheds disturbing light on the fact that the 'demonic' music his musician invents, the twelve-tone composition, is not just predicated on a freedom from any considerations of musical conventions. It entails above all a strict style ('einen strengen Satz', 2007: 280–1) that ideally leaves no more free notes ('keine freie Note mehr', ibid.).[2] Each tone in the complete composition is to be determined by this series. Put another way, the series allows for no note to exist outside what it determines.

What links Leverkühn's aesthetic ideal to the ideal of fascism is the fact that both repudiate anything subjective, contingent or random. Read as a trope for a different demonic liberation, namely the Nazi regime, our attention is uncannily drawn toward a proximity between the avant-garde and political totalitarianism here. The neat distinction that attributes a transparent and harmonious articulation to the political realm and the embrace of opacity and disjunction to the aesthetic gives way to a different ordering, in which both the aesthetic and the political, by presupposing a freedom from all considerations of conventions, are shown to be aligned in that there is no outside allowed by their totalizing claim. The demonic – when read as a political trope – proves to be difficult to fix in place. On the one hand, pitted against the humanist project which Mann's bourgeois citizen Zeitblom represents, it entails a mistrust of the progress of enlightenment and goes against any return to the ordinary predicated on a containment of excessive desire in the interest of human benefit. On the other hand, the demonically inspired political system imposes on the ordinary an all-encompassing law, predicated on radical exclusion, sacrifice and extermination of all those forms of life that do not fit the determining series.

Mapping Mann's notion of the demonic as inspiration for a series which contains no free notes back onto Shakespeare, a poignant difference for the political implication in the early modern dramatist's aesthetic design emerges. Polyphony, on the level both of his poetic language and of his constellations of character, brings with it an awareness of the fragility and provisionality of any all-embracing power in the theatre or in politics. Rosaline and the Princess of France may seek to put an end to all wanton wit, and yet the return to gravity they insist on does not preclude the existence of free notes. Indeed, at the end of Shakespeare's plays there is always something that doesn't fit into the series: be it the discontented Malvolio in *Twelfth Night*, who threatens to have his revenge on the whole pack of courtiers who had their fun with him; be it Antonio, who, bereft of his lover at the end of *The Merchant of Venice*, has only the hope that his ships will come home safely; be it the hysteric Ophelia, who, drawn from her delirious singing to muddy death, subverts the lethal theatre of conspiracy into which Hamlet has drawn the entire court at Elsinore. The ordinary these plays ultimately return us to is precisely one that defies a structuring of the world so strict that nothing cannot *not* fit. To return once more to our primary example: in *Love's Labour's Lost* the answer to an academy in which women's voices have no place is not only including them contrapuntally, but, in following their lead, to force open the imposition of a strict series in order, instead, to confront the incalculabilities and contingencies of the real, especially where death and suffering must be accounted for. In light of the fact that the experience of military destruction throughout the twentieth century has caused critical theory not only to feel uncomfortable with any celebration of harmonious totality but also to doubt the humanist project, asking of art to reflect this two-fold distrust, Rosaline's command that Berowne test the effect of poetic wit not by repudiating life's fragility but in the face of real suffering continues to be timely.

Indeed, as Jonathan Dollimore points out in his contribution to the present volume, a particularly suggestive line of association between Thomas Mann and Shakespeare emerges when discussing *Hamlet* in relation to a knowledge which shatters in that it puts into question psychic, social and political well-being – a knowledge, that is to say, which makes this well-being questionable by turning it into a question and an issue of self-questioning. It is precisely in the turn toward all that is excluded from the ordinary – the nocturnal, the excess of desire, fantasy as a violation of others, death – that a resilient cultural afterlife of Shakespeare in modernity can be located. Though shattering to any comfortable notion of the self, the community or the nation, this dangerous knowledge pertains to something we cannot afford *not* to know. Yet most pertinent about a conception of modern art as that which disturbs any unquestioned experience *of* and existence *in* the world is that, by rendering the ordinary uncanny, the cognitive gain is a double-edged ethical insight. Revisiting the conversation between Mann and Shakespeare, Dollimore offers a keen rethinking of the term *Barbarei*, so as to suggest that barbarism is not the opposite of the civilization it seeks to destroy but its creation – a self-destructive force that civilization itself engenders. Art, in turn, emerges not only as a corrective, but also a particularly potent articulation of the virulent intensity this second degree barbarism unleashes.

In Shakespeare, of course, the proximity between evil and good harks back to an omnipotent God who, having created both, emerges as the source of evil. There is nothing outside or beyond divine power. For Mann, in turn, the proximity between barbarism and civilization speaks to the way that the 'demonic evil' of Nazism cannot be neatly severed from the German people at large and instead must be tracked back to the bourgeois humanist project against which it was pitted. Linking both, the scene in *Doktor Faustus* during which Leverkühn assures the devil that the tempter is telling him nothing save things that are already in him recalls *Macbeth* in more than one sense. On the one hand, the eponymous hero of the play, like Satan, so brilliantly portrayed in Milton's *Paradise Lost*, was once a loyal subject whose rebellion against his sovereign is inspired by both the barbarism of the battlefield and the conjuring powers of the witches, who give him the script of ambitious promotion which he will follow, once circumstances favour him. Yet these allegedly demonic forces, rendering manifest the latent rebellious thoughts in this particular warrior, are themselves subject to Hecate, goddess of dark places, who allows her wanton subordinates to trick Macbeth so as to bring about his destruction and reassert the royal lineage he, for the duration of the play, seems to subvert. As such, her nocturnal force orchestrates a drama in which a powerful general is drawn into the realm of revolt and regicide, so as to prove not only the temptability of even the most loyal subject but, by virtue of his ultimate defeat, also to make an example of his subversive defiance.

The bloodshed and destruction of the world we witness on stage is not in opposition to, but in alliance with the sovereignty of King Duncan's family line. Violation is engendered *by*, but also once more results *in*, the civilization this weak king represents. At the same time, the murky interface between good and evil is also explicitly addressed by Malcolm, heir to the throne, as an equally conflicted expression of the proximity between evil and good. In the fourth act, Malcolm gives voice to the black scruples that devilish Macbeth has inspired in him, claiming, to his astonished companion Macduff, that in his voluptuousness and avarice he is equal to the evil usurper. After listing all his vices, he proclaims 'Nay, had I power, I should / Pour the sweet milk of concord into hell, / Uproar the universal peace, confound / All unity on earth' (4.3.98–100). Only the despair his companion utters in response, regarding the fate of Scotland, compels Malcolm to unspeak his own detraction and abjure the stains and blames he initially laid upon himself. Yet the point is that in order to renounce evil, Malcolm chose to acknowledge it as being – at least potentially – part and parcel of the sovereignty he is about to claim. In so doing, he raises the possibility that he could be one in a series of evil rulers, engendered by his father King Duncan's weak regime. Choosing civilization over barbarism only cements the proximity between these two political forces.

What Shakespeare thus maps is not the narrative of a logical sequence in which the barbaric is conceived as coming before and then being overwhelmed by enlightened civilization, such that its re-eruption marks a reversion to a prior state. Instead, with Mann's notion of shattering knowledge in mind, we see barbarism as the logical consequence of a particular civilization, in *Macbeth* the medieval Scotland of King Duncan. There it finds two embodiments, as the usurper and his challenger, and only the triumph of the latter puts an end to the sequence of bloodshed by regrouping all the Thanes loyal to Malcolm into a far stricter bond of Earls, led by him as their new sovereign. The king-maker Macduff is demonstratively holding the head of his vanquished opponent in his hand as Malcolm proclaims this new political regime. Mann calls the re-eruption of violence in the midst of civilization a double barbarism, as the devil puts it to Leverkühn, coming after bourgeois humanism. As Dollimore suggests, this is an answer to the bourgeois civilization which, by privileging a project of humanitarianism without allowance for excess, not only re-engenders but actually intensifies the very violations it seeks to contain, be these sexual passions, mystical passions or the passion of violence. Rethought in Shakespearean terms, this also brings us back to the excess to be found in Rosaline's final call for gravity's revolt against wantonness. At the height of modernity, in the form of European fascism, the gravity of civilization found itself giving in to wanton political action, whose violence in its excessive cruelty can be conceived as an alarmingly grave wantonness. While it is relatively acceptable to think of gravity and wantonness conjoined in the Elizabethan court, where civilizing love and destructive desire existed side by side, when gravity and wantonness come together in the Nazi regime it blurs together things we would far rather keep distinct. German totalitarian politics was everything but undisciplined and lawless, even while committing crimes against humanity. It puts on display how a lasciviously wanton violence could emerge as part and parcel of an extremely organized project of modernity.

What is timely about the notion that evil is not external to but inherent to the good, and as such not what civilization triumphs over but what it also produces, is not simply the deconstruction of familiar binaries. Rather than collapsing the distinction between barbarism and civilization, crossmapping Shakespeare and Mann suggests that it may be more fruitful, given the proposed proximity, to isolate those historical moments as well as those literary passages that address their cross-over. Our attention is then drawn to the fact that, by both correcting and articulating a barbarism which comes after and as a result of civilization, modern artistic practices participate in a dynamic dialogue. Along the lines of what Freud calls the uncanny return of latent primordial material, it is this dialogue that gives voice to the repression of a dangerous knowledge. Freud himself explicitly conceived the primordial aspect of psychic life in terms of a barbarism that had to be repressed in favour of both individual and collective culturation. As Dollimore notes (in his contribution to this volume, p. 28), while repression thus proves to be a 'necessary aspect of what it means to be humane', the demonic force it seeks to contain is part and parcel of what it means 'to be fully human'. Like Satan, returning from Hell to challenge the God who exiled him, repressed psychic material returns in the form of personal and collective symptoms and fantasies, giving voice in encrypted form to something we cannot afford *not* to know because, as shattering as this knowledge is, it is also all too human.

Freud begins his 'Thoughts for the Times on War and Death', written one year after the outbreak of World War I, with a confession of his own distress. The war, he explains, that 'we had refused to believe in broke out, and it brought – disillusionment' (1964: 278)[3] regarding all trust in humanism, civilization, progress. The furore driving his fellow Europeans into this Great War, which within the first year had resulted in such unexpectedly high casualties, Freud took to be an expression of discontent with the pressure of civilization. So as to make sense of the violence and destruction of war, he suggested an analogy between the early psychic condition of the human subject and what he called 'primaeval man' (1964: 292).[4] This allowed him to think about the war in terms of a re-eruption of barbarism in the heart of European civilization both in personal and in collective terms; as the uncanny return of something which was not so much strange as it was all too familiar.

For Freud, the shattering knowledge which the outbreak of war forced upon all those who had refused to believe it could break out, however, at the same time revealed a troubling association between aestheticism and barbarism. The tendency of civilized society 'to exclude death from our calculations in life' (1964: 291),[5] which is to say to repress the human in support of the humane, entails a 'loss in life' which finds compensation in the world of fiction: 'There we still find people who know how to die – who, indeed, even manage to kill someone else. … In the realm of fiction we find the plurality of lives which we need. We die with the hero with whom we have identified ourselves; yet we survive him, and are ready to die again just as safely with another hero' (ibid.).[6] And yet Freud, adding the following chilling remark, underscores the proximity of death and life, evil and good, barbarism and civility: 'It is evident that war is bound to sweep away this conventional treatment of death. Death will no longer be denied; we are forced to believe in it. People really die; and no longer one by one, but many … and death is no longer a chance event. To be sure, it still seems a matter of chance whether a bullet hits this man or that; but a second bullet may well hit the survivor; and the accumulation of deaths puts an end to the impression of chance. Life has indeed become interesting again; it has recovered its full content' (ibid.).[7]

Dollimore's provocative claim that 'humanism involves a repression of what it is to be fully human, and that such repression is a necessary aspect of what it is to be humane' (this volume, p. 33), locates a potential in modern art that places it not only in the service of human values which support the containment of lethal fantasies and desires on which civilized life is predicated. Instead, as a cognitive instrument, modern art also supports the shattering knowledge that exceeds and violates civilized life by forcing into view again all that humanism feels compelled to exclude and repress. It is not an anaesthetic insensitivity to pain that Rosaline prescribes to her witty lover's skill with words. The aesthetic she has in mind at the end of *Love's Labour's Lost* is not one that aims even to heal the wounds which life inflicts on human beings, but one which actively brings the ugliness of disease, decay and death back into the equation. Rosaline's final, hopeful prescription for the aesthetic involves wantonness once more turning alarmingly grave.

The humane, intent on civilizing and refining so as to reduce pain, and the human, mutually implicated in good and evil, relate to each other in such a way that the former covers up the latter even though it never fully screens it out. If the humane speaks to that part of our existence that is steeped in suppressing all that is in discord with notions of benevolence and civility, we may think of the letter 'e' with which this word ends as the decisive mark of something more than the repression of what it is to be fully human. It also marks the limit to any civilizing effort in excluding what doesn't fit in with the humanist project. Dropping the 'e' allows us to find in the human the dissident and dangerous knowledge which the humane seeks to avert. And the human thus returns in full force, recovering, as Freud puts it, life's full content. My intuition is to turn the screw one notch further regarding the proximity of aesthetics and an attack on bourgeois humanism. If the human is that which brings back into the conversation what the humane seeks to disavow, the absent 'e' opens up an artistic practice in which barbarism is harnessed not in the name of human values, but in opposing aesthetic compositions of strict series in which nothing is contingent, incalculable, or out of place.

To return to Shakespeare *after* and *with* Thomas Mann could entail putting the human back into the artistic equation by tuning our ears to those textual passages that challenge, threaten and repudiate any ideal – be it aesthetic or political – that allows for no free notes. This, I have argued, is what Rosaline speaks for, in the form of a discipline she teaches to her excessively cultivated man. Rather than seeking redemption from the past (and with it our cultural legacy of barbarism), the double-edged challenge to art is to foreground the human in all its ugly inconsistency and disjunction even while recognizing our need for the civilizing assuagement which the humane offers. Yet if, as Dollimore points out, modern culture's sublation of the human into the humane also produces the return of a knowledge that shatters, albeit transformed and re-encoded by virtue of its repression, this rhetorical turn is also applicable to Shakespeare's effective cultural survival in modernity. What a transhistorical crossmapping uncovers are not just the lines of connection and correspondences between early and late modern texts, but that Shakespeare's meaning returns to us inscribed by and intensified by the history of his rearticulations. The aesthetic energies emanating from his poetic refiguration of the cultural anxieties and crises of his own times are both prior to our contemporary concerns and the product of rethinking our historical moment in light of his plays.

Notes

1 All Shakespeare quotations are from the Norton edition, based on the Oxford text, edited by Stephen Greenblatt, Walter Cohen, Jean Howard and Katherine Eisaman Maus (New York 2008).

2 'I will tell you what I understand by "strict style". I mean the complete integration of all musical dimensions, their neutrality towards each other due to complete organization … There would no longer be a free note' (Mann 1999: 191). *Ich werde Dir sagen, was ich unter strengem Satz verstehe.*

Ich meine damit die vollständige Integrierung aller musikalischen Dimensionen, ihre Indifferenz gegen einander kraft vollkommener Organisation. ... Es gäbe keine freie Note mehr. (Mann 2007: 280–1).

3   *Der Krieg, an den wir nicht glauben wollten, brach nun aus und er brachte die – Enttäuschung* (Freud 1999: 328).

4   *dem Urmenschen* (ibid.: 347).

5   *den Tod beiseite zu schieben, ihn aus dem Leben zu eliminieren* (Freud 1999: 341).

6   *Dort finden wir noch Menschen, die zu sterben verstehen, ja, die es auch zustande bringen, einen anderen zu töten. ... Auf dem Gebiete der Fiktion finden wir jene Mehrheit von Leben, deren wir bedürfen. Wir sterben in der Identifizierung mit dem einen Helden, überleben ihn aber doch und sind bereit, ebenso ungeschädigt ein zweites Mal mit einem andren Helden zu sterben* (ibid.: 344).

7   *Es ist evident, daß der Krieg diese konventionelle Behandlung des Todes hinwegfegen muß. Der Tod läßt sich jetzt nicht mehr verleugnen; man muß an ihn glauben. Die Menschen sterben wirklich, auch nicht mehr einzeln, sondern viele .... Es ist auch kein Zufall mehr. Es scheint freilich noch zufällig, ob diese Kugel den einen trifft oder den anderen; aber diesen anderen mag leicht eine zweite Kugel treffen, die Häufung macht dem Eindruck des Zufälligen ein Ende. Das Leben ist freilich wieder interessant geworden, es hat seinen vollen Inhalt wiederbekommen* (ibid.).

Works Cited

Freud, Sigmund, 1964 [1915]. 'Thoughts for the Times on War and Death', in *The Standard Edition of the Complete Psychological Works of Sigmund Freud*, ed. and trans. James Strachey, vol. 14. London: The Hogarth Press and the Institute of Psycho-Analysis, pp. 275–300.

Freud, Sigmund, 1999 [1915]. 'Zeitgemäßes über Krieg und Tod', in *Gesammelte Werke*, vol. 10. Frankfurt am Main: Fischer Taschenbuchverlag, pp. 323–55.

Mann, Thomas, 1999 [1947]. *Doctor Faustus*, trans. H. T. Lowe-Porter. London: Vintage.

Mann, Thomas, 2007 [1947]. *Doktor Faustus*, eds Ruprecht Wimmer, Stephan Stachorski. Große Kommentierte Frankfurter Ausgabe, vol. 10.1. Frankfurt am Main: S. Fischer.

Shakespeare, William, 2008. *The Norton Shakespeare*. Based on the Oxford Edition, eds Stephen Greenblatt et al. New York: Norton.

Index

CPSIA information can be obtained
at www.ICGtesting.com
Printed in the USA
LVHW031718241019
635246LV00010B/225/P